Netscape Navigator™ 3 Starter Kit

Netscape Navigator™ 3 Starter Kit

Mark R. Brown

with

Steven Forrest Burnett, Tim Evans, Heather Fleming,
Galen Grimes, David Gunter, Jerry Honeycutt,
Peter Kent, Margaret J. Larson, Bill Nadeau,
Todd Stauffer, Ian Stokell, John Williams

Netscape Navigator 3 Starter Kit

Library of Congress Catalog No.: 96-69457

ISBN: 0-7897-1181-8

98 97 96   6 5 4 3 2

Interpretation of the printing code: the rightmost double-digit number is the year of the book's printing; the rightmost single-digit number, the number of the book's printing. For example, a printing code of 96-1 shows that the first printing of the book occurred in 1996.

Screen reproductions in this book were created using Collage Plus from Inner Media, Inc., Hollis, NH.

Composed in *Palatino*, *ITC Highlander*, and *MCPdigital* by Que Corporation.

Credits

For my parents, Robert and Margaret Brown, who brought me up right.

About the Authors

Mark R. Brown has been writing computer magazine articles, books, and manuals for over 13 years. He was managing editor of *.info* magazine when it was named one of the six best computer magazines of 1991 by the Computer Press Association, and was nominated by the Software Publisher's Association for the 1988 Software Reviewer of the Year award. He is currently the manager of technical publications for Neural Applications Corporation, a major player in applying cutting-edge artificial intelligence techniques to industrial control applications, such as steel making and food processing. A bona fide personal computing pioneer, he hand-built his first PC in 1977, taught himself to program it in hexadecimal, and has since dabbled in dozens of different programming languages. He has been telecomputing since 1983, and is currently Webmaster of two World Wide Web sites: **http://www.neural.com**, and a personal Web site on the topic of airships, which will have moved to a new URL by the time this is published. (Chapters 10-13)

Steven Forrest Burnett is a technical writer, editor, and teacher of artificial linguistics, with a master of science in technical communication from North Carolina State University. Having dealt with Internet issues for several years, Steve also contributed to the book *Programming Client/Server Applications with RPC and DCE*. (Chapter 7)

Tim Evans is a UNIX system administration and network security consultant. Employed by Taratec Development Corporation, his full-time contract assignment for the past three years has been at the DuPont Company's Experimental Station in Wilmington, Delaware. Tim pioneered development of DuPont's own World Wide Web, known as DuPont-Wide Web, used within the company for information sharing via its worldwide network. Previously, Tim worked for the U.S. Social Security Administration in various staff jobs for more than 20 years. In 1991, before the Internet got hot, he brought that government agency onto the Internet. At both DuPont and SSA, he provided support for large numbers of UNIX users, running UNIX on a variety of computer systems ranging from PCs to workstations to mini-computers. He can be reached via Internet e-mail at **tkevans@dupont.com**. (Chapter 11)

Heather A. Fleming received her first lessons on a computer when she was given an Apple IIe for a Christmas present at the age of 12. Working her way to a Stephens College graduation with a BA in mathematics and computer science, she landed a job working at a lumber mill in Oregon, where, besides pulling green chain, she studied machinery automation. The next year was spent studying Human and Computer Interaction at the University of Nebraska—Lincoln, the University of Missouri—Columbia, and Stephens College set her on a career path that has kept her in mid-Missouri writing training manuals for Datastorm Technologies, Inc. (Appendix B)

Galen Grimes lives in Monroeville, Pennsylvania, a suburb of Pittsburgh, with his wife Joanne. Galen is also the author of several other Macmillan Computer Publishing books, including Sams' *First Book of DR DOS 6*, Que's *10 Minute Guide to NetWare* and *10 Minute Guide to Lotus Improv*, and Que's *Windows 3.1 HyperGuide*. Galen has a master's degree in information science from the University of Pittsburgh, and by trade is a project manager and NetWare LAN administrator for a large international bank and financial institution. (Chapter 1)

Ray Gronberg is a journalist in Chapel Hill, North Carolina, where he specializes in government and public affairs reporting. He has an MA in journalism from the University of North Carolina and a BA in political science from the University of North Carolina at Charlotte. His practical experience with computers, as a hobbyist, dates from the late 1970s and early 1980s, when the gee-whiz operating system was CP/M and "mass storage" was a cassette deck. He uses Internet Web and e-mail services heavily in the course of his daily reporting. Ray can be reached via e-mail at **gronberg@nando.net**. (Chapter 8)

David Gunter is a consultant and computer author based in Cary, North Carolina. His areas of interest include UNIX systems management and network and systems programming. David holds a master's degree in computer science from the University of Tennessee. During his free time, David enjoys traveling, reading, and spending as much time as possible with his wonderful wife. (Appendix A)

Jerry Honeycutt is a business-oriented, technical manager with broad experience in software development. He has served companies such as The Travelers, IBM, Nielsen North America, and most recently, Information Retrieval Methods as director of windows application development. Jerry has participated in the industry since before the days of Microsoft Windows 1.0, and believes that everyone must eventually learn to use the Internet to stay in touch with the world.

Jerry wrote *Using Microsoft Plus!* and was a contributing author on *Special Edition Using Windows 95* for Que. He has also been printed in *Computer Language Magazine* and is a regular speaker at the Windows World and Comdex trade shows on topics related to software development and corporate solutions for Windows 95.

Jerry graduated from the University of Texas at Dallas in 1992 with a BS degree in computer science. He currently lives in the Dallas suburb of Frisco, Texas, with Becky, two Westies, Corky and Turbo, and two cats, Scratches and Chew-Chew. Please feel free to contact Jerry on the Internet at **jerry@honeycutt.com**, on CompuServe at **76477,2751**, or on the Microsoft Network at **Honeycutt**. (Chapter 9)

Peter Kent lives in Lakewood, Colorado. He's been training computer users, documenting software, and designing user interfaces for the last 14 years. Working as an independent consultant for the last nine years, Peter has worked for companies such as Mastercard, Amgen, Data General, and Dvorak Development and Publishing. Much of his consulting work has been in the telecommunications business.

Peter is the author of *Using Microsoft Network, Using Microsoft Internet Explorer*, and the best-selling *The Complete Idiot's Guide to the Internet*. He's also written seven other Internet-related books—including *The Complete Idiot's Guide to the Internet for Windows 95* and *The Complete Idiot's Guide to the World Wide Web*—and a variety of other works, such as *The Technical Writer's Freelancing Guide* and books on Windows NT and Windows 3.1. His articles have appeared in many periodicals, including *Internet World, Dr. Dobb's Journal, Windows Magazine, The Dallas Times Herald*, and *Computerworld*. Peter can be reached via CompuServe at **71601,1266** and the Internet at **pkent@lab-press.com**. (Chapter 14)

Margaret J. Larson is a founding partner of Wintergreen
Associates, located in western Massachusetts. She has worked as a computer programmer and software designer for 15 years. Originally from
Ohio, Peg (as she is commonly called) got her BA in economics from
UMass/Amherst and spent five years in graduate school focusing on
computerized economic forecasting and simulation models. Her work has
involved software design, testing, documentation, technical writing,
statistics, and data analysis.

In late 1994, when the company for which she worked was sold and
moved to Boston, she and her husband, Bill Nadeau, reorganized their
consulting business and founded Wintergreen Associates. They specialize
in design and maintenance of commercial Web sites with a focus on
forms/CGI programming, management and analysis of large databases,
and market research. You can contact Peg at Wintergreen's Web site—
http://www.wintergreen.com/. (Chapter 5)

Bill Nadeau is a founding partner of Wintergreen Associates, and
develops Web sites with his wife and partner, Peg Larson. Bill is a designer, writer, and programmer, and has worked as a consultant and
contractor on a variety of projects in the field. Peg and Bill co-authored the
FreeThink Users Guide and developed tutorials in multi-dimensional data
modelling for clients such as The World Bank while working at Power
Thinking Tools before FreeThink was purchased by Praxis International in
late 1994. Bill has a BS in regional planning & environmental design, and
some graduate training in architecture, as well as some schooling in music
and visual arts. He is currently enmeshed in developing multimedia/CGI
applications. (Chapter 5)

Todd Stauffer has been writing nonstop about computers and the
computer industry since he graduated from Texas A&M University,
where he studied a bizarre combination of English literature, managment
information systems, and entirely too much golf. A die-hard fan of the
Macintosh, Todd is the author of *Using Your Mac, Easy America Online*, and
the coauthor of *Special Edition Using the Internet With Your Macintosh*—
all Que publications.

Todd has recently finished a stint as editor of Texas Computing Magazine and is currently a freelance writer and author. He has worked previously as an advertising, technical, and magazine writer—all in the computer industry. He can be reached by Internet e-mail at **TStauffer@aol.com**. (Chapter 3)

Ian Stokell is a freelance writer and editor living in the Sierra Foothills of northern California with his wife and three young children. He is also Managing Editor of Newsbytes News Network, an international daily news-wire covering the computer and telecommunications industries. His writing career began with a 1981 article published in the UK's New Statesman and has since encompassed over 1,500 articles in a variety of computing and non-computing publications. He wrote the Networking chapter of Que's *Special Edition Using the Macintosh*, and has also written on assignment for such magazines as *PC World* and *MacWeek*. He is currently seeking representation for two completed novels and a screenplay. (Chapter 4)

John F. Williams began his work with multimedia and personal computers after purchasing Director's predecessor, VideoWorks. At about the same time, he created one of the first commercial programs demonstrated for HyperCard's release in 1987. John continued to work in the infant multimedia industry, founding the startup development company Midnight Design in 1989, speaking at universities and conferences on multimedia, and honing his skills while working with some of the best multimedia design firms in the business. Since then, he has gone on to help create dozens of commercial and private CD-ROMs, as well as over 30 interactive demo disks for various companies (most recently the *Director 4.0 Guided Tour for Macromedia*). Today, John is working on a variety of next-generation CD-ROM "titles" that Apple Computers, and some as-yet-to-be-found companies, will publish for Midnight Design. (Chapter 10)

Acknowledgments

It takes a lot of hard work to put together a book of this size and scope in such a short time.

All the writers associated with this project put forth a tremendous effort and deserve all the laurels we can heap upon them. The editors and staff at Que books certainly earned their kudos as well; special thanks go to Cheryl Willoughby, Mark Cierzniak, and Benjamin Milstead for their invaluable assistance and infallible guidance. And I'd like to add a special "thank you" to Oran J. Sands at Que for bringing me into this project.

Of course, we wouldn't have a book at all if it weren't for the excellent product produced by the programmers, planners, and management of Netscape Corporation. And the authors and developers of all the Netscape support programs mentioned in this book deserve our thanks, as well.

Then there are "all those wonderful people out there in the dark" who make up the World Wide Web. Certainly, to the people at CERN in Switzerland who first conceived and implemented the Web, our thanks. But the Web is made up of the efforts of literally millions of people, many of whom selflessly contribute the thoughts, ideas, articles, stories, graphics, movies, sound clips, and all the other elements that make up the multinational, multilingual, multimedia stew that is the World Wide Web. To all of them, our thanks for making Web surfing such an entertaining, enlightening, and engaging activity!

Finally, I'd like to thank my friends and family for their patient understanding of all the hours I had to spend away from them while working on this book. A special thanks goes to my wife, Carol, who has supported me wholeheartedly in this and all my other writing projects, with more patience than anyone could ever ask for or expect from another human being.

—Mark R. Brown

We'd Like to Hear from You!

As part of our continuing effort to produce books of the highest possible quality, Que would like to hear your comments. To stay competitive, we really want you, as a computer book reader and user, to let us know what you like or dislike most about this book or other Que products.

You can mail comments, ideas, or suggestions for improving future editions to the address below, or send us a fax at (317) 581-4663. For the online inclined, Macmillan Computer Publishing has a forum on CompuServe (type **GO QUEBOOKS** at any prompt) through which our staff and authors are available for questions and comments. The address of our Internet site is **http://www.mcp.com** (World Wide Web).

In addition to exploring our forum, please feel free to contact me personally to discuss your opinions of this book: I'm **jminatel@que.mcp.com** on the Internet.

Thanks in advance—your comments will help us to continue publishing the best books available on computer topics in today's market.

Mark Cierzniak
Publishing Manager
Que Corporation
201 W. 103rd Street
Indianapolis, Indiana 46290
USA

Contents at a Glance

Table of Contents

*Other Internet services
accessed through the Web
see page 19*

How to move around the Web

see page 40

Part II: Mastering the Web with Netscape

3 Finding Information on the Web

Changing a Bookmark link

see page 117

5 Web Forms

6 Netscape and Web Security

Setting certificate options in Netscape

see page 173

Part III: E-mail, News, and Other Parts of the Net

7 FTP, Gopher, and Telnet with Netscape

8 E-Mail with Netscape

9 UseNet News with Netscape

see page 258

Part IV: Sound, Graphics, Multimedia, and More!

10 Netscape Plug-Ins

see page 289

11 Netscape Helper Applications

12 Online Conferencing with CoolTalk

see page 348

13 Adding on to Netscape with Power Pack

Part V: Creating Your Own Web Pages

14 Creating Web Pages with Netscape Navigator Gold

see page 400

Part VI: Appendixes

A Connecting to the Internet

*Connecting
to the
Internet*

see page 436

see page 465

Introduction

On the Web site

Netscape is constantly undergoing changes. In fact, you may find that Netscape releases new versions of software more often than you want to buy a book to find how to use new features. While we'd be happy to see you buy every new Netscape book we publish, we realize that a book is not a minor investment and should be something that has lasting value.

With that in mind, we've set up a special Netscape section on our Web site (The Information Superlibrary). This section will include new chapters and coverage of new or changed features in Netscape. The address for this Web site is **http://www.mcp.com/que/et/netscape**. So you can connect to this site and get all of the latest information you need and this book will never go out of date. Then, when you find that enough features in Netscape have changed that you need a whole new book, we'd encourage you to go back to your favorite bookstore or retailer and pick up the latest Netscape book from Que.

Everywhere you turn you find people talking about the World Wide Web. Corporations now include Web addresses in their TV commercials. Television show and movie debuts are accompanied by the launch of promotional pages on the Web. Newspapers and magazines supplement their readership with an online presence. Celebrity fan clubs set up houses of worship on the Net. TV news shows blare excited warnings about kids accessing pornography on the Web.

In just a few short years, the World Wide Web has become a part of daily life. Every day, millions of people all over the world browse the Web for news, product information, entertainment, and even good, hard data. And the browser of choice for the majority of them is Netscape Navigator.

People have always liked Netscape for its solid reliability, generous allotment of features, and free preview offer. And now, with the release of version 3, Netscape is even more useful and powerful than before.

Of course, there's more to learn, too—like JavaScript, the Netscape scripting language, and plug-ins, which allow multimedia files to display right in the Netscape window without launching helper applications.

That's why we're here. *Netscape Navigator 3 Starter Kit* gently guides you through all the steps to get Netscape set up and working to its full potential on your machine.

Who should use this book?

This book is intended for anyone and everyone who wants to get the most out of Netscape and the World Wide Web.

Novices will find information on how to obtain, install, and configure Netscape. Intermediate users will discover tips, tricks, and techniques to make Netscape even more fun and useful. And advanced users will learn the nuts and bolts of Netscape operation, including how to use powerful Netscape 3 features like plug-ins and the JavaScript scripting language.

How this book is organized

Netscape Navigator 3 Starter Kit is organized into six logical sections.

Part I, "Netscape Fundamentals," explains what the Internet and World Wide Web are, and what they are likely to become in the future. It explains how the Web is organized and how it works.

Part II, "Mastering the Web with Netscape," tells you how to navigate on the Web using links, online search engines and indexes, and bookmarks. You'll also find information on how to use online forms, including a discussion of security.

Part III, "E-mail, News, and Other Parts of the Net" gives you information on using Netscape to access Internet services other than the World Wide Web, like e-mail, FTP, Gopher, and UseNet news.

Part IV, "Sound, Graphics, Multimedia, and More!," guides you through the process of finding and configuring Netscape plug-ins and helper applications for audio, graphics, and video. There's a chapter apiece on

Netscape 3's new CoolTalk phone utility and the new Power Pack 2. collection of Netscape add-ons and plug-ins. You'll even learn about Netscape-specific and proposed future HTML commands. Finally, you'll discover how to work with the Web's most advanced page development tools, forms, and CGI-bin scripts.

Part V, "Creating Your Own Web Pages," gets you started with HTML (HyperText Markup Language), the language used to create Web pages. You'll learn how to create links and use advanced graphics techniques like imagemaps to make your Web pages dynamic.

Appendixes finishes out the book with information on how to connect to the Internet, how to install and configure Netscape Navigator on a variety of platforms, and what you'll find on the book's CD-ROM.

The book's CD-ROM

Inside the back cover of this book you'll find a CD-ROM containing multi-megabytes of helper applications, links, tips, and programs that will help you get the most out of Netscape.

Whenever we mention a program in this book that is included on the book's CD, you'll see the icon at the right. Keep an eye out for it.

Conventions used in this book

This book uses various stylistic and typographic conventions to make it easier to use.

Keyboard shortcut key combinations are joined by + signs; for example, Ctrl+X means to hold down the Ctrl key, press the X key, then release both.

Menu items and dialog box selections often have a mnemonic key associated with them. This key is indicated by an underline on the item on screen. To use these mnemonic keys, you press the Alt key, then the shortcut key. In this book, mnemonic keys are underlined, like this: File.

This book uses the following typeface conventions:

Typeface	Meaning
Italic	Variables in commands or addresses, or terms used for the first time
Bold	Text you type in, as well as addresses of Internet sites, newsgroups, mailing lists, and Web sites
`Computer type`	Commands, HTML tags

 Notes provide additional information related to the topic at hand.

 Tips provide quick and helpful information to assist you along the way.

 Cautions alert you to potential pitfalls or dangers in the operations discussed.

 Troubleshooting boxes address problems that you might encounter while following the procedures in this book.

Netscape Navigator 3 Starter Kit uses marginal references like this one to point you to other places in the book with additional information relevant to the topic. Right-pointing arrows guide you forward; left-pointing arrows guide you back /to previous chapters.

Part I: Netscape™ Fundamentals

1

World Wide Web and Netscape 3

● In this chapter:

● **What is the Internet and how is it related to the World Wide Web**

● **What URLs are and how they are used to locate Internet resources**

● **How the World Wide Web works**

● **What future projects are being planned for the Web**

● **What's new in Netscape 3**

The explosive proliferation of Internet usage and Web browsing has led many new users to freely exchange the terms Internet and World Wide Web, as if they are the same entity. Well, let's begin by setting the record straight—the Internet and the World Wide Web are not the same!

Internet is a collective term used to describe an interconnection of world-wide computer networks. Operating on the Internet are a variety of computer services such as e-mail, UseNet newsgroups, FTP, Telnet, Gopher, and the World Wide Web.

Even though the World Wide Web (most often referred to simply as the Web or WWW) has only been around since 1992 (the first Web server prototype was developed in 1990 at CERN, the European Laboratory for Particle Physics in Geneva, Switzerland), its growth on the Internet has been nothing short of phenomenal. In 1993, when the alpha version of Mosaic—the first graphic Web browser—was initially released, there were a total of 130 Web servers. Today, there are more than 13,000 Web servers worldwide, displaying more than 10 million Web pages!

The release of a version of Mosaic for Windows in late 1993 was one of the milestones that spurred Internet and Web activity. Netscape, a second generation Web browser, appeared on the scene not long after the PC version of Mosaic. Netscape forced open the door that Mosaic had been knocking on. Netscape's improved performance and added features helped create the near stampede to the Internet that has occurred in the last year or two.

Before diving into Netscape 3, to help give you a better idea of how we've gotten this far and what's going on behind the scenes, this chapter covers the operation of the Internet and the World Wide Web.

Who uses the World Wide Web

The World Wide Web is one of the most accessible places because it is available to virtually anyone worldwide who has access to a computer and a modem. For this reason, the Web has literally become "the kiosk for the entire planet." Because of the potential for getting a message to a very large and diverse audience, it's no wonder that there are now more than 10 million Web pages available for viewing, all posted on the Web in just the last three years.

As I stated earlier, the initial release of Mosaic for Windows was one of the keys to the success of the Web because Mosaic on the "common" PC made the Web accessible to the masses of ordinary PC users.

So who are these masses of ordinary PC users who have posted those 10 million Web pages? The answer is literally anyone and everyone. Major corporations, small businesses, government agencies, politicians, social organizations, historical societies, and a burgeoning industry of would-be Web authors are among those who have Web pages they are trying to get you to view.

Many Web authors are simply trying to supply information over the Web, but more often you will see businesses either advertising their presence and products, advertising their services, or directly trying to sell you their wares.

When you look out on the Web, you will see Coca-Cola, IBM, CNN, the National Football League, the World History Archives, and the Virtual Quilt home page, just as an example of some of the diversity you'll find (see figs. 1.1 through 1.6).

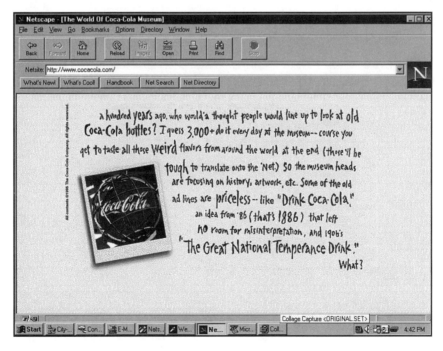

Fig. 1.1
The Coca–Cola home page.

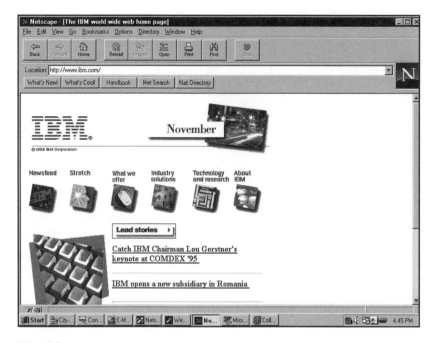

Fig. 1.2
The IBM home page.

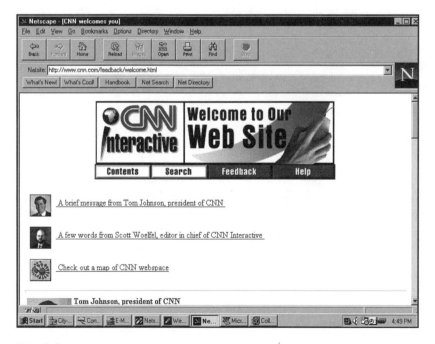

Fig. 1.3
The CNN Interactive home page.

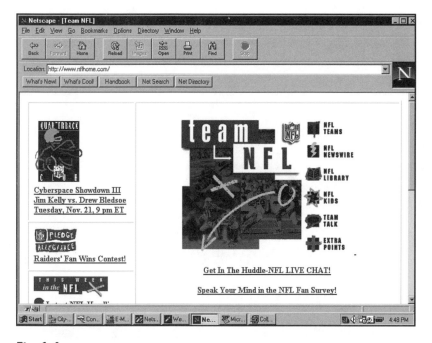

Fig. 1.4
The NFL home page.

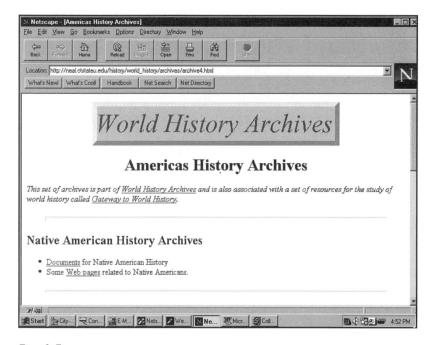

Fig. 1.5
The World History Archives home page.

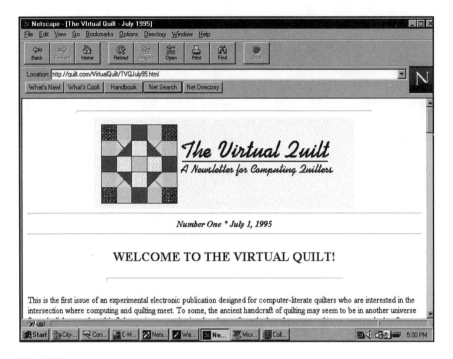

Fig. 1.6
The Virtual Quilt home page.

Hypertext and Hypermedia concepts

Understanding what URLs (Uniform Resource Locators) are and how they function is key to understanding how the Internet and the Web function and how Internet resources are located and accessed.

URLs are a very convenient method of identifying the location of devices and resources on the Internet. All URLs follow this format:

<scheme>:<scheme-dependent-information>

Some examples of <scheme> are http, FTP, and Gopher. This scheme tells you the application you are using:

- What type of resource you are trying to locate (for example, a Web page, a file, a Gopher menu, or a Gopher document)

- What mechanism you need to access the resource (for example, a Web browser, an FTP utility to download the file, or a Gopher client)

The `<scheme-dependent-information>` usually indicates:

- The Internet host making the file available
- The full path to the file

A more recognizable pattern for most users is:

scheme://machine.domain/full-pathname-of-file

Here we see the scheme describing the type of resource separated from the computer and its Internet address by two slashes (//) and then the Internet address separated from the path and file name by one slash (/). URLs for http, FTP, and Gophers generally fit this pattern.

To make this example a bit clearer, let's use a real-world URL as an example. Here is the URL for my home page:

http://www.city-net.com/~gagrimes/galen1.html

Figure 1.7 shows you how my home page appears.

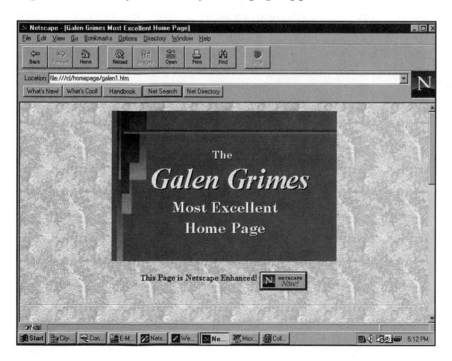

Fig. 1.7
The Galen Grimes Most Excellent Home Page.

Here's the scheme for this URL broken down into its component parts:

- http:—indicates that you are using the HyperText Transfer Protocol to access the resource, which usually means you want to use your Web browser

- www.city-net.com—identifies the host computer and its Internet address (its domain name to be precise)

- /~gagrimes/galen1.html—identifies the path and file name on the host computer for the desired resource

Most Web pages follow this scheme. You may have noticed that when accessing http, FTP, or Gopher URLs, the "full pathname" sometimes ends in a single slash (/). This is used to point the URL to a specific directory instead of to a specific file. In this case the host computer will usually return what is called the default index for that directory. In http the default index file is usually named index.html, but can also be named home.html, homepage.html, welcome.html, or default.html.

So, let's say you're sitting in front of your PC in Phoenix (or anywhere for that matter) and decide to visit my Web page. You start Netscape, and enter **http://www.city-net.com/~gagrimes/galen1.html** in the location window, press Enter, and in a few seconds my home page appears.

How the domain name service works

One of the key components responsible for helping Netscape run on your computer and locate my home page file, galen1.html (which is stored on the Web server of my service provider, City-Net) is a program, or more precisely, a series of programs called the domain name service.

Here's how the domain name service, or DNS for short, works its magic. When you initially set up the connection to your Internet Service Provider (if you used Microsoft Plus! you did it using the Internet Setup Wizard) you were asked to enter the IP address of your DNS Server. The IP address you entered, which your service provider supplied, looked something like the IP address shown in figure 1.8.

Fig. 1.8
Entering the IP address of your DNS Server in Microsoft Plus! Internet Setup Wizard.

An IP address is a unique number, in the format nnn.nnn.nnn.nnn (where nnn is a number between 0 and 255) that is assigned to every physical device on the Internet. Your service provider is assigned a block of IP addresses (by the InterNIC Registration Services) that are in turn assigned to each user who is provided access to the Internet. Your provider either assigns you a permanent IP address that doesn't change, or each time you log on to your provider, you are assigned a dynamic IP address, which could be any number in your provider's assigned block of IP address numbers.

When you enter the URL for my home page, **http://www.city-net.com/ ~gagrimes/galen1.html**, Netscape parses the domain name from this URL according to the URL scheme explained previously. The domain name Netscape gets from this URL is city-net.com. Netscape, working in conjunction with Windows and your TCP/IP protocol stack, passes the domain name, **city-net.com**, to your domain name service.

You may have noticed that domain names often end in .com, .edu, or .org. These identifiers are used with the domain name to help identify the type of domain. The most common identifiers are shown here, along with examples of each:

- .com for commercial organizations, for example, netscape.com, ibm.com, fedex.com

- .edu for educational institutions, for example, psu.edu for Penn State Univ., cmu.edu for Carnegie-Mellon Univ., mit.edu for the Massachusetts Institute of Technology

- .gov for government agencies, for example, whitehouse.gov for the White House, fbi.gov for the FBI

- .mil for the military, for example, army.mil for the Army, navy.mil for the Navy

- .org for nonprofit organizations, for example, red-cross.org for the American Red Cross, oneworld.org for Save the Children Fund

- .net for network service providers, for example, internic.net for InterNIC, si.net for Sprint International

There are also identifiers for countries:

- .uk for United Kingdom

- .ca for Canada

- .ch for Switzerland (Confoederatio Helvetica); you may have noticed that the domain name for CERN is cern.ch

- .li for Liechtenstein

- .cn for China

- .jp for Japan

- .br for Brazil

The lack of a country identifier usually indicates the domain is in the United States.

Your domain name service in one sense is a very large database program running on one of your service provider's computers. (Other computers are running other services such as mail service, news service, and FTP to name a few.) When the domain name is passed to the domain name service, the DNS returns the corresponding IP address.

NOTE   **If by some chance your DNS does not contain the domain name, your** DNS will attempt to locate the IP address by requesting the domain name from another DNS, in this case a centralized DNS containing .com domain names. If the domain name is still not located, the DNS will finally return an error message indicating the requested domain name does not exist.

In the previous example using my home page, the domain name city-net.com is passed to your DNS, and your DNS should return 199.234.118.2. The IP address is not only used for identification, it is also used to route the request to the appropriate host computer. The starting sequence of this IP address, 199., routes the request to North America. Additional routers connecting various Internet segments in North America, and containing routing tables for the segments they connect, eventually route the request to Pittsburgh and to City-Net. Once the request arrives at the domain city-net.com, it is routed to the appropriate host computer and finally to the appropriate directory path until the file galen1.html is located.

Because the request for galen1.html was made using http, the host computer, a Web server, returns the requested file for display by the requesting client, which in this case is Netscape, a Web browser.

The Web metaphor hypertext links

Now you have an understanding of how URLs work, and how URLs are used to help route files to the computers that request them. Figure 1.9 does a good job of illustrating Internet connections in the U.S. and how requests to various host computers could possibly be routed over the various interconnected Internet segments.

The World Wide Web is a means of supporting hypertext across the Internet. Hypertext is simply text that contains links, and these links provide additional information about certain keywords or phrases. Links are just what they sound like, and on Web pages, these links are used to connect one page (or file) to another page. We can use my home page as an example of Web page hypertext links. Figure 1.10 shows three links on my home page. These links are references to three additional Web pages, which also happen to be located on the same computer as my home page, which is the Web server of my service provider, City-Net.

 NOTE   **You can easily identify links when using Netscape because links will** usually appear as either blue or magenta underlined text.

Selecting the link Author Stuff will send another request from your PC across the interconnected segments of the Internet to the City-Net Web server, requesting the file galen-a.htm, which is the file name of the Author Stuff Web page. The URL for the Author Stuff page is included in this link.

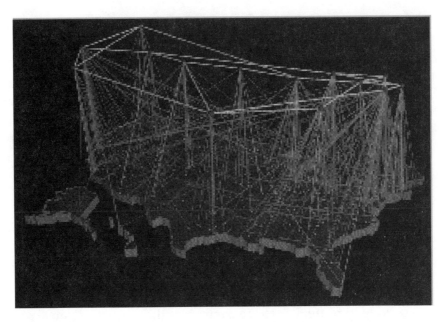

Fig. 1.9
Map of the U.S. illustrating how Internet network segments are interconnected.

Scroll down this page and you will see additional links to more Web pages. These links, however, are to Web pages on the Web server operated by Macmillan Computer Publishing, the owner of Que, and this Web server is located in Indianapolis.

Selecting any of these links will send a request from your PC across the interconnected segments of the Internet to the Macmillan Web server in Indianapolis, requesting the file referenced in the URL in this link.

NOTE   **Netscape will let you see the URLs in links even before you select the** link. Use your mouse and place the pointing finger Netscape cursor on the link without clicking your mouse. Look down at the status bar and you'll see the URL for that link.

You should have a much better understanding now of how the hypertext metaphor applies to the Web and to Web pages. You can see that the World Wide Web resembles a spider's web with connections from any one point or Web page, branching outward to various other connection points, or other Web pages, which in turn can also contain connections to even more Web pages.

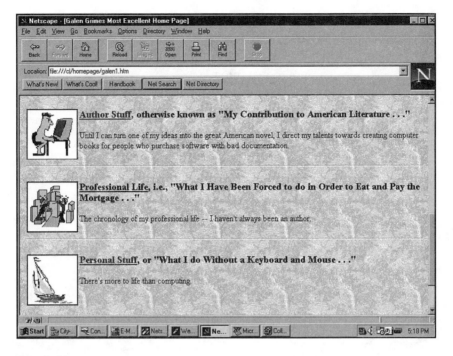

Fig. 1.10
Galen's home page links.

Other Internet services accessed through the Web

In the past year or so, many Web browsers have exceeded their original purpose of simply displaying HTML pages. Many Web browsers are becoming all-purpose Internet tools that can also be used for accessing non-Web Internet services such as FTP, e-mail, newsgroups, and Gophers.

FTP

FTP, short for file transfer protocol, is an Internet protocol that allows you to upload or download text or binary files. FTP is most often used to download files from an archival storage site. In the past few years, numerous FTP sites have sprung up all over the Internet as repositories for shareware, freeware, and general PC utilities and various support files.

It has also become fairly common for computer hardware and software manufacturers to set up FTP sites for customer support. These FTP sites are stocked with software updates and hardware support drivers, which are free for customers to download.

FTP sites that are used for hardware and software support are usually advertised so users who need access to their contents can easily find the sites and the files they store. Unfortunately, many FTP sites do not fall in this category and largely remain unknown, except when passed from user to user, or when these sites are included in a list of FTP sites in books like this. Fortunately, there is another way to locate files on FTP sites. A program called Archie can be used to locate files stored (or archived, hence the name Archie) on FTP sites. A listing of Archie servers can be found at **http://pubweb.nexor.co.uk/public/archie/servers.html** (see fig. 1.11).

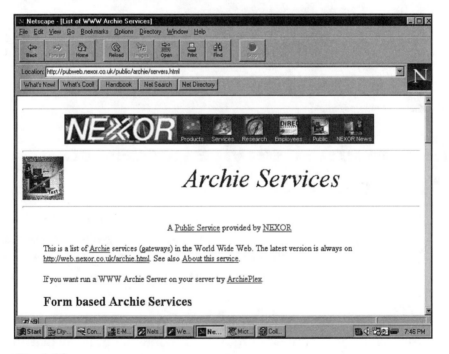

Fig. 1.11
NEXOR List of Archie Servers.

Until you become more familiar with using Archie servers, go to this Web site for a listing of FTP sites you might find helpful: **http://hoohoo.ncsa.uiuc.edu/ftp/** (see fig. 1.12).

Fig. 1.12
The Monster FTP Sites List.

For more information on FTP and how to use this protocol, especially in Web browsers, see chapter 7, "FTP, Gopher, and Telnet with Netscape."

E-mail and UseNet newsgroups

E-mail, short for electronic mail, is a simple system designed to allow the sending and receiving of messages across a network. For most of its history on the Internet, e-mail has been used primarily by businesses and academicians, but in the past few years a large percentage of e-mail messages have been created and read by individuals.

E-mail access is another traditional non-Web service that Web browsers are starting to encroach on. E-mail was one of the earliest services available on the Internet. E-mail today, probably the widest used of all Internet services, is still used primarily for sending messages, but an increasing percentage of e-mail messages now include some sort of file attachment.

UseNet newsgroups are strikingly similar in operation to e-mail, since both involve sending messages that often have file attachments, and like e-mail, newsgroup functionality is also starting to turn up in Web browsers.

Gophers

Accessing Gopher servers is another non-Web function being taken over by Web browsers. Gopher servers, or simply Gophers, first appeared on the Internet in 1991.

Gophers are similar in operation to FTP sites in that they are established as repositories for files. Gopher files, however, are largely academic and informational text documents, and are meticulously arranged by subject under a hierarchical menu structure. Accessing a Gopher server to search for documents by subject is similar to using a Web search engine such as Lycos (**http://www.lycos.com**) or WebCrawler (**http://www.webcrawler.com**). The only problem is that Gophers differ in the subjects they contain documents for. To solve this problem, developers devised a Gopher database search program, which they dubbed Veronica. Veronica works to create its database of Gopher documents and menus like the robot search tools used in many Web search engines. It continuously scans Gopher servers to see what menus and documents are being stored.

If you want to see how Gophers and Veronica work, point your (Gopher-functioning) Web browser to **Gopher://veronica.scs.unr.edu/11/veronica**.

You can also get more information on Gophers in chapter 7, "FTP, Gopher, and Telnet with Netscape."

The future of the Web

The Web, just like the Internet, is still growing, and more importantly, still evolving. As you might expect, numerous groups and organizations are developing new projects to assist in the evolution of the Web, most notably, the World Wide Web Consortium, or W3C for short, at CERN in Geneva, Switzerland. The W3C has posted on its Web server a list of some of the projects it currently has under development. If you want more information on these projects, go to **http://www.w3.org/hypertext/WWW/Bugs.html** to see the entire listing. The following sections are a sampling of some of the projects.

HTML style sheets

Most high-end word processors have some sort of style sheet capability, as do some HTML editors, until recently there was no HTML standard for style sheets. The style sheet standard is so new that it has yet to be included in this version of Netscape.

SGML and the Web

SGML, Standard Generalized Markup Language, is another HTML discussion hot button at W3C. The focus of the discussion is on extending HTML to encompass more of the SGML standard language.

To get more information on this discussion and project:

> **http://www.w3.org/hypertext/WWW/MarkUp/SGML/**

Internationalization of character sets

This will likely be one of the hot areas to watch for future HTML and Web development. Everyone now agrees that the Web has a severe bias toward English and the western-European/Latin writing system. There are several factors that have contributed to this bias, primarily 7-bit ASCII.

NOTE   **ASCII is the American Standard Code for Information Interchange. The** 7-bit ASCII code, which most computer manufacturers recognize, allows for the creation of only 128 characters and symbols, which does not include foreign or non-Latin-based characters. There are several 8-bit character sets that allow for 256 characters, but not an agreement on which one will be universally accepted.

Currently the greatest concentrations of Internet computers and domains are in the U.S. and Western Europe (see fig. 1.13).

With the Internet spreading into more countries that do not use the ISO-8859 Latin-1 character set (an 8-bit character set), there is pressure to approve a 16-bit character set (which would permit a total of 65,536 characters) standard, which will provide character sets for Eastern Europe, Asia, and the Pacific rim.

For more on this discussion see

http://www.w3.org/hypertext/WWW/International/.

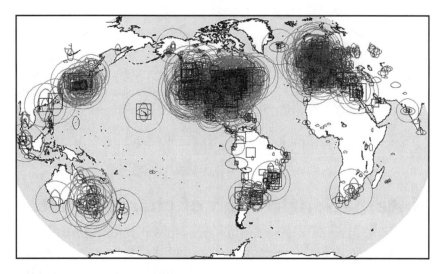

Fig. 1.13
Internet domain concentrations worldwide.

Virtual reality

This is a hot topic, not just at W3C, but all over the Web. Virtual reality is considered the next step for multimedia on the Web, and there are several proposals for how best to handle 3-D VR graphics. Much of the discussion extends to how best to implement VR on the Web—should it be through VRML, Virtual Reality Markup Language; should it be through PostScript extensions; or should a new VR platform be done "from the ground up." The discussion in W3C can be found at **http://www.w3.org/hypertext/ WWW/Bugs/GraphicalComposition.html**.

Emerging technologies

Several emerging technologies that could have an impact on the Web and the Internet in the next few years are just on the horizon—specifically ISDN and cable modems.

ISDN

ISDN, Integrated Services Digital Network, simply stated is digital telephone. ISDN's main advantage over the current analog telephone system is speed. With ISDN your connection to the Internet will be 4 1/2 times faster (128 Kbps) than the current top speed using analog telephone lines and 28.8 Kbps modems.

ISDN's main drawbacks now are availability and cost. As of November 1995, ISDN was available to only about 70 percent of available telephone service areas in the U.S., with the heaviest concentrations in the northeast. Also, many Internet service providers are not set up to provide ISDN connections to their subscribers but are scrambling to offer ISDN connection.

The other drawback is cost. Each of the Regional Bells in the U.S. has established a separate pricing scheme for ISDN service. Through Bell Atlantic, there is a one-time installation charge of only $169.00, but there is a monthly charge of $39.00, plus an online charge of $0.02 per minute per channel ($0.04 per minute if you're multiplexing the two 64 Kbps channels into one 128 Kbps channel). Other Bell service providers have dropped the online charge but charge upwards of $500-700 for installation.

The other cost for ISDN is in the equipment. Equipment prices are dropping as more companies begin offering ISDN equipment, but costs for an NT-1 terminal adapter are still in the $300-500 range.

Cable modems

The other emerging technology, which many experts feel is still several years away, is what is being called cable modems. Cable modems are, in effect, 2-way digital communications lines tied in over the same line used for cable TV. With many cable TV operators upgrading their service line to fiber optic, the potential here is for communications connections to the Internet in the 1-10 Mbps range. Cost will be another factor driving this technology as well, both for the user and the provider. Early speculation for cable modems estimate prices in the $500-700 range. Also, cable operators will have to install fiber optic hubs and routers at an estimated cost of $2,000-5,000 for every 30-50 users.

Obviously there are problems associated with both of these technologies, but once these are solved and either (or both) of these technologies are more widespread, the Internet backbone could begin to face serious bandwidth constraints. Apparently, this concern is being addressed. In April 1995 the NFSNET backbone was phased out and replaced with a new "very high speed Backbone Network Service" (vBNS). The vBNS is currently running at 155 MBps. In 1996, it is scheduled to be upgraded to operate at 622 MBps. While no mention is made of upgrading other segments of the Internet backbone in this country, this example clearly shows that bandwidth concerns remain a high priority.

Exploring the WWW with Netscape 3

Netscape has managed to remain the leader of the pack among Web browsers due in large part to the fact that Netscape has most often been the first Web browser to incorporate new features and new extensions to HTML.

Version 3.0 pushes the limits of a Web browser even further by incorporating new features both for end-users who will use Netscape primarily as a Web browser, and for HTML authors and developers who will be incorporating many of the proposed HTML 3.0 features into their Web sites.

The following gives a cursory overview of some of the new features you'll be seeing in Netscape 3.

LiveAudio

LiveAudio is a new plug-in (this plug-in and others are discussed in detail in chapter 10) that is included with Netscape. This plug-in allows you to hear music and voice audio directly within web pages (see fig. 1.14). This plug-in plays the most popular audio file formats that you'll find on the Web and it's likely that it's the only audio player you'll need.

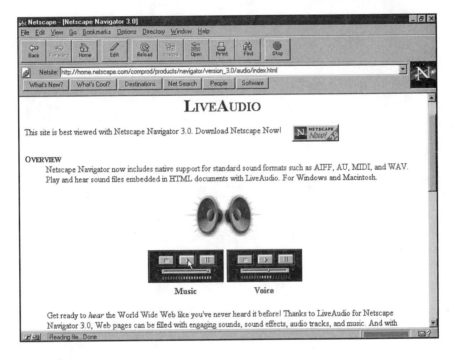

Fig. 1.14
You can see the controls for the audio player here embedded in this Web page, but you'll need speakers to hear the sounds.

LiveVideo

LiveVideo is Netscape's built in player for AVI movie files. AVI is Microsoft's popular Video for Windows movie file format. With LiveVideo you no longer need a separate player to see AVI videos embedded in Web pages, like the one shown in figure 1.15. However, there are many other popular file formats for video that you will still need plug-ins (see chapter 10) or helper applications (see chapter 11) to use.

Fig. 1.15
Near the upper-left side of this page is a video of a sculture in Italy. This AVI movie file is a part of the Web page it is in.

Live3D

VRML is supposed to be the interactive future of the Web. The Virtual Reality Markup Language (VRML) is used to make 3D "worlds" that you can travel through and interact with through your computer. Live3D is Netscape's built-in support for VRML. VRML can be used to create separate Web pages that are "worlds" or to embed VRML objects in a standard Web page as shown in Live3D in figure 1.16.

CoolTalk

If you've heard about people using the Internet for chat or to make long-distance phone calls for free, CoolTalk is Netscape's way for you to do this and more. With CoolTalk you can "chat" via text-based messages along with a shared whiteboard where you and a friend can edit an image together over the Internet. With the audio portion of CoolTalk, you and a friend (who will also need a computer using Netscape and CoolTalk) can talk over the Internet just like a telephone, except there are no charges beyond your Internet connection costs. CoolTalk is explored in detail in chapter 12.

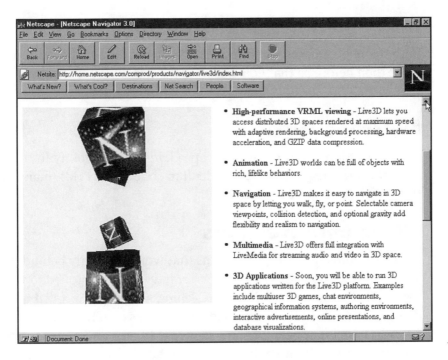

Fig. 1.16
These Netscape cubes are a simple collection of VRML objects that rotate in the left side of this Web page.

Enhanced security

With the new security features in Netscape, you can have your own "personal certificate" in Netscape. With personal certificates you can identify yourself from everybody else. This is particularly useful when you're submitting a form, so that the recipient will know for sure the information is from you, and nobody else. Personal certificates are described in detail in chapter 6.

Frame navigation

Netscape introduced frames in version 2. Frames make it possible to divide Web pages into several sections on-screen called frames. While these made for some nice Web pages, many users soon found that navigating Web pages with frames had some hidden surprises. With version 3, Netscape has made it easier to navigate frames as you'll see in chapter 2.

Mail and news improvements

Both the mail and news windows in Netscape can now be customized more than before so that you can view them in a way that suits the way you work.

Netscape Gold

The biggest improvement in Netscape Gold is its capability to create and edit tables. Tables can be very difficult to code with HTML manually so this is a welcome improvement.

Other improvements

There are some other improvements that work primarily behind the scenes in Netscape. Java and JavaScript have been improved to work better together and with plug-ins. Caching has been improved to allow developers to include "pre-cached" Web pages on CD-ROM to speed up access. There is support for some new HTML tags and network administrators have an administration kit to facilitate installing Netscape in a corporate setting with common setup preferences.

Moving Around the Web

● **In this chapter:**

Some people characterize the Web as confusing. They complain that it's not linear. It doesn't present you with a logical sequence of choices that you must make in order to move forward. You'll find through your own experience, however, that this is precisely why the Web is so intuitively easy. It's free-form, not linear. It more closely matches how people think: jumping from topic to topic as we see fit, as opposed to having order forced upon us.

Do you watch television, read the news, or listen to your technically adept friends talk about the Web? If so, you've probably encountered a variety of metaphors that people use to explain how the Web works. Here are two examples:

- The Web is like our national highway system. It connects countless destinations together in a Web.

- The Web is similar to a spider's Web. Nodes are joined together by tiny strands of silk.

The one concept that both of these metaphors have in common is that of joining, or linking, things together. This is, in fact, what the Web is all about, and represents one of the most important things you need to know about it. For example, you need to know that you can jump from one Web page to another by clicking a link. You also need to know some other ways to get to a Web page without using links.

Understanding links

As you read this book, you may notice the references to other chapters that you sometimes find in the text. They serve a similar purpose as links do on a Web page—albeit a little low-tech. They refer you to other places in this book that might be useful or interesting to read. Without these references, you would have to resort to flipping through the pages looking for what you need.

Links on a Web page are even more vital. You have all the pages of this book right in front of you. At least you would know where to start looking. On the other hand, you have no idea where to find all the Web pages on the Internet. And there are too many to keep track of, anyway. Therefore, links are the only reasonable way to go from one Web page to another related Web page.

NOTE **Hypertext and hypermedia are two terms you'll frequently hear** associated with the Web. A hypertext document is a document that contains links to other documents—allowing you to jump between them by clicking the links. Hypermedia contains more than text, it contains multimedia such as pictures, videos, and sounds, too. In hypermedia documents, pictures are frequently used as links to other documents.

A link really has two different parts. First, there's the part that you see on the Web page—called an anchor. There's also the part that tells Netscape what to do if you click that link—called the URL reference. When you click a link's anchor, Netscape loads the Web page given by the link's corresponding URL reference. You'll learn about both parts of a link in the following sections. You'll also learn about the different resources to which a link can point.

Anchors

A link's anchor can be a word, a group of words, or a picture. Exactly how an anchor looks in Netscape depends largely on what type of anchor it is, and how the person who created the Web page used it. There are only two types of anchors though: text and graphical. You'll learn about both types in this section.

TIP **When you move the mouse cursor over a link's anchor, it changes from** a pointer to a hand.

Text anchors

Most text anchors look somewhat the same. A text anchor is one or more words that Netscape underlines to indicate that it represents a link. Netscape also displays a text anchor using a different color than the rest of the text around it.

TIP **In Windows 95, click and drag a link's text anchor onto your desktop.** You can return quickly to that Web page by double-clicking the shortcut.

Figure 2.1 shows a Web page that contains three text anchors. In particular, notice how the text anchors on this Web page are embedded in the text. That is, they aren't set apart from the text, like the references in this book, but are actually an integral part of it. Clicking one of these links will load a Web page that is related to the link. You'll find many text anchors used this way.

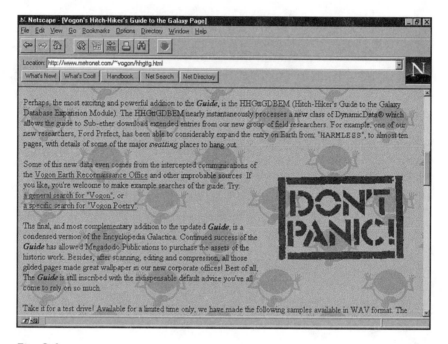

Fig. 2.1

You'll find Vogon's Hitch-Hiker's Guide to the Galaxy Page at **http://www.metronet.com/ ˜vogon/hhgttg.html**.

Figure 2.2 shows another Web page with a lot of text anchors. These anchors aren't embedded in the text, however. They are presented as a list or index of links from which you can choose. Web page authors frequently use this method to present collections of related links.

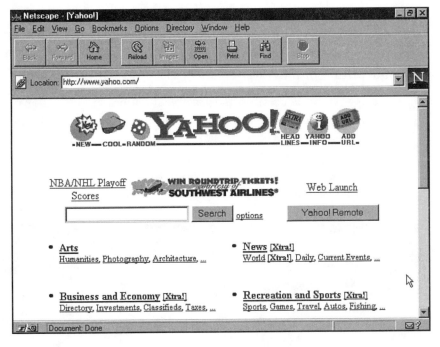

Fig. 2.2
Yahoo (**http://www.yahoo.com**) is one of the most popular indexes on the Web. To learn more about Yahoo, see chapter 3, "Finding Information on the Web."

Graphical anchors

A graphical anchor is similar to a text anchor. When you click a link's graphical anchor, Netscape loads the Web page that the link references. Graphical anchors aren't underlined or displayed in a different color. And no two graphical anchors need to look the same. It depends entirely on the picture that the Web page's author chose to use.

TIP **Right-click a graphical anchor, and choose Save This Image As to save** the image in a file on your computer.

Versatility is the strong suit of graphical anchors. Web page authors effectively use them for a variety of reasons. Here are some examples of the ways you'll find graphical anchors used on a Web page:

- Bullets—Graphical anchors are frequently used as list bullets. You can click the picture to go to the Web page described by that list item. Frequently, the text in the list item is also a link. You can click either the picture or the text.

- Icons—Many Web sites use graphical anchors in a similar manner to the way Windows 95 uses icons. They are common on home pages, and represent a variety of Web pages available through that site. Figure 2.3 shows a Web site that uses graphical anchors in this manner. Click the ProShop icon to open the ProShop Web page, for example.

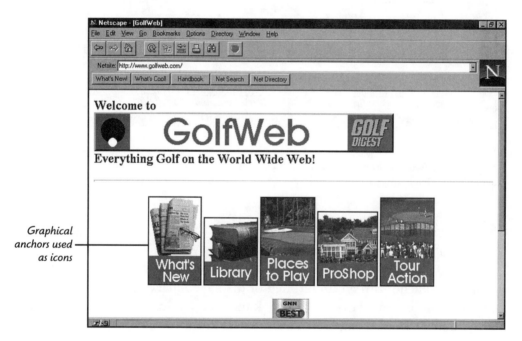

Graphical anchors used as icons

Fig. 2.3
You'll find GolfWeb at **http://www.golfweb.com**. GolfWeb's home page uses graphical anchors to represent a variety of pages that you can load.

- Advertisements—Many Web sites have sponsors that pay to advertise on the site. This keeps the Web site free to you and me, while the site continues to make money. You'll usually find advertisements, such as the one shown in figure 2.4, at the top of a Web page. Click the advertisement, and Netscape will load the sponsor's Web page.

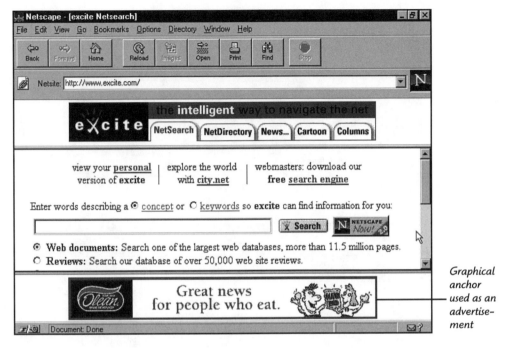

Graphical anchor used as an advertisement

Fig. 2.4
Excite (**http://www.excite.com**) is an up-and-coming Web search tool that uses sponsors to keep the service free to you and me.

URL references

The other part of a link is the URL reference. This is the address of the Web page that Netscape will load if you click the link. Every type of link, whether it uses a text or graphical anchor, uses either a relative or absolute reference. You'll learn about each type in this section, but when you're "surfing" the Web it really doesn't matter which type of URL reference a link is using—as long as Netscape loads the Web page you want.

An URL reference to a file on the same computer is also known as a relative reference. It means that the URL is relative to the computer and directory from which Netscape originally loaded the Web page. If Netscape loads a page at **http://www.mysite.com/page**, for example, then a relative reference to /picture would actually refer to the URL **http://www.mysite.com/page/picture**. Relative references are commonly used to refer to Web pages on the same computer. Figure 2.5 shows a Web page that contains relative references to other Web pages on that site.

TIP Choose **V**iew, Document **S**ource to tell for sure if a link is using relative references.

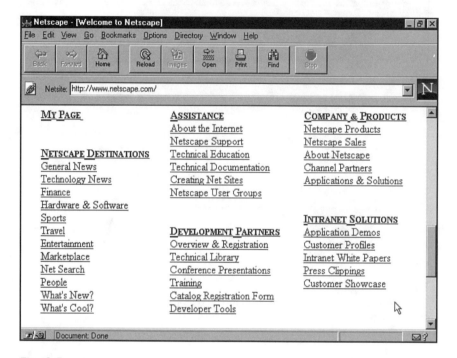

Fig. 2.5
Netscape's Web site is at **http://www.netscape.com**. You can find various information about Netscape and its products.

The primary reason Web authors use a relative reference is convenience. It's much simpler to just type the file name instead of the entire URL. It also makes it easier to move Web pages around on a server. Since the URL references are relative to the Web page's computer and directory, the author doesn't have to change all the links in the Web page every time the files move to a different location.

Absolute references

An URL reference that specifies the exact computer, directory, and file for a Web page is an absolute reference. Whereas relative references are common for links to Web pages on the same computer, absolute references are necessary for links to Web pages on other computers.

TIP Hold your mouse over a link and look at Netscape's status line to see its URL reference.

NOTE If you're curious about what a link with an absolute reference looks like in HTML, however, here's an example:

    <A HREF="http://www.yahoo.com/">Yahoo</A>

The first part of this link, the bit between the left (<) and right (>) brackets, is the URL reference. The word yahoo is the text anchor that Netscape underlines on the Web page. The last part ends the link.

Corporate bulletin boards

Many corporations, such as Hewlett Packard, have created corporate bulletin boards that their associates view with Web browsers such as Netscape. These Web pages aren't on the Web, however. They're stored on the companies' internal network servers. They contain a variety of information that is useful to their associates such as the following:

- Meeting schedules and meeting room availability

- Announcements about corporate events

- Information about policies and benefits

- Recent press releases and financial statements

- Technological information

You can easily create a bulletin board for the corporation you work for, too. Part V, "Creating Your Own Web Pages," shows you how to build pages for the Web. The only difference between that and building a corporate bulletin board is in the type of information you choose to include on the page.

Resources to which links can point

Links can point to more than just Web pages. They can point to a variety of files and other Internet resources, too. A link can point to a video, pictures, or even a plain text file. It can also point to an FTP server, Gopher server, or a UseNet newsgroup. Table 2.1 describes the other types of things a link can point to, and shows you what the URL looks like.

Table 2.1   Resources to which a link can point

Type	Sample URL
Web Page	http://www.mysite.com/page.html
Files	file://C:/picture.bmp
Multimedia	http://www.mysite.com/video.avi
E-mail	mailto:info@netscape.com
FTP	ftp://ftp.mysite.com
Gopher	gopher://gopher.mysite.com
Newsgroup	news:alt.fan.que
Telnet	telnet://mysite.com

How to move around the Web

You didn't buy this book to learn how to load a Web page in Netscape, then sit back and look at it all day. You want to "surf" the Web—jumping from Web page to Web page, looking for entertaining and useful information.

In fact, surfing is such an important part of the Web that both Netscape and the Web itself provide many different ways to navigate. You can use the links and imagemaps that you find on a Web page, for example. You can go directly to a Web page if you know its URL. You can also use some of the more advanced Netscape features such as bookmarks and frames. In this section, you'll learn how to use those features to move around the Web like a pro.

Clicking a link

You learned about links earlier in this chapter. They are the primary method you use to go from the Web page you're viewing to another related Web page. All these links are provided by the Web page's author, and are usually accurately related to the context in which you found it.

Figure 2.6 shows a Web page with both text and graphical links. You can click Collabra Software, for example, to go to the Collabra Web site. The next time you see this link, its color will change, indicating that you've been there before. This helps you keep track of the links you haven't visited, so you don't waste time. You can also click the graphical link at the right side of the Web page to get more information about testing out Netscape's server software.

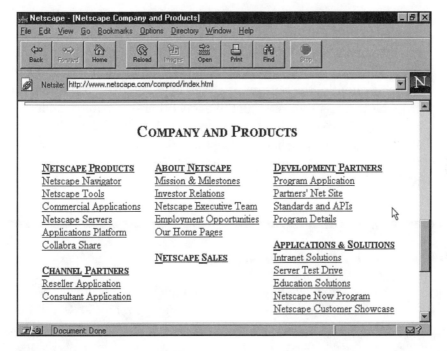

Fig. 2.6
This Web page (**http://home.netscape.com/comprod/index.html**) has a complete list of Netscape products and services at the bottom.

Clicking an imagemap

Imagemaps are similar to graphical anchors, in that if you click an imagemap, Netscape will load another Web page. Imagemaps can load more than one Web page, however, depending on what part of the image you click. The image itself usually indicates the areas you can click to load a particular Web page.

Figure 2.7, for example, shows the imagemap that Microsoft uses at its Web site. Each region of the imagemap is clearly defined so that you know where you need to click, and you know what Web page Netscape will load as a result. Click the Microsoft Windows 95 area and Netscape will load a Web page about Windows 95. Click the area that reads "Support" and Netscape will load the Microsoft Support Desktop.

A common use for imagemaps on the Web is button bars. Button bars are similar to the toolbars you've used in Windows 95 and other windowing environments. They don't appear to toggle in and out like buttons, however. They are, after all, just imagemaps. You'll find them at the top or, more frequently, the bottom of a Web page. Figure 2.8 shows a button bar from Netscape's Web site. Just like any other imagemap, each area you can click is clearly defined. You can click different areas to load different Web pages. You can click the Netscape Search button to search Netscape's Web site, or you can click the Table of Contents button to get a roadmap of Netscape's site.

Client pull on the Web

You'll eventually run across a Web page that says something like "We've moved" or "This Web page has a new location." It'll display a link that loads the Web page at its new location if you click it. If you wait long enough, however, Netscape may automatically load the Web page at its new location.

Client pull is the technology behind this behavior. Client pull allows the Web server to tell Netscape to reload the current Web page or load a different Web page after a set amount of time. One of the most common uses for client pull is the situation described previously. It's also used for simple sequences of Web pages, however, that work just like slide shows.

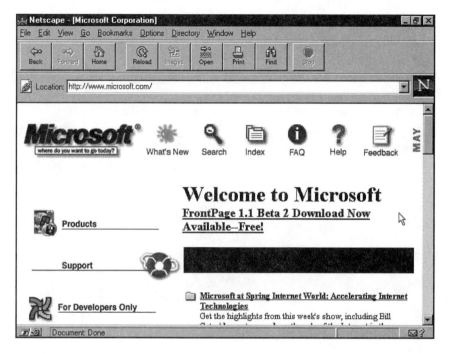

Fig. 2.7
Microsoft's Web Site is at **http://www.microsoft.com**.

TIP If you're having trouble deciphering a button bar, look for text links just below it.

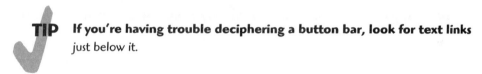

Fig. 2.8
You'll find this button bar at the bottom of all Netscape Web pages.

Going directly to a resource

Which came first, the link or the Web page? If the only way to load a Web page was by clicking a link, you'd never get anywhere. If a friend gives you an URL, for example, you need a way to tell Netscape to open that Web page without having to use a link. That's why Netscape lets you go directly to a Web page by specifying its URL in either the location bar or Open Location dialog box.

TIP **URLs are case sensitive. If you can't open a Web page, check for** strangely capitalized letters such as **http://www.mywebsite.com/ MyPaGe.html**.

Figure 2.9 shows the Netscape location bar with the drop-down list open. Type the URL of a Web page in Netscape's location bar, and Netscape will load the Web page. Netscape keeps the addresses of all the Web pages you've opened this way in the location bar's drop-down list. It keeps this list from session to session, too. That way you can always go back to a previous site by dropping down the list, and clicking on the Web page's URL.

Location bar or Netsite if you're viewing a Netscape Web page

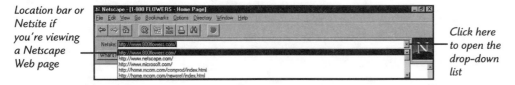

Click here to open the drop-down list

Fig. 2.9
The drop-down list keeps track of only those Web pages you've opened using the location bar.

 NOTE **You don't have to type the http:// part of an URL for a Web address** in the location bar, because Netscape will add this for you.

The Open button requires a few more mouse clicks, but it's just as easy to use. Click the Open button on the Netscape toolbar. Type the URL of a Web page in the Open Location dialog box, and click Open. Netscape loads the Web page that you specified.

Moving forward and backward

After you've clicked on a few links and opened a few Web pages, you may want to go back to a Web page you looked at earlier. Maybe you forgot something you just read, or something didn't seem that interesting then, but it does now. Netscape provides two useful features to look at previously viewed Web pages: the history list and the Back/Forward buttons on the toolbar.

TIP **In the History window, select a Web site from the list, and click Create** Bookmark to add it to your bookmarks.

- The history list keeps track of all the Web pages that you've visited during the current session. You can access the history list in one of two places: the Go menu, shown in figure 2.10, shows the last 15 Web pages that you've loaded in Netscape. Choose Go from the Netscape main menu, and then choose any of the Web pages on the menu. If you want to see a list of all the Web pages that you've visited during the current session, choose Window, History from the Netscape main menu. Figure 2.11 shows the History window. You can scroll up and down the list, and double-click a Web page to open it in Netscape.

- The Forward and Back buttons move you up and down the history list shown in figure 2.11. If you click the Back button, Netscape moves the highlight down the list and opens that Web page. If you click the Forward button, Netscape moves the highlight up the list, and opens that Web page. Once you've reached the bottom of the list, the Back button is disabled. Likewise, when you reach the top of the list, the Forward button is disabled.

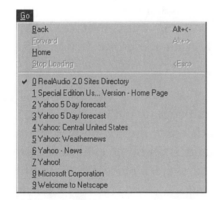

Fig. 2.10
The checkmark in this menu indicates the current Web page.

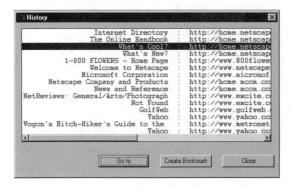

Fig. 2.11
The highlight in this list indicates the current Web page.

Using a home page

The home page, as you've likely discovered, is simply the first Web page that you see when you launch Netscape Navigator. By default this is Netscape Communications Corporation's Web site, but you have the option of changing your home page to just about any Web page on the Internet you want, as well as to a local (on your computer) HTML file. (You'll see how to do that later in this chapter in the section "Changing Your Home Page.")

You'll also see the term "home page" used in a general sense to describe the main, or first, Web page of other people's and organizations' Web sites on the Internet. In my opinion, this is really the wrong way to use the term but it's fairly well entrenched, so there's not much chance of changing it. If a page is the first page of a particular site, it's more correct to call it the index page or default page for that site. As far as Netscape (the application) is concerned, your home page is the first page that loads when you start your browser.

Clicking the Home Page button once takes you to your home page at any time during a browsing session. Alternatively, you may also select Go, Home from the drop-down menu bar.

You can think of the Home Page button as a mini-bookmark that contains only one hyperlink—a very important link with which you begin your Web session. Loading that page from the Home Page button is a bit different, though, than loading it at the start of a session, because of the way Netscape stores the home page in its cache.

The first time you load in your home page it does not use the files on your hard drive's cache. Netscape always travels to that first URL, updates the Web page, and then caches its contents in memory. This is especially important if you decide to change your home page to a site other than Netscape Corp.'s pages. Since Netscape must download all the files from your home page without the speed and support of the cache, connecting to a heavily used site or a Web page with a slow server can be frustrating.

Fortunately, the Home Page button—unless you've designated other- wise—acts as a regular URL, and uses the files from your cache.

Saving bookmarks to Web pages

The easiest way to get back to a Web page that you visit frequently is to use Netscape bookmarks. Bookmarks let you save and organize links to your favorite Web pages. Unlike Netscape's history list, the bookmarks hang around from session to session. They are always easily accessible. Choose Bookmarks from the Netscape main menu. Figure 2.12 shows you what the Bookmarks menu looks like.

Fig. 2.12
Open a submenu or click a Web site to load it in Netscape.

Navigating a Web site with frames

Frames are a feature that is currently specific to Netscape. They allow the Netscape window to be split into multiple sections. Each frame on the window can point to a different URL. Figure 2.13 shows a Web page that uses a frame to present a button bar that's always available to you.

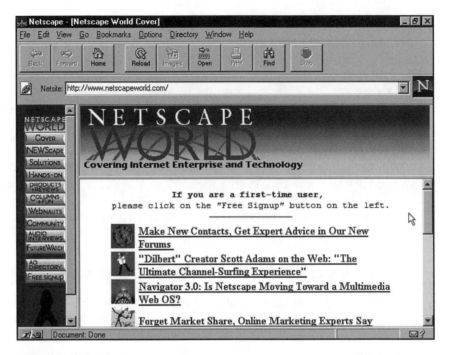

Fig. 2.13
At this site, the button bar will always be available in the bottom frame, regardless of which Web page the top frame is displaying.

With the addition of frames, Netscape added an extra bit of complexity in navigation. Each frame was treated independent of each other, which meant that you couldn't easily go to a previous frame. With Netscape 2.0, you had to put your mouse cursor in a particular frame, click the right mouse button, then select Back in Frame. If you had pressed the Back button, it would've loaded the previous complete page. Netscape 3 greatly simplifies navigation with frames by making the Back button smarter. Now, when you press it, you automatically go back to the most recently modified frame.

 NOTE **You'll run across many Web sites that say "Netscape Enhanced,"** "Best Viewed with Netscape," or something similar. They mean it. Many Web sites implement Netscape specific features that can't be viewed with other Web browsers. Frames are a typical example.

Many Windows 95 programs divide their windows into panes. They do it to make the organization of the windows' contents more obvious. A program that makes the résumés of a list of people available might have two panes: one to display a list of people and another to display the résumé of the currently selected person. Netscape frames can serve a similar purpose as well. Figure 2.14 shows a Web page that does the same thing as the résumé program. It has three frames: one that shows a list of people, another for the résumé of the currently selected individual, and a pane at the bottom to select a category.

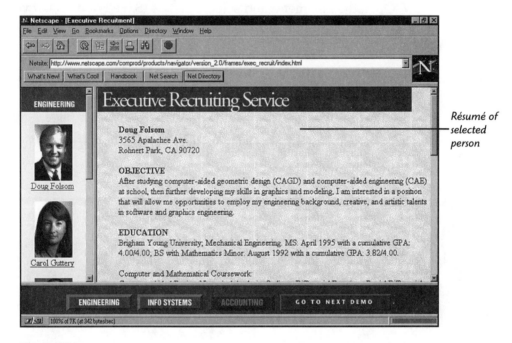

Résumé of selected person

Fig. 2.14
Frames make a Web site easier to use by organizing its contents in a logical fashion.

Saving and printing copies of a Web page

Because the Web is used as a source of information on a myriad of topics, you often need to keep a copy of the material that you read. Sometimes you need to incorporate some of this information in another document, or you may simply need a hard copy to give to someone else. In either case, Netscape allows you to retain that Web site permanently with a click of your mouse.

Saving an HTML file for future reference

All Web pages are created from a text file that has special key commands stored in it that the Web browser reads. These codes allow us to see graphics, colorful backgrounds, bold text, and brightly colored links to other sites. You can save a copy of the original HTML file for future reference by following these steps:

1 Open the File menu and select Save As (Save Frame As, if you are visiting a site that uses Frames) or press Ctrl+S.

2 The Save As dialog box appears, which allows you to direct Netscape to save a copy of the HTML code to a directory of your choosing. The default directory is c:\Program Files\Netscape\\Program.

3 Select the directory in which you want to save this page.

4 Place your cursor in the File Name: field and enter a name for this HTML document.

Watching Netscape's status

Netscape gives you a lot of feedback about what's happening after you click a link, or open an URL. Stars shoot past the Netscape logo while Netscape is transferring a Web page or file, for example. It also updates the status bar with information that'll help you keep track of what Netscape is doing. Here are some of the messages you'll see in the status bar:

Message	Description
http://server/file	The URL reference of the link to which you are currently pointing.
X% of YK	Netscape has completed X percent of a Y kilobyte transfer.
Connect: Contacting hostserver:	Netscape is trying to contact the given server.
Connect: Host contacted. Waiting for reply	Netscape has contacted the server and is waiting for a reply.
Document: Done.	The Web page is finished loading.

5 Click Save. You have now saved a copy of this World Wide Web page that you can view at any time without actually connecting to the Internet.

Because you are saving pages, you must need to look at them at least every once in a while. The following steps assist you in reading a saved HTML document.

1 Open the File menu and choose the Open File option, or press Ctrl+O.

2 The Open dialog box appears. Change to the c:\Program Files\Netscape\\Programs directory, if you are not already there.

3 Click your mouse pointer on the name of the file that you want to open.

4 Click Open.

Netscape opens the file, allowing you to continue working with that Web site. You do not have to retrace your steps. You can forge ahead finding the information you need to complete your tasks.

Printing Web pages

Sometimes you simply need to capture the information that is on a Web page in the fastest way possible and you do not necessarily have to be able to look at it in electronic form. That is where Netscape's printing feature enters the picture.

1 Open the File menu and select the Print option (Print Frame if you are looking at a site that uses Frames), or press Ctrl+P.

2 Select the name of your printer from the Name drop-down list.

3 Set the number of Copies and the Print Range options to meet your needs.

4 When you're done setting up the printer, click the OK button.

A window appears telling you that your document is being retrieved from the main Web site and that it is being formatted for the printer. This process should only take a few moments, and you can resume your search of the World Wide Web.

TIP **If you end up with a stack of printed pages and you're not sure where** they are from, you will find the URL for that Web page located in the upper-right corner of the printout. This URL also allows you to go back to that site to get more or updated information.

Displaying information on a Web page

Netscape 3.0 allows you to look at a Web page in three different views. The first, and most common, is through the browser with all the HTML tags activated. This is the way you are going to automatically see all sites when you first jump to them.

The second method involves looking at the text file that makes up the body of the Web page. This is viewing the document source, and it is useful if you want to know how the Webmaster at that site achieved a specific look in his or her Web page. Of course, if you are just starting to program with HTML, you will want to look at a lot of Web sites in this view. It helps you learn the language, and the conventions that are used when writing HTML documents.

To view the source document of any Web page, open the View menu and select the Document Source option. This opens a document viewer, generally the Netscape viewing utility that comes with Netscape, unless you have asked the program to use another. In this view you see the source code that is interpreted by the Web browser to create the graphical pages that you see on your screen.

The third method shows you specific information about the Web page. Open the File menu and select the Document Info option. This opens another Netscape window using a frame. In the top half of this window you see a copy of the main document. In the bottom half of this screen you see a summary listing about that Web page, as you can see in figure 2.15.

 TIP **With Netscape Gold, there is also another way to view Web pages.** We'll look at that in chapter 14 "Creating Web Pages with Netscape Navigator Gold."

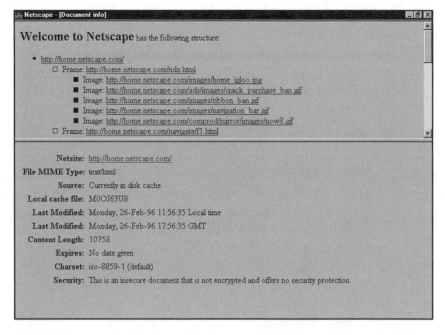

Fig. 2.15
The Netscape browser window showing both the main Web page and the appropriate summary information on that file.

Getting around faster

If you're using a 14.4Kbps or slower modem, you'll eventually become frustrated with how long it takes to load some Web pages. Many Web pages have very large graphics that take a long time to download. Unfortunately, the use of large graphics is becoming more common as Web authors take it for granted that everyone on the Internet is using at least a 28.8Kbps modem.

 TIP **Many Web sites provide links to text-only versions. Look for a text link** that says "Text Only."

Fight back. Netscape provides a few features that make Web pages containing too many graphics more tolerable:

- You don't have to wait for the entire Web page to finish loading before you can click a link. Click the Stop button, and Netscape will stop transferring the Web page. If you change your mind and want to reload the page, click the Reload button. Also, most of the text links are available before Netscape has finished transferring the images for the Web page. You can click any of these links. Netscape will stop loading the current page, and start loading the Web page referenced by the link.

- Most of your time is spent waiting for inline images to load. The irony is that the images on many Web pages aren't really worth the time if you have a slow connection. If you don't want Netscape to automatically load inline images, make sure that Options, Auto Load Images is not checked. If you want to view the images on a particular Web page, and you've disabled Auto Load Images, click the Load Images button on the Netscape toolbar. Figure 2.16 shows what a Web page looks like when it's loaded without inline images. Notice that Netscape displays placeholders where it normally displays the images. Netscape also displays alternative text to help you figure out what the link points to.

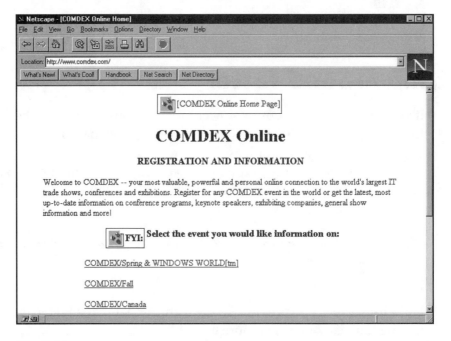

Fig. 2.16
You can click one of the placeholders to load the Web page it refers to, or you can click the Load Images button to see the inline images

Changing the way Netscape works with links

Netscape gives you a bit of control over how it displays links. It lets you choose whether or not they're underlined and what color it uses to display them.

Underlining links

You learned earlier in this chapter that Netscape underlines a link's text anchor on a Web page. You can change that. Here's how to configure Netscape so that it doesn't underline a link's text anchor:

1 Choose Options, General from the Netscape main menu.

2 Click the Appearance tab, and Netscape displays the dialog box shown in figure 2.17.

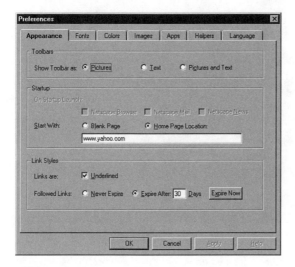

Fig. 2.17
The Appearance box allows you to change the toolbar, start up options, and link styles.

3 Deselect Underlined, and click OK.

Beginning with the next Web page that Netscape loads, text anchors won't be underlined. You can still figure out where the links are, however, because they are displayed in a different color than the text around them.

Using a different color for links

If you don't like the colors that Netscape uses for links, you can change them. If the default colors are hard to tell apart on your computer, for example, you'll want to change the colors so you can easily see the links. Use the following steps to change the colors Netscape uses for a text link's anchor:

1 Choose Options, General from the Netscape main menu.

2 Click the Colors tab, and Netscape displays the dialog box shown in figure 2.18.

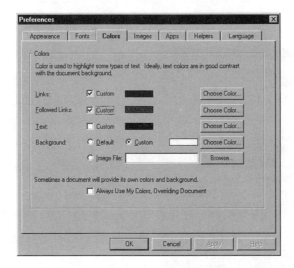

Fig. 2.18
Most of Netscape's options can be configured on one of this dialog box's tabs.

3 Select Links, and click the corresponding Choose Color button. Choose a color from the Color dialog box, and click OK.

4 Select Followed Links, and click the corresponding Choose Color button. Choose a color from the Color dialog box, and click OK.

5 Click OK to save your changes.

Beginning with the next Web page that Netscape loads, Netscape will display text anchors that you've never visited using the color you chose in Links, and text anchors that you've already visited using the color you chose in Followed Links.

Controlling link expiration

Netscape caches Web pages so they'll load faster the next time you visit that Web page. It takes much longer to load a Web page from the Internet than it takes to load it from the hard drive. So, Netscape stores every Web page it loads to your hard drive. The next time you point Netscape to that URL, it loads it from the hard drive instead of the Internet.

The problem is that if Netscape is loading Web pages from your hard drive instead of the Internet, you may be looking at a Web page that's out of date. Even if the Web page's author changes it, you'll still be looking at the older version.

Netscape let's you configure how long it will continue to get a Web page from the cache before it loads it from the Internet again. This is called the expiration. By default, Netscape expires a link after 30 days. If you find that the Web pages you use are updated more frequently, you can easily change it. Here's how:

1 Choose Options, General Preferences from the Netscape main menu.

2 Click the Appearance tab, and Netscape displays the dialog box.

3 Type the number of days you want Netscape to wait before expiring each link in Days. Alternatively, you can expire all of the links in the cache by clicking Expire Now.

4 Click OK to save your changes.

Changing your home page

Selection of a home page is personal, and it depends on how you use the Web. Whether your interests are business, pleasure, or both, you'll have little problem finding a Web page out there that will suit your needs as you begin each browsing session. There are, however, some important things to know about the home page:

- Netscape's own home page (**http://home.netscape.com**) is a great place to begin, especially if you're new to the Web.

- Netscape doesn't load the home page from cache on startup (though it does cache after loading), so expect lag-time if you set your home page to a heavily accessed server or URL that has specific time constraints.

- If you copy the source file for a Web page from another site and use it as your home page (loading it off your hard drive), you won't see any changes or updates from the original Web site.

- You may set your bookmarks file as the home page; however, your history file will not work as a home page.

 TIP **When upgrading from Netscape version 1.x or 2.x to 3.0, install** Netscape in the same directory as the previous version (the Windows 95 default is c:\Program Files\ Netscape\Navigator). This will retain your current home page settings, as well as your bookmarks file and any shortcuts you have in your Start menu or on your desktop. If you've not yet installed Netscape or you install to a different directory, Netscape automatically sets your home page to its Web site. For more information on downloading and installing Netscape, see the appendixes.

Using another Web page for home

As comprehensive as Netscape's home page is, you'll probably, at some point, find another you like better. You may discover that you change your home page as your needs change. For example, if you're heavily into e-mail, you may want your home page to be set to Netscape's e-mail window. If you become interested in a particular newsgroup, you may find yourself specifying the Newsgroups window as your starting point.

In fact, you can set your home page to load any valid, accessible URL on the Internet. And it's as easy as a few clicks. Just remember to watch out for slow servers or heavy Web sites—otherwise you'll become more intimate with the Stop button than you probably want to be.

To change your home page settings, select Options, General Preferences and then the Appearances tab (it's the default tab). The dialog box shown in figure 2.19 pops up.

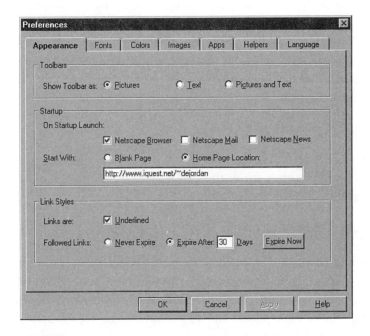

Fig. 2.19
Enter your new home page in the Start With text box.

Midway down you'll see the Start With text box. Enter the new URL there. You don't have to enter the protocol tag for most URLs, though some will require it. For example, if I'm setting my home page to Que's Web site, I type in

http://www.mcp.com/que or just www.mcp.com/que

Notice that there is no Browse button that allows you access to your history file, bookmarks file, or address box. You'll also find that Netscape doesn't allow you to paste a copied URL into this text box. This is an annoying setup that Netscape should eventually fix in later releases. For now—unless you have a photographic memory—you have to resort to pen and paper to write down the URL, and then type it directly into the box.

Notice the two radio buttons above the box. The first one, labeled Blank Page, should be checked if you don't want a startup page to begin your Web sessions. Why do this? It keeps Netscape from loading anything when it starts up. Perhaps you have different URLs you like to load first, depending on the work at hand. Sometimes, for instance, I know I want to go straight to the WebCrawler Web site to search for something. Other times I might want to set off for Netscape's home pages or some other site I often call home.

The second radio button is the one you'll need to check if you're specifying a home page other than Netscape's site.

Above the radio buttons are three check boxes where you can specify whether you want to start up with your home page, with Netscape's built-in e-mail, or with the Newsgroups browser.

Using a local file as your home page

There are some distinct advantages to using a local HTML file on your hard drive as your home page. A local file will load fast, and will always load (barring a badly fragmented hard drive or other local system problem). Again, a heavily accessed site sometimes means it takes quite a while for a remote home page to load. And, even if you specify an URL on the Web that's not heavily accessed, it's always possible that the site's server is down.

Perhaps the most important advantage to a local home page, however, is the control it gives you over the content of your start page. Write your own home page, and you can include exactly what you need and want—your own favorite links and graphics.

Of course, in order to specify a local file for your home page, you've got to have a file. One option is to create your own HTML page and use it as your home page.

NOTE **Controlling just how you want to display your home page is an exciting** idea—and a lot easier to do than you may realize. Part V of this book shows you how to design and create your own home pages.

Another option is to save the source code to any one of the millions and millions of URLs your browser can access. If you spend even a few minutes a day on the Web—and many of you spend far more time than that— you'll have already lost count of the number of Web pages you've visited. Just point your browser to the Web page you want to save, and:

1 With the page you want saved displayed in Netscape, open the File menu and choose Save As. The Save As directory box appears (see fig. 2.20).

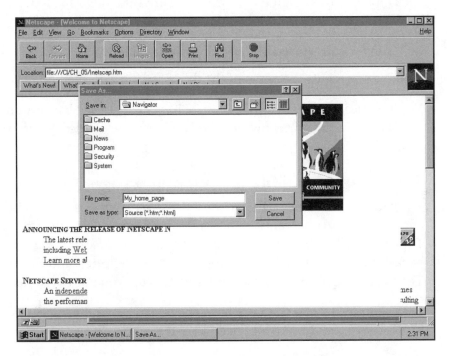

Fig. 2.20
Save the downloaded file using the Save As option in the File menu.

2 Select the directory or subdirectory where the file will reside using the Save in: drop-down menu.

3 Enter a name for the file.

4 Select the file type in the Save as type drop-down menu. In this case, you want source (*.htm, *.html) option.

5 Click the Save button and the file will be downloaded to the location you specified.

To verify that the page was downloaded successfully, go ahead and load it into Netscape Navigator. From File, Open File, click the Browse button and find the folder you saved it in, highlight the file and double-click it or click Open. Look first in the address box after the file is loaded. Netscape, by default, displays your local file structure with UNIX specifiers:

file:///c | directory/subdirectory/filename.htm

where c represents the name of the drive the file is located on.

You'll notice, too, that your Web page has changed; the background and any inline graphics are now replaced by Netscape's little broken picture icons.

Specifying a local file as your home page

To change your home page to a local file, select Options, General Preferences, and the Appearances tab. Place your cursor inside the text box. Type the letter of the drive where the file is located, followed by a colon, backslash, the appropriate directories or subdirectories, and the file name. The file can be from any drive and any directory on your system.

For example, if I'm setting my home page to a file in the windows directory on my hard drive c, all I need to enter is:

c:\windows\myhome.htm

Ensure that the .htm extension is used (see fig. 2.21).

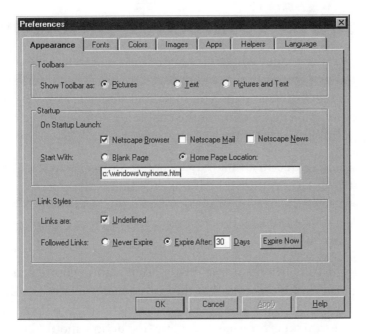

Fig. 2.21
Setting up a local file for your home page is no more difficult than setting up an URL.

Specifying the bookmarks file as your home page

You can also set your Bookmarks file as your home page. After you've been on the Web for a while and catalogued many of your favorite sites, this is a quick and easy option—it's also less clunky than fiddling with Netscape's View Bookmarks window. The file is located in your Navigator subdirectory and is simply named bookmarks.htm. Netscape's default installation for Windows 95 sets up the directory structure like this, where c is the letter of the hard drive:

> c:\Program Files\Netscape\bookmarks.htm

You may be tempted to try to use your History file as your home page. This would make some sense—the History file makes it easy for you to remember some of those dynamite Web sites you visited during your last session, but forgot to put in your Bookmarks file. Unfortunately, the file, netscap.hst, located in your navigator subdirectory, is just a text file that's used for reference to your cache, and is useless as a home page.

Troubleshooting connection problems

Sometimes you do not get where you want to go on the Internet. A site may be down, or a connection may have exactly too much interference in the lines to connect. A Web page you looked at yesterday may be deleted or moved today. This last section of the chapter offers some advice to improve your ability to get where you want to go.

Any address embedded in a link may be entered directly in the Locations field of your Netscape application. If the Web link is not the full link text, you can always see the link by moving your cursor over the link and not clicking the link. The full link description can be seen in the bottom edge of your Netscape window.

Normally, if the full URL (example: **http://www.yahoo.com/Recreation/**) has a slash at the end indicating that the last part of the URL is a directory, Netscape adds the slash for you as it loads the default page there. If Netscape gives you an error Not Found, your first action should be to select the Reload command (either from the View menu, or the Reload button to the right of the Home button on the Netscape toolbar).

 NOTE **An immediate Reload is not just an impatient, "Why won't this thing do what I want?" behavior, it's often the solution.** Small errors happen all the time, and reloading may work more often than you think. Reloading is an especially good idea if images on a page are downloading badly and Netscape displays a "broken picture" image where the picture should have been.

Reloading is exactly the right answer if you get a Too busy, try again later message when attempting to start an FTP or Gopher session. Gopher and FTP servers are often busy, and trying again is the same as redialing a telephone after you get a busy signal.

Your second attempt (if you were using a link from another page) is to look at the destination link displayed in the Location field between the two rows of buttons in the toolbar, and see what it looks like. Leaving the closing end off an anchor causes the rest of the page—from the beginning of the anchor, including the text label (if it was one), the image (if you used an image as the visible part of the link), and everything else to the end of the page—to become part of the destination address. If the location looks like an URL followed by words or file names, select the part of the address that doesn't look like an URL, and delete it. Try again.

Similarly, if you are typing in the address yourself, proofread the destination address. Fix any problems you see such as spaces accidentally inserted into the middle of the URL or capitalization errors, then select the Reload command. I recently encountered a non-functional link in a large Web site discussing HTML authoring. The Web page builder had typed /hyperext/ in the directory path where he meant to type /hypertext/. If a reload of the page doesn't work, or if you saw no problems with the URL, retype the URL, and try again anyway. If you got the URL from e-mail or an article you have electronically, try to copy the URL from where it is and paste it into the Location field in order to reduce interference from typing errors.

Part II: Mastering the Web with Netscape™

3

Finding Information on the Web

● In this chapter:

- Use Netscape's home page

- Use the What's Cool and What's New buttons

- Perform category searches with Yahoo and other subject-search tools

- Find information using the most powerful Internet search engines

You've probably heard some of the staggering numbers associated with the rise of the Internet and the World Wide Web: Forty million global users increasing by millions each month, millions of Web pages containing countless documents—hundreds of new servers popping up almost daily. Just realizing that the enormous resources of sites like the Library of Congress are only one small part of all this vastness does a lot to explain the phrase "information age."

How do you navigate such a universe? As a diligent infonaut perched at your computer—modem screaming, hard drive whining—you may begin to feel like a small spaceship drifting from one planet's gravitational pull to the next, with only the occasional burst from a new Web page's thrusters to point you in a new direction.

What we need is a map. All of this clicking around on links is great; but when you really need to find something (for instance, because your boss wants you to), surfing is about the last thing you want to do. But what if the Web had a table of contents—and some really strong search engines? Well, it does—sort of. And, Netscape makes the best of these engines easily accessible from the directory buttons on the browser window.

Using Netscape's home page

As a veteran of the World Wide Web, Netscape has had the time and resources to put together an informative, flexible, and useful Web site (**http://home.netscape.com**), shown in figure 3.1.

Netscape's home page offers a variety of resources and features a clickable imagemap with the following six options:

- Exploring the Net duplicates the same options that are reachable from the Netscape Directory buttons, namely, What's New, What's Cool, Handbook, Net Directory, and Net Search.

- Company Products divides itself into links about Netscape Products, Development Partners, About Netscape, Netscape Sales, Channel Partners, and Business Solutions.

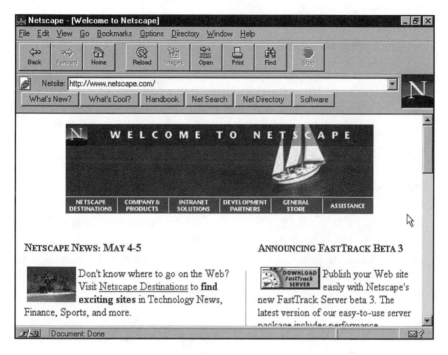

Fig. 3.1
Netscape's opening page is now even easier to return to or reload, thanks to client-side imagemaps.

- Netscape Store keeps you informed about Netscape software and publications with four links to Software, Publications, Support, and Bazaar, which allows you to buy t-shirts and boxer shorts sporting the Netscape Mozilla logo.

- Assistance points to sources that teach you more about the Internet.

- Community includes links to user groups and White Pages directories.

- News & Reference gives you access to a variety of news and information links, including Internet Headlines, Netscape Press Releases, Standards Docs, and Reference Material. A lot of technical information is available here.

NOTE **Reloading Netscape's home page is faster than ever, since the main** imagemap that contains the most important links is now stored in your cache.

One of the most important links on this page is to the latest version of Netscape Navigator. You'll find it at the bottom of the Company & Products page under Netscape Products. You'll want to check this from time to time as Netscape updates the speed, reliability, and functions of its browser. Be aware, though, that the process of obtaining the latest version will take you through several pages of links to get to the download. You may be able to circumvent this to some extent by going directly to Netscape's FTP site. Do this by typing **ftp.netscape.com** in the address box, or use File, Open Location on the menu bar. Netscape's FTP server is often overloaded, but don't worry; if you get an error message you'll also get a list of dozens of mirror sites—FTP sites that contain the same files as Netscape's—that you can immediately access.

The Netscape directory buttons

Built into Netscape's interface are links to certain pages on its Web site that can be of particular use to almost any Netscape user. Netscape, by default, displays these five buttons near the top of the browser. If you don't see these buttons, go to the Options menu and make sure that the Show Directory Buttons option is checked. Save your selection by clicking Options, Save Options.

Later in this chapter we look at the Net Directory and Net Search options for our discussion of search engines and techniques; right now let's look at the other three buttons.

What's Cool?

The What's Cool? button brings you to a collection of favorite Web pages, compiled and updated by Netscape. This is a good starting point for finding interesting Web sites. Figure 3.2 shows you what to expect.

Also, check out the growing list of Netscape Server sites from the Galleria link; sites that use Netscape's Server software have native security features built-in for special use with Netscape Navigator.

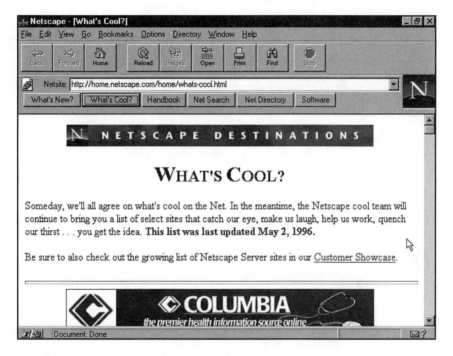

Fig. 3.2
The Netscape Cool team is on the job, so there's some great surfing here!

Be on the lookout for other cool-sites listings as you travel the Internet—
many other Web sites compile, post, and update their favorite Web pages.
You'll find a number of sites that also follow Netscape's practice of requesting you to submit your own cool links for inclusion in their pages. If
you have some really cool Web sites you'd like to see in Netscape's What's
Cool?, submit them via Netscape's online form.

What's New?

The What's New? button takes you to an assortment of new Internet
resources, archived monthly. This is an excellent place for introducing you
to new Web sites; it will give you a good feel for just how fast the surface
of the Web is spinning. Just as with the What's Cool? pages, Netscape is
interested in any new Web sites you want to tell them about. Of course
this area is updated quite often, so your version of figure 3.3 will most
certainly be a bit different.

Fig. 3.3
Netscape lists a What's New? section of links to its own site.

TIP **Want some other examples of What's New? sites? To keep up with the** latest software on the Net, point your browser to Stroud's WSApps List, **http://www.cwsapps.com/**, and Tucows, at **http://www.tucows.com/**. Both of these sites are meticulously maintained and updated daily, include reviews of the newest and best programs, and have direct links to FTP sites to download the freeware and shareware.

Software

Netscape 3 also sports a new addition to the directory toolbar. The Software button is linked to Netscape's Web page on software products, and upgrades (see fig. 3.4). From here, you can purchase Netscape Navigator directly from Netscape, or download the latest version. This makes it easier for you to keep up-to-date with the latest software happenings of Netscape.

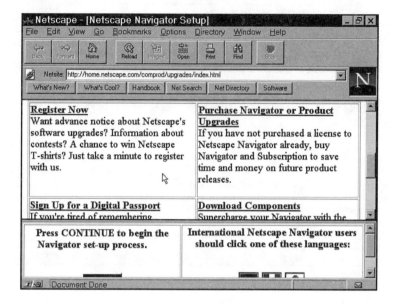

Fig. 3.4
The new Software button takes you to Netscape's page that lets you purchase Netscape, or get the latest version.

Using the Netscape Handbook

You already may have noticed that the Netscape browser really doesn't have much in the way of an online help file. That's because most of the documentation for the program is actually provided in Web format on Netscape Corp.'s Web site. The Netscape Handbook button takes you to all the information Netscape provides about the most current version of Navigator. In addition to the basics of using the Netscape browser, some elementary concepts of the Internet are explained (see fig. 3.5).

Perhaps among the most important links available from the Handbook button are links to the Release Notes for the current version of Navigator. It's on these pages that you can see what advances (and what problems, if any) have been introduced with the latest version of the program.

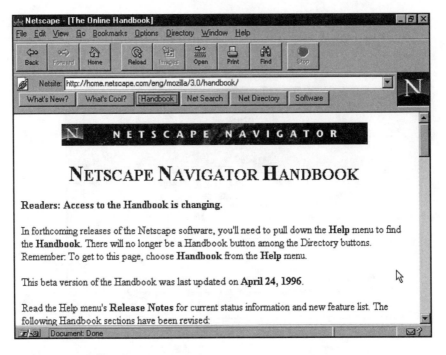

Fig. 3.5
Netscape's own list of some of the latest sites to appear on the Web.

Net Directory searching the Internet by subject

There's no question that using Netscape and the World Wide Web is the wave of the immediate future on the Internet, and it's an amazing tool for gathering information. The Web metaphor, in fact, with its links spiraling out into the unknown, is an ingenious method of information retrieval—if only because it mimics the way most humans think—relationally.

But, sometimes things can feel a little disorganized. Especially when you're on a deadline or sick of surfing to find something. If you've ever used Gopher for information retrieval, then maybe you're feeling a bit nostalgic. Isn't there some way this silly Web can be organized?

Enter the Net Directory pages provided by Netscape. Click once on the Net Directory button on Netscape's interface and you're presented with a listing of available Internet directories scattered around the Web. This page is almost guaranteed to save you hours of surfing frustration more than once in your Web life.

What do we mean by directory? Directories generally provide an editorial service—they determine the best sites around the Web and include them in categorized listings to make finding information easier. Some directories actually combine two features—a directory of categorized sites and a search engine for searching both the category listing and the Internet.

There are a number of directories listed in Net Directory, the most well-known of which is Yahoo, known by many as the most outstanding attempt at organizing the Web yet.

The following are the options currently available in Net Directory:

- Yahoo is the grandfather of Internet guides. Easily the most comprehensive attempt at creating a table of contents for the Internet, Yahoo lets you get directly at listings of Web sites by category. Internet users send submissions to Yahoo, whose editors screen the sites for suitability. There are a lot of sites that aren't covered in Yahoo, but many of the quality sites are.

- The McKinley Internet Directory lists a database of World Wide Web, Gopher, FTP, Telnet, newsgroup and mailing-list links that are divided into categories. The database is searchable, and the sites are rated by an editorial team.

- Point offers reviews of what they consider to be the top five percent of Internet sites. Sites are also allowed to submit their own selling copy, which is edited.

- World Wide Arts Resources offers a digital outlet for more than 2,000 artists. This index page for the arts features links to galleries, museums, arts sites, an antiques database, and arts-related educational and government sites.

- World Wide Web Servers offers a huge listing of Web servers. United States servers are listed by state.

- Virtual Tourist is similar to the World Wide Web Servers information, but presented as a clickable graphical map.

The Yahoo directory

The Yahoo Internet directory **(http://www.yahoo.com)** was created in April 1994 by David Filo and Jerry Yang, two Ph.D. candidates in Electrical Engineering at Stanford University, as a way to keep track of their personal interests on the Internet. The directory grew quickly in popularity after they made it available to the public and spent more and more time organizing sites into their hierarchy. In early 1995, Netscape Corp. invited Filo and Yang to move their files from Stanford's network to computers housed at Netscape.

Using Yahoo is a little like shopping for the best Internet sites. Instead of blindly following links to different Web sites, hoping that you'll eventually come across one that's interesting, you deal with Yahoo's pages for a while. As you move deeper through Yahoo's menu-style links, you get closer to Web sites that interest you.

 TIP   **Although Yahoo's primary role is as a directory for the Web, it also** offers access to breaking Reuters NewMedia newswire stories. If you're a newshound, click the Headlines button at the top of Yahoo's index page.

First, you need to get to Yahoo. From the Net Directory page, click the link to Yahoo once. Starting at the top-most level, you choose the category of Web site you're interested in seeing, for instance, Computers and Internet (see fig. 3.6).

 TIP   **Yahoo's direct URL is http://www.yahoo.com. I'd even go so far as** to recommend creating a Bookmark for Yahoo (or using it as your home page)— sometimes Netscape's Net Directory page is a bit slow to respond.

From there, it's as easy as clicking your way through the hierarchy as you get closer and closer to the type of site you're trying to find. In figure 3.7, for instance, I've moved down the line a little bit, having chosen to view Connectivity, Access Providers, Regional and U.S. States. Now I'm looking at a listing of different parts of the country. Pick one, and I'll get a list of links to the Web pages of Internet providers in that part of the country.

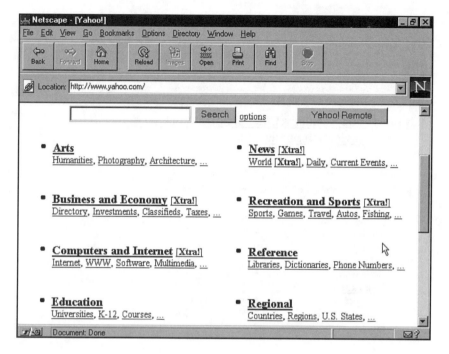

Fig. 3.6
Yahoo offers a directory listing of subjects from the Internet.

How Yahoo works

What you first notice about the Yahoo directory is its 14 top categories. These categories, determined by the folks who designed Yahoo, are the basic structure of the Table of Contents approach. But how do you get your Web site included in this hierarchy?

Web site creators decide what category they feel is most appropriate for their Web site's inclusion in the directory. Once you get to the part of the directory you'd like your site to appear in, you click the Add URL button at the top of Yahoo's interface. You're then asked by Yahoo to fill out a Web form with information on their site, the URL, a contact's address, and other tidbits (see fig. 3.8). After reviewing the entry, Yahoo's staff decides if the site merits inclusion.

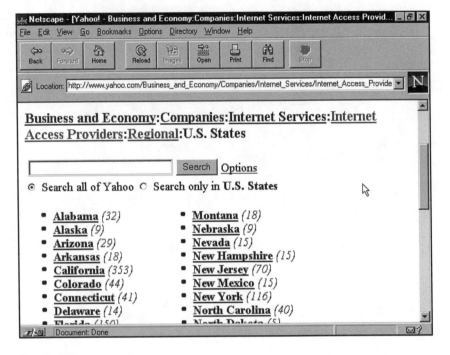

Fig. 3.7
Digging a little deeper into Yahoo gets you closer to the Web sites you're seeking.

Why is this important? Two reasons. First, whether you're a Web user or a Web creator, it's significant to recognize that being included in the Yahoo directory is something of a make-or-break proposition. That's not to say that you can't have a successful site if you're not in the Yahoo directory (or, that it will be successful just because it does get included). But being in the Yahoo directory does, at least in a sense, suggest that you've arrived.

Second, it's important to note that being in the Yahoo directory is something you generally have to actively seek. These are, then, sites that want to be accessed. A lot of these sites are high-traffic areas with broad appeal—in fact, a good percentage of them are commercial sites. That is by no means always bad, but you should recognize that it is a limitation to what you'll find using the Yahoo directory.

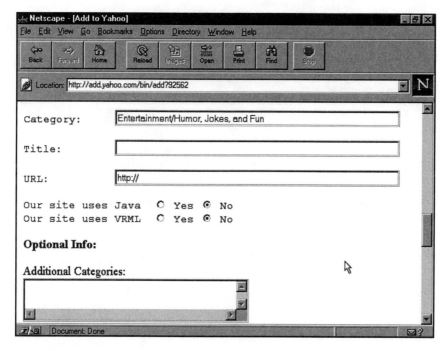

Fig. 3.8
Submitting your own Web site for inclusion in the Yahoo directory.

Searching with Yahoo

Clicking through the directory isn't the only way to get at Yahoo's listed sites. There's also a basic search engine that uses keywords to find interesting pages for you. Where do you do this searching? From Yahoo's main index page, enter a search phrase in the text box that sits above the category listings (see fig. 3.9).

By search phrase, I simply mean a few keywords to help Yahoo limit the search. This takes some experimentation (as it does with all of the Internet search engines), and we'll discuss that later in this chapter in the section "Searching on the Web." This simple search from the Yahoo index page assumes you want to find all the keywords you enter. By default it searches the names, URLs, and descriptions of all its Web pages.

What results from this search is a list of possible matches in Yahoo's database, with hypertext links to the described pages (see fig. 3.10). This gives you an opportunity to look at a number of different pages that may or may not include the information you're seeking.

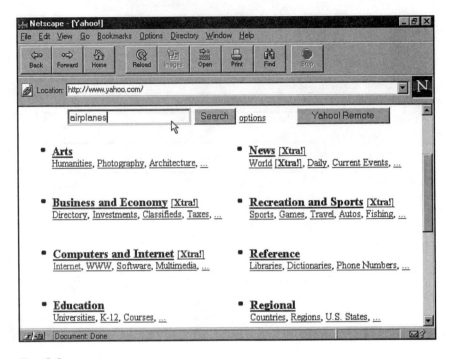

Fig. 3.9
Yahoo lets you search its database for relevant sites.

This is a pretty basic search, and, as I pointed out, it's based on a number of default assumptions about the type of search you want to use. If you're not having much luck, you may want to try taking a little more control over the search variables. For a more advanced search, follow these steps:

1 From the basic Yahoo index page, click the Options link next to the Search button. The advanced Yahoo Search page appears (see fig. 3.11).

2 Type your search phrase or keywords into the text box.

3 Put a check in the boxes next to the type of information you want Yahoo to examine as it performs the search. The more checkboxes you have selected, the more results you'll probably get.

*Results were found in these
Yahoo categories*

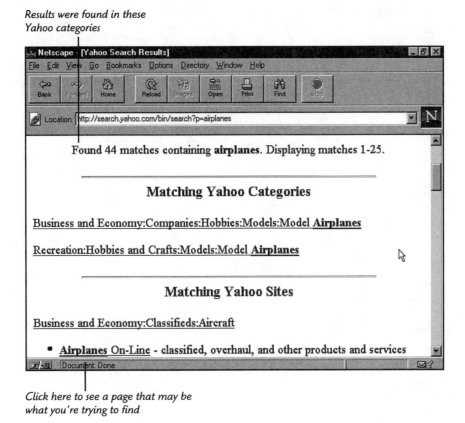

*Click here to see a page that may be
what you're trying to find*

Fig. 3.10
The Yahoo search results page. Each of these results is actually a link to the site that's being described.

4 If you'd like to see more results, click the radio button that allows results that contain less than all of your search phrases. To narrow the search even further, you can click the radio button for All keys as a single string, which looks for all of the words you entered in the text box—in exactly that order, with no words.

5 Then determine whether or not Yahoo treats your keywords as substrings (potentially parts of larger words) or only complete words.

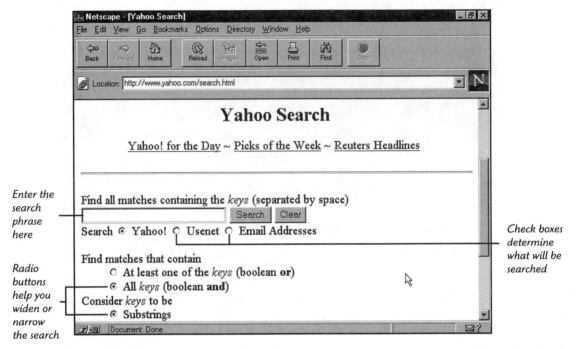

Enter the search phrase here

Radio buttons help you widen or narrow the search

Check boxes determine what will be searched

Fig. 3.11
If you don't get good results from the simple Yahoo search, you can take more control of the variables.

TIP **You can eliminate a lot of erroneous results by telling Yahoo to** assume your keywords should be complete words only. Why? Consider the keyword "net." As a substring, it may appear as Net, Internet, and Netting. It may also, however, result in pages referencing the Netherlands and garnets.

6 Finally, choose the number of results you want shown. You can choose 100, 200, 300, or Unlimited. The more results you ask for, the longer it takes to get through them all.

7 Click the Search button to initiate the search.

What results is a page very similar to the search results page we saw with the simple Yahoo Search except, hopefully, it's more likely to have links to the sites you need to access. If not, you might want to keep trying if you feel like you can narrow or widen the search with the advanced options. If you feel like you've done all you can, it might just be that Yahoo doesn't have what you're interested in.

Don't worry, though. We've got plenty more directories and Internet search engines to consult.

The McKinley Internet Directory Magellan

Offered by the McKinley Group, Magellan **(http://www.mckinley.com)** is another Internet directory and search service available from Netscape's Net Directory page (see fig. 3.12). Magellan offers a listing of over 1,000,000 sites—30,000 of which are reviewed, evaluated, and rated Web, Telnet, Gopher, and FTP sites. Like Yahoo, Magellan allows you to search its database directly for links that match certain keywords. You can also access the staff's recommended sites through a hierarchy of menus.

Fig. 3.12

From Magellan's index page you can search over 1,000,000 sites or browse around 30,000 reviewed sites.

Magellan isn't quite identical to Yahoo—it's both less and more of a directory than Yahoo is. While searching is more tightly integrated into the directory portion of Magellan, it does offer more description and recommendations than Yahoo does—at least for a limited number of sites.

Browsing the Magellan Directory

If you're looking for some of the best possible sites on the Internet, choose the Browse Categories link on Magellan's index page. This gives you a listing of categories to choose from, much like Yahoo's directory. Eventually you'll dig deep enough to find some sites that have been reviewed by the McKinley Group staff (see fig. 3.13).

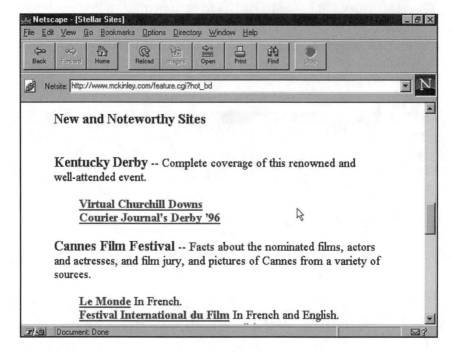

Fig. 3.13
After choosing a category and a subcategory, here's a list of possible sites.

Notice also that you can limit the number of reviewed sites that appear in the listing by entering keywords at the top of the page and clicking the Focus Search button. This results in fewer listings in a particular category—most of which, hopefully, will include information that interests you.

Searching Magellan

As I mentioned before, you can also search Magellan for interesting Web sites. For a simple search, enter a search phrase in the text box on

Magellan's index page and click the Search Magellan button. For a more advanced search, click the graphic marked Advanced Search. That presents you with the page in figure 3.14.

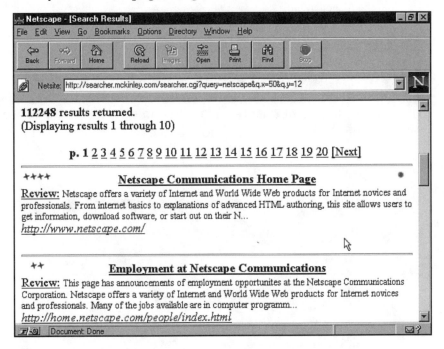

Fig. 3.14
Magellan's advanced search page helps you find exactly what you're seeking.

Enter your search keywords in this box, then you've got some choices to make. Magellan allows you to do a straight keyword search or a concept search. For a concept search, Magellan generates a series of words that are related to the keywords you enter, and also searches for these. This generates resulting Web sites that don't necessarily include the specific keyword you entered, but may contain related information.

You are also asked to choose whether AND or OR should be assumed between your keywords (to, respectively, broaden or limit your search), the minimum rating for the pages to be returned, and how much description you want to see in the resulting list. Once you've made these decisions, click the button marked Search the Magellan. Now you're off and running.

TIP The advanced Magellan search engine can actually accept very involved (and somewhat complicated) keyword phrases. For more on Magellan's searching abilities, choose Help from Magellan's graphical interface, then click the Search the Magellan link.

Point

Point **(http://www.pointcom.com)** is another widely recognized repository of Internet site reviews. Claiming to have links to the "top 5 percent" of Internet sites, Point is a great place to find some of what's cool on the Web (see fig. 3.15). To see a directory of the reviews that Point has to offer, click once on the Top 5% Reviews graphic in the top-left corner of Point's index page interface.

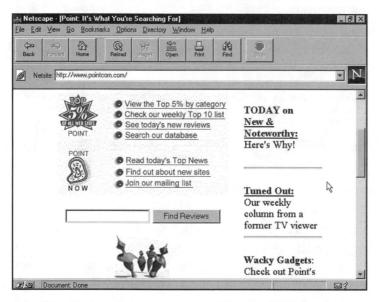

Fig. 3.15
Point offers reviews of what it considers to be the best Internet sites in various categories.

The reviews can sometimes be a little irreverent, fun and, as the Netscape Net Directory page puts it, pointed. Internet sites can also submit their own descriptions, which are duly edited. You search the reviews using keywords via the Point Search feature. If you want to submit your site for inclusion in Point's listing, use the Submit feature.

Interestingly, Point Communications, which puts out the Point direc- tory and ratings, has recently been acquired by Lycos, one of the premier search engines on the Internet. According to the Point index page, this gives you access not only to the top five percent of sites, but, through Lycos, access to 90 percent of all the Internet sites around the world. We'll discuss Lycos in the "Net Search searching on the Internet" section of this chapter.

The best of the rest

There are a few other Internet directories available behind Netscape's Net Directory button. They're a little more specialized, but, if you're interested, you may find tons of links to the kinds of sites you want to visit.

World Wide Arts Resources

For anyone interested in the arts, the World Wide Arts Resources (**http:// www.concourse.com/wwar/default.html**) offers access to galleries, museums, an antiques database, related arts sites, as well as arts-related educational and governmental sites. The directory also presents the digital work of over 2,000 artists. There are a variety of resources within the directory, which have been actively compiled for well over a year now.

For example, if you are looking for the work of a particular artist, then use the Artist Index. Other resources include: Art Galleries & Exhibits; Museums, for international listings; USA Museums, which features a 20-page preview and has categorized both the museums and what is available at those museums; Important Arts Resources, which lists related arts sites; and Arts Publications, which features both electronic and conventional publications.

World Wide Web Servers

The World Wide Web Servers directory (**http://www.w3.org/pub/ DataSources/WWW/Servers.html**) is a huge list of available Web servers from the CERN educational institution. The servers are presented alphabetically by continent, country, and state. Clicking the top-level country, for instance, lets you "drill-down" to the next geographic level, where you find listings of individual servers according to region.

North America is sub-divided into states, which are listed alphabetically. Also available is a listing of Federal government servers for North

America. The directory is actually a listing of HTTP (HyperText Transmission Protocol) servers whose administrators have sent requests to **www-request@w3.org**, and other sites.

Virtual Tourist

The Virtual Tourist **(http://www.vtourist.com)** is similar in content to the World Wide Web Servers directory, but is presented in a visually appealing clickable map (see fig. 3.16).

When you click a specific area of the map, another screen appears to help you narrow down your search for geographically sited Web servers.

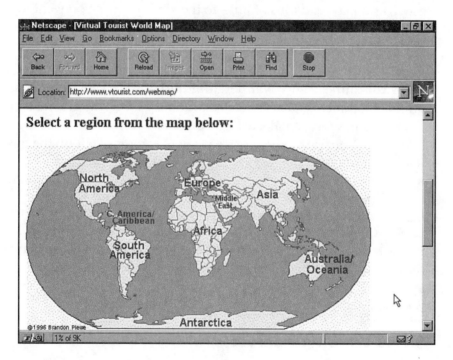

Fig. 3.16
Virtual Tourist offers a clickable map listing of Web servers around the world.

NOTE **Information about individual countries and states is not provided by** Virtual Tourist. That sort of information is evidently available in The Virtual Tourist II, which is operated in cooperation with City.Net.

Net Search searching on the Internet

Now for that other button on Netscape's browser window, Net Search. Although some of these services overlap with the directories we found on Netscape's Net Directory page, you'll find that all of these are a little more oriented toward searching—and a little less interested in editorializing. For the most part, these search engines are here to help you find keywords in titles of Web pages. You won't see many reviews in these pages. You will, however, see hundreds of results to your queries—chosen from among millions and millions of possible Web pages.

The Net Search directory button takes you to the Internet Search page at Netscape Corp.'s Web site. Here you'll find a collection of easy-to-use search engines that allow you to find information and documents on the Internet.

There are a number of useful search engines listed, offering a variety of search techniques—for example, some search headers and document titles, some search their own extensive indexes of Internet documents and pages, and others rummage through the Internet itself.

The different search options available in Net Search are discussed in the next section. Here are some of the more popular engines:

- InfoSeek Search allows you to search the Web using plain English or keywords and phrases. Special query operators let you customize your search. Results include the first few lines from each Web site— often making it clear how your keyword is used, and thus, whether or not a site is actually interesting to you.

- The Lycos Home Page is an extremely comprehensive search engine that reportedly features a database of millions of link descriptors and documents. The engine searches links, headings, and titles for key-words you enter. It also offers different search options.

- WebCrawler lets you search by document title and content using words you enter into the search box. It's not as comprehensive as Lycos, but it's a quick and easy way to find a few hundred sites that match your keywords.

- Deja News Research Service allows you to search UseNet newsgroups in, what the company claims is, the world's largest UseNet news archive. A variety of search options are available.

- Excite allows you to search a database with over one million Web documents. You can also search through the past two week's worth of classified ads and UseNet news. Internet site content quality evaluations are also available through Excite.

- W3 Search Engines offers a variety of topics and subjects from the University of Geneva, although the list is not updated as often as the more mainstream search engine databases.

- CUSI (Configurable Unified Search Interface) features a single form to search different Web engines, provided by Nexor U.K.

How these search engines work

Each one of these search services on the Net Search page is designed to give you access to a database of information related to Internet sites around the world. Some are Web-specific (like Lycos and WebCrawler) while others, like InfoSeek and Excite, allow you to search not only Web pages, but also UseNet newsgroups, online publications, and other archives of information.

What all of these do have in common is that they require you to come up with keywords to facilitate the search. There's definitely an art to this search—the more you try it, the more you'll see that it takes some patience and creativity. Let's discuss some of the basic concepts.

The key to a good search is good keywords. What you're trying to do is come up with unique words or phrases that appear only in the documents you want to access. For instance, one thing to definitely avoid are common terms, such as www, computer, Internet, PC, Mac, and so on. These terms come up time and again on pages that may or may not have material that interests you. Also consider that words like Mac not only appear in words like Macintosh, but also in Mace, Mach, Machine, Macaroni—you'll probably get a lot of bizarre results with such a common keyword. Articles and common English words like a, an, the, many, any, and others are generally unnecessary.

Most of these search engines also give you a choice of Boolean operators to use between keywords (AND, OR, NOT). Take care that you understand how these operators work. If you enter them yourself (in the search phrase text box), then an example might be:

Windows AND shareware NOT Mac

This results in pages that discuss shareware programs for Microsoft Windows, while it eliminates pages that include the word Mac, even if they also discuss Windows shareware. Remember that AND and NOT are used to limit searches; OR is used to widen them. Notice, for instance, that

Ford OR Mustang

generates many more results than either

Ford AND Mustang

or

Ford NOT Mustang

Presumably, the first only returns pages that have references to both, while the second returns pages that do reference Ford, but do not reference Mustang.

InfoSeek Search

InfoSeek **(http://www.infoseek.com)** is a very popular search engine that generates not only search results but also offers the first few lines from pages to help you determine if a Web site may have what you need before you leave InfoSeek to view it. While this can often save you time, the way InfoSeek reports its results (a maximum of 100 results, 10 to a page) can take a little while to flip through. InfoSeek, therefore, is really designed for digging deep for a subject—perhaps when you've had less luck with other search engines.

What is InfoSeek Search?

You access InfoSeek by clicking the InfoSeek Search button on the Internet Search page at Netscape. You can also start searching straight away by entering search words in the text box under InfoSeek Search and pressing the Search button on Netscape's Net Search page. This is a quick way to get results. The InfoSeek index page offers this same text box, but also includes a quick directory of popular sites (see fig. 3.17).

InfoSeek is very easy to search. Simply enter keywords in the text box and click the Search button. InfoSeek assumes an AND between each of your keywords, although it returns pages that don't include every keyword. Capitalization is important, though, so only capitalize words that you want recognized as proper nouns.

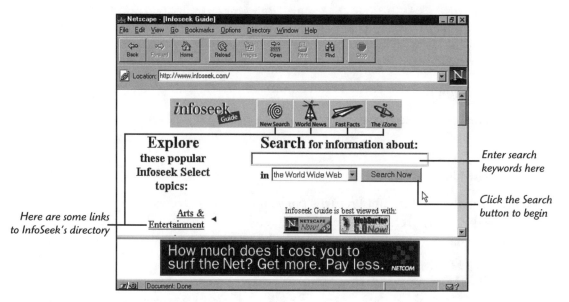

Fig. 3.17
InfoSeek's index page is a little spartan, but it gets the job done.

InfoSeek offers this ability to search the Internet as a free service to the Internet community; however, free searches are limited to 100 results per search, and they don't cover the breadth of services that InfoSeek offers. InfoSeek's commercial searching accounts may end up being something that interests you, and more information is provided on their Web site.

Lycos

Lycos (**http://www.lycos.com**) is a very comprehensive and accurate search engine that is also very popular. It consists of a huge catalog that, as of August 1995, claimed to include more than 90 percent of the Web. As a result, you may find it often too busy to let you use it, especially during peak business hours. However, it is worth the wait; Lycos claims to already have included more than 7.98 million URLs and is adding to that number every day.

Lycos was developed at Carnegie-Mellon University, Pittsburgh. However, in June 1995, Lycos Inc. was formed to develop and market the Lycos technology. Lycos Inc. says that Lycos will remain free to Internet users, although, as a commercial venture, it will gain revenue from advertising and licensing the Lycos catalog and search technologies. Non-exclusive license holders of the Lycos technology already include Frontier Technologies and Library Corp., as well as Microsoft Corp. for use in the company's newly introduced Microsoft Network online service.

Searching with Lycos

The Lycos interface is similar to InfoSeek's in that you can just enter words and click the Search button. However, Lycos includes more options and contains a much larger database of indexed Web documents. You can begin by selecting the Lycos link on Netscape's Net Search page. That brings up the Lycos index page, where your search begins. A simple Lycos search works just like most of the other search engines. Enter your search keywords in the text box and click the Search button. Lycos finds any pages or documents matching any of the words you type into the search box.

For a more advanced search, choose the Search Options button next to the text box on Lycos' index page. Now you're presented with a new page, where you can spend a little more time tailoring your search (see fig. 3.18).

Here is where you can take a little more control of the search phrase. For instance, if you enter a number of keywords and you'd like to expand the search to show pages that match any of your keywords, pull down the first Search Options menu and choose Match Any Term (OR). You can also choose to match a certain number of keywords with this same menu.

 TIP If you're unsure how a keyword is spelled, type in a couple of different ways you think it might appear, then choose to match the number of terms that you know are spelled correctly. For instance, entering Heron Hearon Huron senate candidate, then selecting to match three terms would give me a good chance of finding information about this public figure whose name I'm not sure how to spell.

Advanced InfoSeek searches

At its most basic, InfoSeek is a quick and easy way to search the Internet. In fact, it's one of the few search engines that doesn't offer an advanced page with more control over the results. What you see is basically what you get with InfoSeek.

That is, at least, until you dig a little deeper. Then you realize that there is some customizing you can do to your searches. It all takes place in your search phrase (what you enter in the text box). The following little tidbits may help you get faster, and more reliable, results.

- Before authorizing any search for documents on the Internet, make sure there are no misspelled words or typographical errors in the text box.

- Don't use characters such as an asterisk (*) as wildcards.

- Unlike some other search engines such as Lycos, don't use Boolean operators such as AND and OR between search words, as InfoSeek looks at all words as search terms.

- When searching for documents, try both word variations (plural, adjective, and noun forms of the same word) and synonyms.

- If you want both the upper- and lowercase occurrences of a term, use only the lowercase word in the search text box.

- You need to separate capitalized names with a comma (for example, Bill Gates, Microsoft). You can also use a comma to separate phrases and capitalized names from each other.

- Quotation marks and hyphens can be used to identify a phrase.

- You can use a plus sign (+) to distinguish terms that should appear in every document. The + appears at the beginning of the term, with no space before the first letter of the first word (for example, +skiing Colorado, Utah).

- As an alternative to a plus sign, you can use a minus sign (-) to designate phrases or words not to be included in any document. This is useful if you have a word that is often used with another word in unison, but you want only documents containing the word and not both words to be retrieved (for example, desktop-computer).

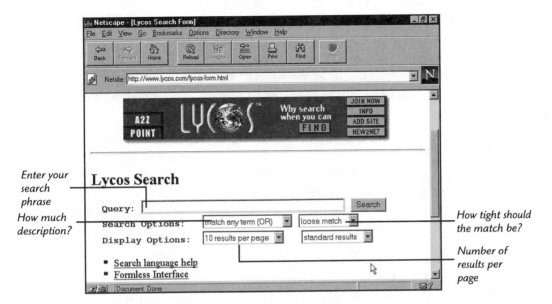

Enter your search phrase

How much description?

How tight should the match be?

Number of results per page

Fig. 3.18
The Lycos Search Options page for a more advanced search.

The second Search Options pull-down menu allows you to specify if you want close or not-so-close matches. If you are really just "fishing" for some leads as to where to concentrate your next search, make sure the "loose match" option is selected from the second Search Options menu. If you are pretty sure of the search criteria you typed in the Query box, then select "strong match." There are a number of choices in between, each becoming about 20 percent more lenient as they move down the list.

There are two Display Options pull-down menus—one dictates how many results are displayed on the page, and the second determines the level of detail for the specified search.

Although Lycos always allows you to access all the "hits" that resulted from your search, obviously all of them cannot be displayed at once. You can choose to display between 10 and 40 links on a page at any one time. This is done using the first of the two Display Options pull-down menu. To specify how many search results are displayed on the page at any one time, pull down the first menu and select the number you'd like to see.

The second pull-down menu lets you determine the level of information detail to be displayed about each search result. With this menu there are three levels of detail, each one on the list being a little more detailed than the one above it. The level of detail you specify will probably change with each search you do, depending on the documents you are seeking and the research you are trying to accomplish. If you don't specify any level, the default "standard results" takes the middle ground, reporting with a reasonable amount of detail.

How Lycos works

So how does Lycos manage to cover so much ground on the Internet? There are actually three parts to Lycos, all of which are interconnected, and each requires the others to work properly. The first part of Lycos are groups of programs, called spiders, that go out and search the Web, FTP, and Gopher sites every day.

The results are added to the second part of Lycos—the "catalog" database—which contains such things as the URL address of each site found, along with information about the documents found at that site, the text, and the number of times that site is referenced by other Web addresses. As a result of the advanced search performed by the spiders, the most popular sites are indexed first. Whatever information and new sites are found by the spiders is added to the existing catalog.

The final element is the "search engine" itself. It's the real strength of the system for the end-user (us) because it can manage to access all of this information so smoothly and accurately. The engine sorts through the catalog and produces a list of hits according to your search criteria, listed in descending order of relevance. This means that, according to the search engine, the best and most accurate hits are at the top of the Lycos results list. So, the deeper you dig into Lycos' results, the less likely you are to find what you want—at least, according to Lycos.

WebCrawler

WebCrawler is one of the best search engines on the Web, not least because it is so easy to use and very fast. It is owned and maintained by America Online, which provides it as a public service to the Internet community. It's a great search engine to use when you're fairly sure that what you're looking for will appear in the title of a Web page—WebCrawler only searches titles of Web pages, not all text. For direct access, its URL is **http://www.webcrawler.com/**. You can, of course, also access it from the Net Search page.

TIP **WebCrawler is also a great way to start out on a directed surfing** expedition—that is, when you're not searching too closely. If you want to see 500 hits with the word Microsoft in the title, you'll find them the most quickly and easily with WebCrawler.

WebCrawler's interface is designed to be as uncomplicated as possible (see fig. 3.19).

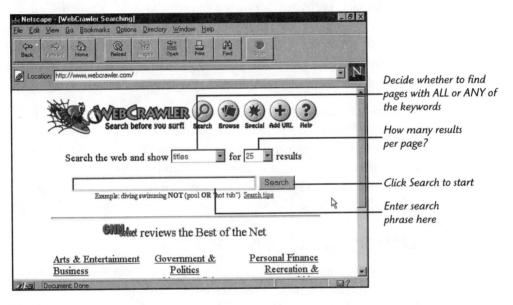

Fig. 3.19
WebCrawler allows for easy searching and quick results.

Instead of searching the entire World Wide Web for instances of your typed keywords, WebCrawler searches its own index of documents. This makes for quicker searches, although, with documents and pages being added to the Web at such an astounding rate, newer resources can be missed.

The result of your WebCrawler search is a list, with each item on the list underlined and colored indicating it is a hypertext link that you can click to retrieve that page from the Internet.

Down the left side of the search results is a list of numbers, with one number corresponding to each item on the list. The highest number is next to the first item on the search results list. This indicates that the first item is the most relevant according to your search keywords, which is why the numbers (from 100 to 001) are called relevance numbers. As you move down the list you notice that the number along the left side decreases for each item on the list—indicating that each of these pages offers fewer occurrences of your keywords than the previous item.

With a large search, not all the results are necessarily displayed on the first page. In fact, WebCrawler limits the results to 10, 25, or 100, depending on how many pages you specified in your search criteria. But if WebCrawler finds, for example, 500 pages that correspond to your search keywords and you chose to view 25 at a time, only 25 are going to be shown on the Netscape screen.

That doesn't mean you can't view the rest of the search results. To view the next 25 items in the resulting search list, click the Get the Next 25 Results button under the resulting list, and the next 25 items in the search are displayed. Keep doing that until you have viewed all the items in the list, if you need to see them. But don't forget, the further down the list you go, the less relevant the search results, according to your keywords.

Other search engines

There are a variety of other search engines available on the Internet, and some of the best have also been made available to users of Netscape's Internet Search page. These engines tend to be either more specialized—focusing on searching UseNet newsgroups instead of the entire Internet, for instance—or simply convenient ways to access the search engines we've already talked about.

Deja News Research Service

If you want to search UseNet newsgroups exclusively, then the Deja News Research Service **(http://www.dejanews.com)** is the place for you. Currently claiming over four gigabytes of searchable data, Deja News is updated every two days. You can even follow an entire newsgroup thread by just clicking the subject line when it appears at the top of your screen.

To get to the search engine page, choose Deja News from the Net Search page. Then, click the Search link on Deja News' index page. The Deja News query form page appears (see fig. 3.20).

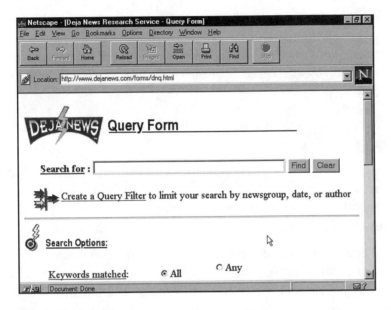

Fig. 3.20
Just enter words and click Find for simple searches. But you can perform more complex queries from this page as well.

For the simplest search, just type search words into the text box, click the Search button, and use the default options. However, for the best results, you should customize your search a little by following these steps:

1 Type your search words into the text box. You don't need to worry about capitalizing words because the search engine isn't case-sensitive. The engine automatically assumes there is an OR between multiple words.

2 Choose the maximum number of hits you want retrieved by checking either 30, 60, or 120 in the Maximum Number of Hits option. The default is 30. If more than the number specified is returned, a link appears at the bottom of the screen allowing you access to the next set of hits.

3 The amount of information retrieved about each site is determined by the Hitlist Format option. Click Terse for less information, or Verbose for more.

4 The Sort By option lets you emphasize score, group, date, or author.

 NOTE **Score is just another way to say relevance number, as we discussed** earlier. It's how Deja News determines how close each result is to your search phrase.

5 You can choose between default boolean operators using the Default Operator: OR or AND option.

6 Use the Create a Query Filter option if you want to use a filter to narrow down your search. A filter can be used to specify a date range, if you only want postings from a specific author, or if you know which newsgroups you want to retrieve.

7 The age of the record can also be a factor in your search. If you want newer postings, check the Prefer New box, or if you want older ones, check the Prefer Old box. In addition, you can use the Age Matters option to tell Deja News how important it is that a message is relatively recent or a few months old.

There are some groups that are not included in the indexing, such as *alt., *soc., *talk., and *.binaries. Deja News says that this is either because they contain a large volume of postings that are mostly "flames," or else they don't lend themselves well to text searchings, such as binary groups.

In any event, Deja News is worth using if you want to search the enormous amount of UseNet newsgroups available. There are reportedly as many as 80MB of traffic posted on newsgroups each day! Newsgroups can be very useful for retrieving information if you know how to search and where to look.

Excite

Excite **(http://www.excite.com)** allows you to search through more than a million Web documents and the past two weeks-worth of UseNet newsgroups and classified ads. The user interface is as simple as other search engines available (see fig. 3.21).

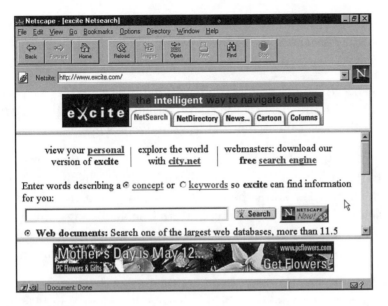

Fig. 3.21
The Excite database lets you search Web documents, UseNet newsgroups, and classified ads.

Searching Excite is only slightly different from searching the other search engines. You start by selecting the type of search you want Excite to carry out—click the Enter Keywords box if you want documents retrieved using regular keywords. You can also click the Enter Words Describing a Concept box if you want the search engine to retrieve documents that seem to involve a subject that's related to the words you typed in the search box, and not just those documents that contain those words.

After you type in your keywords, you have another set of checkbox options. Check Web Documents if you want Excite to search its database of Web documents. Check UseNet Discussion Groups if you want to search through the last two weeks-worth of UseNet messages, or select Classifieds if you want Excite to search the last two weeks-worth of classified advertisements.

Excite uses both color-coded icons and percentage-style scores to indicate the relevance of retrieved results. When there's a red icon at the beginning of the result line, that is an indication that Excite thinks it's a good search match. On the other hand, a black icon means that it may not be such a good match. The colors are a quick way of identifying good matches at a glance.

The percentage is a better way of identifying the relevance of a search result, relative to the next search result. Obviously, the higher the percentage score, the better the match—at least in Excite's eyes.

The title of each result depends on whether it is a Web page or site, or a UseNet article. If it is a Web page, the page's title is displayed, or (if there is no title) it may just show the URL. If it is a Web site, then an Excite editor-selected site title is displayed. With UseNet listings, things are different. If a UseNet group is indicated, the name of the group is displayed. If a UseNet article is referenced, its Subject text is shown.

Excite also offers NetReviews (some of the best Web sites as chosen by the Excite staff) along with its database of Web pages and UseNet newsgroups. In fact, that's why you'll find Excite both on the Net Search and Net Directory pages. To access these reviews, click the NetReviews tab on the Excite index page.

Alta Vista

AltaVista **(http://www.altavista.digital.com/)** is another up and coming Web search engine, backed by Digital Equipment Corp. DEC, well known for their powerful Alpha chip, has provided a very powerful Web search engine. Superficially, it functions the same as most other Web search engines (see fig. 3.22). But under the hood, is an extremely fast and powerful Web indexer. Speed is easily Alta Vista's strongest suit. In the middle of a work day, Alta Vista found over 8,000,000 matches on the word "Netscape." All in under a second.

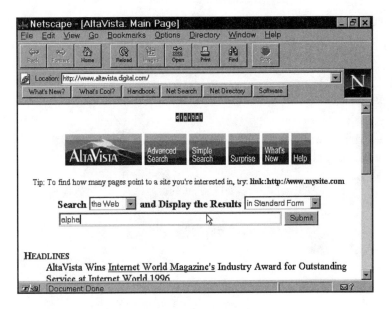

Fig. 3.22
Alta Vista is a remarkably fast and powerful Web search engine.

OpenText

OpenText **(http://www.opentext.com/)** is yet another Web search engine available. It's pretty much like any other search engine (see fig. 3.23), in that all you have to do is type in some keywords, then press the Submit button. If you want a more sophisticated search, simply select the "Search the World Wide Web" button. This will allow you to refine your search on OpenText's database to narrow down your search options.

Probably the most notable aspect of OpenText is that it's linked into Yahoo search results. With the list of matching Yahoo categories and sites, you have the ability of performing the same search with OpenText. Because OpenText is much more automated than Yahoo, there's a good chance it'll find more matching Web pages.

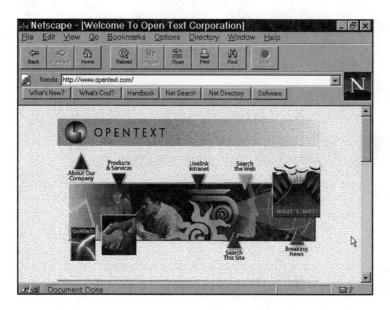

Fig. 3.23
OpenText is a Web search engine that is automatically updated, unlike other engines.

W3 Search Engines

There are, in fact, many more searching services available on the Internet than we've even begun to touch on in this chapter. While InfoSeek, WebCrawler, and Lycos are some of the largest and most popular, that won't always mean they're the best for what you need to find. If you're not having much luck with the big name engines, head over to the W3 Search Engines page.

The W3 Search Engines page **(http://cuiwww.unige.ch/meta-index.html)** is basically an interface to many different types of search engines around the world (see fig. 3.24). You can search information servers (Web and Gopher, primarily), UseNet news, publication archives, and software documentation. You can even use these pages to search for people on the Internet in a variety of ways.

To use the individual search engine, just type in your search words in its text box and click the Search button next to that engine's description. You'll notice that you really don't have many options for these engines, but it is a convenient way to initiate simple searches for many different services.

CUSI (Configurable Unified Search Interface)

The Configurable Unified Search Interface **(http://web.nexor.co.uk/susi/cusi.html)** allows you to quickly check related resources, without retyping search keywords.

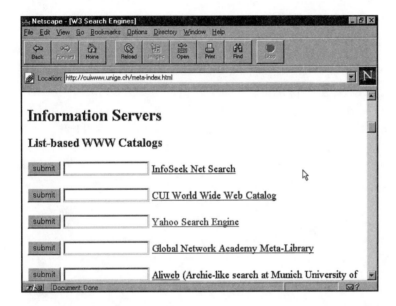

Fig. 3.24
Here are a few of the search engines you can use from the W3 Search Engines page.

This configurable search interface for a variety of searchable World Wide Web resources was developed by Martijn Koster in 1993 and is now provided as a public service by Nexor, which can be contacted at **webmaster@nexor.co.uk**.

CUSI offers a search text box for both manual Web indexes and robot-generated Web indexes, such as Lycos and WebCrawler.

Tracking Favorite Sites with Netscape Bookmarks

● In this chapter:

● **Using Bookmarks and why they are useful**

● **How to create and delete Bookmarks**

● **Creating Bookmarks from your History list**

● **How hierarchical menus work**

● **Effective menu management**

● **How to turn your Bookmark list into a Web page**

This chapter covers the use of Netscape's Bookmark feature. You can use Bookmarks to keep track of your most visited Internet sites. Placing them in your Bookmark list makes the site address instantly accessible from the Bookmarks pull-down menu in the menu bar.

What are Bookmarks?

The World Wide Web is a tapestry of millions of different documents and sites, all linked via references from other sites and documents. It is no surprise then that help was considered necessary for those exploring the links. One option available to all end users of Netscape is the Bookmarks feature.

Bookmarks are an extremely useful feature of Netscape. They basically allow Netscape to remember whatever places on the Web you tell it to remember. Having taken note of the Internet address of a site, Netscape lists it in a pull-down menu that you access from the menu bar.

When you select an item on the list, Netscape enters the item's URL that it has saved in your Bookmark file and tries to connect to the site, document, graphic, or whatever it corresponds to.

Because of the complexity of Web URLs, it would be enormously tedious if you had to remember and manually enter every page's address each time you wanted to read it. And while you should always try to save a document or image on your local drive so as not to have to connect to it over the Internet, you will likely have a great many remote pages that you will want to access on a regular basis, because they will be continually updated with new information by the remote site's administrator.

Bookmarks take away that tedious task of having to write down or otherwise save each page's or document's URL address.

When you add an item to your Bookmark list, you are essentially keeping a record of that item's address on the Internet, along with a description of that item, and placing it in a pull-down menu that you can quickly access from the menu bar in Netscape.

When you want to go to that site or document or graphic, pull down the Bookmarks list, and select the item. Netscape automatically enters the item's URL and tries to access the address. Chances are you will be able to access the item without any problems, although, the Internet being a global network, difficulties do sometimes occur.

TIP **The Bookmark list contains all the elements that go into making a** normal Web page. However, when viewed as a hypertext document, the special HTML coding takes over and displays it with enlarged fonts and a visually pleasing composition that is easy on the eyes.

TIP **If a link doesn't work, one reason may be that the filename on the** remote server has changed or it has been moved to another directory. Instead of using the entire URL, type in a truncated version listing just the main server address. That should get you into the remote server from which you can rummage around and look for the old file.

Saving Web pages

Before you can begin to categorize and separate your Bookmarks into different sections, you need to create them by notifying Netscape that you want to save the URL of a specific Web page. Fortunately, Netscape makes adding a Bookmark to your Bookmark list a simple matter of pulling down a menu.

Creating a Bookmark

There are two ways to add a Bookmark to your Bookmark list. The first involves just pulling down a menu, while the second requires an extra step or two. Let's take the simple way first.

The easiest way to add a Bookmark to your existing Bookmark list is to just select Add Bookmark (Ctrl+D) from the Bookmarks pull-down menu. The current page is added to the bottom of the list.

NOTE **Just as you can use your Bookmark file as your home page, you can also** use it as any other Web page. This is because it is actually a normal hypertext document just like any other you come across when you go "Web crawling."

The second way of adding a Bookmark allows you to add a Bookmark without having to be at the actual site on the Internet in question.

To add a new Bookmark the long way, follow these steps:

1 Select <u>B</u>ookmarks from the Windows menu. The Netscape Bookmarks list window appears (see fig. 4.1).

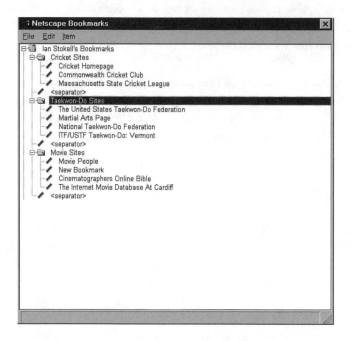

Fig. 4.1
The Netscape Bookmarks list includes all your saved Bookmarks with their addresses.

2 Select a current item in the Bookmark list window. The new Bookmark appears directly below the current selection in the list. Alternatively, you can skip this step and go straight to step 3. Then, when the bookmark has been added to the list, drag-and-drop the bookmark in the appropriate folder.

3 Select Insert <u>B</u>ookmark from the Item menu. The Bookmark Properties General sheet appears (see fig. 4.2).

4 Name the Bookmark in the Name text box.

5 Enter the URL address of the new link in the Location (URL) text box.

Fig. 4.2
To add a new Bookmark's details, select Insert Bookmark from the Item menu in the Netscape Bookmarks list window.

6 You can include a lengthy description of the Bookmark in the Description text box.

7 The Select Aliases button lets you select all aliases (or copies) of this bookmark in the Bookmark file. If there are no Aliases, the button is dimmed.

8 The Last Visited field shows when the site was last visited.

9 The Added on message shows the date that you added the Bookmark.

10 When all the particulars of the new Bookmark have been entered, click OK. The new Bookmark appears in the Bookmark list.

To go directly to your new Bookmark, either double-click the item in the list, or make the item the current selection and select Go To Bookmark from the Item menu, or drag the bookmark to the Netscape content area. Alternatively, if you want to exit, click the close box in the upper-right corner of the Netscape Bookmarks window.

The newly added Bookmark now appears in the Bookmark list each time it is shown, or it can be accessed via the lower section of the Bookmarks menu. By default, the bookmark list file is called Bookmark.htm.

NOTE **After you begin categorizing a large Bookmark list, by adding headers** and separators, for example, make sure you make a backup copy of the resulting file. If you get a hard disk crash and you have not saved the file, you will have to start constructing the Bookmark file again from scratch, which can be a very time-consuming process.

Deleting a Bookmark

Deleting a Bookmark from your Bookmark list is just as easy as adding it. Follow these steps to delete a Bookmark from your list:

1 Select Bookmarks (Ctrl+B) from the Window menu. The Netscape Bookmarks list window appears.

2 Select the item to be deleted from the Bookmark list.

3 Select Delete from the Edit menu, or press the Del button. The item disappears from the Bookmark list, or click the right mouse button over the bookmark. Choose Delete from the pop-up menu.

4 Click the close (x) box in the upper-right corner to exit.

Creating Bookmarks from your History list

Your History list keeps a record of the most recently visited Internet sites in case you want to return to a specific site while you are still in the Internet session. The History list disappears when you quit Netscape and end your current Internet session.

The History window consists of two columns, one displaying the title of the page visited, and the other showing the full URL. The most recently visited page is at the top of the list.

You may decide that you want to add an item from your History list to your Bookmark list, but for some reason or another, you neglected to do it when you visited the site and had the page displayed in the main Netscape screen. However, don't fret, you can still create a Bookmark from the current History list by following these steps:

1 Select History from the <u>W</u>indow menu. The History window appears (see fig. 4.3).

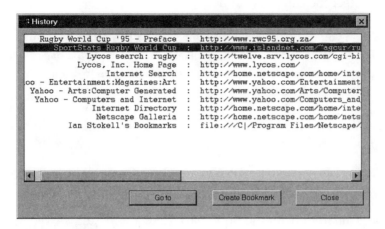

Fig. 4.3
You can create a Bookmark from the History list.

2 Select the History item you want to make a Bookmark.

3 Click the Create Bookmark button under the list window. The selected item is added to your permanent Bookmark list.

4 Click the Close button to exit the History window.

 TIP **You can access a numbered History list from the Go menu. Just click** the numbered item you want to return to.

Changing Bookmark properties

You may decide to change any number of Bookmark properties after you have placed the Bookmark in your Bookmark list. This next section tells you how to change such properties as the name, the URL link address, and the description. It also explains how to create a Bookmark shortcut using a function key.

Changing Bookmark names

At some point, you may decide to change the name of a Bookmark. For example, the site name may change on the Web and you may want to have your Bookmark name correspond to the current name, or you may have organized your Bookmark list into categories and you want the name to reflect the category name.

 TIP **When you initially save a Bookmark using the Add Bookmark option** from the Bookmarks menu, the bookmark is saved as per the original file or document name. You rename it via the Properties option of the Item menu in the Netscape Bookmarks list window.

Whatever the reason, changing the name of a Bookmark list item is a simple procedure; follow these steps:

1 Select Bookmarks (Ctrl+B) from the Window menu. The Netscape Bookmarks list window appears.

2 Select the item from the Bookmarks list.

3 Select Properties from the Item menu. The Bookmark Properties list appears.

4 Change the name of the Bookmark in the Name field.

5 Click OK when you have finished.

Adding a description

As you add more and more Bookmarks to your list, and you find additional interesting sites that you want to return to, remembering what exactly it was that you liked at the site becomes more difficult. As a result, it is always a good idea to add a description to your Bookmark in order to remember exactly what the site includes. To add a description, follow these steps:

1 Select Bookmarks (Ctrl+B) from the Window menu. The Netscape Bookmarks list window appears.

2 Select the item from the Bookmarks list.

3 Select Properties from the Item menu. The Bookmark Properties dialog box appears.

4 Add or change the description of the Bookmark in the Description field.

5 Click OK.

Changing a Bookmark link

The Internet is a continually changing environment. Every day there are tens of thousands of documents added. In addition, documents are often moved from server to server, or directory to directory on the same server.

When this happens, the remote server administrator often places a note where the document used to be, telling anyone that comes to that address hoping to find the document that it has moved. In this case, there is usually a referring Web URL for you to change in your Bookmark list. Make a note of the new address and do the following to change the Book-mark URL:

1 Select Bookmarks (Ctrl+B) from the Windows menu. The Netscape Bookmarks list window appears.

2 Select the item from the Bookmark list.

3 Select Properties from the Item menu. The Bookmark Properties dialog box appears.

4 Change the URL address in the Location (URL) text box.

5 Click OK.

The new URL is now in effect.

 TIP   **Make sure you have included all the different sections of the URL** correctly—the protocol used, the server name, the directory path, and finally, the filename. Without all these parts you may not be able to access the desired file.

 TIP   **Instead of trying to remember or physically copy a URL from the Go to** location text box in the main Netscape screen, use Netscape's cut and paste features to cut it from the Go to box and paste it into the Bookmark properties dialog box.

Organizing Bookmarks

Bookmark lists are an extremely useful feature of Netscape. However, after you have added more than a dozen Bookmarks to your list, it needs to be organized in some way or else you will find that it is difficult to retrieve saved Bookmarks. The next few sections include advice on how to organize your Bookmark lists.

Hierarchical Bookmark menus and menu management

A Bookmark list is extremely simple to use if all you do is keep adding Bookmarks to it and know exactly where each book item is in the drop-down list when you want to return to it on the Web. Unfortunately, things get a little more complicated than that.

As you travel the Web, you keep adding Bookmarks to your list, and before you know it, the list is long and cluttered. At this point, you need to think about organizing and categorizing the list into a hierarchical one, most likely with different subject categories divided into sections using headers and separators.

A well-planned Bookmark list, with common-sense headers and catego-ries, and a visually uncomplicated set-up using separators, can take a lot of the frustration out of navigating the Web. A few seconds of forethought can save you many minutes in search time when you mislay that just-added Bookmark somewhere in your list of 300 items.

A Netscape hierarchical Bookmark list works much the same way as the Mac's folder-nested-within-another-folder, or the Windows 3.x/DOS subdirectory-within-a-directory format. With a hierarchical listing, you have top-level items, within which are at least one other sub-level cat-egory of Bookmarks.

That's how hierarchical Bookmark lists work. They have categories of items contained beneath headers or category titles. The items on the second-level appear indented in the Bookmark list to show they are on a sub-level (see fig. 4.4).

A major benefit of a hierarchical system is that it allows you to display only the items that you want. You can just display the top-level headers by clicking each one header folder in turn. Top-level folder icons are shown as either closed or open. When the folder is closed, the items within it are hidden. When the folder is open, items are displayed in the Netscape Bookmarks window in a hierarchical listing.

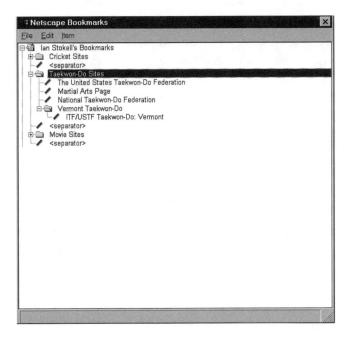

Fig. 4.4
A hierarchical Bookmark list contains indented items beneath higher-level folders.

If you want only the main folders displayed, just close all the folders in the window. Then, when you want to open up a specific header folder and access a particular Bookmark item, just double-click the top-level folder and the indented items appear in the list window.

If you have a lot of nested items within your Bookmark list and you want to locate one that is not immediately visible, use the Find Bookmark dialog box, which you access by selecting the Find option from the Netscape Bookmarks list in the Bookmark list window.

Organizing and categorizing your Bookmark list

When you get so many Bookmarks in your list that it overruns the list window, it is time to think about categorizing and organizing it. You can use headers and separators to visually distinguish between the different sections.

The categories you choose, of course, depend on the Bookmarks that you have listed, and the emphasis you want to place on the Bookmarks themselves; maybe you want them listed in order of importance, for example.

Bookmark items should be grouped in logical categories wherever possible, so you don't have to hunt through a large number of header folders in order to locate them, which defeats the purpose of organizing the Bookmark list in the first place. The next sections cover using header folders and separators.

Header folders and separators

Having decided what form your Bookmark list is going to take, one way to divide it up into easily recognizable sections is by using headers and separators. A header is essentially the title of a specific category group within your Bookmark list, and is represented in the newer versions of Netscape for Windows as a folder icon, while a separator is a physical line separating categories.

With both, you need to strike a balance between using too many headers and separators and not enough. Too many separators, for example, break up the flow of the Bookmark list and make you scroll further down the list to get where you want. Not enough separators, on the other hand, can make deciphering a long list more difficult.

 TIP   **You will typically be accessing your bookmark list from the Bookmarks** menu, which displays only second-level folders. Scrolling down the list from the Bookmarks menu allows you to open up submenus.

Not enough header folders can also lead to you having to scroll down long lists of unrelated files in order to find the one you are looking for. Too many folders can also be a problem, as it often means you have to keep opening folders and sub-folders in order to display multiple lists and sub-lists, looking for the one item you need.

Bookmark list organization and planning are very important for efficient management once your list begins to get long.

Creating header folders

In the Netscape Bookmarks list window, folders represent category headers, into which you place individual Bookmark items. You should have a new header folder for each category in your Bookmark list.

Headers appear as folder icons, each with its own name, and are either open or closed. When open, an indented list of items within that folder are displayed in the Netscape Bookmarks window. When you double-click the opened folder, it closes and all items within it become hidden from view. To reopen that folder and display the enclosed list of Bookmarks, double-click the closed folder.

Creating a new folder header is a simple process; follow these steps:

1 Select Bookmarks (Ctrl+B) from the Windows menu. The Netscape Bookmarks list window appears.

2 Select the current item in the list, under which the new header folder is to appear.

3 Select Insert Folder from the Item menu. The Bookmark Properties General sheet appears (see fig. 4.5).

Fig. 4.5
The Bookmark Properties General sheet is where you fill in the details of the new folder header.

4 Name the new folder in the Name field.

5 Add a general description of the contents of the folder in the Description text box.

6 Click OK.

The new folder header appears in the Bookmark list, directly beneath the current item previously selected.

TIP   **If you move or delete a header folder, all those items contained within** that folder are also affected. Moving a folder is less cumbersome if you first hide the contents by double-clicking the open folder icon.

Just as you can have Bookmark items contained within header folders, so you can have folder icons within folders. To add a folder inside a folder, or indented beneath a folder in the Bookmark list window, just make the top-level folder the current item before selecting Insert Folder from the Item menu. The result will be a folder within a folder in the Bookmark list (see fig. 4.6).

Fig. 4.6
You can have folders nested within header folders in your Bookmark list.

The more Bookmarks you add to your list, the more useful nested folders become. Without the header folders, a long Bookmark list quickly becomes unmanageable.

In addition, because the bookmark list appears at the bottom of the Bookmarks menu, higher-level folders containing sub-lists of bookmarks are vital to maintaining order. Without folders, the Bookmarks menu can become unwieldy very quickly.

Drag-and-drop Bookmarks

One of the primary benefits of upgrading to the Windows 95 operating system/graphical user environment is the ability to drag-and-drop files on the desktop. This is also true for using Netscape. It is a feature that is particularly useful for managing your Bookmark list.

To move Bookmark items within the list, just click the item to be moved and, while still holding down the mouse button, drag the icon to the new location. When you get to the new location, release the mouse button and the icon moves.

If you are moving an item into a folder nested within another folder, make sure the sub-folder is displayed in the list. To do this, just double-click the top-level folder and the item/folders in the level immediately below the top-level folder are displayed.

If the current selection to be moved is a folder header, the header alone does not move. Everything belonging to that header—the sub-items attached and indented underneath it—also move up or down the list. In this way, you can save large amounts of time if you want to move entire categories of Bookmarks up the list. Think how long it would take to move everything individually after you have moved the header if drag-and-drop wasn't a feature of Netscape! Not to mention the time it takes to indent all the items that belong to the header!

Additionally, you can rearrange your Bookmark list items in the same way, simply by clicking the item and then dragging it to a new position in the same folder, or to another folder altogether.

TIP   **Before moving items up the Bookmark list, it may be a good idea to** collapse all the header items by clicking the individual headers, so just the headers and not their sub-items are visible. Then you don't have so far to move the item.

Adding items to a specific header

Having established your header category, you now need to indicate what items belong to it. You can specify which Bookmark items belong to a specific folder header by dragging-and-dropping them within that folder.

Dropping an item on a folder indents that item directly beneath the folder. This signifies that the item belongs to that folder. To hide the list of items in the folder, double-click the folder icon.

Adding and deleting a separator

Adding a separator is a similar process to adding a header, except you obviously don't get to name it! But be careful not to add too many. Separators can be very visually effective when used in the right amount, but too many can make a list look messy—especially if you want to use the list as a regular Web page as well as within the Bookmark menu.

To add a separator, follow these steps:

1 Select Bookmarks (Ctrl+B) from the Windows menu. The Netscape Bookmarks list window appears.

2 Select the current item in the list, under which the new separator is to appear.

3 Select Insert Separator from the Item menu.

The separator appears directly beneath the item you selected as the current list item.

If you want the separator to appear directly beneath a header folder, and not as the first item in that folder's list, you need to close that folder icon, then make it the current item, before selecting Insert Separator from the Item menu. If the folder is open and selected as the current item when you click Insert Separator, the separator appears as the first item in that folder's list.

There will often come a time when you need to delete a separator from your Bookmark list. Deleting a separator is a simple two-step process; follow these steps:

1 Click the separator that needs to be deleted from your Bookmark list, making it the current selection.

2 Select Delete from the Edit menu, or press the Delete key on the keyboard.

The separator is immediately deleted.

Using the Find option in Netscape Bookmarks

When you first start saving Bookmarks, it's pretty easy to find items that you have added to the list. However, as time goes by and you begin to organize your Bookmark list into categories with headers, finding the Bookmark you want can get a little time-consuming. Sometimes you have to scroll through pages of items to get the one you want. Fortunately, Netscape includes a Find feature in the Netscape Bookmarks window that helps solve that very problem.

The Find feature allows you to search for titles in the Bookmark list. Found items match whatever you type into the Find dialog box, except that the word or letters are not case sensitive unless you enable the Match Case checkbox. To use the Find feature, follow these steps:

1 Select Bookmarks (Ctrl+B) from the Windows menu. The Netscape Bookmarks list window appears.

2 Select Find from the Edit menu. The Search Headers dialog box appears (see fig. 4.7).

3 Enter the word, phrase, or letters that you want to find in the Find what box.

4 Select Find Again in the Edit menu, or press F3.

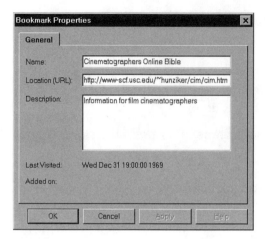

Fig. 4.7
The Find feature allows you to easily find Bookmarks in your Bookmark list.

When you click the Find Next button, the search begins with whatever is the current selection and work its way down the list.

Obviously, if you want to search the entire list, it is best to make the top-most Bookmark item the current selection. That way the search begins from the top and works its way right through the list.

The item found becomes selected, at which point you can press the Find Next button again and wait for the next instance of the requested word, phrase, or letters to be located. The text you typed in the Find what box becomes selected if there is no match in your list.

The search also locates matches even if they are found within folder headers. If this happens, the header's folder list automatically unfolds, and the item that matches the search parameters becomes selected.

Using the What's New? option

Instead of hunting through your entire list of bookmarks each time you sign onto the Web to see if there is anything new at the sites, you can have Netscape do it for you using the What's New? option. Here's how:

1 Select Bookmarks from the Windows menu.

2 In the resulting Bookmarks window, select the What's New? option from the File menu. The What's New? window appears (see fig. 4.8).

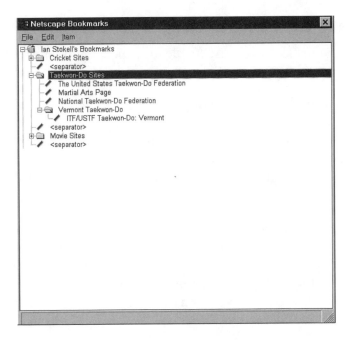

Fig. 4.8
The What's New? option allows you to track new additions to your bookmarks automatically.

3 If you want to check all the bookmarks on the list, click the <u>A</u>ll bookmarks radio button.

4 If you want to choose individual bookmarks from your list, check the <u>S</u>elected Bookmarks radio button.

5 Click the <u>S</u>tart Checking button.

Netscape will check the selected sites and report any new changes.

Importing/exporting Bookmark files

There may come a time when either you want to let someone else use your Bookmark list—especially if you are involved in a workgroup project at work—or you want to use someone else's Bookmark list. This next section covers importing and exporting Bookmark lists.

Importing and exporting Bookmarks

You can make your Bookmarks available for exporting to other users, just as they can make their Bookmarks available to you.

As you travel around the Web looking for information or research locations pertaining to your collective interest, you will no doubt run across a variety of sites you want to share with a group of friends or co-workers. If you create a Bookmark list for that day's search, for example, or update an existing Bookmark category list, you will then be in a position to export that list to other users.

Because documents on the Web are formatted using the platform-independent HTML language, the Bookmark list you save and want to export can be read on another platform without any converting. You just have to save it in the HTML format and pass it on, either via "sneaker-net" across the workspace, over a local area network within your building, or over the Internet as an e-mail message.

How to import a Bookmark list

You can import another Bookmark list via the Netscape Bookmarks window. This is a particularly useful feature for office or education environments where a number of people are working on the same project and need to share research and information.

If your PC is connected to a local area network, you will probably be able to access other team members' hard drives, or at least a centralized server that can act as a holding pen for information collected by the different team members.

To import a list, follow these steps:

1 Select Bookmarks from the Windows menu. The Netscape Bookmarks window appears.

2 Select the current item from the Bookmark list window. The imported Bookmark list is added to the list directly under the current item selected.

3 Select Import from the File menu. The Import Bookmarks File dialog box appears (see fig. 4.9).

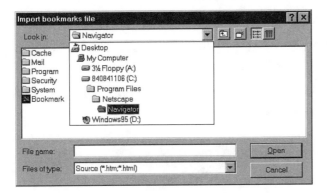

Fig. 4.9
You can import a Bookmark using the Import Bookmarks File dialog box.

4 From the Import Bookmarks File dialog box, select the file you are interested in from the list of available folders, drives, and file types. The selected file's name appears in the File name field at the bottom of the dialog box.

5 When you have the desired file listed under File name, click Open. The imported file appears in the Bookmark list immediately below the current item.

How to export or save a Bookmark list

After you have completed a new search or updated an old Bookmark list file, you can either send the file directly to other users using the company e-mail system, connect to their hard drives and place it in a place where they will find it, store it on the central information repository server, or leave it in a place on your own drive where those users will be able to retrieve it. Of course, the latter means you will have to keep your PC on all the time to allow them to access the new file.

TIP   **Because your bookmark list is already in the form of an HTML file,** called Bookmark.htm, you can save it as a straight text file and send it to someone else on the Internet via e-mail.

Turning your current Bookmark list into an export file for use by someone else is just as simple as importing a file.

To export your Bookmark list file, follow these steps:

1 Select Bookmarks from the Windows menu. The Netscape Bookmarks window appears.

2 Select Save As from the File menu. The Save bookmarks file dialog box appears (see fig. 4.10).

Fig. 4.10
Use the Save bookmarks file dialog box to export your current booklist to another location.

3 Type the name of the file as it will appear to others in the File name field.

4 Select the type of file it will be saved as (for example, .htm for hypertext markup language) from the Save as type drop-down menu.

5 Select the drive where the exported file is to reside from the Save in drop-down menu. If you are connected to a local area network, this can either be your own local drive, a drive on a distant user's PC, or a server on the network.

6 Select the folder where the exported file is to reside from the folder list.

7 Click the Save button. The file has now been exported to the specified location.

 NOTE **You can also use your bookmarks as your home page. To see how to do** this, see the section "Specifying the Bookmarks File as Your Home Page" in chapter 2.

5

Web Forms

● In this chapter:

● **What diffrent kinds of forms there are on the Web**

● **What the parts of a form are**

● **How to fill out and submit an online form**

● **What happens when you submit a form**

Browsing the Web is mostly a matter of downloading files from a Web server to view with your browser. But when you fill out an online form, you're sending data the other way—from your computer back to the server you're connected to.

Web forms are like paper forms; they are comprised of data entry fields, check boxes, and multiple-choice lists. They open the electronic door to all kinds of exciting transactions on the Web. You can sign a guest book, sign up for a service, ask to be added to a mailing list, join an organization, request a catalog or brochure, and even make purchases by submitting forms over the World Wide Web.

What are forms good for?

Forms are the Web's standard method for letting you submit information to a World Wide Web server. They are used for four major functions:

- Searching for information in an online database
- Requesting a user-customized action, such as the creation of a custom map or table
- Registering for a service or group
- Online shopping

In each of these cases, forms give you the means to send specific information to the server you're connected to, so that you can receive a customized response.

NOTE How does a Web site send a customized response when you submit a form? Usually by running an associated program on the server called a CGI-BIN script.

In contrast, normal page links only allow you to click a link from a list to retrieve a "canned" response from the server. Forms let Web page creators send you information and services that are tailored to your specific needs, rather than broad, generic responses built for an audience constrained by "least common denominator" considerations.

Let's take a look at four real-world examples from the Web, one for each of these common uses of forms.

Searching

The most popular site on the World Wide Web is Yahoo at Stanford University. Yahoo is a combination Web directory/search engine that lets you find just about any site on the Web in seconds. There are two different methods built into Yahoo for finding specific Web sites.

 TIP **You can also find some interesting sites by clicking the New, Cool,** Popular, and Random buttons in the Yahoo title bar, though these are more for Web surfers than for anyone trying to find specific information on the Web. You'll find more information about these and about Yahoo in chapter 3.

One search method is a standard hierarchical index. While you can find a site by following the index through its ever-narrowing lists of topics and subtopics, this is definitely the brute-force approach, especially when you consider the tens of thousands of sites that are contained in Yahoo's index space!

The superior way to search Yahoo is to let it build a custom index to your personal specifications. You do this by filling out and submitting the simple one-line form near the top of the page (see fig. 5.1). You just click in this data entry field and type a list of keywords, then click the Search button. Yahoo then searches its database of Web site information and builds a custom index composed only of the entries that contain your keywords. This takes only a few seconds. Finally, Yahoo builds and transmits a custom Web page that contains an index that has been generated "on the fly" just for you.

There are literally thousands of sites like Yahoo on the Web that let you use forms to search online databases and retrieve custom pages containing information on a myriad of topics. Just about every kind of information you can imagine (and some you can't imagine) is available on the Web somewhere in a forms-searchable database. The following are a few good examples:

- Search UseNet postings with DejaNews (**http://www.dejanews.com/**)

- Look up drugs on the Pharmaceutical Information Network (**http://pharminfo.www.com/**)

- Find interesting biographical notes in Britannica's Lives (**http://www.eb.com/calendar/calendar.html**)

- Do a keyword search for jobs (**http://www.occ.com/occ/ SearchAllJobs.html**)

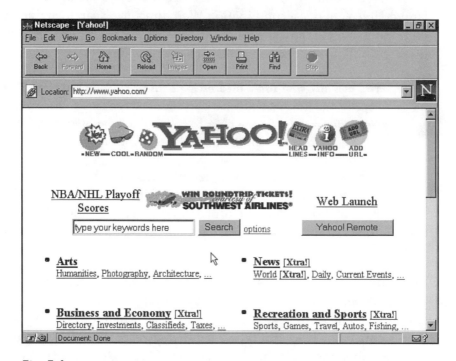

Fig. 5.1
Yahoo lets you search for Web sites in two very different ways. The best, shown here, is to use its online form to search for keywords.

Requesting

Forms can also be used to ask a server to run a program to perform a specific task for you (see fig. 5.2). This is one of the most open-ended (and fun) examples of interactivity on the Web.

Because a Web server is a computer just like any other, it is fully capable of running any program that any other computer can run. So the types of actions you can request of a Web server are limited only by what the server is willing to let you do. The following is a quick list of a few of the actions you can request on the Web by submitting a form to the right site:

- Display an up-to-the-minute satellite view of the earth's cloud cover from a user-definable viewpoint using the Earth Viewer (**http:// www.fourmilab.ch/earthview/vplanet.html**)

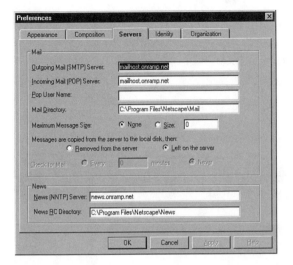

Fig. 5.2
The Earth Viewer form lets you specify latitude and longitude for your point of view, as well as specifying which satellite data to use. You can even generate a custom view from the sun or the moon!

- Say something over the speech synthesizer in Rob Hansen's office at Inference Corporation (**http://www.inference.com/~hansen/talk.html**)

- Operate a model train at the University of Ulm in Germany (**http://rr-vs.informatik.uni-ulm.de/rrbin/ui/RRPage.html**)

- Generate custom tables of 1990 census data (**http://www.census.gov/cdrom/lookup**)

While some of these activities are definitely more useful than others, they serve to illustrate what it is possible to do over the Web if the server you are connected to provides the right forms and support programs.

Registering

You can use online forms to sign up for just about anything somewhere on the Web (see fig. 5.3). You can enter contests and sweepstakes, join organizations, apply for credit cards, subscribe to e-mail lists on hundreds of different topics, and even sign a guest book at some of the sites you visit.

Most online registration forms ask you for the same information you'd supply on a paper registration form: name, address, phone, and—since this is the Internet, after all—e-mail address. Many places also require user registration before they allow you into the deeper, and hopefully most interesting, regions of their Web site. (Some may charge you for this privilege, some not.)

Some of the places on the Web that ask you to fill out a registration form are the following:

- Neural Applications Corporation wants you to fill out a short registration form before you take a look at their home page (**http://www.neural.com**).

Fig. 5.3
Many sites, like this one, ask that you fill out a registration form before you are allowed to access the rest of their site.

- Follow the links and enter your personal information and some keywords to win a new Toyota from Oxyfresh (**http://www.oxyfresh.com/Oxyfresh/Contest/**).

- Apply for an AT&T "universal card" credit/phone card (**http://www.att.com/ucs/app/app_intr.html**)

- Subscribe to an e-mail list of properties for sale in San Francisco (**http://www.starboardnet.com/form.html**)

Shopping

You can shop 'til you drop without ever leaving home by cruising the electronic malls on the World Wide Web (see fig. 5.4).

Web shopping generally involves filling out an order form (or registering as a shopper) with your name, address, and credit card information. Many sites now even include an electronic "shopping cart." This allows you to browse a site, reading product descriptions and price information; when you find something you like, you just click the check box (an online form, of course) next to the item you want and it is added to your cart. When you get ready to leave the online store, you go through a "checkout" where your items are totaled and you are presented with a bill, which you can then pay with your credit card or "electronic cash." For more information on electronic cash, see the "Digital Money" section in chapter 6.

By "shopping" we really mean the process of requesting goods, "hard copy" information like catalogs or brochures, or services that require either the action of human beings or the transfer of physical objects through delivery services. Though this certainly can involve buying things, it also includes many other services. The following is a list of some more or less random examples: (Please note that we are not endorsing or recommending any of these products or services. Use at your own risk.)

- Enter Liechtenstein's $1,000,000 InterLotto lottery (**http://www.interlotto.li/**).

- Order free and low-cost government pamphlets from the Consumer Information Center (**http://www.pue.blo.gra.gov/**).

- Click check boxes to receive hundreds of free catalogs at the Mall of Catalogs (**http://www.csn.net/marketeers/mallofcatalogs/**).

- Request books or research services from a library. Though you'll have to check with your local or university library to see if they offer such services via the World Wide Web, Jim Robertson maintains a list of links to the kinds of forms commonly used by libraries at **http://hertz.njit.edu/~robertso/LibForms.html**.

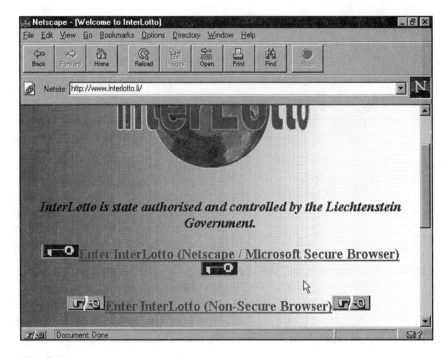

Fig. 5.4
You can enter Liechtenstein's national lottery directly through their secure server connection by
filling out an online form.

A generic online shopping trip

Just so you'll know the steps that are involved, let's take a quick virtual
shopping trip on the World Wide Web.

The first question is "Where to go?" A good place to begin is the All-
Internet Shopping Directory at **http://www.webcom.com/~tbrown/**. It lists
hundreds of online malls, catalogs, and stores.

From this list, a good choice might be The Awesome Mall of the Internet
(**http://malls.com/awesome/**). How could you pass by a place with a name
like that?

The Awesome Mall lists the CyberWarehouse online store (**http://
www2.pcy.mci.net/marketplace/cyber/**); it's intriguing because they list a
28.8 modem for only $99.99, if you're tired of your slow 14.4 kilobit-
per-second dial-up connection to the Web.

Scrolling down to the bottom of the page, you find a short form that lets you specify your preferred Delivery method, and Quantity to purchase (see fig. 5.5). Normal delivery is okay, and you only want one unit, so you can accept the default answers by clicking the button marked Add to Basket. This adds the item to your virtual shopping basket. Though you could add more items, you decide to be done for now. Selecting Shopping Basket from the bottom-of-page menu lets you examine your shopping basket's contents.

Fig. 5.5
You can use an online order form like this one to buy things on the Web.

The shopping basket is private. Netscape pops up a Security Information dialog box to warn you that you're about to enter a secure space, and that all data transmissions from here on will be encrypted. Note that you haven't accessed any secure data yet, which means that the key icon in the lower-left corner of the screen will still look broken.

The shopping basket screen lists what you've purchased. At this point, the key icon is unbroken, reminding you that this page is secure. (And you didn't have to do a thing to get a secure connection—Netscape did it all for you.) You could change your order now, but you decide you're happy so you just click the button marked Checkout.

That takes you to an online form where you fill out your shipping and credit card information (see fig. 5.6). The process is very similar whether you use a credit card or digital money, though many more sites take credit than "ecash." The key shows you still have a secure link.

Scrolling down to the bottom of this page, you find the credit card information part of the form. You know you can fill this out safely because your link is secure, and the data you send will be safely encoded by Netscape. When done, you press the Continue Checkout button, proceed though a couple of final messages, and you're done.

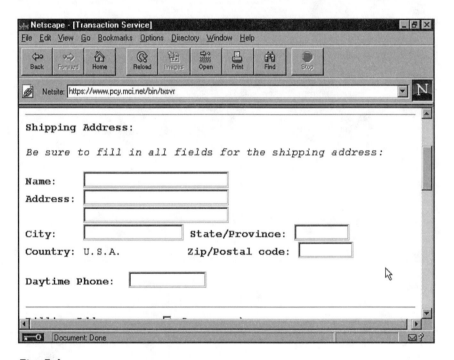

Fig. 5.6
When ready to make an online purchase, you are asked to fill out an order form through a secure connection (note unbroken key in lower-left corner of screen).

Form formats

Web forms are created using the <FORM></FORM> HTML tag. Within this structure, many options are available to the Web forms designer to create a wide range of form elements. Online forms can include data entry fields, check boxes, scrolling lists, and even push buttons.

You'll run into a wide variety of form formats on the Web. Among them are inline forms, full-page forms, multiple forms on a single page, and even hidden forms.

Inline forms

If the Web page you're visiting needs only a single item of information from you, it's likely to present you with a much simplified form called an inline form.

The Lycos search engine is a good example of an inline form (see fig. 5.7). There is only one field to fill in and a single button to push when you're done. In fact, most forms that have only a single field don't even require that you push a button to submit the information you've filled in; if you just hit the Enter key when you're done, the information is sent to the server automatically.

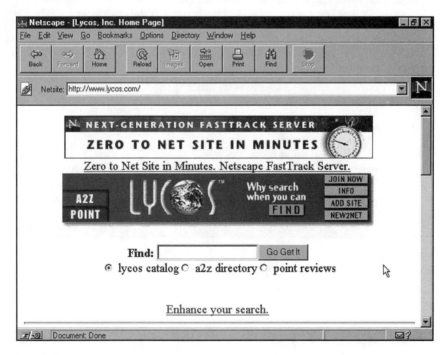

Fig. 5.7
Lycos uses a single inline form field to ask for a list of keywords to search for.

Full-page forms

You'll find many examples of full-page forms on the Web. These ask for a variety of information, and may make use of all the available form elements (push buttons, check boxes, fields, scrolling menus, and so on). However, they probably also incorporate many other HTML design elements like style tags, formatted text, inline images, hypertext links, links to objects that launch helper applications, and even links to other sites. Sometimes it's hard to sort out which parts are the form and which parts are collateral material.

Yahoo's Search Options form is a good example of a full-page form with a variety of input field types (see fig. 5.8).

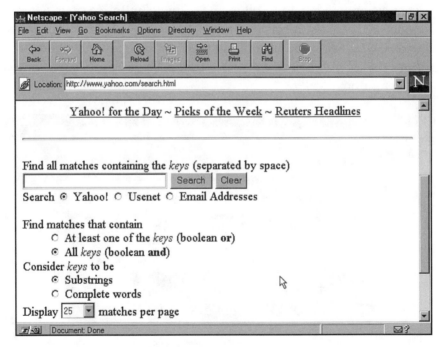

Fig. 5.8
Yahoo's Search Options screen is a good example of a full-page form, and it includes most of the input field types you'll see on online forms.

Multiple forms

You can also put several separate forms on a single Web page. If there are multiple forms on one page, they are independent, each with its own SUBMIT button.

Each individual form has its own associated program or script that is invoked when its SUBMIT button is pressed. Only the data from the associated form is passed to the server. Figure 5.9 shows an example of a Web page with multiple forms.

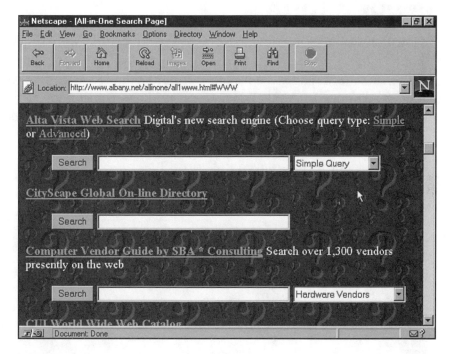

Fig. 5.9
Multiple forms occupy William D. Cross's All-in-One Search Page at **http://www.albany.net/allinone**.

 NOTE If you put more than one form on a Web page, make sure you don't nest one <FORM></FORM> construct within another. Forms cannot be nested within forms. According to proposed HTML 3.0 specifications, forms can only be nested within the following "parent" elements on an HTML page: BANNER, BODYTEXT, DD, DIV, FIGTEXT, FN, LI, NOTE, TD, and TH. Some older browsers have reportedly had problems displaying forms within tables; similar problems might arise from nested constructs.

Hidden forms

You may have used forms without even knowing it. Sometimes forms are completely hidden. Forms can consist of nothing but hidden fields that send pre-defined data when an associated button, image, or link is clicked. Since there is nothing to see on a hidden form, we won't show an example here; however, we will discuss how they work a little later in this chapter.

Filling out a form

Now that we've covered what forms are good for, and what different kinds of forms you're likely to run into on the Web, let's step through filling out a form page. We'll choose as our example a form that contains almost all of the different elements you're likely to encounter in real life. We'll concentrate on what forms look like on the Web page, and how to fill them in.

Our sample form is displayed in figure 5.10.

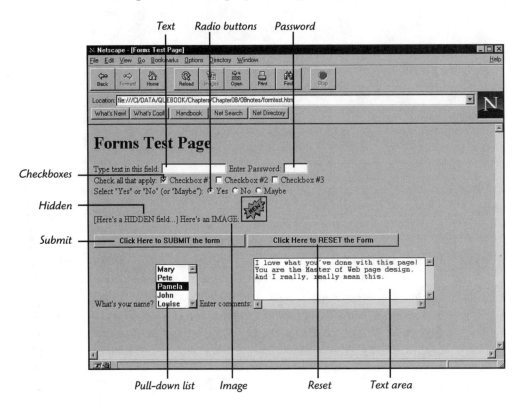

Fig. 5.10
Examples of the most visible parts of an HTML form.

The INPUT areas

There are eight commonly used input type options, each of which looks and acts differently on-screen.

- The TEXT type is used for entering a single line of text. To fill in a TEXT field, point and click in the field, then type. To move from one TEXT field to the next, use the Tab key.

 TIP **When any form field is "active," your cursor and page up/down keys** don't work to scroll the Netscape window anymore. Instead, they work to move around in the form field. To use them for scrolling the window again, just click anywhere in the window background.

- A PASSWORD field is the same as a TEXT field, but for security purposes the screen doesn't display what you type. Instead, you see a string of asterisks (*). You fill in a password field the same way you fill in a text field.

- The CHECK BOX type is for Boolean variables, variables which can take only one of two values. Sometimes, a check box will be checked by default. You check a check box by clicking it; you uncheck a checked check box by clicking it again.

- The RADIO input type is for variables that can take any one of several different specified values. Selecting one of the buttons causes any previously selected button in the group to be deselected. A radio button can be checked by default. You select a radio button by clicking it. If the radio button you click has the same variable NAME as a radio button that has already been selected, the previous button will automatically be unselected when you select the new one.

 TIP **Want to know which radio buttons share the same variable NAME, or** what the default VALUE of a variable is? If the Web page creator hasn't been nice enough to tell you on-screen, the only way to know is to choose View, Document Source (Alt+V,S) from the Netscape menu and comb through the HTML code.

- An input field of the HIDDEN type does not appear anywhere on a form, but the VALUE specified is transmitted along with the other values when the form is submitted. HIDDEN fields are not usually used on pre-defined Web page forms. They usually only appear on customized forms that are created "on the fly" by the Web server you're connected to. They are used to keep track of information specific to your request. For example, if you request information from a server and it sends back a form asking for additional details, that form might include a hidden field type that defines a request number. When you submit the second form, the server is then able to tell which request number your second form referred to. You don't (and can't) fill out a HIDDEN field. Its value is predefined. In fact, you probably won't even know it's there.

- The IMAGE type is an advanced form of the SUBMIT type. Instead of providing a push button, the IMAGE type lets you use a bitmapped image to submit a form. When clicked, the IMAGE field submits the entire form to the Web server, and can also be used to transmit the coordinates of exactly where the image was clicked. If the INPUT type is IMAGE, you'll probably be asked to "Click somewhere on this image to submit this form," or something similar. If it is set up to transmit the coordinates of your mouseclick (that is, if it has a variable NAME), you'll probably be asked to click in different specific spots depending on what you want to do. In any event, you shouldn't click the IMAGE bitmap until you have filled in all the other fields on the form.

- The SUBMIT input type creates a push button which, when selected, activates the ACTION specified in the FORM definition. In most cases, this means it sends the data from all of the form fields on to the server. The VALUE attribute of the SUBMIT type is actually the label that appears on the button. When you are done filling out a form, click the SUBMIT button to finish.

 TIP **SUBMIT buttons are often labeled something else, like "Done" or** "Send." Don't let labels fool you. If it's a push button and it sounds like something you should only click when you're finished, it's probably a SUBMIT button.

- RESET also manifests itself as a push button, but selecting it resets all of a form's fields to their initial values as specified by their VALUE attributes. Like the SUBMIT button, it can be labeled with different text. If you've totally mucked up filling out a form, click the RESET button to reset all the fields to their default values so you can start over.

There are other less-often-used or proposed-for-future-versions types for INPUT, but the types just cover 99 percent of what you'll run into on the Web.

There are two other common types besides INPUT that are used to create online forms: SELECT and TEXTAREA.

Pull-down lists

RADIO and CHECK BOX fields can be used to create multiple choice forms. But the <SELECT></SELECT> element pair can be used to produce a neat multiple-choice field in the form of a pull-down list. It is possible to have one of these lists that allows for more than one option to be selected.

To choose a SELECT option, click it. To select more than one option in a MULTIPLE-enabled list, click one option and drag to select more. To select non-contiguous options, hold the Ctrl key when you click additional items. Selected items are highlighted; if you can only highlight one option, then the MULTIPLE attribute isn't enabled.

Text areas

The TEXTAREA HTML construct lets you type in multiple lines of text in a scrolling text box. These can include default text.

To fill in a TEXTAREA field, just click it and type. You can use all of the standard editing keys (arrows, Delete, Page Up/Down, etc.) to move around and edit in the TEXTAREA box.

Filling out a form by uploading a file

Version 2 of Netscape added the ability to upload the data for a form, rather than having to fill it all out online. This can save you lots of connect time when filling out long online forms. (Unfortunately, you can't upload data for just any old form—the Web form you're looking at has to be specially configured to accept a file as input.)

For an example of a short form that accepts file input, see figure 5.11.

Fig. 5.11
A short example of a Web form that accepts a file as input.

The new INPUT TYPE="file" not only lets you upload a file in response to the form request, it even adds a BROWSE button that, when clicked, brings up a standard Windows file requester dialog box. It couldn't be much easier.

For every action

Every FORM definition has an associated ACTION that determines how the server deals with the information it receives from the form. There are two possible form actions: GET and POST.

Fortunately, all of this is totally invisible to you. You don't have to worry about how it works at all, because the process is fully automatic.

Another possibility is the MAILTO command which mails the form data to the specified Internet mail address. Though not all browsers support the MAILTO command, Netscape does, and you'll find it used quite often on the Web.

The form submission process flowchart

So what really happens when you submit a form? The whole process is summarized in the flowchart shown in figure 5.12.

The following is the step-by-step process that occurs when you submit a form.

1 While filling out the form, you can move around and edit, and even press the RESET button to clear the form back to its default VALUE settings.

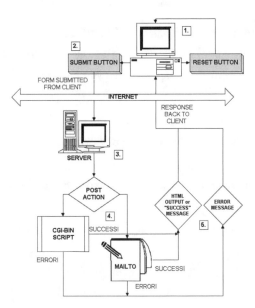

Fig. 5.12
This diagram shows the sequence of events when submitting a form.

2 When you are satisfied with the data you've entered, pressing the SUBMIT button sends the form data to the server you got the form from via the Internet.

3 The server receives the data and performs the ACTION defined in the FORM statement.

4 If the METHOD is POST and the ACTION references a CGI-BIN script (or program), the CGI-BIN is run with the form data as input. If the ACTION is MAILTO, the form data is mailed to the address specified in the ACTION statement.

5 The server then sends a response to you. If the action was successfully completed, you get a confirmation message or custom page, depending on the actions defined in the CGI-BIN script. If unsuccessful, you (hopefully) are sent an error message. If the action was MAILTO, the only feedback you get may be a Document Done message in Netscape's status bar at the bottom of the screen.

Q&A *I pressed the SUBMIT button, but all I got back was some weird error message that I couldn't interpret. What gives?*

There are a number of things that can happen when you press the SUBMIT button that result in an error message. The following are just a few:

- Between the time you received the form and the time you submitted it, the server you were connected to may have gone down.

- The server you're connected to may submit its CGI scripts to another server to be run, and that server may be down. (Hey, nobody said this would be easy!)

- The CGI program may be buggy, and might have choked on your particular data.

- The CGI program may be telling you that you filled out the form incompletely or incorrectly. Read the error message carefully to see if it's specific about the problem.

The fix is often no more complicated than pressing the Back button on the Netscape toolbar and filling out the form correctly. If you continue to get errors, your only solution may be to e-mail the Webmaster of the site where you're experiencing the problems. There's usually an address or link on most home pages for this purpose.

6

Netscape and Web Security

● **In this chapter:**

● What security issues are associated with the Web

● Do forms present unique security issues

● How to make sure that your transactions (including credit card purchases) are secure and safe

● What the future holds for Web security

The first time you use the Web to order something using an online form, you may wonder if you should be afraid to use your credit card on the Web. But you might also wonder why no one seems to care about how much "insecurity" there is in more traditional uses of credit cards in stores, by mail order, and over the phone. It's really much more likely that someone will pull a receipt out of the trash at a store and steal your credit card number than it is that some hacker will latch onto it on the Web.

The real issue is this: How trustworthy is the party you're dealing with? Your major worry should probably be the chance of running into a dishonest employee or a bogus company—online or not—that wants to steal your number outright.

That being said, it should also be noted that there really are a few dishonest hackers out there who revel in gathering information through any means possible. Some of them even go on to use it for personal gain. When this happens, it doesn't matter that the percentages are low if it's your credit card number they're playing with! And, as commerce increases on the Web, it's likely to draw larger numbers of out-and-out professional thieves, too.

If nothing else, business and government are extremely concerned about security, and they won't trust their transactions to the Web until they're convinced that no one else can illegally tap in and see what's going on.

Clearly, the security of online transactions is not an issue that can simply be ignored.

Encryption and security

Enter encryption. Public-key encryption, to be exact. Encryption uses a "key" number to change readable text into unreadable code that can be sent and decrypted back into a legible message at the receiving end. A public key system uses two keys: a public key number and a private key number. Messages encrypted with the public key can only be decrypted with the associated private key, and messages encrypted with the private key can only be decrypted with the public key. You keep the private key private and make the public key as public as you want, and you've guaranteed that all of your communications will be secure. Netscape incorporates public-key cryptography as part of its built-in Secure Sockets Layer (SSL) security.

(For more on public-key encryption, see the discussion on Netscape's Secure Sockets Layer technology later in this chapter.)

Of course, it's more complicated than that, or this chapter would end right here.

TIP **Point your Netscape newsreader to the comp.security newsgroups for** the latest discussions of security on the Web.

The following are some of the other issues involved in making sure your online communications are really secure:

- Is your computer (the client in the transaction) set up in a secure manner?

- Is the server you're connected to secure?

- Is the connection between the two systems secure?

- Is there some way you can be sure your transaction is secure?

We'll address all four of these concerns (see fig. 6.1) in this chapter.

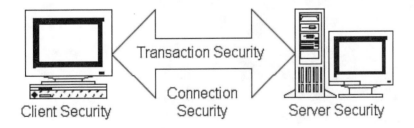

The four areas of security concern

Fig. 6.1
This diagram illustrates the four areas of security concern.

Client security

Frankly, client security is the only area in which you have much say. Your computer is yours, and you can choose how to set it up. The chain being only as strong as its weakest link, you want to make sure that your link in the security chain is not the one that's going to snap first.

There are three areas where you can have some major effect on the security process: how you configure helper applications, how you set up proxy servers, and how carefully you keep your passwords.

Configuring helper applications

You can get into some real security problems if you configure helper applications without first thinking about security issues (see fig. 6.2). (See chapter 11, "Netscape Helper Applications," for detailed information on using the Netscape Helpers dialog box to set up helper applications.)

Fig. 6.2
You get to this dialog box for configuring Helpers
by selecting Options, General Preferences (Alt+O,G) from the Netscape menu.

For example, if you configure Microsoft Excel as a helper application to view files with an extension ending in .XLS, what happens if a spreadsheet file you view while you're browsing the Web has an auto-execute macro that runs some hidden (and sinister) procedures? At that point, your system has been breached.

You expose your PC to a great many security risks if you configure helper applications that aren't simply passive viewers or players, unless you are certain that downloaded files can never contain any malicious content.

Be careful about helper applications. Don't configure fancy helper applications that can be programmed to run sinister macros via the Web.

NOTE **Concern about sinister macros is no mere bugaboo. Recently, Microsoft** addressed the issue of what it called a "prank macro" that was being distributed via a MS Word document on the Web. This macro and variations on it have caused a great deal of problems for Word users.

Microsoft immediately issued a prank-macro-swatter program that would kill the macro and scan all Word documents for it, to eliminate it from your system completely. Microsoft and several anti-virus companies have issued updates to programs to better combat macro viruses.

Proxy servers

Proxy servers—also called application gateways or forwarders—are programs that handle communications between a protected network and the Internet. Most proxy programs log accesses and authenticate users.

If you run Netscape from a machine on a network that is protected with a firewall (see "Firewalls" later in this chapter), you'll need to set up a different proxy server for each Internet application you want to use in conjunction with Netscape—for example, one for FTP, one for Telnet, one for UseNet news, and so on.

Your major responsibility in this area is to make sure the proxies you use are secure and a good match to your network's firewall. In short, you should never use a proxy application that hasn't been approved by your system administrator.

If you connect to the Web via a commercial dial-up service like America Online or CompuServe, you don't need proxies and don't need to worry about them (see fig. 6.3).

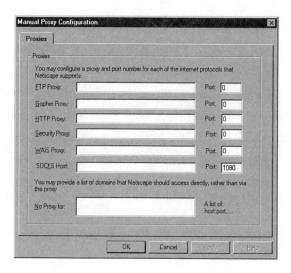

Fig. 6.3
You get to this dialog box for configuring Proxies by selecting Options, Network Preferences from the Netscape menu.

Passwords

If you ever want to rob a bank, just walk in at noon and check around the computer terminals of people who are out to lunch. The odds are very, very good that you'll find at least one person who has left their system password on a sticky note in public view.

Of course, you'll never have to worry about anyone stealing your password, because you follow the Five Basic Rules of Password Security, which are as follows:

1 Choose a password that isn't obvious.

2 Commit your password to memory.

3 Never write your password down anywhere that's accessible by anyone but you.

4 Change your password often.

5 Don't ever share your password with anyone.

If you're on a network, you already have a password for network access. Odds are, you'll register for additional access passwords on many Web sites, as well.

But there's also a password you can set for access to Netscape itself. To set your password, follow these steps:

1 Select Options, Security Preferences from the Netscape menu.

2 Click on the Passwords tab to bring it to the front (see fig. 6.4).

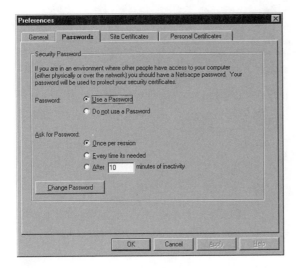

Fig. 6.4
Netscape's Preferences dialog box lets you set access password options.

3 Click the Use a Password radio button.

4 Under the Ask for Password option, click one of the following buttons, depending on your preference:

  • Once per session

  • Every time it's needed

  • After __ minutes of inactivity

If you select the last option, enter an appropriate number in the minutes field.

5 Select the Change Password push button. You'll see the screen as shown in figure 6.5.

6 Click the radio button that indicates you want a password, then select the Next> button.

7 You are prompted to enter a password of more than eight characters, then retype it to confirm (see fig. 6.6). REMEMBER YOUR PASSWORD!!! Netscape cannot tell you what it is if you forget.

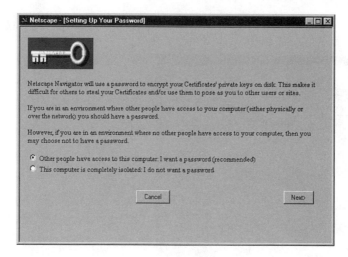

Fig. 6.5
Confirming that you really want to use a password.

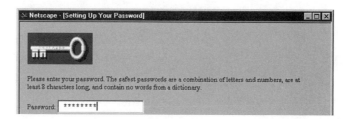

Fig. 6.6
Entering a password.

8 Choose the Next> button.

9 When the last window appears, select Finished. You'll be sent back to the Password window.

10 Choose OK to end.

Server security and firewalls

A poorly managed Web server can be the source of many security compromises. For example, a poorly written CGI script can accidentally allow malicious intrusions into a system. The Web server administrator is responsible for managing the server in such a way as to prevent such security compromises.

It's also important that the Web server software installed on the server system be capable of handling secure transactions over the Internet. For example, the Netscape Commerce Server (Netscape's server software package) incorporates SSL (Secure Sockets Layer) security, with support for acquiring a server certificate and communicating securely with SSL-capable browsers like Netscape Navigator.

But perhaps the most important security concern regarding servers is the installation of a good firewall.

A better name for firewall might be traffic cop, because the main function of the group of programs that comprise a firewall system is to block some Internet traffic while allowing the rest to flow. There are a variety of ways that this can be implemented on a server system, but all firewalls perform similar functions.

Some allow only e-mail traffic, which limits security concerns to "mail bombs" and other e-mail-based attacks. Others allow a full range of Internet accesses. In any event, a firewall performs two major functions: user authentication and access logging. The first keeps out intruders; the second provides an accurate record of what happened in case one gets through.

Since all firewalls provide a single access point between the Internet and a network, they make it relatively easy to monitor communications should there be any suspected breaches of security.

Without some kind of firewall installed, a network system hooked up to the Internet is open to all kinds of security attacks.

TIP **For more information on firewalls, point Netscape to ftp://ftp.greatcircle.com/pub/firewalls,** which contains the Firewalls mailing list archives.

Connection security

Between point A (your computer) and point B (the Web server you're connected to on the Internet), there may be dozens of other computers handling the communications link. Obviously, the more computers in the chain, the more chances for some unknown person to break into your transmission and steal your data.

Unfortunately, you don't have much control over your Internet connection. That's even more reason to make sure you do as much as you can to make the things you do have some control over as solid and secure as possible.

Transaction security

Transaction security is the area that most people think of when they think of security on the Web. Maybe it's because it's the area that encompasses the most high-tech and dramatic aspect of computer security: cryptography.

There is, of course, much more to transaction security than just data encryption. Message verification and server identification are at least as important, if not even more so. After all, what difference does it make if a message is securely encoded if its source is someone impersonating you and trying to use your credit card or steal your data, or if a message that you legitimately sent has been intercepted and altered in transit?

NOTE **What if your major concern is not making sure that data is transmitted** securely, but making sure that it doesn't get transmitted at all? Many parents are concerned about (admittedly overblown) media reports about pornography and other objectionable materials that are available on the World Wide Web. They don't want their children to be able to access such data.

Parental lock-out systems can work in much the same way as the security measures employed in ensuring secure transactions. For example, a Web browser might have different accounts set up with different passwords and different encryption keys for parents' and kids' accounts. The parents' account might allow unlimited access, while the kids' account wouldn't properly decode transmissions from restricted sites. Such sites could be defined by looking for specific "ratings" tags sent by the Web server, or by setting up a list of forbidden sites.

There are many ways that parental lock-out could work. Netscape and two other leading Internet software companies (Microsoft and Progressive Networks) have formed the Information Highway Parental Empowerment Group to work on the problem.

The rest of this chapter is devoted to the topic of transaction security and how Netscape handles it.

Netscape security

NOTE **Additional information on Netscape security is just a couple of mouse** clicks away. From the Netscape menu, select <u>H</u>elp, <u>O</u>n Security for access to the following helpful documents from Netscape Corporation's World Wide Web site:

- Netscape Navigator Handbook: Security
- Netscape Data Security
- Using RSA Public Key Cryptography
- The SSL Protocol

The security features built into Netscape Navigator (and the Netscape Commerce Server) attempt to protect your Web transactions in the following three important ways:

- Server authentication (thwarting impostors)
- Encryption (thwarting eavesdroppers)
- Data integrity (thwarting vandals)

Netscape's visual security cues

Netscape Navigator includes some visual security indicators to let you know about security conditions. These indicators include identification of secure URLs, changing color bars, a broken/solid key icon, and the ability to view identification and security information associated with a Web page. You'll also see various warning dialog boxes from time to time, depending on how you have your security options set.

URL identification

You can tell whether a Web page comes from a secure server by looking at the URL (location) field at the top of the Netscape window. If the URL begins with https:// instead of http://, your connection is secure

The cracking of SSL

You may have read about it in the papers: Two University of California–Berkeley students and a researcher in France almost simultaneously posted messages to the Internet detailing their success in decoding a message that had been posted as a "Netscape security challenge." They discovered how Netscape 1.2 generates session encryption keys, enabling them to replicate the keys for that specific message with a moderate amount of computing power and, within a few days, they had deciphered it.

The researcher in France used 120 workstations and two parallel supercomputers at three major research centers for eight days—approximately $10,000 worth of computing power. While this seems like a lot of effort to put into decoding just one simple little one-page message (and it is), it did serve to show that Netscape's security was crackable. If the same techniques had been applied to a security-critical message (for example, a hostile takeover bid for a major corporation), the consequences could be substantial.

The 40-bit key used in the "challenge" message is the international encryption mode used in export versions of Netscape Navigator. The 128-bit key encryption used in the U.S. version is export-restricted under government security regulations. It is much more robust; it would have taken many years to break the challenge message if the same amount of computing power had been used had it been encoded with the U.S. version.

While no actual thefts of real-world information have ever been reported to Netscape Corporation, they worked quickly to provide updated software for free downloading from their home page on the Web. The new version 1.22 security patch increased the amount of random information used to generate keys from 30 bits to approximately 300 bits. With 10 times as much pseudo-random data to start with, keys in the latest versions of Netscape Navigator are now effectively immune from similar "brute-force" attacks.

(see fig. 6.7). Similarly, a news URL that begins with snews: instead of news: indicates that a document comes from a secure news server. In both cases the s stands for secure, of course, and in both cases, it indicates that the HTTP requests are traveling through a Secure Sockets Layer.

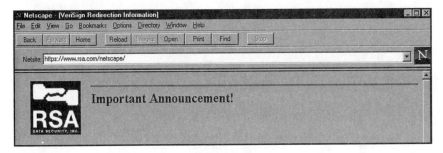

Fig. 6.7
If the server you're connected to is secure, Netscape's URL bar shows the address as beginning with https:// instead of http://.

The key and the color bar

To the left of the status message at the bottom of the Netscape screen, you'll find a key icon. The status of this key indicates whether or not you are viewing a secure document. A broken key icon on a gray background indicates an insecure document (see fig. 6.8); a solid key on a blue background indicates a secure document. The secure key icon varies slightly depending on the grade of encryption: The key has two teeth for high-grade and one tooth for medium-grade. A mixed document with insecure information omitted is shown as secure; if the insecure information is included, the status is displayed as insecure.

Likewise, a blue color bar above the Netscape display window indicates a secure document, while a gray color bar indicates an insecure document.

Netscape security dialog boxes

Several notification dialog boxes (or alerts) inform you of the security status of documents.

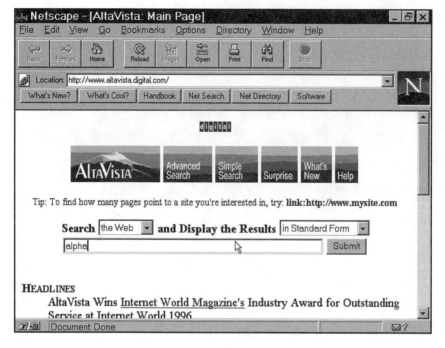

Fig. 6.8
The key in the lower-left corner of the Netscape window is broken (top) if your connection is insecure or mixed.

When entering a secure document space, you are notified that the secure document is encrypted when it is transferred to you, and any information you send back is also encrypted (see fig. 6.9).

When leaving a secure document space, you are notified that the insecure document can be observed by a third party when it is transferred to you, and any information you send back can also be read by a third party.

When viewing a document with a mix of secure and insecure information, you are notified that the secure document you just loaded contained some insecure information that will not be shown. If an insecure document contains secure information (either inline or as part of a form), this alert is not displayed. The document is simply considered to be insecure.

Fig. 6.9
One of Netscape's security alert dialog boxes; this one is to notify you of encrypted data transfers.

When you submit a form using any insecure submit process, you are notified that the submission process you are about to use is insecure (see fig. 6.10). This means that the information you are sending could be compromised by a third party.

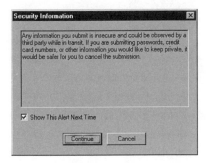

Fig. 6.10
If a form you submit is insecure, you'll see this alert.

You are notified if the document was expected to be a secure document but is actually an insecure document (the document location has been redirected to an insecure document).

You can choose whether to receive these dialog boxes by setting the panel items in the Netscape Options menu.

Here's how to turn Netscape's security alert dialog boxes on or off:

1 Select Options, Security Preferences from the Netscape menu.

2 Click the General tab to bring it to the front (see fig. 6.11).

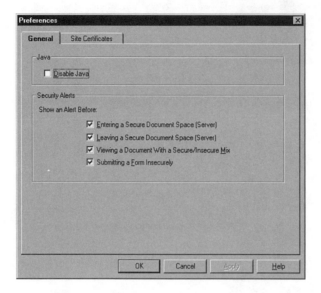

Fig. 6.11
You use Netscape's Preferences dialog box to set alert display options.

3 You'll see the following four different Security Alerts selections, labeled Show a Security Alert Before:

- Entering a Secure Document Space (Server)

- Leaving a Secure Document Space (Server)

- Viewing a Document With a Secure/Insecure Mix

- Submitting a Form Insecurely

Click the appropriate spaces to select or deselect the dialog boxes you want to see.

4 Choose OK to finish.

You can also simply uncheck the dialog box's Show this Alert Next Time check box if you decide you never want to see it again.

View document information

To view information about a displayed Web page, choose <u>V</u>iew, Document I<u>n</u>fo from the Netscape menu. A new Netscape window (see fig. 6.12) displays the document title, the URL of the file, and document info, which includes file type, source, modification date, file length, expiration date, character set, and security level. This information is taken from the header of the document and from the server that supplied the page.

The Document Info window displayed in Netscape uses another new feature, Frames, which enables independent sub-windows, or frames, within one page display window. In the Document Info window, the top frame shows the document title and its URL, and the bottom frame shows a list of information about the document. If you click the link to the document in the lower frame, the document itself is shown in the lower frame. If you then click the link in the upper frame, the lower frame displays the document information again. You can resize the relative sizes of the frames in the window: just put the mouse on the boundary until you see the mouse icon change into a split pair of arrows, then click and drag the boundary between frames.

 Depending on where the Document Info window appears on your screen when it is invoked, you may need to move it (click and drag the title bar) to be able to use the scroll bar in the lower frame. You may need to scroll the lower frame down to where the security information line is, at the bottom of the list of document information, so you can see the lines of security information for the document.

If a document is insecure, the security information panel notifies you that encryption is not used and there is no server certificate. If a document is secure, the security information panel notifies you of the encryption's grade, export control, key size, and algorithm type, and, in a scrolling field, the server certificate presents coded data identifying the following:

- Certificate version and serial number

- Issuer of the certificate

- Subject (organization) that is being certified

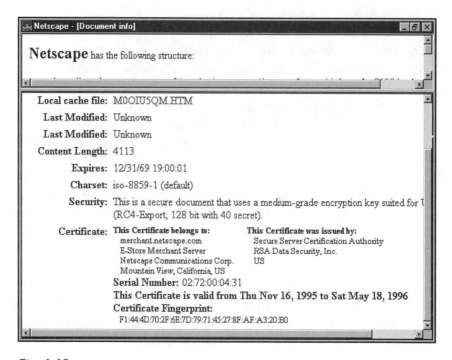

Fig. 6.12
Netscape displays document information using its new Frames capability. This info is for a page at
RSA, Inc.'s secure WWW server.

To ensure that you are communicating with the organization you want,
examine the subject of the server certificate. The organization should
identify itself with the name and location you expect.

Certificate information is protected by encryption to ensure authenticity
and integrity. You can interpret the coded data as follows:

- Country: Two-character country code

- State or Province (ST): Unabbreviated state/province name

- Organization (O): Legal, registered organization name

- Organizational Unit (OU): Optional department name

- Locality (L): City the organization resides or is registered in

- Common Name (CN): The server's fully qualified host name (such as
  hostname.netscape.com)

To return to the main Netscape window, choose <u>F</u>ile, <u>C</u>lose to close the Document Info window, or use the window Close button.

Personal certificates

Netscape 3 now provides for the ability to definitely identify who you're sending data to. Previously you could never be sure that the Web page you're looking at was created or maintained by the person who said it was. That is, somebody could've put up a Web page and claim to be somebody else, and you would never have been able to tell the difference.

Personal certificates allow you to identify yourself from everybody else. This is particularly useful when you're submitting a form, so that the recipient will know for sure the information is from you, and nobody else. You can control your personal certificates by selecting Options, Security Preferences, and choosing the Personal Certificates tab. This dialog box (see fig. 6.13) lists your existing personal certificates.

Fig. 6.13
The Personal Certificates tab is used to help you control how you identify yourself to others.

Site certificates

Certification for an entire domain or company is performed in a manner similar to personal certificates. The only difference is that it's applied to a larger entity, rather than an individual. As with personal certificates, all site certificates must be issued from a Certifying Authority (CA). A CA can be any trusted central administration, a person or a computer, willing to acknowledge the identities of those to whom it issues certificates. For example, a company would probably be the Certifying Authority for any certificates it issues its employees.

SSL

The Secure Sockets Layer (SSL) protocol is Netscape's answer to transmission security over the World Wide Web. SSL is application protocol-independent and provides encryption, which creates a secured channel to prevent others from tapping into the network; authentication, which uses certificates and digital signatures to verify the identity of parties in information exchanges and transactions; and message integrity, which ensures that messages cannot be altered en route.

The Netscape Commerce Server and Netscape Navigator incorporate SSL technology, and both (or compatible programs) are needed in order to establish a secure SSL connection.

SSL is layered beneath application protocols such as HTTP, Telnet, FTP, Gopher, and NNTP, and layered above the connection protocol TCP/IP (see fig. 6.14). This strategy allows SSL to operate independently of the Internet application protocols. With SSL implemented on both the client and server, your Internet communications are transmitted in encrypted form, ensuring privacy.

SSL uses authentication and public-key encryption technology developed by RSA Data Security, Inc.

Server authentication uses RSA public key cryptography (see the "RSA Public Key Cryptography" sidebar that follows) in conjunction with ISO X.509 digital certificates. Netscape Navigator and the Netscape Commerce Server deliver server authentication using signed digital certificates issued by trusted third parties known as certificate authorities. A digital certificate verifies the connection between a server's public key and the server's identification (just as a driver's license verifies the connection between your photograph and your personal identification). Cryptographic checks using digital signatures ensure that information within a certificate can be trusted.

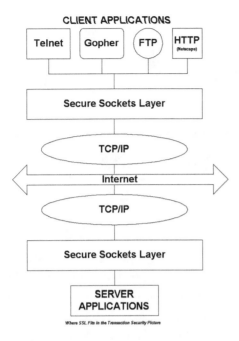

Fig. 6.14
This diagram shows how SSL fits into transactions on the Internet.

 NOTE **The security of this system comes from the fact that the numbers used** are very large. Though the numbers can be discovered by factoring, the amount of computer time required to do so is highly impractical, often running into hundreds of years.

Server certificates

To operate using security features, the Netscape Commerce Server requires a digitally signed certificate, which is a kind of trustworthy "electronic driver's license"—it's a unique identifier. Without a certificate, the server can only operate insecurely. If you are a server administrator and want to obtain a signed certificate, you need to submit a certificate request to a certificate authority, a third-party organization that issues certificates, and pay an associated service fee.

When you request a server certificate from an online service, your server software generates a public key/private key pair and you choose a distinguished name. Online forms guide you through the process of submitting the form to the certificate authorization company.

The authenticity of each certificate request is verified (making sure requesters are who they claim to be). Upon approval, the certifier digitally signs the request and returns the unique digitally signed certificate through e-mail. You can then install the signed, valid certificate to enable security.

RSA public key cryptography

RSA (Rivest-Shamir-Adleman) public key cryptographic technology is at the heart of most Web security schemes, including Netscape's built-in Secure Sockets Layer protocol. The following is how it works, in a nutshell.

Encoding and decoding of messages is accomplished by using two large random numbers. One is called the public key, and is made public. The other is the private key, and is kept secret. Messages encoded with the public key can be decoded only using the private key, and vice versa. So messages sent to you can be decoded only by you, and messages you send can be verified as coming from you, since only your public key decodes them.

Because encryption is considered a national security issue by the federal government, U.S. products can't be exported to foreign countries with really high-level security built in. That's why the international version of Netscape uses only 40-bit keys, while the domestic version uses 128-bit keys.

The RSA encryption technology used in Netscape is owned by RSA, Inc., which also makes a stand-alone security product for Windows called RSA Secure. RSA Secure integrates into the Windows File Manager to provide RSA encryption for the Windows file system. The company offers a trial version for 30-day evaluation, and checking it out is a good way to learn more about RSA encryption. For more information on RSA, Inc., or to download the free evaluation version of RSA Secure, go to their secure (naturally) WWW server at **http://www.rsa.com**.

Public key cryptography has been around only a couple of years longer than the World Wide Web. Pretty Good Privacy (PGP) is a stand-alone public-key encryption program from MIT for multiple platforms that lets you play around with and learn about public key cryptography. You can also use it for serious purposes, like encrypting mail and files on your hard disk.

The latest version of PGP for Windows can be downloaded from **ftp://net-dist. mit.edu/pub/PGP**.

To learn more about PGP and public-key cryptography, point Netscape to **http:// bs.mit.edu:8001/pgp-form.html**.

Setting certificate options in Netscape

You can examine and change Netscape's installed security certificates through the Options, Security Preferences section on the menu bar.

Select the Site Certificates tab for a scrolling list of server certificates that Netscape is configured to handle (see fig. 6.15).

Fig. 6.15
You can set Site Certificate preferences through this Preferences dialog box.

You can highlight an entry and select Delete Certificate to remove a certificate from the Netscape setup. You'll probably want to do this only if there is some major flap over bugs or breaches of a particular certification authority's certificates.

The Edit Certificate button brings up the certificate information dialog box shown in figure 6.16. Clicking check boxes here lets you choose to allow or disallow connections to sites using the chosen certificate. You can also elect to see an alert dialog box when you encounter a site with the specified certification.

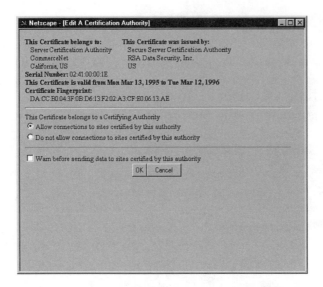

Fig. 6.16
Netscape displays detailed information about a site certificate.

NOTE   **Cookie files seem to be mentioned in passing in a lot of discussions** having to do with security, without much associated definition or clarification.

Briefly, a cookie file is a small amount of data sent back from the server to be stored on your computer, which the server can then access later. This might be account information or any other information associated with your specific session that the server doesn't want to keep on hand, but needs to refer to later.

Cookie files may be transmitted to your computer and back to the server in a secure or insecure manner (that is, with or without SSL security). So security with cookie files is, as with any data transfer, a separate issue to itself.

There are two things you can say about cookie files and security in general: There might be some extra measure of security in keeping your personal information on your machine rather than on the server, but there is also some additional security risk involved in transferring cookie file data back and forth between your machine and the server every time it's needed.

Business transactions

First there was television, which from the very beginning included commercials. Then there were those late-night infomercials for Ginsu knives and the Popeil Pocket Fisherman. Finally, with the advent of cable TV, there was the Home Shopping Network (and its many clones).

Though the Internet began life as an infrastructure for the exchange of scholarly information, it didn't take long for someone to figure out how to turn a quick buck online with mass postings and mailings. And it took even less time for those annoying all-text "spam" messages to give way to a plethora of Web-based online shopping malls.

Not that there's anything wrong with that (though some old-timers whine all night about the commercialization of the Web). Let's face it—people like to buy things. And buying things on the Web is no worse than buying them on the Home Shopping Network, or even at Wal-Mart. It's just different.

One of the toughest things to work out is how to pay for something you've ordered electronically. Cash and checks can't be squeezed down the wires, and most people are leery about posting their credit card numbers where they might be grabbed by unscrupulous hackers.

But enterprising Web entrepreneurs have already figured out how to take the electronic equivalents of credit cards and money electronically.

There are differences between using credit cards and using electronic cash, but the range of services available blurs the lines of distinction between the various methods of conducting financial transactions electronically on the Internet. Some schemes deal directly with banks, while some use second-tier arrangements, bonding-houses, or third-party secure-server services.

Digital money

Digital money is a totally new concept. Even more radical in concept than the once-preposterous idea that paper bills could represent real gold, in its most basic form digital money involves transmitting an encoded electronic packet of information that is as secure and difficult to counterfeit as a dollar bill. (More so, really.)

Digital money is based on the same security encoding schemes as other secure transactions on the Web—encryption and authentication. But some of the proposed schemes go a step beyond.

For example, the two companies examined next have very different ideas of how digital money should work.

CyberCash

CyberCash has set up both debit and credit systems, but we're mostly interested here in the debit, or "cash" system.

In the CyberCash scheme, participating banks let a customer open accounts that amount to "electronic purses." Using the company's software, a customer moves money from the checking account into the electronic purse. As with an automatic teller machine, the customer then withdraws digital tokens from the purse and uses them to make purchases on the Net. Upon receipt, the seller queries the CyberCash computer to verify that the token is valid and instructs CyberCash where to deposit the money.

To use the CyberCash system, you must install the client version of CyberCash software to work with your browser. It also requires that the Web server handling the transaction form must use the CyberCash system to decrypt order information.

CyberCash believes that most consumers want to have a record of their transactions to budget and account for their spending.

For more on CyberCash, visit their Web site at **http://www.cybercash.com/**.

DigiCash

DigiCash operates a debit system that is similar to an electronic checking account. To set up a DigiCash account, you deposit money in a bank that supports the DigiCash system, and you are issued Ecash that can be used to purchase things through the Web.

But DigiCash has a philosophy that is much different than CyberCash's. DigiCash sees records as a threat to privacy, and has developed a method to create completely untraceable, anonymous digital cash. Without anonymity, they say, electronic transactions leave a detailed trail of activity that could enable governments, personal enemies, or commercial marketers to easily trace an individual's activities, preferences, and beliefs.

DigiCash, based in the Netherlands, has created electronic tokens that can be trusted as valid money regardless of who is spending them. An ingenious double-blind encryption method makes it impossible to trace transactions unless there is mathematical proof that fraud has occurred.

But the idea of total anonymity has scared off most bankers and has government officials worried as well. Total anonymity, they fear, could provide a haven for money launderers, arms dealers, and kidnappers.

For more info on DigiCash, check them out on the Web at **http://digicash.support.nl/**.

 TIP **For more information on digital money and the companies making it** happen, check out the Yahoo index on the topic at **http://www.yahoo.com/ Business_and_Economy/Electronic_Commerce/Digital_Money/**.

Credit card transactions

If you're concerned about security risks when using your credit card over the Web, then you also should be concerned about giving out any personal information through a Web page. But then again, maybe you shouldn't buy raffle tickets from the neighborhood kids, either. Who knows what people will do with your personal information?

Using your credit card anywhere poses risks. Those risks are certainly more complex in the realm of Internet servers, browsers, and complex multi-functional systems. Secure communications does not eliminate all of an Internet user's concerns. The situation is analogous to telling someone your credit card number over the telephone. You may be secure in knowing that no one has overheard your conversation (privacy) and that the person on the line works for the company you wish to buy from (authentication), but you must also be willing to trust the person and the company.

That being said, let's look at a few of the schemes that are surfacing on the Web that claim to make using your credit card online as secure as (or even more secure than) using it at your local supermarket.

Netscape's Secure Courier

Netscape's Secure Courier protocol builds on their existing Secure Sockets Layer (SSL) protocol. Secure Courier observes the MasterCard and Visa security specification for bank card purchases on open networks.

While SSL encrypts data passing along the network between a client system and a server, Secure Courier keeps a transaction encrypted in a secure digital envelope when it arrives at a merchant's server or at other intermediate points on the Net. This means that the data remains wrapped, or protected, at any site at which it stops.

To find out more, connect to Netscape's Web page for the Secure Courier protocol at **http://home.netscape.com/newsref/std/credit.html**.

First Virtual

First Virtual Corporation is an online transaction handling company that operates a system that is designed for selling downloadable products, such as executable software files and information in text files. To get an account, you call them and give them your credit card information, and they issue you a First Virtual account number.

Whenever your First Virtual account number is used to purchase something online, you are notified by e-mail, and you must confirm the transaction before your credit card is charged. Once you verify, your card is charged for the purchase and the money is deposited in the vendor's First Virtual checking account.

The First Virtual method needs no software or hardware on either end of the transaction. It's designed to be simple, fast, and efficient.

For more detailed information, go to **http://www.fv.com/** on the Web.

VeriSign

VeriSign, a spin-off of RSA, Inc., is collaborating with Netscape to provide Digital IDs (digital certificates) for direct online transactions through the Netscape Commerce Server and Netscape Navigator version 3.0. The following four classes of ID are available:

- Class 1—A low level of assurance, to be used for secure e-mail and casual browsing. Non-commercial and evaluation versions are offered for free, with a VeriSign-supported commercial version for $6 per year.

- Class 2—Provides a higher degree of trust and security. Used for access to advanced Web sites. $12 per year.

- Class 3—A higher level of assurance for valued purchases and inter-company communications. $24 per year.

- Class 4—Said to provide "a maximum level of identity assurance" for high-end financial transactions and trades. Pricing is by quote.

The Digital ID system from VeriSign is being marketed as "The Driver's License for the Internet." RSA has the good fortune to own the patents on the encryption schemes used by SSL and SHTTP, so this gives the VeriSign system a boost.

For more info, see **http://www.verisign.com/**.

Open Market

Open Market acts as its own credit card company in a scheme that relies on their own Open-MarketPlace Server. It is unique in that it depends on the end-user having a browser that supports the S-HHTP protocol, not Netscape's SSL protocol. They'll be worth watching, if just to see whether a company other than Netscape can help set security standards on the Web.

You can check out their Web site at **http://www.openmarket.com/**.

 TIP **For lots of links relating to credit cards, point Netscape to the Credit** Card Network Home Page at **http://www.creditnet.com**.

For an excellent detailed discussion of how credit card transactions work on the Web, check out this Netscape page: **http://www.netscape.com/newsref/std/ credit.html**.

The future of WWW security

TIP   For a lengthy discussion of current Web security issues, check out http://www-genome.wi.mit.edu/WWW/faqs/www-security-faq.html.

With a topic as hot as security, it's about as easy to get an agreement on the question of what's secure as it is to get two politicians to agree on a plan to balance the federal budget.

Though Netscape Corporation is in a powerful position, it's not powerful enough to simply dictate security standards for the World Wide Web. There are a lot of people out there—powerful, influential, and monied people in banking and credit and the government—who simply aren't convinced that Netscape's SSL protocol can protect their important transactions over the Internet.

That's why there are dozens of alternate proposals for security protocols for WWW transactions. Because of Netscape's position in the Web community, it's likely that SSL will be with us well into the future, but you're still likely to start running into some sites that want you to use another protocol. The following pages offer an overview of some of the most likely contenders for real-world implementation as WWW security protocols in the months and years to come.

S-HTTP

S-HTTP (Secure HTTP) has emerged as the major competitor to Netscape's SSL security protocol. In fact, it has gained such a following that most commerce on the Web will be supporting both protocols—including Netscape Navigator!

Developed by EIT, CommerceNet, OpenMarket, and others, S-HHTP extends the Web's standard HTTP data transfer protocol by adding encryption and decryption using paired public-key encryption, support for digital signatures, and message authentication.

Several cryptographic message format standards can be incorporated into S-HTTP clients and servers, including PKCS-7, PEM, and PGP. S-HTTP clients can also communicate with non-secure standard HTTP servers, though without security.

S-HTTP doesn't require (though it does support) client-side public key certificates or public keys, which means that you can initiate spontaneous transactions without having an established public key first.

S-HTTP also provides for simple challenge-response freshness authentication—that is, an "are you really you" and "yes, I'm really me" secure message exchange—to make sure no one is intercepting and changing transmitted messages. It can even consider HTTP's DATE header when determining freshness.

For more information on S-HTTP, visit the following sites: **http://www.eit.com/**, **http://www.openmarket.com/**, or **http://www.commerce.net/**.

Shen

CERN (the organization in Switzerland that created the World Wide Web) is developing a new high-level secure protocol called Shen. It approaches security by providing for weak authentication with low maintenance and no patent or export restrictions, or strong authentication using public key encryption. Since it's coming from CERN, which has the ear of the whole Web, Shen is bound to become a standard itself, or at least influence the development of other security standards.

For more info on Shen, point Netscape to **http://www.w3.org/hypertext/ WWW/Shen/ref/shen.html**.

Fortezza

One of Netscape Corporation's latest security additions is integrated support for the Fortezza security card, which is based on U.S. government standard cryptography. Developed by the National Security Agency, Fortezza is a cryptographic system delivered in a PCMCIA card format, and is now mandatory for use in many government agencies. Fortezza cards are already being used by the Department of Defense and the U.S. intelligence community.

Support for Fortezza has been added to Netscape's Secure Sockets Layer (SSL) open protocol, and Netscape Corp. will be upgrading Netscape Navigator and other Netscape products to support the use of Fortezza cards.

Netscape is currently working with Litronic Industries to further develop the Fortezza cryptographic interface.

Because of its status as a top-secret government security protocol, information on Fortezza is difficult to come by. I know of no site on the Web that offers more than just a terse sentence or two on the subject.

TIP **Security is a hot topic on the Web. A good place to find out more** about security online is the Virtual Library Subject Catalogue entry on the topic at **http://www.w3.org/hypertext/DataSources/bySubject/Overview.html**.

For more details on Netscape's security technologies, see **http://home.netscape.com/newsref/ref/netscape-security.html**.

An excellent source of links to security sites on the Web is at Xenon Laboratories WWW site: **http://www.xe.net/xenon/security.htm**.

Part III: E-mail, News, and Other Parts of the Net

FTP, Gopher, and Telnet with Netscape

● **In this chapter:**

- ● **How to access an FTP site**

- ● **How to use Gopher to find information**

- ● **How FTP and Gopher are integrated into Netscape**

- ● **How to search FTP sites and Gopherspace with comic book characters**

- ● **The ancient art of Telnet**

The World Wide Web was only created in 1991, and has since experienced explosive growth. However, the Internet was more than 20 years old when the Web was first developed as a graphical, point-and-click interface that would reduce the learning curve associated with navigating it. Finding anything on the Internet then was associated with understanding UNIX, and the tools developed for searching the Internet were only marginally more intuitive than being a systems administrator yourself.

This chapter will discuss some of Netscape's other capabilities in addition to looking at World Wide Web pages. One of the newest tools for navigating the Internet, Netscape incorporates many of the Internet access techniques that formerly required separate tools.

Accessing and downloading from an FTP site

FTP (File Transfer Protocol) lets you examine the directories of remote systems on the Internet, and lets you transfer files between your computer and other computers. Almost as old as the Internet itself, FTP was designed to work with the systems of the time. You can think of FTP as being very much like using the CD and Dir commands in DOS to move from one directory to another, and to see what's in that directory only when you get there. FTP lets you transfer both text files and binary files (programs).

Using Netscape for FTP

As a Netscape user, you have FTP incorporated into Netscape so that you really don't notice any difficulty. Netscape displays FTP information as a single column of links, each link being either a file or a directory link. An FTP directory viewed with Netscape looks very similar to the File Manager in Microsoft Windows. Each line of the FTP directory displays a small icon (either a file or a directory), the name of the file, the size of the file, and the date that file was added to the directory. FTP directories may include a README or an INDEX text file, which describes the contents of the directory, or the policies of FTP access for that site.

To reach an FTP server in Netscape, type the URL of the FTP server. If a link to an FTP server is on a Web page, select that link to jump to that FTP server. Netscape reduces the effort needed to access an FTP site if the hostname starts with ftp. For example, typing the hostname ftp.foobar.com into the location field (without ftp:// before it) takes you to the URL **ftp://ftp.foobar.com/**. For example, typing ftp.kli.org into Netscape's Location field takes you to the FTP archive of the Klingon Language Institute shown in figure 7.1, just as **ftp://ftp.kli.org/** does.

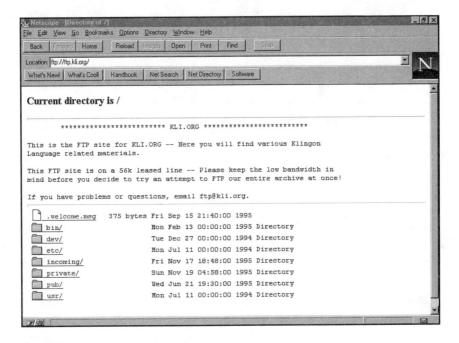

Fig. 7.1
The Klingon Language Institute's FTP server.

If, for whatever reason, a Web site you are trying to reach has named its Web server as ftp.whatever.com/, you can avoid the new default by specifying the protocol identifier. So typing the URL as ftp.foobar.com/ or as ftp://ftp.foobar.com/ starts an FTP session with the FTP server ftp.foobar.com/, but typing the URL as http://ftp.foobar.com/ attempts to retrieve a Web page from the Web server. When you have found the file you want, downloading from an FTP archive with Netscape is as simple as selecting the appropriate link, and the file is transferred to your local system.

TIP **FTP directories and subdirectories almost always have a link at the top** of the page named "Up to higher level directory." Clicking this link takes you one step higher in that FTP site's directory hierarchy—not back one Web page as the Back button in Netscape does.

Most FTP servers are set up to allow anonymous access—meaning that you do not need a login and password account set up specifically for that server. Typically, an anonymous FTP server accepts "anonymous" as the login, and your e-mail address as your password. Netscape is designed to try to log in anonymously when it encounters an FTP server.

 NOTE **Because Netscape tries to log in anonymously, you need to have your** electronic mail preferences set up in the Mail and News window of Netscape's Options window before you try. Most anonymous FTP servers request that you use your e-mail address as your password. See chapter 8 to see how to set your e-mail preferences.

Downloading files

Downloading a file (getting a file from an FTP site to your computer) is as simple as clicking a link in Netscape. When an FTP site is displayed in Netscape, you can click any of the directory links to see the contents of that directory. When you click the link for a file, Netscape will prompt you to see what you want to do with the file. You'll see the same dialog box that you see when Netscape encounters any file type for which it has no helper or plug-in. (See chapters 10 and 11 for a discussion of plug-ins and helper applications.) Generally, you'll want to click the Save File button and then choose a location to save the file.

For files such as text and graphics that Netscape can display, Netscape will display them if you simply click on them. You can do this and then choose the File, Save As command to save it. Or, you can save it directly by clicking the link with the right mouse button and choosing Save Link As from the shortcut menu.

Uploading files

There may be times when you need to upload a file (send a file to an FTP site from your computer). Not all FTP sites allow uploading so you'll need to check to see if you have permission to upload files. If you do have permission:

1 Click the directory links until you are in the directory where you want the file uploaded.

2 Choose the File, Upload File command.

3 Find and select the file to upload in the dialog box and click Open.

This uploads your file. You can also use drag and drop to upload a file. To do this, drag a file from your desktop file manager (or Explorer) to the Netscape window. Netscape will ask you to confirm that you want to upload the file to this location.

Using Netscape to FTP non-anonymously

In some instances, you have a username and password for a network, and need to log in to that network and download files. Netscape does support FTP access with a username and password. To start a non-anonymous FTP session with Netscape, add your username and the at (@) symbol before the FTP server's hostname. For example, if you had access to the servers at startup.com, and the FTP server's name started with ftp, you would type the following URL into the Location field at the top of the Netscape window:

ftp://username@ftp.startup.com/

The next window Netscape displays is a prompt asking for your password. After you type in your password, you are logged into the FTP server, and may start downloading files.

Archie: how to search for files to remotely transfer

The original problem with FTP was that, while FTP lets you transfer a file from a remote computer system, you had to go to that remote directory with FTP first and find what you wanted. If the person administering the FTP server had not included an index text file describing the files in the directory, you had to guess if the file name you were reading was the one you wanted.

Archie was designed to create a centralized indexed list of files that are available on anonymous FTP sites. The Archie database, which as of this writing indexes over 1,000 anonymous servers and an aggregate of 2.4 million files, is mirrored at several locations around the world to reduce the load on individual systems. Over 50,000 queries are made to Archie databases every day. Many of the Archie servers now support inquiries using the Web forms capability discussed earlier in this chapter. Archie is accessible in three ways:

- Netscape

- Archie-specific client software

- Telnet

The Telnet protocol will be discussed later in this chapter. Archie clients are available for almost every platform, and may be found with the Web interfaces to the Archie database. To use Netscape to conduct Archie searches, use the URL **http://pubweb.nexor.co.uk/public/archie/servers.html** (see fig. 7.2).

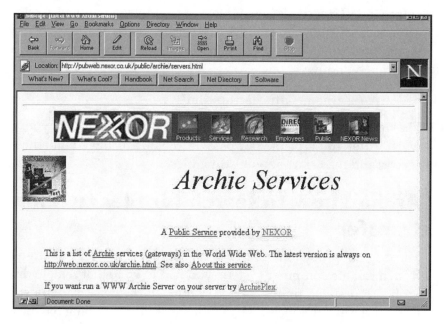

Fig. 7.2
The central index of Archie servers on the World Wide Web.

This Web page presents you with links to many of the mirror sites of the Archie database. One Archie server you can use is located at **http://www.lerc.nasa.gov/archieplex/doc/form.html**, which gives you the form shown in figure 7.3.

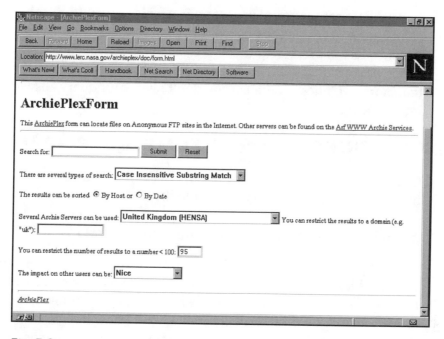

Fig. 7.3
The Archie form for searching FTP servers, as provided by the NASA Lewis Research Center.

NOTE **Whenever you are presented with a choice of multiple sites to connect** to, it is polite to try the one closest to you first. International connections are often heavily loaded, and you may get a faster response from a host computer on the same continent that you are. However, if closer hosts don't respond, try the other hosts from the menu.

You may choose many ways to customize your Archie search. The default setting for matching your entry is a case-insensitive substring match, but you may choose other options from the drop-down list box. The results of your search may be given to you sorted by host or by date of the files, and you may choose a specific server from the next list box, or enter a domain in the field below that list box to restrict the search to only part of the world. To speed up your reply, you can reduce the number of answers.

This is helpful if you have a good idea of what you're looking for. For example, if you know the exact name of the file you want, you probably don't need to receive the location of more than the first 10 or so files matching that exact file name.

You can also set the "niceness" of your Archie search, from "Nicest" to "Not Nice at All." Niceness is a priority tag that determines how fast your Archie query is processed. If you are just about to leave for your lunch break, be considerate of other people and set your query as lower priority than normal ("Nice"), because you don't need your query answered immediately.

Gopher: burrowing through the Internet

Gopherspace is a common way to refer to the interlinked set of Gopher menus. Gopherspace, with its individually designed menus and no unifying taxonomy, but with frequent links from one Gopher menu to others, is generally considered to be the forerunner to the World Wide Web.

Gopherspace lacks some of the most visible features of the Web. Firstly, Gopher is text-based only, so there are no cool pictures, no odd little images usable as buttons or dividing rules on pages, and no large images used as menus. Second, Gopher servers don't know how to accept anything back from the Gopher client program you are running on your computer, so Gopherspace is one-way only. With no CGI-bin support, nothing like a Webform for shopping or surveys exist in Gopherspace. With no e-mail capability, there are no hypertext links for sending e-mail with a single click. If you want to interact with someone or some site in Gopherspace, you will need to send e-mail or use the telephone.

However, Gopherspace has some strong points. The World Wide Web didn't exist five years ago, so anybody who wanted to set up a Web-like access before 1991 that didn't require the user to have a thorough understanding of UNIX had to use Gopher.

For you, the Netscape user, the biggest advantage Gopherspace has is that you don't have to do anything special. Netscape has full Gopher capability integrated into the point-and-click graphical interface of Netscape. A Gopher page appears to be a plain, but ordinary, Netscape page (see fig. 7.4).

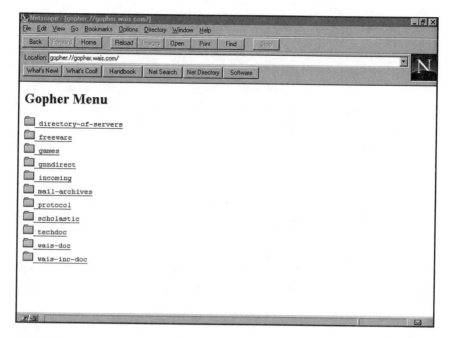

Fig. 7.4
A Gopher page viewed with Netscape.

Netscape displays a Gopher page as a single column of text links. Each
entry in a Gopher menu consists of a small icon indicating the type of the
file, and a description of the file. One major distinction between FTP
directories and Gopher menus is that Gopher descriptions are typically in
plain text, whereas FTP directories look like a directory listing from an
operating system.

Some of the common Gopher link types you might see are:

- Menu—Another Gopher menu or directory
- Text—A text file
- Binary—An application (transferred via FTP if you select it)
- Telnet—Starts a Telnet session
- Search—Starts a simple Gopher search

A full list of Gopher document types is presented in table 7.1, in the
section "How to Ask Veronica a Question: Search Strategies."

Veronica: a Gopher search tool

Gopherspace is too large to search randomly. In addition to the fact that Gopher has been around for several years longer than the World Wide Web, every Gopher menu was organized by the individual who created it, and there are no particular standards for organizing menus. "Tunneling through Gopherspace" may be almost as much fun as surfing the Web, but you are likely to take longer to find what you're looking for if you don't take advantage of some additional tools.

NOTE **The name Veronica is a crowning example of Silly Acronym Syndrome** (SAS). Just as the UNIX variant GNU means GNU's Not UNIX, and the name of the e-mail reader PINE is an acronym meaning Pine Is Not Elm, Veronica's creators were inspired to create a somehow-meaningful acronym around the name of one of Archie's cartoon girlfriends. Officially, Veronica means Very Easy Rodent-Oriented Net-wide Index to Computerized Archives.

You be the judge of whether you believe the words, or the acronym, came first.

Remember how Archie searches directories and file names available on anonymous FTP servers? Veronica is like Archie, but Veronica searches Gopher servers. While Archie is a good search tool to use if you know the exact file name you are looking for, Veronica can find items where Archie can't. Veronica's success derives from the fact that, while Gopher menus may be descriptive names, FTP shows just the file and directory names. For example, giving Veronica the words "martial arts pictures" may find you a GIF of Bruce Lee. On the other hand, Archie won't find the same picture of Bruce Lee unless you ask Archie to search for GAM_DTH2.GIF. If you don't know exactly what you're looking for, but have a good idea of what kind of thing you're looking for, Veronica is probably better than Archie.

Using Veronica is simple. After you get to a Veronica server from a Gopher server, you can enter keywords to search for. Veronica searches its index of Gopherspace looking for matches to your keywords. When Veronica's done, you receive a Gopher menu consisting of all the matches to your search.

A Veronica menu of Gopher items is the same as an Archie page of FTP files and directories: you may not get the same result twice. If you run a Veronica search today and then again tomorrow, new files may have been made available by tomorrow, old files may have been removed, whole servers may be offline (or back online) tomorrow, and so on. The Veronica page you get today is an answer to your question today; the exact details of the answer may change tomorrow.

The following steps demonstrate a search from the home Gopher site at the University of Minnesota:

1 Once you have your Internet connection up and Netscape is running, enter the URL **gopher.micro.umn.edu** to jump to the University of Minnesota's Gopher server, as shown in figure 7.5.

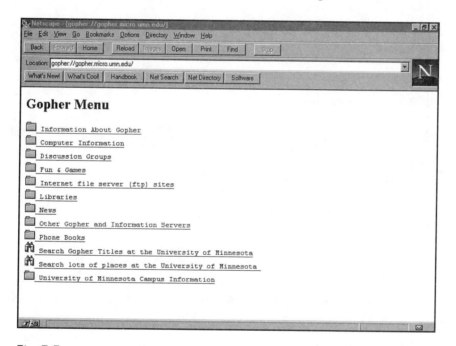

Fig. 7.5
The home of Gopher.

 Remember that Netscape 2.0 allows you to skip entering the gopher:// portion of the URL if you are jumping to a Gopher server whose hostname starts with gopher.

2 Select the Other Gopher and Information Servers item and the Gopher menu displayed in figure 7.6 appears.

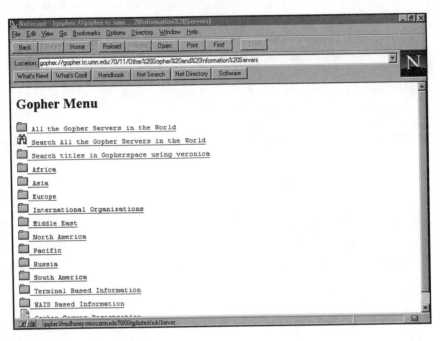

Fig. 7.6
Other Gopher and Information Servers menu.

3 Select the Search Titles in Gopherspace Using Veronica item to see the Gopher menu shown in figure 7.7.

You should notice the two text file items in the middle of figure 7.7. The Frequently Asked Questions (FAQ) about Veronica and How to Compose Veronica Queries text files can provide additional information on this search tool.

4 Select the Search Gopherspace by Title words (via PSInet) item to retrieve an Index Search dialog box as shown in figure 7.8.

5 Place the cursor in the text entry field and type anything you like. You may get a message that looks like Too many connections, please try again soon, or some variation. If you get this response, try another Veronica server, or just try again in a minute or two. Some servers may be busy at different times of the day or week.

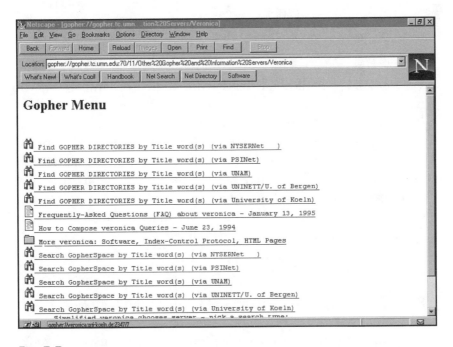

Fig. 7.7
Several Veronica servers.

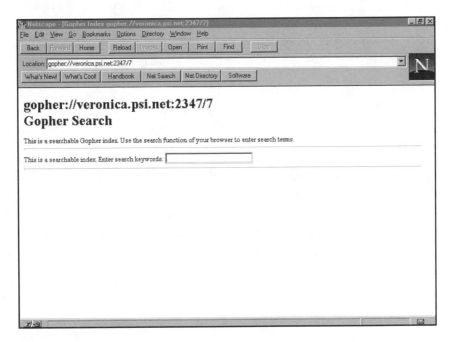

Fig. 7.8
A Veronica search input page.

How to ask Veronica question search strategies

Veronica, like a hammer, extends your ability. A hammer lets you put nails into wood. However, a hammer also lets you hit your other hand (the one holding the nail) *really* hard if you miss. Like any tool, Veronica can be used correctly or incorrectly. Because Veronica servers are always busy, search results can take time. If your search criteria are too narrow or just not quite right, you can eliminate the material you are looking for. If your search criteria are too wide, you can get a huge result (huge searches take even longer) that is not much better than tunneling through Gopher-space until you find the right file yourself. (What's the right file? The one you think fits the answer.) Here is some advice on how to ask Veronica the right question.

Remember that Gopher servers are set up individually—sometimes very individually. You can be creative in your search keywords as long as you are creative in the way others might have been creative before. You can use multiple words to quickly narrow your search. Veronica supports the Boolean operators NOT, AND, and OR. For example, the search TELEVISION AND DRAMA NOT DAYTIME gives you Gopher items for evening drama television shows, but TELEVISION AND DRAMA increases the size of the search result to include all Gopher items also relating to daytime soap operas.

You can use an asterisk (*) as a wild card at the ends of words. A Veronica search for the keyword "director*" returns Gopher items for director, directory, directories, directorate, and so on.

A useful way to narrow your search is by file type. To narrow your search to return only results of a specific file type, add -t# to your Veronica search keywords, where the number sign (#) is a character representing a Gopher file type. The official Gopher document types and their signifying characters are presented in table 7.1.

Table 7.1   Official Gopher document types

Type value	Description
0	Text file
1	Directory
2	CSO name server—read as text or HTML
3	An error of some sort
4	.HQX (also called BinHex, a Macintosh compression format)
5	PC binary (an uncompressed application)
6	UUEncoded file (a UNIX compression format)
7	Full text index (a Gopher menu)
8	Telnet session—if you have a Telnet application configured, it will launch
9	Binary file
s	Sound (an audio file)
I	Image (any format that's not GIF)
T	TN3270 session—if you have a TN3270 application (a fancy Telnet) configured, it will launch
g	GIF image
;	MPEG (a video file)
h	HTML (HyperText Markup Language)—a Web URL (Universal Resource Locator)
H	HTML URL Capitalized
i	Information (text) that is not selectable (like a comment line in a program)
w	A World Wide Web address
e	Event (not supported by Netscape)
m or M	Unspecified MIME (multi-part or mixed message)

For example, if you want to find Web pages on paleobotanical research in Turkey, you could use the Veronica search string paleobotany AND Turkey -th. If you know the Bruce Lee movie photo mentioned earlier was in GIF format, you could search for it using bruce AND lee -tg.

Jughead: another Gopherspace search engine

Another Gopherspace search tool is Jughead, which was written by Rhett "Jonzy" Jones at the University of Utah. In keeping with the Archie comics motif for Internet search engine names, the acronym came first, and the name Jughead was justified as Jonzy's Universal Gopher Hierarchy Excavation And Display

Like Veronica, Jughead is a Gopherspace search engine. However, Veronica searches widely, over all of Gopherspace. Jughead is most commonly configured to search only the one Gopher server it is installed on, but Jughead can search that one Gopher server very thoroughly.

For an example of how Jughead works, go to North Carolina State University's library Gopher server at **gopher://dewey.lib.ncsu.edu:300/7**. The Jughead search index of NCSU's library is shown in figure 7.9. Because the server's hostname does not start with gopher, you have to type the gopher:// portion of the URL.

Entering search text into the field and pressing the Enter key gives you a Gopher menu made up of all matching items in the site that the Jughead server indexes.

Jughead: If it's there, use it

System administrators rarely bother to install Jughead on a Gopher server with a small file collection. If you find a Jughead search engine on a specific Gopher server, it's because someone thought it was better to install Jughead than to do without it.

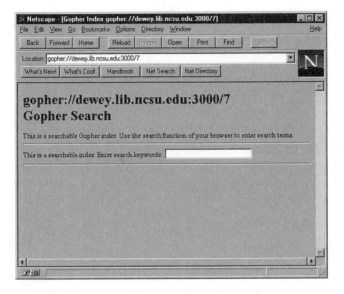

Fig. 7.9
North Carolina State University's Jughead search index.

How to ask Jughead a question

Jughead accepts the same kind of Boolean search requests Veronica does, but Jughead has some special commands. The generic form for these commands is a question mark followed by the command (no spaces between the question mark and the command), followed by the string of characters to search for.

The special Jughead commands are as follows:

Command	Result
?all string	Returns all matches to the string
?help string	Returns the Jughead help document, as well as any matches for the string
?limit=x string	Returns up to x matches for the string
?range=x1–x2 string	Returns the matches between x1 and x2

The ?range command is useful if the string matches a very large number of Gopher files.

NOTE **You can use only one special command per query. However, you can** limit your Jughead queries to improve the response time. (It's also polite; other people may want to use that server, and asking Jughead for all matches to "IBM" may be a waste of processor time if the item you want turns out to be the third one returned.)

Jughead also restricts special characters for its own use. Almost all of the standard special characters are treated as a space. These special characters are:

!"#$%&'()+,-.?/\[@]{^}'~

This entire line is read as 24 spaces. Jughead treats a space as a Boolean AND, so it's probably best to use letters and numerals only in your search string.

Accessing a Telnet site

Telnet is an ancient (as old as the Internet) way to access services on the Internet. When people speak of the Internet, they are generally referring to those computers that are on and connected to the Internet all the time.

NOTE **If you have a SLIP or PPP dial-up connection, your computer has an IP** (Internet Protocol) address and is "part of the Internet." However, this only lasts as long as the connection. Generally, you need to have at least a leased-line connection before you can consider your local system as part of the Internet.

Telnet, like the World Wide Web, works because all the computers of the Internet are on and connected all the time, barring system crashes, backhoes accidentally cutting the T1 cable, and other things system administrators don't really like to think about.

You can think of Telnet as making your computer a dumb terminal for the system you are "telnetting" to. A dumb terminal was called such because it was only a keyboard and screen, directly wired into the host computer. Dumb terminals are called dumb because they have no processor inside. Terminals were manufactured in standard designs so they would be compatible with many different computers. A common type of terminal was the VT series manufactured by Digital Equipment Corporation. VT terminals came in several models (VT100, VT102, VT220, and so on). Your personal computer is enormously more powerful than a VT100 terminal, so a Telnet terminal emulator acts like a terminal in order to let your computer communicate with computers that are set up to connect to VT100 terminals. In other words, every time you run Telnet, you are reducing your high-end state-of-the-art personal computer to the level of a keyboard and screen.

What you get for lobotomizing your great workstation is the ability to connect to many computer systems that, in some cases, don't have any other connectivity available. Also, because Telnet is the lowest common denominator of computer power, almost everyone can participate. Windows 95 and Windows NT include Telnet applications in the Windows folder. The filename should be c:\windows\telnet.exe.

If you aren't using Windows 95 or Windows NT (or don't like the version of telnet that comes with them), you'll need to get a Telnet application. Telnet applications are available from Netscape's Helper Applications Web page at URL **http://home.netscape.com/assist/helper_apps/index.html**. To use these applications with Netscape, you need to download and uncompress the files.

Regardless of which telent application you use, you can configure Netscape to launch a Telnet application as a supporting application. Then configure the application as a helper application in the General window of the Options menu. You can find information on how to configure helper applications for Netscape in chapter 11, "Netscape Helper Applications," of this book.

 NOTE **One specific Telnet application is Wintel, NCSA's Telnet application for** Windows. Wintel is available through Netscape's Helper Applications Web page as listed earlier, or it may be downloaded directly from the FTP site **ftp://gatekeeper.dec.com/pub/micro/msdos/win3/winsock/wintelb3.zip**.

Because Telnet and Gopher are both early Internet tools, many Telnet sites are most easily found through Gopher menus. For example, use Netscape to view the Gopher menu at URL **gopher://gopher.micro.umn.edu**, as you did earlier in this chapter. The Gopher menu shown in figure 7.5 is displayed. As you did earlier, choose the Other Gopher and Information Servers item and the Gopher menu displayed in figure 7.10 appears. Choose the Terminal Based Information from the bottom of the Gopher menu.

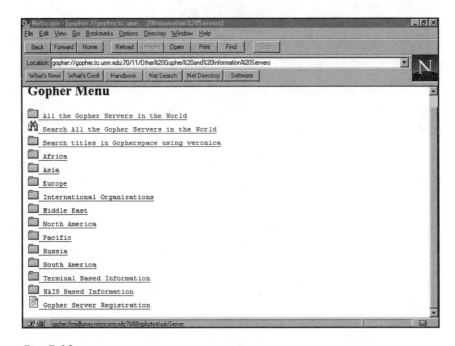

Fig. 7.10
Choose Terminal Based Information on this Gopher menu to see a menu of Telnet applications.

When you choose the Terminal Based Information item, a Gopher menu appears as shown in figure 7.11.

Select the Telnet connection for Appalachian State University. If you have Netscape configured correctly, your Telnet supporting application launches, and the informational message Log in as 'info' appears before the Telnet window displays. When you see the "Enter username" prompt appear in the Telnet window, type INFO as your username. The main menu for Appalachian State University's information distribution server will appear, as shown in figure 7.12.

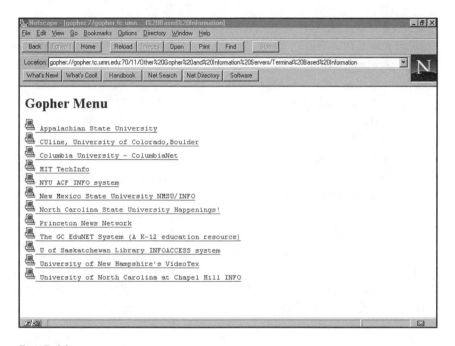

Fig. 7.11

Netscape displays Telnet session links in Gopher menus as small terminals.

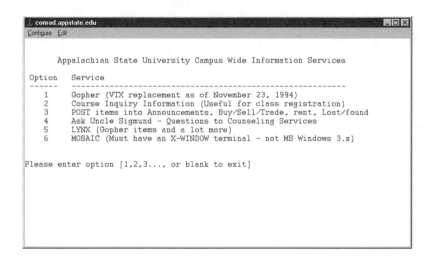

Fig. 7.12

A Telnet session with Appalachian State University.

Appalachian State University provides a great deal of information to its students via its Telnet host computers. However, not all Telnet sessions are used for information gathering. Multi-User Dungeons (MUDs) are computer programs that people can explore by adopting a character and typing commands for the character to move, talk, and do other things. MUDs are commonly used for social interaction between people. There are many different types of MUDs, both in types of programming involved in their creation and extension, and in the types of interaction typically occurring. Some MUDs are socially oriented chat discussion, some are fantasy role-playing in nature, and others are oriented to foreign language practice. While Telnet applications may be used for MUDs, many of the various types of MUDs have specific client applications that were created to optimize some aspects of performance on a given type of MUD. For more information on multi-user games, see Yahoo's directory of multi-user games at **http://www.yahoo.com/Recreation/Games/ Internet_Games/MUDs_MUSHes__MOOs_etc_/**.

E-mail with Netscape

● **In this chapter:**

- **Configure Netscape 3's e-mail servers and preferences**

- **Send and receive mail**

- **Organize your mail using folders**

- **Create an address book to speed your correspondence**

Netscape started life as a dedicated Web browser, and there's never been a doubt that it's a superior piece of software for that purpose. Netscape has also bent over backwards, for the most part successfully, to make other Internet services like FTP and Gopher accessible from Netscape.

But in one key area—e-mail—Netscape fell short. Early, 1.x versions of Netscape provided only the most rudimentary capability to access the Internet's most popular service. Users could only send mail with Netscape; they couldn't receive it. Needless to say, the designers of dedicated e-mail managers didn't find Netscape a threat to their business.

This is changing fast. In a bid to make its flagship program a full-service Internet client, Netscape has given version 3 a powerful mail manager that many users—particularly those at home—may find suits their needs.

Netscape's new e-mail manager

In their first attempt to make their Web browser a full-service Internet client, Netscape's programmers have done a pretty fair job. The new e-mail manager provides most of the functionality that veteran Net users have come to expect from their software. It also offers a couple of very useful, Netscape-only twists.

The feature that, above all others, sets Netscape's mail package apart from its established competitors is the fact that it treats incoming messages basically as HTML documents. The mail reader is able to detect any URL mentioned in the text of a message and highlight it for one-click access by the user. Your mail becomes a separate, hotlinked gateway to the World Wide Web and the rest of the Internet.

Netscape doesn't stint on the standard stuff, either. You've always been able to use it to write and send messages, but now you'll find that you can easily reply to, forward, and carbon copy messages, just as users of third-party mail packages can. Message management is a snap because you have the ability to transfer your traffic to a set of custom, user-defined mail folders. Within those folders, you can tell Netscape to sort your mail by subject, sender, or date. You can also keep and maintain a list of your most frequently used addresses.

If you're a casual e-mail user, you'll likely find that Netscape's new built-in mail capabilities are all you need. And if it's important that you have the ability to tap into the Web directly from your message traffic, you'll find Netscape's mail manager indispensable.

But if you're accustomed to using other mail packages, programs like Eudora and cc:Mail, you'll soon see that Netscape's package isn't quite complete. Although some rough edges present in the Address Book and file attachment features of Netscape's early betas have been smoothed over, power users will miss high-end features like automatic message filtering.

All in all, if you're happy with your current mail program, you'll have to make the call as to whether you want to switch to Netscape just yet. You'd be well-advised, however, to watch carefully as it evolves in the future. It's quite clear that Netscape is serious about making its leading program the only Internet client most people will ever need.

But if you're a new mail user, or if you haven't found a package quite to your liking just yet, you'll probably want to give Netscape's e-mail facility a try. You may find that it meets your needs completely.

Setting mail preferences

Before attempting to use Netscape's mail facility, you must provide some basic information about yourself, your Internet provider, and your computer. Begin by choosing Options, and then select Mail and News Preferences. Netscape responds with a tabbed dialog box.

The best way to familiarize yourself with Netscape's mail settings is to step through each of the five tabs sequentially as you set up the program for the first time.

Appearance

The options on this tab, seen in figure 8.1, affect the way Netscape displays message text. Under Messages and Articles Are Shown With, your choice tells Netscape whether to use a fixed-width or variable-width font when it displays the text of your mail. The default is Fixed Width Font; in most cases you'll want to stick to that setting because Variable Width Font can ruin the formatting of many Internet messages. The settings under Text Beginning With > (Quoted Text) Has the Following Characteristics affects the display of message excerpts included in a mailing to establish its subject and context. They're largely self-explanatory; change them to suit your taste.

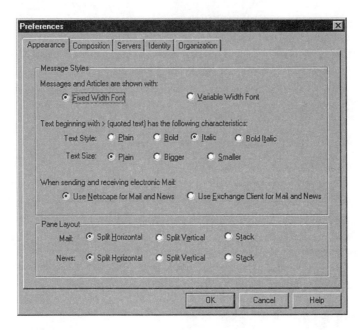

Fig. 8.1
The settings on the Appearance tab give the user control over the fonts Netscape uses to display the text of mail messages.

The remaining buttons on this tab, found under heading When Receiving Electronic Mail, tell Netscape whether to use its own built-in e-mail capabilities or those provided with every copy of Windows 95 by Microsoft Exchange. If you want to use Netscape's, click Use Netscape for Mail and News.

New to Netscape 3 is the ability to configure the window layout of Netscape Mail. You can have Netscape Mail's window panes use one of three basic configurations. The default, Split Horizontal, lists your mail folders in the upper-left pane, the mail headers in the upper-right pane, and the letters themselves in the bottom pane. The Split Vertical option (see fig. 8.2) has the folders in the upper-left, the headers in the lower-left, and the messages on the right.

Finally, the Stack option puts the folders on top, the headers in the middle, and the mail body at the bottom. Just choose the window pane layout you want and click the OK button. The new layout won't be used until you quit Netscape Mail, and start it up again.

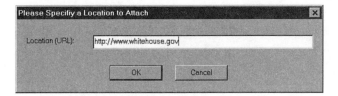

Fig. 8.2
This is one of the new Netscape Mail window pane layouts that's available with Atlas.

Composition

There are several key settings on this tab, seen in figure 8.3:

- The Send and Post setting determines how file attachments are coded. Allow 8-bit is the default and is recognized by most mail programs.

- The Deliver Mail setting tells Netscape whether you want to send each message when you're done writing it, or to hold it on disk. Choosing Automatically tells Netscape to send when you're done writing; Queue for Manual Delivery holds your message.

 TIP **You'll probably want to queue your messages on disk if you do most of** your work offline, as a dial-in Internet user. Send them by clicking File and choosing Deliver Mail Now.

- You can have Netscape send a copy of all your outgoing messages to a single address by entering that address in the Mail Messages field.

- The entry in the Mail File field tells Netscape where to store copies of your outgoing messages on disk. This is a key setting; in the following discussion of the Directories tab, we'll tell you how to avoid problems by reconciling it with that tab's Mail Directory field. If you don't care to keep copies of your outgoing traffic, you can avoid problems entirely by leaving this field blank.

- Checking Automatically Quote Original Message When Replying tells Netscape to insert the text of any message you answered with the Message menu's Reply option into the body of your answer.

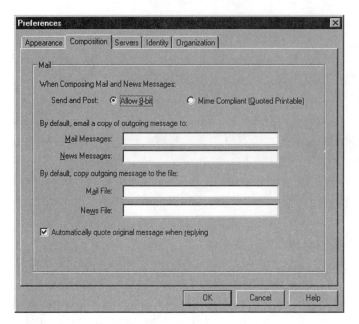

Fig. 8.3
The Composition tab controls key settings for file encoding and message queuing.

Servers

This tab is probably the most important of the five on the Mail and News Preferences dialog box. On this tab, seen in figure 8.4, you tell Netscape how to get to your mail.

Do the following:

1 Type the Internet addresses for your service provider's SMTP (send mail) and POP3 (receive mail) clients in the Mail (SMTP) Server and Mail POP Server fields, which are near the top of the tab. Get this information from your service provider if you don't already have it.

2 Type your e-mail name (in all likelihood, the one you use when you log into your Internet provider) in the Pop User Name box.

3 You should make sure Netscape's setup routine has provided access to the directory where your mail folders are stored by looking in the Mail Directory field. There should be some entry like C:\Program Files\ Netscape\Navigator\Mail, as seen in figure 8.3. The actual listing will vary depending on your Netscape setup.

4 If there's no path in the Mail Directory field, or you have reason to believe the path is incorrect, open Explorer, find the folder Netscape's installed in, and then find the Mail subfolder. Note the Windows 95 path, go back into Netscape, and type the path into the Mail Directory field.

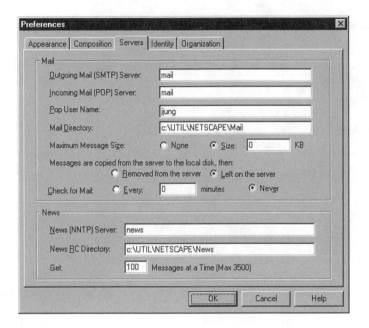

Fig. 8.4
Many of the controls that affect your use of Netscape's e-mail features are on the Mail and News Preferences dialog box. Here we're using it to enter information about our mail server.

 TIP **You can use the Mail Directory field to tell Netscape to store your mail** in any Windows 95 folder you want. Simply type its path in place of the one provided by Netscape.

5 Click the Composition tab. Look in the Mail File field, near the bottom of the tab. The Windows 95 path listed there should match that in the Mail Directory field, with the addition of the characters, \Sent (see fig. 8.5). Netscape stores a copy of your outgoing messages in this file.

6 If it doesn't match, type the path in yourself. For example, if your Mail Directory is C:\Program Files\Netscape\Navigator\Mail, type

C:\ Program Files\Netscape\Navigator\Mail\Sent in the Mail File field.

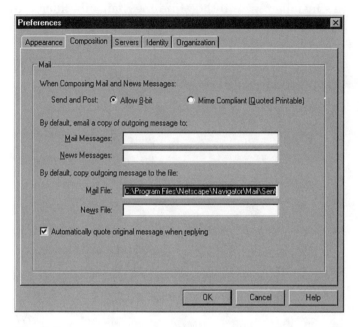

Fig. 8.5
Make sure the Composition tab's Mail File field refers to the same path as the Directories tab's Mail Directory field.

Q&A **When I try to send mail, Netscape responds with an error message that says Can't open FCC file. I've searched the Netscape directories and the rest of my hard drive and can't find an FCC file. Should I create one?**

No. This cryptic message is Netscape's way of telling you that the Composition tab's Mail File field isn't referring to the same Windows 95 path as your Mail Directory field. The Sent file has to be located in the same folder as the rest of your mail files.

This problem originally cropped up because the installation routines for the early betas of Netscape 3 wouldn't update the Mail File field when asked to install the program to any folder other than their default settings.

There are three ways to fix the resulting mess. Check the Mail Directory field, and then enter this path in the Mail File field, tagging the characters "\Sent" on the end. Alternatively, open Windows 95's Registry Editor and, using its search facility, find the phrase "Default FCC." It'll turn up among the HKEY_CURRENT_USER settings, as in figure 8.6. Click Edit, choose Modify, and enter the proper path in the field provided.

Your remaining option, if you don't consider it important to keep copies of your outgoing messages, is to leave the Composition tab's Mail File field blank. If you do, Netscape won't save any copies, but it won't pop up an error message either.

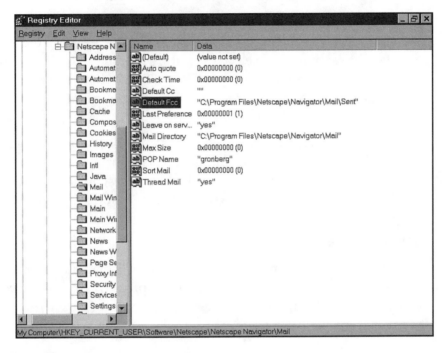

Fig. 8.6
You can use Windows 95's Registry Editor to reconcile the Mail Directory and Mail File fields. The path to the Sent file listed beside Default FCC should match the path beside Mail Directory.

7 After you're comfortable with Netscape's mail features, you'll likely want to click the Removed from the Server button so old mail doesn't clutter your Internet provider's disk.

Identity

Netscape personalizes your outgoing messages by adding bits from the settings on this tab. You'll want to do the following:

1 Type your real name in the Your Name field.

2 Type your e-mail address in the Your Email field.

3 If you want replies to your outgoing messages sent to an address other than the one listed in Your Email, type it in the Reply-to Address field.

4 Fill in Your Organization if you want the name of your employer or the group you represent to appear on your mail.

5 If you want Netscape to append a signature file to your outgoing messages, use the Browse key next to Signature File on the Identity tab to search for and select a signature file from your hard drive. Your signature must be an ASCII text file. It should be hard-formatted and less than 80 characters wide. Internet etiquette would also suggest that you keep it short.

6 If you're concerned about retaining your privacy on the Internet, click either the Nothing: Anonymous User or A Unique ID Number button at the bottom of the tab. In most cases, however, you'll want your messages identified with Your Email Address.

Organization

The threading and sorting features of Netscape's mail manager are fully controllable from the mail window, but the program does allow you to designate their default settings. They're available on the Organization tab, seen in figure 8.7.

- If you think you'll want your message traffic threaded (that is, with messages and replies on the same topic grouped together for easy reading), click the Organization tab and make sure the Thread Mail Messages box is checked.

- You may also want to change the default sort order for your incoming message traffic. If so, click the Organization tab and choose one of the Sort Mail By selections. The available sort options are by Date, Subject, and Sender.

When you're satisfied with the changes you've made to the various tabs on the Mail and News Preferences dialog box, click OK to save your work. Clicking Cancel abandons it.

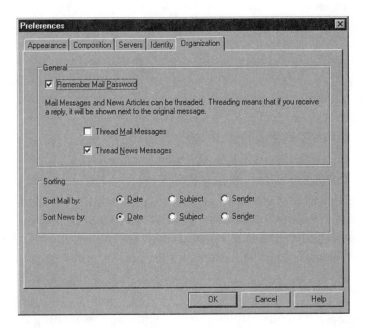

Fig. 8.7
The settings on the Organization tab tell Netscape how to sort and thread your message traffic.

Using the mail package

At first glance, Netscape 3 appears no more a sophisticated mail package than its predecessors. The picture begins to change, though, when you click the Window menu and select Netscape Mail.

The program responds first by asking you to enter a password. In the Password Entry dialog box, enter verbatim the phrase your Internet provider told you to use when logging on to your mail server (see fig. 8.8).

Fig. 8.8
Netscape demands that you enter the password for your Internet e-mail account every time you want to access its mail window.

If you click OK, Netscape immediately tries to log on to your mail server. If it finds that you're not online, or that it can't log on to your server, eventually it will give up and flash an error message. If you've opened a mail window to work offline, you can avoid this problem by clicking Cancel in the Password Entry dialog box.

Understanding the screen

Once in the program, you're confronted by a screen that reminds some users of the Microsoft Exchange e-mail client that comes with every copy of Windows 95. Don't be fooled: Netscape's mail facility is nowhere near as sophisticated as Exchange and nowhere near as resource-hungry. In actual use Netscape's mail facility compares favorably with such light-footed freeware and shareware packages as Eudora and Pegasus.

Let's get oriented.

- On the top left of Netscape's mail screen, you see a listing of your personal mail folders (see fig. 8.9). At minimum, this listing contains your inbox and your trash folder. After you've sent your first message with Netscape, you should see a Sent folder that holds copies of your out-going traffic.

- On the top right, you see a scrollable listing of the message headers for every piece of mail in the folder you're looking at. The inbox opens by default when you first open Netscape's mail facility.

 NOTE Netscape highlights unread messages in bold. Folders that contain unread messages are also highlighted in bold. You open folders by double-clicking them.

- On the bottom of the screen, you see the text of the open message, along with headers indicating the message's subject, sender, sender's reply-to address, and the date it was sent.

One feature you'll learn to like may not be immediately obvious: If the message contains a URL, Netscape treats it as such, recognizing and highlighting it for immediate use. By clicking a URL, you can jump immediately to the Web page, FTP site, or other Internet service that it points to.

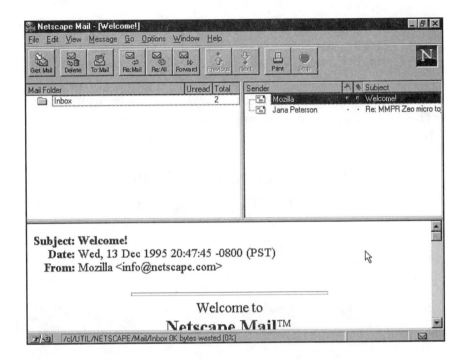

Fig. 8.9
Netscape's clean mail layout provides easy access to your message traffic and your personal mail folders.

TIP Netscape gives you one-click access to any URL embedded in an e-mail message displayed on-screen.

NOTE You may notice at low screen resolutions that Netscape's mail display is a bit cramped. You can adjust the sizes of the various panes by clicking and dragging their frames. You'll find that the only real way to see what you're doing, video card permitting, is to use a higher screen resolution. Open Control Panel's Display properties, click the Settings tab, and set the Desktop Area slider to at least 800 × 600 pixels for a better look.

Atlas now has the ability to show you a variety of e-mail headers. Typically, all e-mail you send or receive has a lot of information stored in its headers. The information is often technical and not intended for most people to figure out. However, some mail headers can be useful to the casual person. Whether it's because of a cute quote that somebody put in, or a particular e-mail address, some header information is useful.

You can determine how much, or how little, of the e-mail header you want to see. Simply click on Options, Show Headers, and select between All, Normal, or Brief. The All option shows you every single bit of header information in the letter body. The Normal option only shows you the subject of the letter, the date it was sent, who it's from, and who it's to. The Brief option shows you pretty much the same information as the Normal option, but puts it into a compact, one-line format.

Composing and sending mail

Netscape 3's mail and news clients use the same front end for message composition. In the case of the mail client, you begin a message either by clicking the New Mail button on the toolbar or by clicking the File menu and selecting New Mail Message. A message form like the one shown in figure 8.10 opens.

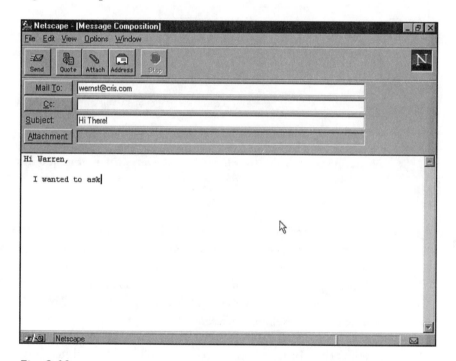

Fig. 8.10
Netscape uses a standard form for outgoing e-mail and UseNet articles. Here's an e-mail message ready to go.

Netscape inserts the text of your signature file, if you use one, in the section of the screen reserved for message text. Fill out the rest of the message by following these steps:

1 Type the address of the person or organization you're writing to in the Send <u>T</u>o field.

2 Type a short phrase in the <u>S</u>ubject field describing the content of your message.

TIP **You don't have to open the Netscape Mail window to create a** message. Click Netscape's File menu and choose New Mail Message to open a Composition window.

3 If you want to send copies of your message to third parties, click the <u>V</u>iew menu and select either Mail <u>C</u>c or Mail <u>B</u>cc. This adds a blank address field of the same name to your message header. Type the addresses of the additional recipients. Use Cc if you want to publicize the fact you've sent copies; use Bcc (blind copy) if you don't.

4 Click once in the main text box to set the cursor at the beginning of your message, and begin writing your text. Standard Windows 95 Cut, Copy, and Paste commands are available on the <u>E</u>dit menu.

NOTE **If the recipient of your message is using Netscape's e-mail manager** also, you can pass along interesting and useful URLs in one of two ways. First, you can simply type the URL into a message. Or, if you're viewing a Web page or some other resource in the browser, you can click the File menu and select Mail Document. When you do, Netscape opens a new message window with the URL listed in the body of the mailing. In either case, when the person viewing your message opens it in Netscape's mail manager, the URL will appear as a hotlink. You need do nothing more than type; Netscape detects the presence of the URL automatically.

5 When finished, make sure you're online and then click the Send button on the Composition window's toolbar.

Netscape sends a new message as soon as you click Send if its Composition preferences are set to deliver mail automatically. If they're set to queue messages, eventually you'll have to click the File menu and select Deliver Mail Now to send your outgoing traffic to your server.

Attaching files and URLs to mail

Most e-mail packages provide the capability to transmit binary files over the Internet by attaching ASCII-coded copies of them to your message traffic. Netscape is no exception. In fact, its attachment facility is one of the most versatile around.

You can attach files to a message any time before sending it. Open the Attachments dialog by clicking the Attachments button, which you'll see just below the Subject field. You may also click the Attach button on the message composition window's toolbar. Figure 8.11 shows the Attachments dialog box.

TIP **If the Attachment button is grayed out, you can enable it by clicking** any of the message's header boxes.

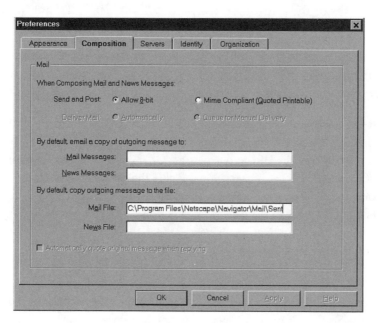

Fig. 8.11
You can attach a binary file to any outgoing message. Netscape will translate it using an ASCII coding scheme intelligible to most mail readers.

Once the Attachments dialog opens, you may add files to your message by clicking the Attach File button. Use the Enter File To Attach dialog box to select the file you want to transmit (see fig. 8.12).

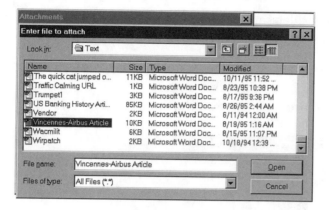

Fig. 8.12
The Enter File To Attach dialog box looks and works like any other Windows 95 file-handling dialog box.

Once you've actually selected the file, you have a decision to make:

- You'll want Netscape to code and transmit true binary files like a spreadsheet or a compressed archive using MIME rendering. Make sure it does so by highlighting the name of the file in the Attachments dialog and clicking the As Is button. Most e-mail software available automatically decodes and stores the attachment when it arrives on the receiving end.

- You may ask Netscape to incorporate ASCII text files, such as those created with Notepad, into the body of the message itself. You do this by clicking the Convert to Plain Text button. Netscape does not, however, let you control where this insertion takes place. It always adds the new text to the bottom of the message. You will not see the text displayed in Netscape's message window, but as long as the file's visible in the Attachments dialog box it will appear in the finished message seen by your correspondent.

TIP **Bear in mind that you can always send an ASCII file As Is. If you do,** Netscape will treat it as a binary file. This is perhaps the best way to handle heavily formatted plain-text files. Sending them in the body of a message could badly disrupt their formatting.

The Attachments dialog box also gives you the ability to e-mail a copy of an entire Web page—not just its Internet address. This new and exciting feature is unique to Netscape. If the recipients are using Netscape, they can view the Web page you're sending within a mail window.

Begin from the Attachments dialog box by clicking Attach Location (URL). Netscape opens the Please Specify a Location to Attach dialog box; type the full Internet address of the page you want to send (see fig. 8.13).

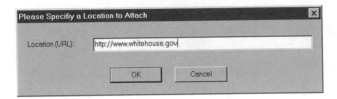

Fig. 8.13
Enter the URL of the Web page you want to send.

As with files, you have to decide whether to send the attachment as is or as plain text. If you know that the person to whom you're sending the URL is using Netscape 3 as a mail reader, click As Is. The result on the receiving end will be rather extraordinary (see fig. 8.14).

What you basically did is ask Netscape to mail the HTML source code of the URL to your correspondent. Because Netscape's mail facility treats every message as an HTML document, it is able to reconstruct a fully formatted and hotlinked Web page. Whatever you can do with that page from within a normal browser window, your friends can emulate within a Netscape mail window.

If your friends don't have Netscape, all is not lost. By clicking Convert to Plain Text, you instruct Netscape's mailer to strip the HTML codes out of the page and send the remaining text. You may send it As Is anyway; they'll see pure HTML, but after saving a copy to disk they can always open and view the page in any Web browser. Bear in mind that they won't get any of the artwork that gives a Web page its distinctive look and feel.

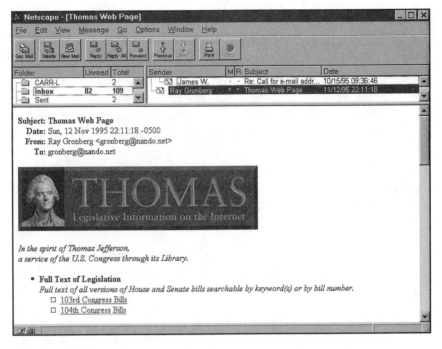

Fig. 8.14
Your friends don't have to seek out Web pages like this one from the Library of Congress. If they're using Netscape as a mail reader, you can send them a copy.

Receiving and replying to mail

As explained earlier, Netscape tries to log on and retrieve messages from your mail server the first time you open the Netscape Mail window.

Q&A *When Netscape tries to deliver my mail, it responds with a message that it's unable to locate the server. What's wrong?*

One of four things—three of which you can do something about.

The first thing you want to do is note the name of the server Netscape's trying to access. It'll be listed in the error message. It should be the name of your Internet provider's mail server. If it isn't, open the Preferences dialog box, click the Directories tab, and correct the entry in the Mail (SMTP) Server field.

If Netscape has the right address but can't get through, you may be working offline or you may have another program open that's got the mail server tied up. Get online by dialing in or logging on. Close any other program that uses SMTP or POP service before you try to use Netscape's mail manager.

The remaining possibility is that your Internet provider's mail server is down. If that's the case, you can do little but wait. If your provider has a help desk, you may want to call to let them know there's a problem.

You can also retrieve messages any time while the Netscape Mail window is open either by clicking the File menu and selecting Get New Mail, or by clicking Get Mail button on the toolbar. If you haven't already entered your mail server's password, Netscape requests it.

Netscape dumps all new mail into the inbox. Unlike some mail software, it can't automate the sorting of messages into user-specified folders. That's a job you have to handle yourself.

Like most e-mail packages, Netscape lets you respond directly to a message without having to address a new one from scratch. You do this by using the Reply, Reply All, and Forward buttons on the mail screen's toolbar.

By clicking either Reply or Reply All, you can tell Netscape to create a pre-addressed message. You can include the text of the message you received by clicking the mail window's File menu and selecting Include Original Text (see fig. 8.15). The Quote Icon on the Netscape Mail Composition Toolbar performs the same function. Trim the length of your quotation using the Edit menu's Cut, Copy, and Paste commands.

The Forward button works a bit differently. As with Reply and Reply All, clicking it creates a new message. This time, however, you supply the address of your intended recipient. But you'll notice that Netscape has filled in the Attachment field for you. By doing so, it tacks a copy of the text open in Netscape Mail window to the bottom of the message you're creating, including it for the benefit of your correspondent.

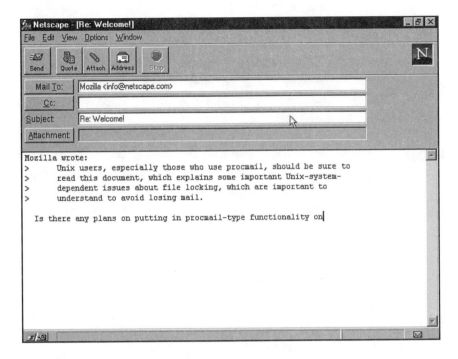

Fig. 8.15
By using the Reply and the Include Original Text commands located on the mail window's File menu, you can draft understandable answers to your mail quickly and easily.

Organizing your mail

Fortunately, Netscape doesn't make mail sorting hard. You can add and name an unlimited number of folders and shift messages between them at your discretion (see fig. 8.16).

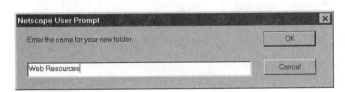

Fig. 8.16
User-created message folders simplify the task of organizing your mail.

Create a folder by clicking the Netscape Mail window's File menu and selecting New Folder. A Netscape mail folder is nothing more than a Windows 95 file, so you can give it a name up to 255 characters long. You may want to keep your names shorter than that, though. As it displays your folders, Netscape truncates the names of any that are too long to fit in the available window.

NOTE **Unlike many full-featured e-mail packages, Netscape does not offer** any method of nesting folders within folders. High-volume mail users may find this a serious limitation that argues for keeping their current software. Low-volume users should be able to get along fine, but they may find it advisable to keep their filing system short and understandable.

Conversely, you kill an unused folder by clicking it once to highlight its name, and then selecting Delete Folder from the Edit menu.

The commands for shifting mail between folders—Move and Copy—are at the bottom of the Message menu (see fig. 8.17). Highlight either, and you'll find a list of your folders nested beneath them.

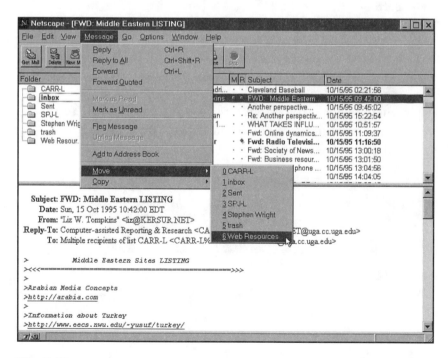

Fig. 8.17
The Move and Copy commands take only a single click. Highlight the directory you want to send the message to and release the mouse button.

The Move and Copy commands work the same way:

1 Highlight the message you want to move or copy in the Message Headers pane by clicking it.

2 Click the Message menu and select Move or Copy.

3 A list of your folders will pop up next to the Message menu. Select the folder you want the message transferred to.

Choosing Move places the selected message into the destination folder and deletes it from the source. Copy puts a copy in the destination folder while leaving the contents of the source folder unchanged.

Within folders, Netscape gives users several options for sorting messages. All are accessible by clicking the View menu and highlighting Sort.

The three major options—Sort by Date, Sender, and Subject—are largely self-explanatory. Toggling the Ascending command tells Netscape to arrange messages in ascending or descending order.

Netscape's capability to organize messages into threads is both unusual and powerful. By toggling Thread Messages, you're ordering the mail client to override normal sort order in cases where a single message has inspired at least one reply. It groups the original and any replies, making the conversation easy to follow as it develops over time (see fig. 8.18).

You can send any highlighted message to the trash folder by clicking the Delete button on the toolbar, by clicking Edit and selecting Delete Message, or by transferring it there using the Message menu's Move command. Trash stays on your disk, however, until you click the File menu and select Empty Trash Folder. Unlike many mail packages, Netscape provides no way of automating deletions.

Using the address book

Any good e-mail software provides some quick and simple way of storing and retrieving the addresses of your most frequent correspondents. Most are very easy to use. See figure 8.19.

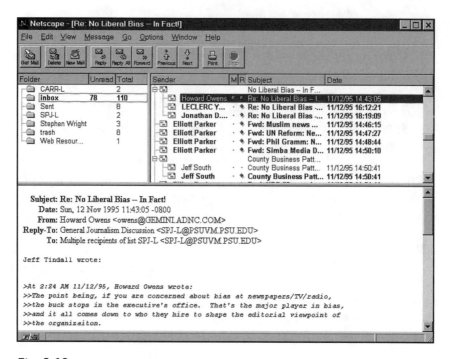

Fig. 8.18
The Windows Explorer-like tree structures indicate message threads.

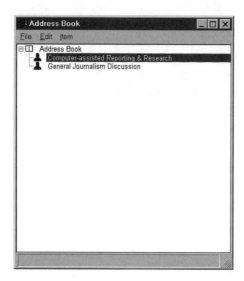

Fig. 8.19
Netscape's address book simplifies mailing chores by storing the names and addresses of the people you write the most.

Setting up an address book isn't difficult. In fact, Netscape gives you a couple of ways to do it. The easiest method is to open a message from someone you want to correspond with regularly, click the Message menu, and select Add to Address Book.

Netscape responds by opening a Windows 95 property sheet that has four fields (see fig. 8.20). If you're adding to your Address Book using the Message menu command, you'll find that two of them, Name and E-Mail Address, are already filled in.

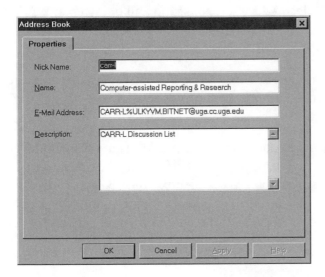

Fig. 8.20
Use the Address Book properties sheet to create and maintain your address list.

Q&A ***Netscape's Add to Address Book function filled out the properties sheet for the addition incorrectly. It didn't use the name and address of the person who wrote the original message. Why not?***

There's an entry in the message's Reply To field. When it's creating an Address Book entry, Netscape always takes the name and address listed in Reply To. This avoids problems with mailings to a list or to a person who takes return mail at a different address. But it means more work for you; you have to take the time to enter the correct name and address yourself. Always check the entries in these fields the first time you create an Address Book entry.

The Description field gives you a place to write a short note about your correspondent.

The remaining field, Nick Name, gives you a place to enter a short, one-word phrase that can serve as a shortcut to your Address Book entry. Be sure to use lowercase characters only; Netscape won't accept a Nick Name that contains uppercase characters.

You can also create Address Book entries from scratch. Click the Window menu and select Address book. Once the address book opens, click the Item menu and select Add User. Netscape will open a blank Address Book properties sheet. You can also modify any existing entry in the Address Book by right-clicking the entry and selecting Properties.

Once you've created your Address Book, Netscape gives you three ways to use it. They work with any of the available address fields, Mail To, Cc and BCc:

- The simplest way, once you've placed the cursor in the Message Composition window's Mail To field, is to click the toolbar's Address button. Netscape opens a dialog box called Select Addresses (see fig. 8.21). Highlight the address you want to use, and then click the button that corresponds to the field you want it placed in. Click OK when you're done.

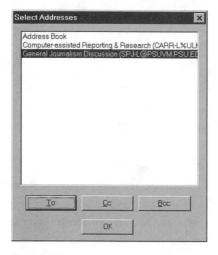

Fig. 8.21
Clicking either the toolbar's Address button or a message's Send To, Cc, or Blind Cc button opens the Select Addresses dialog box. Highlight your choice, click the button for the field you want it placed in, and click OK.

- You may also open the Select Addresses dialog box by clicking any of the labels next to your message's various address fields. Unfortunately, once you've highlighted the address you want to use, you still have to place it in the proper field by clicking the corresponding button on the dialog box. You can't just click OK and expect the address to pop up where you want it.

- If your memory is good, you can address a message quickly merely by typing an Address Book entry's Nick Name property in Mail To, Cc or BCc. Netscape will automatically fill the box with the name and e-mail address associated with the Nick Name as soon you move the cursor elsewhere.

You may notice that Netscape fills the message address boxes differently, depending on an Address Book entry's properties. If you've given the entry a Nick Name, it will use that until you close the Select Addresses dialog box. Once you do, it will fill a field with both the name and the address of your intended correspondent. This is nothing to be alarmed about. As long as the e-mail address itself is bracketed by the < and > symbols, your mail server will be able to find it.

If you haven't given an address book entry a Nick Name, Netscape will only list the e-mail address in the proper field. The recipient's name won't appear. Again, no harm is done.

Because an address book is an HTML document—just like your Bookmarks file—Netscape gives you one other way of getting at it quickly. Just as with your Bookmarks file, you can load your address book directly into your browser.

Close your mail window, and then open the File menu and select Open File. You should find address.htm somewhere in your Netscape folder structure, most likely in the Program subfolder. If it doesn't open readily, use Windows 95's Find Files or Folders utility to search for it. When you find it, double-click to load it in Netscape (see fig. 8.22).

Once the file is there, you can create a new message, complete with pre-completed address information, merely by clicking one of the highlighted links. Because it's HTML, clicking a link opens a message composition window, just as it would if you had clicked an e-mail link embedded on a Web page.

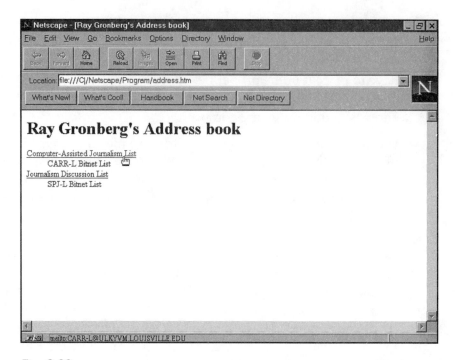

Fig. 8.22
Your address book is an HTML document you can see within Netscape. Load it, and you have the ability to address mail with a single click, just as you would from any Web page.

And, again because it's HTML, you can also add your Address Book to your Bookmarks menu, putting it one click away any time you're using your browser.

Setting up the Microsoft Exchange client

There's more than one way to manage e-mail with Netscape 3. Starting with version 1.2, Netscape has shipped a connection to Microsoft Exchange with every copy of Netscape. Until recently, the Exchange client was the only thing that gave Netscape users full access to Internet e-mail services.

It was, and is, by no means a perfect solution. Exchange is a notorious resource hog that gulps RAM and virtual memory by the megabyte. It's also slow. For all that, it offers the Internet e-mail users little more than freeware programs like Eudora Light. You'll look high and low in Exchange, for example, and never find a high-end feature like automatic message filtering, which in a package like Eudora Pro, lets you tell the program to pre-sort incoming message traffic into mail folders.

Exchange shines as a corporate network messaging client. If you're not part of such a network, you're probably better off using Netscape 3's e-mail service, or acquiring a third-party mail package.

But if you are part of a corporate network, and if you're an Exchange user, you'll probably want Internet mail routed to your Inbox instead of relying on another program.

You don't necessarily need Netscape to use Exchange for handling your Internet mail. Microsoft provides its own POP3 client for Exchange as part of Microsoft Plus!. You can find instructions for setting it up in many publications, including Que's Special Edition Using Windows 95. The same references will tell you more about using Exchange on a day-to-day basis, which we also don't cover.

But we do tell you how to enable the connection to Netscape in the event you don't have Plus!. Just follow these steps:

1 From Windows 95's Start menu, open the Control Panel.

2 Double-click on the Mail and Fax icon.

3 On the Services tab, click the Add button.

4 Highlight Netscape Internet Transport and click OK (see fig. 8.23). A tabbed dialog box labeled Netscape Transport Configuration appears.

5 On the User tab, type your name in the Display Name box and your e-mail address in the Internet Address box.

6 On the Hosts tab, enter the addresses supplied by your Internet Provider in the SMTP Host and POP3 Host boxes (see fig. 8.24). These should match exactly those you entered in Netscape's Mail and News Preferences dialog box.

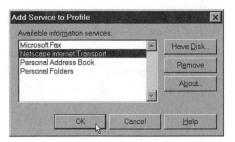

Fig. 8.23
Click OK to add the Netscape Internet Transport to your Microsoft Exchange user profile.

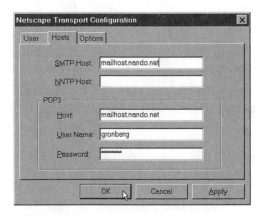

Fig. 8.24
Enter mail server and login information in the indicated boxes.

7 Also on the Hosts tab, enter your login name and password in the POP3 Under Name and Passwords boxes.

8 On the Options tab, be sure to clear the Send RTF Text check box.

9 Click OK twice and close Control Panel.

10 Open Netscape's Mail and News Preferences dialog box by selecting it from the Options menu.

11 On the Appearance tab, click to put a check in the Use Exchange Client for Mail and News box.

9

UseNet News with Netscape

● In this chapter:

● How newsgroups work

● The different types of newsgroups on UseNet

● The organization of UseNet newsgroups

● Using Netscape's newsreader to access newsgroups

● Accessing newsgroups without using the newsreader

CompuServe calls them forums. The Microsoft Network calls them BBSs (bulletin board systems). At your office, they're possibly known as cork boards. They are all places where people come together to exchange ideas and opinions, post public notices, or look for help. The Internet has such a place, too. On the Internet, it's called UseNet newsgroups, or just newsgroups for short.

You learn all about how newsgroups work and how to access newsgroups in this chapter.

A UseNet primer

Newsgroups are a bit more complicated than forums, BBSs, and cork boards. Not in a technical sense, but in a cultural sense. Newsgroups don't have official rules that are enforced by anyone in particular. They have unofficial rules that newsgroup peers enforce. Newsgroups concentrate cultures, from all over the world, in one place—a source of a lot of conflict, as you can imagine.

So, take a few moments to study this section before you dive into newsgroups head first. Make sure that you understand how newsgroups and the UseNet culture works. Then, you'll learn how to use Netscape's newsreader to access one of the most dynamic parts of the Internet—newsgroups—later in this chapter.

 CAUTION **If you're particularly sensitive or easily offended, newsgroups may not** be right for you. Unlike the forums and BBSs on commercial online systems, no one is watching over the content on newsgroups. The material is often very offensive to some folks. You'll find plenty of nasty language and abusive remarks in some newsgroups, just like you'd expect to find in some pubs.

The basics of using newsgroups

If you've ever used a forum or BBS on a commercial online service, you're already familiar with the concept of a newsgroup. Readers post messages, or articles, to newsgroups for other people to read. They can also reply to articles that they read on a newsgroup. It's one way for people like yourself to communicate with millions of people around the world.

Newsgroups are a bit looser, however. A newsgroup doesn't necessarily have a watch dog—other than the readers themselves. As a result, the organization is a bit looser, and the content of the messages is often way out of focus. The seemingly chaotic nature of newsgroups, however, produces some of the most interesting information you'll find anywhere.

Newsgroup variety is good

The variety of content is exactly what makes newsgroups so appealing. There are newsgroups for expressing opinions—no matter how benign or how radical. There are other newsgroups for asking questions or getting help. And, best of all, there are newsgroups for those seeking companionship—whether they're looking for a soul-mate or longing to find someone with a similar interest in whittling. The following is a sample of the types of newsgroups you'll find:

- alt.tv.simpsons contains a lot of mindless chatter about *The Simpsons*.

- comp.os.ms-windows.advocacy is one of the hottest Window's newsgroups around. You'll find heated discussions about both Windows 3.1 and Windows 95.

- rec.games.trading-cards.marketplace is the place to be if you're into sports trading cards.

- rec.humor.funny is where to go to lighten up your day. You'll find a wide variety of humor, including contemporary jokes, old standards, and bogus news flashes.

Alternative and regional newsgroups

Not all the newsgroups available are true UseNet newsgroups. Some newsgroups are created to serve a particular region or are so obscure that they wouldn't make it through the rigorous UseNet approval process. If something looks like a newsgroup and acts like a newsgroup, however, it can find its way onto your news server.

Here are some examples:

- Regional—Many localities, such as Dallas or San Francisco, have their own newsgroups where people exchange dining tips, consumer advice, and other regional bits of information.

- Alternative—The alt newsgroups are responsible for most of the variety on UseNet. Some of these groups have a reputation for being downright nasty (for example, pornography), but also have groups dedicated to your favorite TV shows, books, or politicians.

NOTE **If you have a child who will be using newsgroups, you might consider** finding a service provider that makes the pornographic newsgroups, such as alt.sex.pictures and alt.binaries.pictures.erotica, unavailable.

Moderated newsgroups

Moderated newsgroups are a bit more civil, and the articles are typically more focused than unmoderated newsgroups. Moderators look at every article posted to their newsgroup before making it available for everyone to read. If they judge it to be inappropriate, they nuke it.

So what are the advantages of a moderated newsgroup? You don't have to wade through ten pounds of garbage to find one ounce of treasure. Check out some of the alternative newsgroups and you'll get the picture. Most of the alternative newsgroups are unmoderated. As such, they're a free-for-all of profanity, abusiveness, and childish bickering. The value and quality of the information that you'll find in moderated newsgroups is much higher than their unmoderated cousins.

The disadvantages, on the other hand, are just as clear. Some people believe that moderating a newsgroup is the equivalent of censorship. Instead of the group as a whole determining the content of a newsgroups, the judgment of a single individual determines the content of the newsgroups. Another significant disadvantage is timeliness. Articles posted to moderated newsgroups can be delayed days or weeks.

Participating in a newsgroup

Every Internet resource that you want to use requires a client program on your computer. Newsgroups are no exception. The program that you use to read newsgroups is called a newsreader.

A newsreader lets you browse the newsgroups that are available, reading and posting articles along the way. Most newsreaders also have more advanced features that make using newsgroups a bit more productive.

Later in this chapter, you'll learn how to use Netscape's newsreader to access the news. You'll also find other ways to read the newsgroups without using a newsreader.

Wading through UseNet

Sometimes, you'll feel like you're knee deep in newsgroups. There are over 10,000 newsgroups available. Wading through them all to find what you want can be a daunting task. What's a new user to do?

It's all right there in front of you. There's a lot of logic to the way newsgroups are named. Once you learn it, you'll be able to pluck out a newsgroup just by how it's named. You'll also find tools to help you locate just the right newsgroup, as well as a few newsgroups that provide helpful advice and pointers to new users.

Newsgroup organization

Newsgroups are organized into a hierarchy of categories and subcategories. Take a look at the alt.tv.simpsons newsgroup discussed earlier. The top-level category is alt. The subcategory is tv. The subcategory under that is simpsons. The name goes from general to specific, left to right. You'll also find other newsgroups under alt.tv, such as alt.tv.friends and alt.tv.home-imprvment.

So how do newsgroups work, anyway?

NNTP (Network News Transport Protocol) is used to move the news from one server to another. It's very similar to e-mail in a lot of respects. Instead of all the messages sitting on your machine, however, they are stored on an NNTP news server that many other people can access. Therefore, the news only has to be sent to the server, instead of each user. Each user is then responsible for retrieving the articles she's interested in.

UseNet news makes its way to your news server using a process called flooding. That is, all the news servers are networked together. A particular news server may be fed by one news server, while it feeds three other news servers in turn. Periodically, it's flooded with news from the news server that's feeding it, and it floods all of its news to the news servers that it feeds.

TIP   **alt.tv.* is a notational convention that means all the newsgroups** available under the alt.tv category.

There are many different top-level categories available. Table 9.1 shows some that you probably have available on your news server.

Table 9.1   Internet top-level newsgroup categories

Category	Description
alt	Alternative newsgroups
bit	BitNet LISTSERV mailing lists
biz	Advertisements for businesses
clarinet	News clipping service by subscription only
comp	Computer-related topics: hardware and software
k12	Educational, kindergarten through grade 12
misc	Topics that don't fit the other categories
news	News and information about UseNet
rec	Recreational, sports, hobbies, music, and games
sci	Applied sciences
soc	Social and cultural topics
talk	Discussion of more controversial topics

These categories help you nail down exactly which newsgroup you're looking for. A bit of practice helps as well. If you're looking for information about Windows 95, for example, start looking at the comp top-level category. You'll find an os category, which probably represents operating systems. Under that category, you'll find an ms-windows category.

NOTE   **Exactly which newsgroups are available on your news server is largely** under the control of the administrator. Some administrators filter out regional newsgroups that don't apply to your area. Some also filter out the alt newsgroups because of their potentially offensive content.

Searching for newsgroups on the Web

Scouring the categories for a particular newsgroup may not be the most efficient way to find what you want. Here are a couple of tools that help you find newsgroups based upon keywords that you type:

- Point Netscape at **www.cen.uiuc.edu/cgi-bin/find-news**. This tool searches all the newsgroup names and newsgroup descriptions for a single keyword that you specify.

- Another very similar tool is at **www.nova.edu/Inter-Links/cgi-bin/news.pl**. This tool allows you to give more than one keyword, however.

Newsgroups for new users

Whenever I go some place new, I first try to locate a source of information about it. Likewise, the first few places that you need to visit when you get to UseNet are all the newsgroups that are there to welcome you. It's not just a warm and fuzzy welcome, either. They provide useful information about what to do, what not to do, and how to get the most out of the newsgroups. Table 9.2 shows you the newsgroups that you need to check out.

Table 9.2 Newsgroups for the newbie

Newsgroup	Description
alt.answers	A good source of FAQs and information about alt newsgroups
alt.internet.services	This is the place to ask about Internet programs and resources
news.announce.newsgroups	Announcements about new newsgroups are made here
news.announce.newusers	Articles and FAQs for the new newsgroups user
news.newusers.questions	This is the place to ask your questions about using newsgroups

NOTE **Don't post test articles to these newsgroups. Don't post articles asking** for someone to send you an e-mail, either. This is a terrible waste of newsgroups that are intended to help new users learn the ropes. See the section "Practice posting in the right place" later in this chapter to learn about a better place to post test articles.

Getting real news on UseNet

UseNet is good for a lot more than just blathering and downloading questionable art. There's a lot of news and great information coming from a variety of sources. You'll find "real" news, current Internet events, organizational newsgroups, and regional newsgroups as well—all of which make newsgroups worth every bit of trouble.

ClariNet

You can be the first kid on the block with the current news. ClariNet is a news service that clips articles from sources such as the AP and Reuters news wires. They post these services to the clari.* newsgroups. These newsgroups aren't free, though. They sell these newsgroups on a subscription basis. You wouldn't want to pay for them, either, because they can be expensive. Many independent service providers do subscribe, however, as a part of their service.

ClariNet has more than 300 newsgroups from which to choose. My favorite ClariNet newsgroups are shown in table 9.3. You'll come up with your own favorites in short order. One ClariNet newsgroup that you definitely need to check out is clari.net.newusers. It's a good introduction to all the newsgroups that ClariNet offers.

news.announce.newusers

The news.announce.newusers newsgroup contains a lot of great articles for new newsgroup users. In particular, look for the articles with the following subject lines:

- What is UseNet?

- What is UseNet? A second opinion

- Rules for posting to UseNet

- Hints on writing style for UseNet

- A Primer on How to Work with the UseNet Community

- Emily Postnews Answers Your Questions on Netiquette

- How to find the right place to post (FAQ)

- Answers to Frequently Asked Questions about UseNet

Table 9.3   Popular ClariNet newsgroups

Newsgroup	Description
clari.biz.briefs	Regular business updates
clari.local.State	Your own local news
clari.nb.online	News about the online community
clari.nb.windows	News about Windows products and issues
clari.news.briefs	Regular national and world news updates

For your convenience, table 9.4 describes each ClariNet news category. You'll find individual newsgroups under each category. Under the clari.living category, for example, you'll find arts, books, music, and movies.

Table 9.4   ClariNet news categories at a glance

Category	Description
clari.news	General and national news
clari.biz	Business and financial news
clari.sports	Sports and athletic news
clari.living	Lifestyle and human interest stories
clari.world	News about other countries
clari.local	States and local areas
clari.feature	Special syndicated features
clari.tw	Technical and scientific news
clari.matrix_news	A networking newsletter
clari.nb	Newsbytes, computer industry news
clari.sfbay	San Francisco Bay Area news
clari.net	Information about ClariNet
clari.apbl	Special groups for the AP BulletinLine

Net-happenings

If it seems that the Internet is moving too fast to keep up with, you're right—without help, anyway. The comp.internet.net-happenings newsgroup helps you keep track of new events on the Internet, including the World Wide Web, mailing lists, UseNet, and so on.

The subject line of each article tells you a lot about the announcement. Take, for example, the following announcement:

WWW>Free Internet service for first 100 visitors

The first part tells you that the announcement is about a World Wide Web site. You'll find many other categories such as FAQ, EMAG, LISTS, and MISC. The second part is a brief description about the announcement. Most of the time, the description is enough to tell you whether you want to see more information by opening the article. The article itself is a few paragraphs about the announcement, with the address or subscription information near the top.

Regional newsgroups

Is your geographical region represented on UseNet? A lot are. The Dallas/Fort Worth area has a couple of newsgroups, such as dfw.eats, dfw.forsale, and dfw.personals. Virtually every state has similar newsgroups. Other states might have special needs. For example, California users might be interested in the ca.environment.earthquakes newsgroup.

Using Netscape to read the news

All that news is out there, just sloshing around on the news server, and you need a program to get at it. There are a lot of newsreaders out there, but you already have Netscape's newsreader. It's one of the cleanest and easiest to use newsreaders available.

Starting the Netscape newsreader is easy. Choose <u>W</u>indow, Netscape News from the Netscape main menu. Figure 9.1 shows the Netscape newsreader, and table 9.5 shows what each of the buttons on the toolbar does.

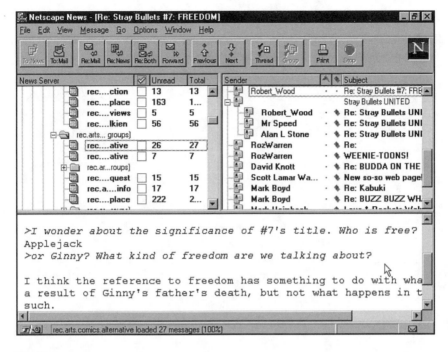

Fig. 9.1
The Netscape newsreader window is divided into three panes: groups list, article list, and article body.

Table 9.5 Buttons on the Netscape Newsreader toolbar

Button	Name	Description
	Post new	Post new article to newsgroup
	New message	Create a new e-mail message
	Reply	Reply using an e-mail message
	Post reply	Post reply to newsgroup article
	Post and reply	Post and e-mail a reply

continues

Table 9.5   Continued

Button	Name	Description
	Forward	Forward article to e-mail address
	Previous Unread	Previous article in a newsgroup
	Next Unread	Next article in a newsgroup
	Mark thread read	Mark entire conversation as read
	Mark all read	Mark entire newsgroup as read
	Print	Print the current article
	Stop	Stop transferring from news server

Configuring Netscape to read the news

To configure Netscape for your service provider, use the following steps:

1 Choose Options, Mail and News Preferences from the Netscape newsreader main menu, and click the Servers tab. Netscape displays the dialog box shown in figure 9.2.

2 Fill in your NNTP (Network News Transfer Protocol) and SMTP (Simple Mail Transfer Protocol) servers as shown in figure 9.2, and click the Identity tab. Netscape displays the dialog box shown in figure 9.3. You can also control how many UseNet messages Netscape will retrieve using the Get test field. If you're paying toll charges to access your UseNet server, or your computer is a bit on the slow side, you'll want to set this to a low number.

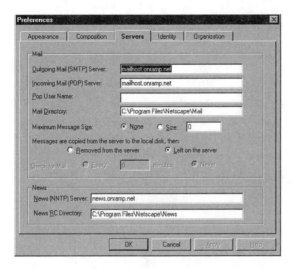

Fig. 9.2
Your service provider should have given you the NNTP news server and SMTP mail server.

3 Fill in Your <u>N</u>ame, Your <u>E</u>mail, and Reply-to <u>A</u>ddress as shown in figure 9.3. If you want to attach a signature file to the end of your postings, select a text file by clicking Browse. Click OK to save your changes.

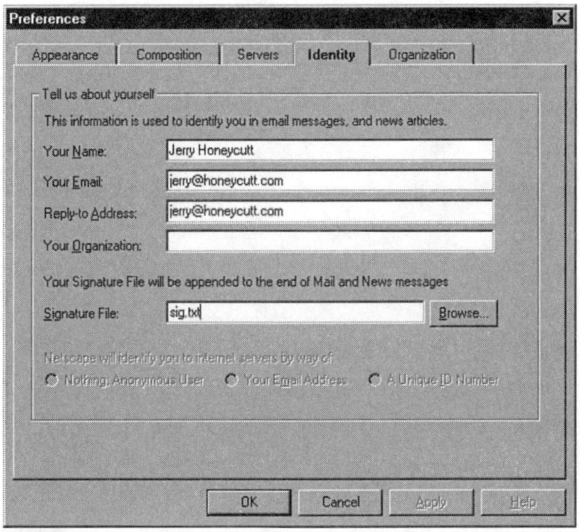

Fig. 9.3
You need to provide a name and e-mail address so that other people can respond to your postings.

Q&A *Why do I get an error message that says Netscape couldn't find the news server?*

First, make sure that you have a connection to your service provider. If you're definitely connected, make sure that you correctly configured your NNTP news server. Don't remember the exact address your provider gave you? Try this: If your domain name is provider.net, then add news to the front of it like this: news.provider.net.

 Q&A *Can I use Netscape to access UseNet through CompuServe?*

Yes. The CompuServe news server is news.compuserve.com and the SMTP mail server is mail.compuserve.com.

Subscribing to newsgroups

After you've configured the Netscape newsreader for your service provider, you need to download a complete list of the newsgroups available on your news server. Highlight your news server in the groups pane, and choose Show All Newsgroups from the Options menu. Netscape displays a dialog box warning you that this process can take a few minutes on a slow connection. Click OK to continue.

A note about signatures

You can easily personalize your postings with a signature. Save about three lines that say something about yourself, such as your address and hobbies, into a text file. Then, in step 3 of "Configuring Netscape to Read the News," select the text file you created. Here's an example of a signature file:

Jerry Honeycutt
  | jerry@honeycutt.com
  | (800) 555-1212
  | Buy Using the Internet, Now!

Your signature can communicate anything that you want about yourself including your name, mailing address, phone number, or a particular phrase that reflects your outlook on life. It is considered good form, however, to limit your signatures to three lines.

Before you can read the articles in a newsgroup, you have to subscribe to it. When you subscribe to a newsgroup, you're telling Netscape that you want to read the articles in that newsgroup. Normally, Netscape only displays the newsgroups to which you've subscribed. Thus, subscribing to a handful of newsgroups keeps you from having to slog through a list of 15,000 newsgroups to find what you want.

TIP **Categories are indicated with a file folder icon; newsgroups are** indicated with a newspaper icon.

Earlier you learned that newsgroups are named in a hierarchical fashion. Netscape takes advantage of this by organizing newsgroups the same way, using folders in the groups pane. Initially, all you see under a news server is the top-level categories. If you click one of the top-level categories, you see the sub-categories underneath it. Continue clicking categories until you see a newsgroup to which you can subscribe.

If you want to subscribe to alt.tv.simpsons, for example, follow these steps:

1 Click the alt top-level newsgroup.

2 Find alt.tv in the list under alt, and click it.

3 Find alt.tv.simpsons in the list under alt.tv, and check the box that is to the right of the name to indicate that you want to subscribe to that newsgroup.

After you subscribe to all the newsgroups you want, you can tell Netscape to display only those newsgroups to which you've subscribed. Choose Options, Show Subscribed Groups from the main menu.

NOTE **You can sample the articles in a newsgroup before subscribing. If you** click a newsgroup to which you haven't subscribed, Netscape displays that newsgroup's articles in the article pane. If you like what you see, subscribe to the group by checking the box next to the name of the newsgroup.

Browsing and reading articles

TIP   **Articles that you haven't read have a green diamond in the R column.**

Select a newsgroup in the groups Pane and Netscape displays all the current articles for that group in the articles pane. You can scroll up and down the list of articles looking for an interesting article. When you click an article in the article pane, Netscape displays the contents of that article in the body pane.

Notice that some of the articles are indented under other articles. These are replies to the articles under which they are indented. All the messages indented under an article, including the original message, are called a thread. Netscape indents articles this way so you can visually follow the thread. Figure 9.4 shows what a thread looks like in Netscape.

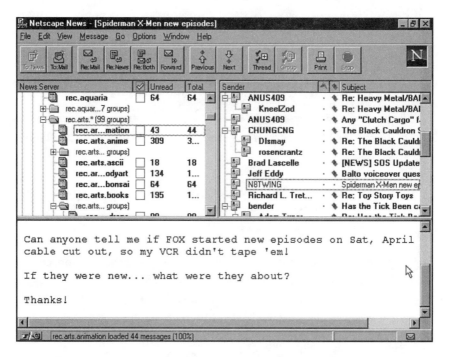

Fig. 9.4
The top portion of the message's body tells you who posted the message and what other groups they posted the message to.

Q&A *What happened to the articles that were here a few days ago?*

It's not practical to keep every article posted to every newsgroup indefinitely. Your service provider deletes the older articles to make room for the newer articles. Another way of saying this is that a message scrolled off. The length of time that an article hangs around varies from provider to provider, but is usually between three days and a week.

Moving around the article pane

When you click an article header in the article pane, the article's contents are automatically displayed in the body pane. After you read the article, you can click another article, or you can use the following options from Netscape's toolbar and menu to move around:

- Choose Go, Next Unread from the main menu to read the next message you haven't read.

- Choose Go, Previous Unread from the main menu to read the previous message you haven't read.

- Click the Next button to read the next article in the newsgroup—whether you've read it already or not.

- Click the Previous button to read the previous article in the newsgroup—whether you've read it already or not.

- Choose Go, First Unread to read the first message in the newsgroup that you haven't yet read.

Q&A *I opened an article, but its contents were all garbled.*

You've probably opened an article that is ROT13-encoded. ROT13 is an encoding method that has little to do with security. It allows a person who is posting a potentially offensive message to place the responsibility for its contents on you—the reader. It essentially says that if you decode and read this message, you won't hold me responsible for its contents. To decode the article, right-click in the body pane, and choose Unscramble (ROT-13).

Downloading files from newsgroups

Posting and downloading files from a newsgroup is a bit more complicated than your experience with online services. Binary files can't be posted directly to UseNet. Many methods have evolved, however, to encode files into text so that they can be sent.

The downloading process works as follows:

1 A file is encoded, using UUEncode, to a newsgroup as one or more articles.

2 While you're browsing a newsgroup, you notice a few articles with subject lines that look like this (headings are provided for your convenience):

Lines	File name	Part	Description
5	HOMER.GIF	[00/02]	Portrait of Homer Simpson
800	HOMER.GIF	[01/02]	Portrait of Homer Simpson
540	HOMER.GIF	[02/02]	Portrait of Homer Simpson

These articles are three parts of the same file. The first article is probably a description of the file because it is part zero, and because there are only five lines in it. The next two articles are the actual file.

3 To download a file from a newsgroup, you retrieve all the articles belonging to that file. Then, you UUDecode the articles back into a binary file.

Replying to an article

You'll eventually want to post a reply to an article you read in a newsgroup. You might want to be helpful and answer someone's question. You're just as likely to find an interesting discussion to which you want to contribute. Either way, the following are two different ways you can reply to an article you have read:

- Follow up—If you want your reply to be read by everyone who frequents the newsgroup, post a follow-up article. Your reply is added to the thread. To reply to an article, click the Post Reply button on the toolbar. Fill in the window shown in figure 9.5, and click the Send button.

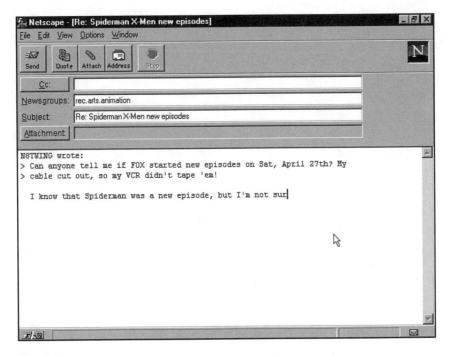

Fig. 9.5
The text that starts with the greater-than sign (>) is the original article. Delete everything that you don't need to remind the reader of what he posted.

- E-mail—If your reply would benefit only the person to whom you're replying, respond with an e-mail message instead. That person gets the message faster, and the other newsgroup readers aren't annoyed. To reply by e-mail, click the Reply button on the toolbar. Fill out the window shown in figure 9.6 and click the Send button.

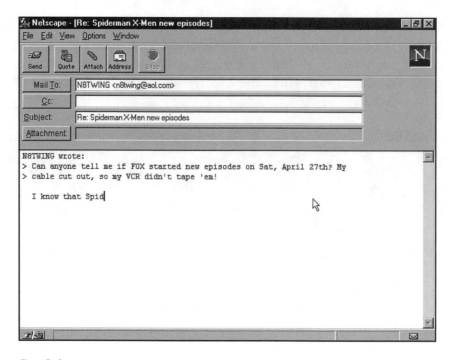

Fig. 9.6
Look carefully—the only difference between this window and the window in figure 9.5 is this window has the Mail To field and the previous window has the Newsgroups field.

Posting a new article

It's no fun being a spectator. You'll eventually want to start a discussion of your own. To post a new article, click the Post New button on the toolbar. Fill in the window shown previously in figure 9.5 and click the Send button.

 NOTE   **Lurk before you leap. Lurking is when you just hang out, reading the**
articles and learning the ropes without posting an article. You'll avoid making a
fool of yourself by learning what's acceptable and what's not before it's too late.

Practice posting in the right place

You'll find a special newsgroup, called alt.test, that exists just for test posting. You can post a test article to that newsgroup all day long and no one will care.

In fact, you should go ahead and post a test article just to make sure that everything works. You'll get a good idea of how long it takes your article to show up, and you'll also learn the mechanics of posting and replying to articles.

TIP   Test your file uploads in the alt.test newsgroup, too, instead of testing them in productive newsgroups.

Posting a file

Netscape makes posting a file easy. Post a new article as described earlier in the section "Posting a new article." Before you click the Send button, however, follow these instructions:

Stay out of trouble; follow the rules

Etiquette, as Miss Manners will tell you, was created so that everyone would get along better. Etiquette's rules are not official rules, however; they're community standards for how everyone should behave. Likewise, netiquette is a community standard for how to behave on the Internet. It's important for two reasons. First, it helps keep the frustration level down. Second, it helps prevent the terrible waste of Internet resources by limiting the amount of noise.

- Post your articles in the right place. Don't post questions about Windows 95, for example, to the alt.tv.simpsons newsgroup.

- NEWSGROUP READERS REALLY HATE IT WHEN YOU SHOUT BY USING ALL CAPS. It doesn't make your message seem any more important.

- Don't test, and don't beg for e-mail. There are a few places where that is appropriate, but this behavior generally gets you flamed (a flame is a mean or abusive message).

- Don't spam. Spamming is posting an advertisement to several, if not hundreds, of newsgroups. Don't do it. It's a waste of Internet resources.

- Don't cross-post your article. This is a waste of Internet resources, and readers quickly tire of seeing the same article posted to many newsgroups.

1 Click <u>A</u>ttachment. Netscape displays the Attachments dialog box.

2 Click Attach <u>F</u>ile, choose the file you want to attach in the Enter File to Attach dialog box, and click <u>O</u>pen.

3 Repeat step 2 for each file you want to attach to your article. Then, click OK to save your attachments.

After you've selected the files you want to attach to your posting, you can continue editing it normally. Click the Send button when you're finished.

Other ways to read the news

If browsing newsgroups with a newsreader seems like too much trouble, the tools described in this section might be just what you need. You'll learn to use DejaView, which lets you search UseNet for specific articles. You'll also learn how to use SIFT, a tool that filters all the newsgroup postings and saves them for you to read later.

Searching UseNet with DejaNews

DejaNews is a Web tool that searches all the newsgroup articles, past and present, for terms that you specify. Point your Web browser at **http://www.dejanews.com/forms/dnq.html**. Figure 9.7 shows you the DejaNews search Web page. To search UseNet, fill in the form as shown in figure 9.7, and click Search.

DejaNews displays another Web page that contains a list of the newsgroup articles it found. You can click any of these articles to read them, or click Get Next 30 Hits to display the next page full of articles. The following are a couple of other things you should know:

- The author's name is the last item on each line. You can click it to see what other newsgroups they typically post to.

- You can click the subject line of an article to display the complete thread that contains that article.

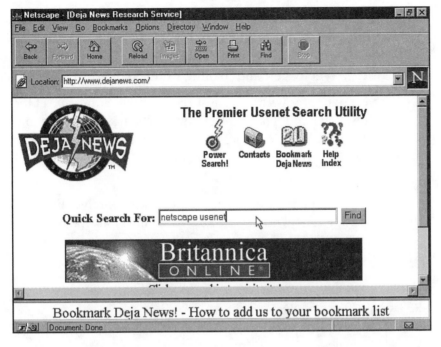

Fig. 9.7
Click the Create a Query Filter link to specify exactly which newsgroup, author, or date range to search.

Filtering UseNet with SIFT

SIFT is a tool provided by Stanford that filters all the articles posted to UseNet. As an added bonus, it filters a lot of public mailing lists and new Web pages, too. You tell SIFT the keywords in which you're interested, and it keeps track of all the new documents on the Internet that match those keywords. Like DejaNews, this is a Web tool, so point your browser at **http://sift.stanford.edu**.

The first time you access SIFT, it asks you for an e-mail address and password. You don't have one, yet. That's OK. Type your e-mail address and make up a password. You'll need to use the same password the next time that you access SIFT. Click Enter to go to the search form.

The most effective way to use SIFT is as follows:

1 Figure 9.8 shows the SIFT search form. Select the Search radio button, and type the topics for which you're looking in Topic. If you want to make sure that some topics are not included, type them in Avoid.

2 Click Submit. SIFT displays a page, containing all of today's new articles that match your keywords, on each line. The most relevant line is at the top; the least relevant is at the bottom. Read some of the articles, Web pages, and mailing list messages by clicking them.

3 If you're happy with these test results, click Subscribe at the bottom of the Web page. Then, click Submit. The next time you log on to SIFT, you'll see additional lines at the bottom of the Web page, as shown in figure 9.8, that let you delete subscriptions or review the current day's hits.

4 If you're not happy with the results, click Search at the bottom of the Web page. Then, adjust the keywords in Topic and Avoid, and click Submit. SIFT displays a similar Web page using your new search keywords.

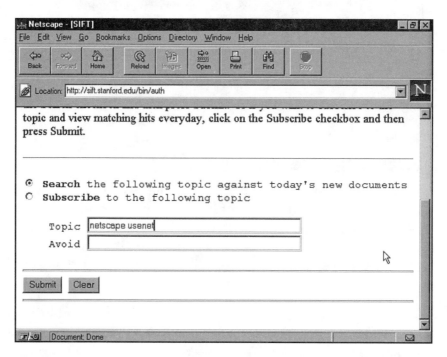

Fig. 9.8
You won't see the Read and Delete Topic choices until you've submitted at least one subscription.

The pros and cons of Netscape's newsreader

There's a wide variety of newsreaders available on the Internet. They range from the most basic (Qnews) to complex (Free Agent). Netscape's newsreader is at the basic end of this spectrum. It doesn't have the features that an avid UseNet junkie needs to be productive. Netscape doesn't let you choose a UUEncoded file, for example, then download and UUDecode it automatically. If you need more advanced features such as this, you should consider some of the freeware and shareware newsreaders available. Free Agent is available on the Web at **www.forteinc.com/forte/agent/dlmain.htm**.

Netscape's newsreader does have everything that a casual user needs, however. You can easily post, reply, and view articles—possibly easier than with the other newsreaders available. You can also view UUEncoded images on UseNet just by selecting the article in the list. This is about all most people use UseNet for anyway. Incidentally, the most important feature of Netscape's newsreader is how solid and well thought out it appears to be. Newsgroups are organized using an outline metaphor and the article list is easy to navigate, for example.

Part IV: Sound, Graphics, Multimedia, and More!

10

Netscape Plug-Ins

● **In this chapter:**

● **What are Netscape plug-ins and what do they do for you?**

● **Where to get plug-ins and how to install them**

● **Multimedia plug-ins**

● **VRML plug-ins**

● **Business productivity plug-ins**

Though a wide variety of plug-in modules is now available for Netscape (more than 100 are described in this chapter alone), and more are under development, they fall roughly into three categories. In this chapter, you will learn about all three types:

- Multimedia—including viewers for video (AVI, MOV, and MPEG movies), audio (speech, music, and digitized sound), and graphics (including vector objects and super-compressed images), as well as multimedia presentation formats like Macromedia Director and Astound

- VRML—Virtual Reality Modeling Language 3D world display plug-ins (sometimes with extra features)

- Business Applications—this includes viewers for application files like Excel spreadsheets and Word documents, Web navigation tools, and plug-ins that link to OLE objects to call other programs, embed applications, or provide custom controls, as well as some interesting miscellaneous applications

We won't list every plug-in ever created for Netscape —some have been merely testbed projects or fun demos ("Animated Widgets" comes to mind). But we *will* try to list all of the most useful plug-ins released so far. Of course, plug-in development proceeds apace, and it's almost impossible to keep up-to-date, even if you're online checking every day. Over 50 were released in the three months which immediately preceded the writing of this book!

 TIP **Look for the icon at the left, which indicates that the plug-in under** discussion is one of the fifteen plug-ins included on Netscape's Power Pack 2.0 CD-ROM.

What is a Netscape 3 plug-in?

Plug-ins are feature add-ons designed to extend the capabilities of Netscape 3. The creation of (and support for) plug-ins by Netscape is significant primarily because it allows other developers to seamlessly integrate their products into the Web via Netscape, without having to launch any external helper applications.

For Netscape users, plug-in support allows you to customize Netscape's interaction with third-party products and industry media standards. Netscape's plug-in API also attempts to address the concerns of programmers, providing a high degree of flexibility and cross-platform support to plug-in developers.

What plug-ins mean for end users

Because plug-ins are platform-specific, you must have a different version of each plug-in for every operating system you use, such as Windows or the Mac OS. Regardless of your platform, however, Netscape plug-ins should be functionally equivalent across all platforms.

 TIP **Many plug-ins ship with the copy of Netscape you purchased, already** designed for your platform. However, if you find other plug-ins that you want to either purchase and/or download from the Internet, make sure the plug-in is designed for your specific platform.

For most users, integrating plug-ins is transparent. They open up and become active whenever Netscape is opened. Furthermore, because most plug-ins are not activated unless you open up a Web page that initiates the plug-in, you may not even see the plug-in at work most of the time. For example, after you install the Shockwave for Director plug-in, you will notice no difference in the way Netscape functions until you come across a Web page that features Shockwave.

Once a plug-in is installed on your machine and initiated by a Web page, it will manifest itself in three potential ways:

- Embedded
- Full-screen
- Hidden

An *embedded* plug-in appears as a visible, rectangular window integrated into a Web page. This window may not appear any different than a window created by a graphic, such as an embedded GIF or JPEG picture. The main difference between the previous windows supported by Netscape and those created by plug-ins is that plug-in windows can support a much wider range of interactivity and movement, and thereby remain live instead of static.

In addition to mouse clicks, embedded plug-ins may also read and take note of mouse location, mouse movement, keyboard input, and input from virtually any other input device. In this way, a plug-in can support the full range of user events required to produce sophisticated applications.

An example of an embedded plug-in might be an MPEG, Video for Windows, or QuickTime movie player, or the Shockwave for Macromedia Director player discussed later in this chapter.

A *full-screen* plug-in takes over the entire current Netscape window to display its own content. This is necessary when a Web page is designed to display data that is not supported by HTML. An example of this type of plug-in is the Adobe Acrobat viewer.

If you view an Acrobat page using the Netscape plug-in, it pulls up just like any other Web page, but it retains the look and functionality of an Acrobat document viewed in Adobe's stand-alone viewer. For instance, you might find an online manual for a product displayed on a Web site with Acrobat, and you'd be able to scroll, print, and interact with the page just as if it were being displayed by the stand-alone Acrobat Reader program.

A *hidden* plug-in doesn't have any visible elements, but works strictly behind the scenes to add some feature to Netscape that is otherwise not available. An example of a hidden plug-in might be a MIDI player or a decompression engine. A MIDI player plug-in could read MIDI data from a Web page whenever it's encountered, and automatically play it through your local hardware or software. Similarly, a decompression engine could function much the way it does on commercial online services, decompressing data in real-time in the background, or saving decompression until the user logs off the Internet.

TIP For more information on Netscape 3 plug-ins, point Netscape to http:// home.netscape.com/comprod/products/navigator/version_2.0/plugins/ index.html.

Regardless of which plug-ins you are using, and whether they are embedded, full-screen, or hidden, the rest of Netscape's user interface should remain relatively constant and available. So even if you have an Acrobat page displayed in Netscape's main window, you'll still be able to access Netscape's menus and navigational controls.

Downloading, installing, and using plug-ins

Downloading Netscape plug-ins couldn't be much easier—Netscape maintains a page which lists many of the currently available plug-ins, with links to the pages from which they can be downloaded, at **http:// home.netscape.com/comprod/products/navigator/version_2.0/plugins/ index.html**. There's also the Plug-Ins Plaza site, which seems to consistently be even more up-to-date than Netscape's own site. It's at **http:// www.browserwatch.com**. For your convenience, we've included the URL of the download site for all of the plug-ins that are listed in this chapter.

On the CD

TIP Watch for the "On the CD" icon throughout this chapter. Many of the plug-ins discussed here are included on the CD-ROM with this book.

You should download a plug-in file into its own temporary directory before installing it. I usually keep a directory called C:\INSTALL on my hard drive just for this purpose. I download a single plug-in to the INSTALL directory, install it, then delete the files in C:\INSTALL so that the directory is empty and available for my next installation. (I usually make sure that the plug-in is actually installed correctly and working properly before I delete the installation files.)

Each plug-in downloads as a single file. Installation involves one of two procedures:

1 If the file is called Setup.exe, you simply have to run it. It will automatically install itself as a Netscape plug-in. You may be given the option to determine which directory the plug-in will be installed to. Don't change the default unless you already have a directory by that name which contains something else.

2 If the file has some obscure name like xx32b4.exe, it's a sure bet that it's a self-extracting archive. In this case, double-clicking the file in Win95 (or opening a DOS shell in Windows 3.1, CD-ing to the INSTALL directory, and typing the filename) will extract the archive into a whole bunch of files in your INSTALL directory. Then close the DOS window and run the program called Setup.exe. From here, the process is identical to step 1 above.

In any event, the download page for a plug-in always contains complete instructions on downloading and installation. Read and follow these instructions carefully. They might just do something different, and you don't want to be caught by surprise. (For example, you can optionally download a bare-bones version of the Crescendo MIDI player plug-in without a setup program, but if you do, you have to unpack and copy the file into the Netscape Plug-ins directory yourself.)

Q&A *I've been playing around with plug-ins, and have installed several. Now I can't remember which ones I have, and which ones I don't! Worse, I had a nice plug-in installed for playing audio [or video, or multimedia, etc.] plug-ins, but some plug-in I installed later seems to have taken over this function, and I don't like it near as well! How can I figure out which plug-ins I have installed, and which ones I still need? Is there any way to get my old plug-in back?*

Unfortunately, Navigator has no easy menu selection or pop-up dialog that just tells you exactly which plug-ins you have installed. However, there are three places you can go to get some good clues.

One is to pick <u>H</u>elp, About <u>P</u>lug-ins from the Navigator menu. You'll get a screen with a list formatted like this:

File name:

Types:

   Description: data

   MIME Type: x-world/x-vrml

   Suffixes: wrl

etc...

This is a list of the MIME types that are registered to launch plug-ins. Each entry on this list was entered when you installed a plug-in. While this list is a good indicator of which file types will launch plug-ins when they're encountered, it won't tell you exactly which plug-ins will be launched.

If the list includes two or more entries documenting the same MIME type and/or Suffixes, then you've installed one plug-in over another, and the more recent one is handling that type of file display.

You can also check out Options, Ceneral Preferences and select the Helpers tab from the dialog box that appears. This box includes a scrolling list of registered MIME types. Look under the Action column, and you'll see either the word "Browser" (which means that file type is handled by Netscape itself), "Ask User" (which means it'll bring up a dialog to ask the user what to do), or the name of a helper application that has been set up to handle that type of file for Netscape. If the Action field is blank, it means that there's a plug-in configured for that MIME type. Though you still don't know *which* plug-in is associated with that file type, at least you know there is a plug-in of some kind handling it.

Note that in the version of Netscape 3 that I'm currently working with, this list has a bug that could throw you off. If you click on an entry with a blank Action field, you may see a filename in the Launch the Application text box. Don't be fooled. This box should be blank; if there's a filename there, it's left over from a previous list selection. Don't make the mistake of thinking it's a helper application configured for that MIME file type. If the Action field is blank, a plug-in is handling that file type. Period. This bug may be fixed in future versions.

The last thing to try is to use Explorer to look in the folder c:\program files\netscape\navigator\program\plug-ins (this is the default folder; if you installed Netscape elsewhere, you'll have to find the path to the plug-ins folder yourself). This folder contains the .dll libraries and other files used by the plug-ins you've installed. Unfortunately, most of them have obscure names like "Npskwav.dll" or "Micrdate.dll." Right-click on a .dll filename under Win95 and select Properties from the pop-up menu, and you'll get a variety of information about the file, including what company created it and any developer's notes associated with it. There's usually enough information for you to be able to figure out which plug-in it is.

By combining the knowledge you glean through your explorations with your memory of which plug-ins you *think* you remember installing, you should be able to figure out which plug-ins you actually have installed and enabled.

If you can manage to figure out what you've got installed, all you need to do to re-enable a plug-in that has been superseded by another is to delete the offending plug-in. Once it's gone, the older one will take over again, provided it's still in the plug-ins directory. If it isn't, you'll have to reinstall it.

Running a plug-in is a piece of cake—you don't have to run a plug-in at all.

They run themselves whenever a Web page or link contains the proper kind of embedded file. You don't have to decide when to run them, you don't have to figure out how to load in the data file, nothing.

However, you do have to learn how the controls work. Many of these programs put a set of specialized controls on the screen for zooming, printing, panning, scrolling, or what have you. Each plug-in comes with detailed documentation explaining what its specific controls are and how they work. (In some cases, there may be a separate manual file to download, or the documentation will be online in the form of Web pages—pay close attention so you get the documentation along with the plug-in itself.) Make sure you read the documentation so you know all about a plug-in *before* you encounter any files it'll be called upon to display. That way you won't spend valuable online time trying to figure it out.

Multimedia plug-ins

It's not an overstatement to say that interest in delivering multimedia content on the Web and on corporate intranets is what's driving plug-in development. Though there are plug-ins for things other than playing audio, video, and multimedia content, these types of plug-ins are, by far, the most pervasive.

This section lists and describes the sound, graphics, video, multimedia, and animation plug-ins currently being distributed for Netscape Navigator.

Sound

Internet audio is growing like gangbusters. It seems like there are more live audio programs, digitized sound files, and MIDI music files on the Web every day. And with the explosion of plug-ins development in this area, it's sure to move even faster in the near future.

In the beginning, the Web was mute. Eventually, some sites began to add a few digitized sounds, which had to be downloaded and played using helper applications. Now there are several sound plug-ins that let Netscape play live audio data streams in real-time. Audio plug-ins are available for several varieties of digitized sound, as well as MIDI music and speech.

LiveAudio

Netscape's LiveAudio plug-in is shipped with Netscape 3.0, so you could call it the "official" Netscape audio player. Unlike the other audio plug-ins discussed here, LiveAudio doesn't use a proprietary sound file format; it plays standard AIFF, AU, MIDI, and WAV files. Sound files can be either embedded in or linked to a Web page. LiveAudio features an easy-to-use console with play, pause, stop, and volume controls.

If your system is equipped with a sound card, LiveAudio lets you listen to audio tracks, sound effects, music, and voice files that have been embedded in Web pages. You can also use it to listen to stand-alone sound files both on the Web and on your own computer system.

LiveAudio is a huge improvement over The NAPlayer audio helper application that Netscape shipped with previous versions of Netscape Navigator. Where NAPlayer only played Sun/NeXT (.au, .snd) and Mac/SGI (.aif, .aiff) sound files, LiveAudio automatically identifies and plays four of the most popular standard sound formats:

- AIFF—Mac/SGI format sounds
- AU—Sun/NeXT format sounds

- MIDI—Musical Instrument Digital Interface music files
- WAV—MicroSoft Windows system sound files

When you encounter a sound file embedded or linked on a Web page, LiveAudio creates the on-screen control console shown in figure 10.1.

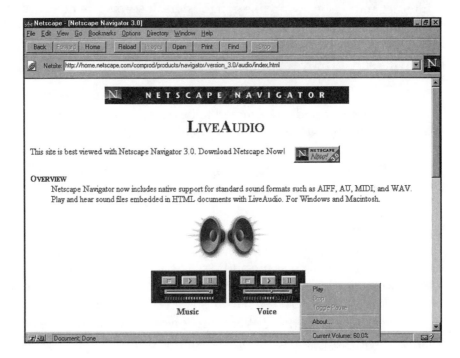

Fig 10.1
The LiveAudio plug-in expresses itself as a minimalist inline audio player control console, shown here in duplicate on a Netscape Web site demo page.

The LiveAudio plug-in works with both embedded sound files, like the two it encountered in figure 10.2, and with stand-alone sound files. In the case of stand-alone files, a blank Netscape window is displayed which contains only a LiveAudio console.

The LiveAudio console controls are intuitive and easy to use (see fig. 10.2).

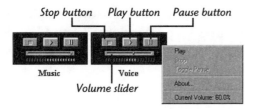

Fig 10.2

The LiveAudio audio player control box features four manual controls and a simple drop-down menu.

The Stop, Play, and Pause buttons work just as they do on a tape or CD player. Clicking on Play plays the sound, selecting Stop stops it, and choosing Pause pauses audio playback. Pressing the Pause button a second time resumes play from the point at which the sound was paused.

Click to the right or left of the Volume slider knob to increase or decrease volume. The volume can only be jumped in increments of 20%—you can't slide the volume smoothly from 0% to 100%. The LED bar graph below the Volume slider indicates the current volume level. The dark green LEDs are for the 0%-40% range; light green LEDs take over for 40%-100%.

Clicking on the LiveAudio console brings up the pop-up menu shown in figure 10.2. This menu includes selections that duplicate the Play, Stop, and Pause buttons. There is also a selection to display the program's "About" dialog box, and a final nonselectable menu item that tells you the volume level as a percent of maximum.

There is a single keyboard hotkey for the LiveAudio player—the spacebar. Pressing it will cause whatever button you pressed last (Stop, Play, or Pause) to be activated again. Re-stopping an already stopped playback is of limited use, to say the least. But if you last pressed Pause, the spacebar becomes an unpause/re-pause toggle. And if you last pressed Play, it's a handy replay key.

LiveAudio is included with the Windows 3.1, Windows 95, Macintosh, and PowerPC versions of Netscape 3. The Windows 3.1 and Windows 95 versions require a minimum of a 386 processor and a compatible sound card.

RealAudio

Progressive Networks' RealAudio plug-in provides live, on-demand real-time audio over 14.4Kbps or faster Internet connections. Users with 28.8 or better connections can now hear true FM-quality tunes. Its controls are like a CD player—you can pause, rewind, fast-forward, stop, and start play with on-screen buttons.

RealAudio is getting a lot of support on the Net from big companies like ABC broadcasting, small independent radio stations, and individual users alike. It's almost a necessity for browsing the Web. The latest version even has synchronized multimedia playback capabilities.

You create RealAudio format sound files using the RealAudio Encoder 2.0 program. It's available as part of the RealAudio Player 2.0 Standard Edition CD-ROM, which is $29. To deliver RealAudio content, your Web server will also have to be set up with the RealAudio Server software.

Available for Windows 95, Windows NT, Windows 3.1, UNIX, and Macintosh, the RealAudio Version 2.0 player plug-in is included on Netscape's Power Pack 2.0 CD-ROM. It can also be downloaded directly from the RealAudio Web site at **http://www.realaudio.com/products/ra2.0/**.

TrueSpeech

On the CD

If nothing else, TrueSpeech is convenient. If you're using Windows 3.1 or Windows 95, the supplied Sound Recorder program can digitize sound files and convert them to TrueSpeech format. The TrueSpeech Player can then be used to listen to them on the Web in real-time. Despite its name, TrueSpeech can be used for any type of audio file. No special server is needed. From the DSP Group's home page at **http://www.dspg.com** you can download TrueSpeech players for Windows 3.1, Win95/NT, Mac, and PowerMac.

Crescendo & Crescendo Plus

Most sound cards go a step beyond merely digitizing and playing back sounds. They can also generate their own. If your sound card is MIDI compatible (and most are), you've got more than a passive record-and-playback system—you've got a full-fledged music synthesizer in there. And with a MIDI plug-in, you can experience Web sites with a full music soundtrack.

LiveUpdate's Crescendo plug-in lets Navigator play inline MIDI music embedded in Web pages. With a MIDI-capable browser, you can create Web pages that have their own background music soundtracks. And don't forget that MIDI instruments can be sampled sounds, so it's possible to create sound effects tracks, too.

Crescendo requires an MPC (MIDI-capable) sound card and Netscape Navigator version 2 or above. It launches automatically and invisibly and is a fun addition to Web browsing.

Crescendo is a 10K self-extracting archive file for Windows 95 and Windows NT, or a 50K file for Windows 3.1. The Win95/NT version is super-tiny—I had to check twice to make sure it had downloaded! A Mac version is now also available. Download Crescendo from **http://www.liveupdate.com/midi.html**. An enhanced version called Crescendo Plus adds on-screen controls and live streaming (you don't have to wait for a MIDI file to completely download before it starts playing), and can be purchased from LiveUpdate's Web site (see fig. 10.3).

More music plug-ins

Can't get enough music on the Web? Here are a few more Netscape music plug-ins.

RapidTransit decompresses and plays music that has been compressed up to 40-to-1. It can provide full 16-bit, 44.1kHz, It's available for Windows 95, Windows NT, and Macintosh from **http://monsterbit.com/rapidtransit/.**

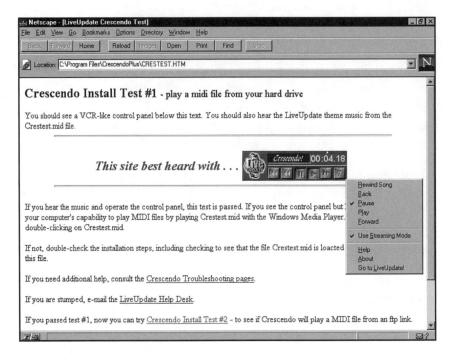

Fig. 10.3
Crescendo Plus features a CD-player style control panel and a convenient pop-up menu.

Do you prefer the sound of the Orient? Then Sseyo's Koan (**http://www.sseyo.com/**) might better fit your preferences. It plays real-time computer-generated Japanese Koan music on Win95 and Windows 3.1 versions of Netscape.

ToolVox

If speech is all you need, there are a variety of speech plug-ins for Netscape. Under this category there are really three kinds of plug-ins:

- Players for digitized audio that is of less-than-music quality
- Text-to-speech converters, currently available only for the Macintosh
- A speech recognition plug-in, also Mac-only

ToolVox provides audio compression ratios of up to 53:1, which means very small files that transfer quickly over the Internet. Speech can be delivered in real-time even over 9600 baud modems. One unique feature is that you can slow down playback to improve comprehension, or speed it up to shorten listening times without changing voice pitch.

Like the higher-fidelity RealAudio, ToolVox streams audio in real-time, so you don't have to wait for a file to download before you can listen to it.

ToolVox doesn't need special server software to deliver audio content from your Web server. Buffering and playback are controlled by the player, in the form of a Netscape Navigator 2.0 add-in. As a result, any standard HTML server can act as a streaming media server. Even the encoder is free. It compresses a speech file from WAV format to an 8kHz, 2400 bps VOX file.

Netscape Communications Corporation has become a part-owner of Voxware, the makers of ToolVox, so expect to hear a lot more about it. Netscape has also licensed key elements of Voxware's digital voice technology, including the Voxware RT24 compressor/decompressor (codec) and ToolVox, for incorporation into the Netscape LiveMedia multimedia standard.

Voxware has also announced plans to release an enhanced version of ToolVox, called ToolVox Gold.

ToolVox Navigator plug-ins are available for Win 95 and Windows 3.1, and Mac and PowerMac versions are promised. Download them from the Voxware site at **http://www.voxware.com/download.htm**.

EchoSpeech

EchoSpeech compresses speech 18.5 to 1. This means that 16-bit speech sampled at 11025 Hz is compressed to 9600 bits per second. Even people with 14.4Kbps modems can listen to real-time streaming EchoSpeech audio streams. Because EchoSpeech was designed to code speech sampled at 11025 Hz rather than 8000 Hz, it sounds better than ToolVox.

Real-time decoding of 11kHz speech requires only 30% of a 486SX-33 CPU's time. EchoSpeech plug-ins are also small—40-50K when decompressed.

No server software is required to deliver EchoSpeech content; your ISP or server administrator only needs to declare a new MIME type and pay a one-time $99 license fee. To add EchoSpeech files to your Web pages, you compress them with the EchoSpeech Speech Coder (available for evaluation via free download) then use the HTML <EMBED> tag to include them in your documents.

EchoSpeech is available for Windows 95 and Windows 3.1, and a Mac version is promised. You can get it at **http://www.echospeech.com**.

Graphics

Though Netscape Navigator displays inline GIF and JPEG images just fine, there's more to graphics than those two file formats. Besides other bitmap formats like TIFF and PNG, Navigator is completely ignorant of vector graphics formats like CGM and Corel's CMX. Graphics plug-ins fill that void. The real-time demands of the Net are also pushing graphics compression to the limit, with new high-tech encoders coming out all the time. Some of the very latest compression techniques can be handled via Netscape plug-ins.

FIGleaf Inline

Bitmaps are the canvas of computer graphics. Every image you see on your screen is a bitmap, a collection of colorful lit pixels in a grid. Computers generally store screen images in bitmap format, too. That is, after all, the easiest way; there is a one-to-one relationship between the dots in the picture and the dots on the screen. Netscape can handle GIF and JPEG bitmap images all by itself, but they are not the be-all and end-all of bitmaps. There are dozens—perhaps hundreds—of different bitmap formats available on the Web. To view them, you'll need to install the appropriate Netscape plug-ins.

Carberry Technology's FIGleaf Inline plug-in lets you zoom, pan, and scroll both vector (CGM format) and bitmap graphics, including GIF, JPEG, TIFF, CCITT GP4, BMP, WMF, Sun Raster, PNG, and other graphics file formats. It even handles Encapsulated PostScript (EPS) files, as well as the new proposed standard PGM and PBM file types. It'll even provide improved display of your GIFs and JPEGs.

FIGleaf Inline adds rotation of all images to 0, 90, 180, or 270 degrees, as well as the ability to view multipage files. Scrollbars are available when zoomed in on an image, or when the image is too large to be displayed in the default window.

The version shown in figure 10.4 is for Win95, though Macintosh and Windows 3.1 versions are planned. The self-extracting archive is 1.5MB big including sample files, but in one fell swoop it practically eliminates the need for other Netscape graphics plug-ins or helper applications. If the file size disturbs you, a smaller version called FIGleaf Inline Lite is also available.

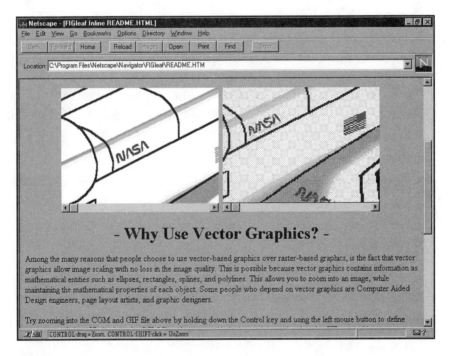

Fig. 10.4
This tight zoom on two graphics being displayed inline by the FIGleaf plug-in demonstrates the superiority of CGM vector graphics (left) versus GIF bitmap graphics (right). Note that, since FIGleaf is now handling the display of Netscape's inline GIFs, they are zoomable as well. This is an excellent example of how plug-ins can even improve Netscape's built-in capabilities.

FIGleaf Inline is available for free evaluation at **http://www.ct.ebt.com/figinline/download.html**. You can buy it for $19.95.

ViewDirector

The ViewDirector Imaging plug-in from TMS displays black-and-white, grayscale and color raster images in TIFF (uncompressed, modified Huffman, G3 1&2D, and G4), CALS Type 1, JPEG, PCX/DCX, BMP, and other image formats. With it, you can zoom, pan, and rotate images embedded in Web pages. ViewDirector even lets you enhance image quality by turning on scale-to-gray and color smoothing functions. A professional version adds the ability to view multipage images, magnify them, and more. Available for Windows 95 and Windows NT, you can download ViewDirector from **http://www.tmsinc.com**.

Autodesk's WHIP!

Most architects, engineers, and designers create their masterworks in AutoCAD, the de facto computer-aided drafting program. Just about every manufactured thing or constructed edifice you encounter started out somewhere as an AutoCAD drawing. With the rise of the corporate intranet, there is increased interest in making these drawings available for viewing in Web browsers. Thanks to a handful of Netscape plug-ins, this is now possible.

Autodesk is the publisher of AutoCAD. Though they were not the first to come out with a Netscape plug-in for viewing 2D AutoCAD drawings on the Web, they are almost certain to end up being the most popular. Their WHIP! plug-in is based on the same rendering technology as the WHIP driver in AutoCAD Release 13. It allows for panning, zooming, and embedding URLs in AutoCAD drawings.

WHIP! uses a new DWF (Drawing Web Format) file type, which will be supported in future versions of AutoCAD. Though WHIP! won't view current DXF AutoCAD files, the new file type is said to be highly compressed and optimized for fast transfer over the Internet. Autodesk is publishing the new DWF file format as an open standard, and other software vendors who use 2D vector data are being encouraged to adopt the DWF file format as well. The DWG file format is the actual editable AutoCAD drawing, so DWF files offer a form of security in that they are not editable by the end user. However, if you want you can bundle the DWG data in a DWF file (for use over a secure corporate intranet, for example) so that the end user can drag and drop the file into a copy of AutoCAD for modification. Though there will be a time lag as existing

AutoCAD files are converted to the new format, with Autodesk pushing it it's bound to become very popular very soon.

The compressed WHIP! Plug-In is less than 1.4 megabytes, so it will fit on a single floppy, and requires Windows NT 3.51 or Windows 95. Also available will be a free WHIP! Development Kit for other software vendors who plan to support the DWF file format. You can download WHIP! from Autodesk's Web site at **http://www.autodesk.com/**.

DWG/DXF Viewer

SoftSource's DWG/DXF plug-in was the first Netscape plug-in to make it possible to view AutoCAD and DXF drawings on the Web (see fig. 10.5). Zoom, pan, and layer visibility controls makes it simple to explore complex CAD drawings online. Its advantage over WHIP! is that it can view standard AutoCAD DXF format display-only or even editable DWG format drawing files, so existing libraries of AutoCAD drawings don't have to be translated before they can be viewed.

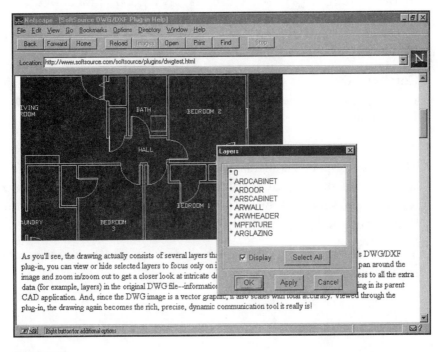

Fig. 10.5
SoftSource's DWG/DXF plug-in makes viewing AutoCAD format drawings an online activity.

Available for Windows 95 and Windows NT, you can download this plug-in from **http://www.softsource.com/softsource/plugins/plugins.html**.

NOTE **European users especially might want to check out NetSlide 95 by Alessandro Oddera, an AutoCAD file plug-in for Win95 available from http://www.archserver.unige.it/caadge/ao/first.htm** in Italy.

Corel CMX

The problem with bitmaps is that they're chunky. Because they're made up of square pixels arranged in a grid, they aren't really scalable. Where a bitmap is an actual map of a picture, vector graphics are more of a description of how to draw a picture. A vector graphic file tells a drawing program how to use lines, curves, fill patterns, rectangles, and other elements to re-create an image. How big to make it is an entirely different question. For this reason, vector graphics can be rescaled to any size and retain their good looks, without losing detail.

There are a plethora of vector graphics formats out there, and with the following plug-ins, Netscape can display a good number of them.

Corel Draw is perhaps the most popular vector graphics creation program for both the PC and the Mac.

Corel's CMX Viewer plug-in for Navigator lets you view Corel CMX vector graphics in Web pages in-line (see fig. 10.6). The CMX viewer is, so far, available only for Win95 and WinNT, though a Mac version is promised.

There are no special controls or considerations with the CMX Viewer—when installed, it simply displays CMX images when they are encountered. It's a kick to see them "draw" in pieces on-screen in real time, rather than coming in like a window shade, as bitmap graphics do.

You can download the Corel CMX viewer from **http://www.corel.com/corelcmx/**.

Fig. 10.6
Corel's CMX vector graphics viewer lets you view smooth Corel format vector graphic images inline in Navigator.

Other vector graphics viewers

SoftSource, the creator of the DWG/DXF AutoCAD plug-in, also has its own vector graphic drawing program. The SVF plug-in for Netscape Navigator lets you view those images on the Web. SVF (Simple Vector Format) uses an officially registered MIME type and features single-download navigational capabilities and scalable vector graphics. You can pan and zoom an SVF image, and hide and display layers. In the way it works, it is unsurprisingly similar to their DWG/DXF plug-in. The SVF plug-in also lets you include HTML hyperlinks (either URLs or textual annotations) in an SVF file. You can download the SVF plug-in, one of Softsource's Vdraft (Virtual Drafter) suite of Internet CAD Tools, for Windows 95 or Win 3.1 from **http://www.softsource.com**.

CGM (Computer Graphics Metafiles) can be created and used by a wide variety of programs; they're an industry standard. The InterCAP InLine plug-in from Intercap Graphics Systems is an online adaptation of their MetaLink RunTime CGM viewer. With it, you can view, zoom, pan, and magnify an image. Animation of intelligent, hyperlinked CGM graphics is also possible. A Windows 95/NT version is available at **http://www.intergraph.com/icap/**.

FutureSplash's CelAnimator is software for creating vector-based drawings and animations for multimedia and Web pages. CelAnimator can be used for creating static or fully-animated cartoons, logos, technical drawings, and interactive buttons. You can export these animations as FutureSplash, animated GIF, Windows AVI, or QuickTime files. You can download a free trial version of CelAnimator for Macintosh or Windows 95/NT from their Web site at **http://www.futurewave.com/**. Since this isn't a plug-in, why should you care? Well, besides the fact that you can use AVI, animated GIF, and QuickTime files with other plug-ins, the FutureSplash plug-in for Netscape (available for Macintosh and Windows 3.1/95/NT) will let you view FutureSplash format animations as well. "Wait," you ask, "what's an animation plug-in doing in this section?" Read those last few lines again, and you'll see that these animations are vector graphics based, which means they're zoomable and scalable. This is a truly unique product. FutureSplash animations can even be displayed as they are downloaded, which allows long animation sequences to begin playing immediately. It even supports antialiasing for the elimination of jagged edges, and scalable outline fonts. Interactive buttons let you get URLs and play animations. The plug-in in small (90-150K uncompressed), and UNIX and a Java versions are planned. All are available from **http://www.futurewave.com/**.

Lightening Strike

On the CD

Graphics are big. Huge, in fact. Graphics files can take up multi-megabytes of hard disk space in no time, and can seemingly take an eternity to load over the Web. JPEG images are better than most, compressing some images dozens of times smaller than they started out. But JPEG has its limitations, and the bandwidth demands of Web browsing have people searching for even better solutions. There are at least three Netscape plug-ins that improve graphics transfer times considerably.

Infinet Op's Lightening Strike plug-in is meant to compete directly with JPEG image compression. Images compressed with Lightening Strike are said to have higher compression ratios, smaller image files, faster transmissions, and improved image quality.

Infinet Op says that JPEG uses a Fourier analysis based method, such as discrete cosine transform (DCT), while they use a form of the wavelet transform. Okay. All I know is that the images look every bit as good as JPEG and come down the line fast. Will they gain a following? Hard to say. But if you are into graphics, you'll definitely want to install Lightening Strike and take a look at some of the sample compressed images on Infinet Op's site. They're awesome.

Macintosh and Windows 3.1/95/NT plug-ins are available from **http:// www.infinop.com/html/extvwr_pick.html**.

FIF Viewer

Iterated Systems' FIF (Fractal Image Format) viewer plug-in for Navigator displays fractally compressed images inline in the Netscape window. FIF images are smaller and load faster than JPEGs, and can be scaled and zoomed on the page. One typical 768x512 image in the Iterated Systems gallery compressed from 1.15MB to only 47KB with remarkable fidelity.

The FIF plug-in is available for Windows 95/NT, Macintosh and Windows 3.1. You can download the FIF Viewer plug-in from **http:// www.iterated.com/cnplugin.htm**.

Summus Wavelet Viewer

Summus' Wavelet Viewer is another plug-in for decompressing images inline which have been compressed using their proprietary wavelet technology.

Versions of this plug-in are currently available for Win95/NT and Windows 3.1. at **ftp://ftp.scsn.net/software/summus/**.

Special graphics formats

Sometimes a "standard" graphics format is just not good enough. When you need a graphic to do something special, you turn to proprietary formats.

On the CD

For example, Freehand. Freehand is the major competitor to Corel Draw as the top-of-the-heap illustration program. If your studio or company uses Freehand, you'll be glad to know that the Shockwave for Freehand plug-in from Macromedia will let you put your Freehand drawings on the Web or on your company intranet. Don't be confused by the name—Macromedia calls *all* of their plug-ins "Shockwave." The first was for Macromedia Director; this one is for Freehand. The Shockwave for Free-hand plug-in lets users view compact 24-bit vector graphics with panning and zooming up to 25,600%. These can contain irregularly shaped hot objects that link to other Web pages. There are actually three modules involved here: the Shockwave for Freehand plug-in for Netscape; the Shockwave Afterburner Xtra module, which is installed into the Freehand drawing program to compress FreeHand images by up to 50% for distri-bution on the Web; and the Shockwave URL Managers, which lets the designer add URL references to hot spots on drawings. Windows 95/NT, Windows 3.1, and Macintosh versions are available at **http:// www.macromedia.com/Tools/Shockwave/Info/index.html**.

Though its end result is a graphic image, the Chemscape Chime plug-in from MDL Information Systems is more of a scientific and chemical engineering tool than a graphics plug-in. Chemscape Chime plug-in lets scientists and engineers display "chemically significant" (that is to say, scientifically accurate) 2D and 3D structures within an HTML page or table. MDL Information Systems supplies of chemical information-management solutions to the pharmaceutical, agrochemical, and chemical industries, so they know what they're about. Windows 95/NT, Windows 3.1, Macintosh, and PowerMac versions can be downloaded from **http:// www.mdli.com/chemscape/chime/download.html**.

Micrografx's QuickSilver is a highly popular business graphics tool, and now their ABC QuickSilver plug-in for Netscape makes QuickSilver files usable over the Web or corporate intranets. You create these vector images with ABC Graphics Suite, which can make drawings move, display mes-sages, or link to URLs. The plug-in uses a 32-bit vector graphics rendering engine for fast display. Available for Windows 95/NT you can download the plug-in from **http://www.micrografx.com/download/qsdl.html**.

Johnson-Grace's ART Press program creates ART image format files, which can be viewed online using their ART press plug-in from **http:// www.jgc.com/aip/artpub.html**. ART compression is already being used in

America Online's TurboWeb browser. Johnson-Grace says ART Press images download and display three times faster than GIF and JPEG images.

Video

Video plug-ins let Netscape Navigator play inline videos in real-time. Video for Windows, MPEG, and QuickTime movies can all be played with the right plug-in.

LiveVideo

Video for Windows is the standard for PC platforms. There are a number of programs and video boards that let you create AVI format animations or digitized scenes. With the following plug-ins, you can deliver them as Web page content in Netscape.

Netscape's official plug-in for AVI video is LiveVideo, which is included with the Netscape 3 distribution. It automatically installs and configures as your Video for Windows player of choice. You click on a movie image to play it and click again to stop. A right mouse click on an image pops up a complete menu of controls including Play, Pause, Rewind, Fast Forward, Frame Back, and Frame Forward.

LiveVideo installs automatically side-by-side with Netscape 3. You don't have to do anything to install, set up, or configure it. Since it's a plug-in, you don't have to do anything to launch it, either. It sits there blithely waiting until you encounter a Web page with an embedded AVI format video, then plugs its video player into the Netscape window, as shown in figure 10.7.

You simply click on the embedded video frame to start playing, click again to pause, then click to resume, etc.

 TIP **You can also use LiveVideo to play stand-alone AVI videos, either from** the Web, your corporate intranet, or your hard drive—just use File, Open File (Ctrl+O) from the Netscape menu and pick a file of type .avi.

To access the LiveVideo player controls, you click the right mouse button on the displayed video frame. You'll get the pop-up menu shown in figure 10.8.

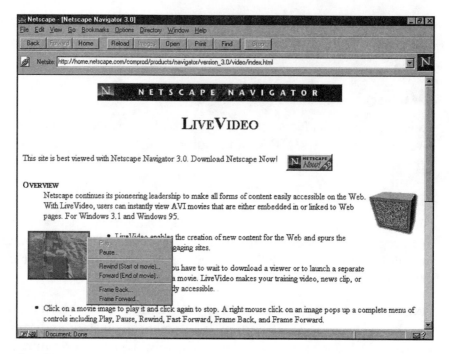

Fig. 10.7
LiveVideo launches invisibly, without any visible controls, and plays AVI videos inline in the Netscape window.

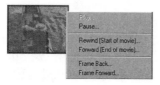

Fig. 10.8
LiveVideo's pop-up control menu gives you a minimal but easily understood set of controls.

There are six basic controls available from the LiveVideo pop-up menu. You can Play, Pause, Rewind to the start of the movie, and Fast Forward to the end.

Like a VCR, once you've played a video through to the end, you have to rewind it before you can play it again.

You can also select Frame Back or Frame Forward to step backwards or forwards through the movie a frame at a time.

LiveVideo is included in the Windows 3.1 and Windows 95 versions of Netscape 3. Both require a system with at least a 386 CPU and a compatible sound card. Win 3.1 also requires the Video for Windows driver. (Video for Windows is automatically installed in Win95.)

VDOLive

The VDOLive Plug-in for Netscape 3 enables inline Video for Windows (.AVI) clips to be included in HTML pages and played back in real-time (see fig. 10.9).

If you are operating over a slow connection, VDOLive will intelligently download a video file, skipping over enough information to retain real-time playback. In cases of severe bandwidth shortage (such as 14.4Kbps PPP connections) you'll get a low frame rate (approximately one frame each 1-3 seconds) but you'll still be able to view videos. In other cases, the VDOLive Player and the VDOLive Server will try to converge at the best possible bandwidth which may sometimes result in blurry display and/or low frame rate. While this can result in jerky playback (especially over a slow modem SLIP or PPP connection), it sure speeds up viewing video over the Web!

Autostart, Stretch, Width, and Height options let HTML designers customize inline Web page video for just about any purpose.

The VDOLive Personal Server is required to deliver motion video from your Web server. The VDOLive Personal Server and Tools 1.0 enable you to deliver up to two streams of video, capture, compress, and serve up to one minute of video and audio, and will scale up to 256Kbps connections.

VDOLive is available for Windows 3.1 and Windows 95/NT from VDONet's site at **http://www.vdolive.com/download/**.

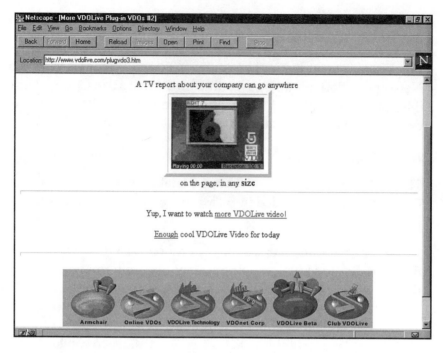

Fig. 10.9
VDOLive displays video files inline, and can deliver reasonable performance over even a very slow Internet connection.

CoolFusion

Iterated Systems' CoolFusion is a plug-in for Navigator which plays inline Video for Windows (.avi) movies. It lets you view videos at any size all the way up to full-screen, and you can stop, replay, and save them using a full set of controls.

The self-extracting archive I looked at (cf_b6_32.exe) is for Windows 95 or Windows NT. It requires only a 256-color graphics card, though a 24-bit or high-color graphics adapter is recommended. You'll also need at least 8MB of RAM.

You can downlaod CoolFusion at **http://webber.iterated.com/coolfusn/ download/cf-set32.htm**.

QuickTime plug-ins

Where Microsoft's standard video format is Video for Windows (AVI files), Apple's video standard is QuickTime. Because a lot of creative types use the Mac, there are a lot of QuickTime movies out there on the Web.

Apple (**http://www.apple.com**) has had a QuickTime movie player plug-in for Netscape in the works for some time. However, there are quite a few third-party plug-ins available that can play QuickTime movies in Netscape.

MovieStar by Intelligence at Large is for QuickTime movie playback. Using their MovieStar Maker, a multimedia editing application also available for download, Webmasters can optimize QuickTime movies so that Navigator users can view them while they download. You can also use autoplay, looping, and many other settings. This one is available for Windows, Windows 95, and Macintosh at **http://www.beingthere.com/**.

Need more choices? There are at least three more QuickTime player plug-ins for Netscape: Iván Cavero Belaúnde's ViewMovie for Win95 and Macintosh at **http://www.well.com/~ivanski/**; TEC Solutions' TEC Player, also for Win95 and Mac, at **http://www.tecs.com/TECPlayer_docs**; and Kevin McMurtrie's Mac-only Multimedia Plug-in at **ftp://ftp.wco.com/users/mcmurtri/MySoftware/**.

MPEG plug-ins

MPEG is the bright and shining star of multimedia right now. The MPEG2 movie compression standard is destined to give us full-screen, full-motion movies on a highly compressed CD-ROM, among other things. Because of its high compression ratios, it's also a good choice for delivery of movies over the Internet.

Of course, it works best with a video board capable of doing hardware decompression. But even running in software on fast Pentium systems, MPEG shows promise.

There are at least four Netscape plug-ins available for playing inline MPEG videos.

Open2U's Action MPEG player plug-in can also play included synchonized soundtracks, or sound-only files that have been compressed using MPEG. Action doesn't require special hardware or even a special Web server. Available for Windows 95/NT, you can download it for trial at **http://www.open2u.com/action/action.html**.

InterVU's PreVU plug-in also plays streaming MPEG video without specialized MPEG hardware or a proprietary video server. It gives you a first-frame view inline, streaming viewing while downloading, and full-speed cached playback off your hard drive. PreVU requires a 486 or Pentium processor and Windows 95/NT; a Mac version is also available. PreVU can be downloaded from **http://www.intervu.com/download.html**.

Xing (**http://www.xingtech.com**), well-known for its MPEG applications, will be providing a Navigator plug-in to support live streaming MPEG and LBR (low bitrate) audio and full-motion MPEG video from Xing StreamWorks Web servers. Check out their Web site for availability information.

Sizzler

Pictures that move—that wonderful concept has brought millions of children (and adults who hold onto their childlike wonder) untold hours of entertainment and enjoyment. When computers got powerful enough, animation made the move to the computer. With powerful animation player plug-ins for Netscape, it's making the transition to the World Wide Web, and even to corporate intranets.

Totally Hip Software's Sizzler plug-in and companion converter program let you create and display Web animation. The Sizzler converter (currently available only in a version for the Macintosh) takes PICS files or QuickTime movies and converts them into sprite files that can be played in real-time in Navigator.

However, Totally Hip's core technology (called Object Scenario) allows for streamed delivery of several media types including text, animation, video, sound, and interactivity. They plan to add all of these to Sizzler in the near future.

The Sizzler plug-in is available as a free download for Windows 95/NT, Windows 3.1, and the Macintosh from **http://www.totallyhip.com/tools/ Win/2f_tools.html**.

Emblaze

GEO Interactive Media Group's Emblaze plug-in is a real-time animation player. It plays a proprietary animation format that GEO says needs only 3MB to 4MB of disk space for approximately 30 minutes of play time. The animations can be displayed at a rate of 12 to 24 frames per second in 256 colors in real time over a 14.4Kbps connection. Animations must be created using the commercial Emblaze Creator program.

Windows 3.1, Macintosh, PowerMac, and Win95 versions can be found at **http://www.Geo.Inter.net/technology/emblaze/index.html**.

Other animation plug-ins

Here are a few more Animation plug-ins for Netscape:

Deltapoint's Web Animator, for the Macintosh only (a Windows version is promised), combines animation, sound, and live interaction. The authoring tool for creating animations to add to your own site is also available from their Web site at **http://www.deltapoint.com/animate/ index.htm**.

Heads Off's Play3D plug-in supports real-time interactive 3D, 2D sprites, and WAVE and MIDI sound playback. Objects can be linked to URLs, media files, or Play3D "scene" files. The free demo version allows for authoring and playback without leaving Netscape. For Win95 only, Play3D is downloadable from **http://www.headsoff.com**.

Shockwave for Macromedia Director

"Multimedia" is a good buzzword, but what does it really mean? Literally "more than one medium," when most people use the term they mean a presentation that includes some combination of sound, graphics, anima-tion, video, and even interactivity. Interactivity is an important part of multimedia. It's the part that puts the flow of the whole thing under the user's control. Though this can be as simple as an on-screen button that you have to click on to move to the next slide, more often it involves making selections from multiple choices.

Multimedia is the hottest topic on the Web right now, so it's not surprising that there are a dozen or more multimedia player plug-ins already available for Netscape.

Perhaps one of the most significant and awe-inspiring plug-ins supported directly by Netscape 3 is Macromedia Shockwave for Director, which allows you to view Director "movies" directly on a Web page (see fig. 10.10). Director movies are created with Macromedia's Director (don't confuse Director "movies" with other file types of the same name, such as QuickTime movies), a cross-platform multimedia authoring program that gives multimedia developers the ability to create fully interactive multimedia applications, or "titles." Because of its interactive integration of animation, bitmap, video, and sound media, and its playback compatibility with a variety of computer platforms including Windows, Mac OS, OS/2, and SGI, Director is now the most widely used professional multimedia authoring tool.

Using Shockwave for Director, a Director movie run over the Internet can support the same sort of features as a Director movie run off a CD-ROM, including animated sequences, sophisticated scripting of interactivity, user input of text right into the Director window (or "stage"), sound playback, and much more. Developers can even include hot links through URLs.

Shockwave for Director consists of two main components, the Shockwave plug-in itself, and Shockwave Afterburner, a compressor program that squeezes a Director file by 40-50% for faster access over the Net. You can download it from Macromedia at **Shockwave http://www-1.macromedia.com/Tools/Shockwave/Plugin/plugin.cgi**.

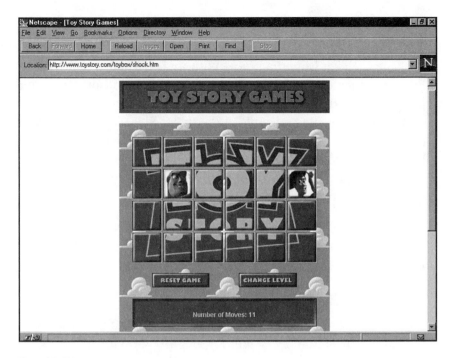

Fig. 10.10
The Shockwave for Director plug-in for Netscape 3 plays interactive multimedia Director files inline in the Netscape window. These can range from simple animations to complex interactive games, like this "concentration" game from the Toy Story Web site.

Shockwave for Authorware

Another in the series of "Shockwave" plug-ins from Macromedia, their Shockwave for Authorware plug-in lets users interact with Authorware interactive multimedia "courses" and "pieces" right in the Netscape Navigator window. Animation, clickable buttons, links to other Web pages, hybrid layout and delivery, streaming PICS movies and sound, and more can be integrated within a piece to deliver an interactive multimedia experience.

Intended for the delivery of large, content-rich multimedia presentations, such as courseware and training materials, Authorware can also write viewer data back to a Web server using FTP, so it's useful for creating market surveys, tests and quizzes, and customer service applications.

Like all Shockwave plug-ins, this one includes an "Afterburner" module for compressing files for delivery on the Web. Authorware developers package their multimedia pieces without the usually-included Runtime Projector, then drag and drop this file onto the Authorware Afterburner program. Afterburner compresses the Authorware file by 50-70% and creates one map file and multiple segment files. Developers can optimize the number and size of segment files to the bandwidth of the network. Developers also are able to create a single map file referencing both Macintosh and Windows segment files for display in the same Web page, making this transparent to the viewer.

Windows 95/NT, Windows 3.1, and Macintosh versions of Shockwave for Authorware can be downloaded from the Macromedia Web site at **http://www.macromedia.com/Tools/Shockwave/Info/index.html**.

ASAP WebShow

Software Publishing Corporation's ASAP WebShow is Netscape Navigator Plug-in presentation viewer for viewing, downloading, and printing presentations created with ASAP WordPower. Similar to PowerPoint presentations, WordPower presentations can contain tables, organization charts, bullet lists, and other graphic and text elements, in a slide show format. Since the files are compressed, they can be transmitted very quickly over the Net.

Presentations and reports can be embedded as icons, as live thumbnails, or in a window on a Web page. Each slide can be viewed in a small live area window, enlarged to fill the current Web page, or zoomed to full screen. You can select one slide at a time or watch a continuously running show.

A Win95/NT version is available, with Window 3.1 promised. You can download a fully functional copy of ASAP 1.0 or ASAP WordPower 1.95, for a free 30-day trial for creating your own WebShow-compatible presentations. It's available at **http://www.spco.com/asap/asapwebs.htm**.

Astound Web Player

Gold Disk's Astound Web Player displays multimedia "greeting cards" and other interactive documents created with Gold Disk's Astound or Studio M programs. These presentations can include sound, animation, graphics, video, and even interactive elements.

I took a look at Version 1 of the Astound Web Player for Win95 and Navigator 2. Versions are also available for Windows 3.1 and for Navigator 1.1. You can even get a stand-alone version for use with browsers other than Netscape.

You can choose to download a "slim" version of the player without chart, texture, and animation libraries if you already own Studio M or Astound. If you plan on including movies in your presentations, you'll need QuickTime for Windows, which is also available from the Gold Disk site.

The Astound Web Player lets you actively view one multimedia slide while it downloads the next one in the background. But the main appeal of Studio M and Astound is that they let nonprogrammers create multimedia presentations by using predesigned templates that integrate animations, graphics, sound, and interactive elements. If you've thought that multimedia might be too difficult to integrate into your site, you might want to check the specs for Studio M and Astound on Gold Disk's site at **http://www.golddisk.com/awp/index.html**.

Other multimedia plug-ins

Though the previous four are arguably the "hottest" multimedia plug-ins for Netscape, here are a few more to keep you busy:

The mBED plug-in for Netscape plays multimedia "mbedlets." The MBD file format and the built-in mBED players are open and license-free. Available for Windows 95/NT, Windows 3.1, Macintosh, and PowerMac, you can find out more and download these plug-ins from **http://www.mbed.com**.

Rad Technologies (**http://www.rad.com**) has a plug-in to play back multimedia applications built in RAD PowerMedia. Designed for corporate communicators and Web designers, PowerMedia provides authoring and viewing of interactive content, presentations, training, kiosks, and demos. It's available for Windows 95/NT.

Asymetrix's ToolBook is one of the top multimedia authoring tools. Now, with their new Neuron plug-in for Netscape, you can deliver ToolBook multimedia titles over the Net. The Neuron plug-in supports external multimedia files, so you can access either complete courseware or multimedia titles, or just the relevant portions of titles in real time. Content that is not requested is not downloaded, saving you download time and making the application more responsive. Jump to **http://www.asymetrix.com/** for more info and the download files.

The mFactory Netscape plug-in promises streamed playback of and communication between fully interactive multimedia "worlds" embedded in Web pages. Here are the supported file formats: Video: QuickTime, QTVR, and Video for Windows (AVI); Graphic: PICT; Text: Dynamic and editable text; Audio/sound: AIFF, snd, and MIDI; Animation: PICT, PICS, QuickTime. Their cel-based proprietary mToon animation format enables ranges of cels to be defined and played. Check out **http://www.mfactory.com/** for info and download availability.

7TH LEVEL has Top Gun in the works, an authoring and playback engine for both Windows and Macintosh. You can read all about it at **http://www.7thlevel.com**.

Powersoft's media.splash plug-in for Windows 3.1 and Win95 resides at **http://www.powersoft.com/media.splash/product/index.html**.

The SCREAM inline multimedia player is for Windows 3.1, Win95, and Mac, at **http://www.savedbytech.com/sbt/Plug_In.html**.

Kaleida will have a multimedia player plug-in for Navigator, too. Kaleida Labs is the developer of ScriptX, an object-oriented programming language for multimedia, and currently offers a free platform-independent Kaleida Media Player (KMP) for playback of ScriptX applications which can be configured as a helper application. To find out when you can get their plug-in, check out **http://www.kaleida.com**.

VRML

VRML (Virtual Reality Modeling Language) promises to deliver real-time virtual 3D worlds via the Web. Though it's arguable whether this has actually been accomplished yet, its promise looms great. And VRML plug-ins bring 3D worlds right into the Navigator window.

Live3D

Moving Worlds is a newly proposed extension to the VRML (Virtual Reality Modeling Language) specification which has been developed by Silicon Graphics and Sony. Netscape and many other online developers, including heavy-hitters like Adobe and IBM, are hoping it will become the VRML 2 standard.

Moving Worlds goes beyond the current VRML standard to include Java and JavaScript integration and support for third party plug-ins which would allow developers to incorporate live content such as video and RealAudio into 3D VRML worlds. A key new element is the ability to link to databases.

Moving Worlds allows 3D data sets to be scaleable for viewing on a variety of computer systems ranging from low-cost Internet PCs to powerful 3D graphics workstations. Integrated Java applets can be used to create motion and enable interactivity.

Advocates say that the Moving Worlds version of VRML will finally allow the development of real "cyberspace" applications, such as 3D shopping malls, collaborative 3D design, 3D visual database and spreadsheet display, 3D interactive real-time online games, and photorealistic geographic landscapes.

Silicon Graphics will make the source code for Moving Worlds application development available to all developers.

Netscape's own Live3D Navigator plug-in is a VRML viewer that implements the proposed Moving Worlds VRML extensions. It's feature-packed, it's fun, and—most of all—it's Netscape's official VRML browser. It comes bundled with Navigator 3 and is automatically installed when you install NS3.0.

That VRML is becoming an important part of the Web is clearly demonstrated by the fact that Netscape is bundling a VRML 3D world viewer plug-in with Navigator 3. Live3D is an enhanced adaptation of Paper Software's WebFX plug-in (see fig. 10.11).

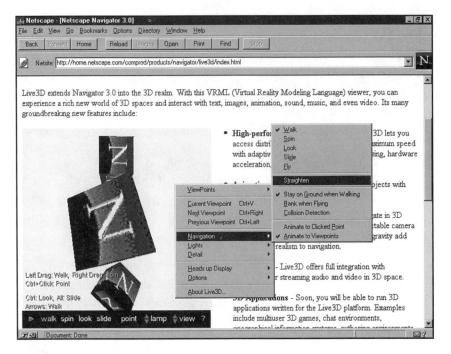

Fig. 10.11
Live3D is Netscape's "official" 3D VRML world browser, and sports a number of nifty features.

Live3D supports GZIP data compression, text, images, animation, sound, music, and video additions to 3D VRML worlds. Live3D even integrates with LiveMedia for streaming audio and video in 3D space.

Netscape promises support in future releases for special 3D applications written for the Live3D platform. Examples include multiuser 3D games, chat environments, geographical information systems, authoring environments, interactive advertisements, online presentations, and database visualizations.

The toolbar along the bottom of a Live3D window gives you control over your movement in the displayed 3D world. Clicking on the arrow at the left pauses any animated movement. Click on Walk, Spin, Look, Slide, or Point to activate movement paradigms with a vastly different "look and feel." Each selection will be highlighted when you click on it; click and move the mouse in the display to move after selecting a mode.

Clicking the up and down arrows by the Lamp selection changes the brightness of the illumination of the scene. Clicking the arrows by the View item changes your point of view.

Right-clicking the mouse button anywhere in the scene brings up the pop-up menu shown in figure 10.12.

Fig. 10.12
This pop-up menu gives you a full complement of 3D movement and scene adjustment controls.

The Viewpoints selection brings up a submenu which lets you pick other points of view, if available. The next three menu items let you pick the Current (Ctrl+V), Next (Ctrl+Right), or Previous (Ctrl+Left) viewpoint.

The Navigation, Lights, and Detail menu items each bring up submenus with a variety of controls for modifying the way you move, the scene lighting, and the level of detail you see. The best way to find out what these selections do is to play with them. VRML worlds are very dynamic environments, and half the fun is changing things and seeing what happens!

The Heads up Display menu selection lets you turn on or off various portions of the heads up display feature of Live3D—the text in the lower left corner of figure 10.11 that tells you how the controls work. These guides are helpful for starters, but as you get more experienced you may want to turn them off.

You can even turn off the toolbar using the Options menu. This menu also sets Motion Blur, Fast Rendering, and other display options, and it's where you can Save the current setting as the default for future use.

Live3D is available with Netscape Navigator 3 for Windows 3.1, Windows 95, Windows NT, and Power Macintosh, and versions for 68K Macintosh and UNIX were under development as this was being written.

VR Scout

On the CD

Chaco Communications' VR Scout VRML plug-in displays VRML worlds inline. Chaco's viewer implements the full VRML 1 standard.

I've found that with VRML viewers, as with Web browsers, the one you like is most often a matter of personal preference, not features. But VR Scout uses Microsoft Reality Lab for fast software rendering and hardware acceleration, and that can't hurt. It's multithreading so different aspects of a scene are simultaneously downloaded. Toys include a headlight with a brightness control, and Walk/Fly/Examiner viewing modes with a heads-up toolbar. It also supports textures (GIF, JPEG, BMP, and SFImage).

The VR Scout 1.22 plug-in is for Win95/NT, and is 2.96MB big. Windows 3.1 users can download a stand-alone viewer to use as a Netscape helper application. Download it from **http://www.chaco.com/vrscout/plugin.html**.

WIRL

WIRL, VReam'S Win95 VRML plug-in for Navigator supports object behaviors (motion, rotation, gravity, weight, elasticity, throwability, and sound), logical cause and effect relationships, multimedia capabilities, and links to Windows applications.

Its "Full Object Interactivity" lets you pick up objects, and throw them around in 3D space. This goes way beyond mere passive VRML viewing. Of course, a VRML world has to include the code to enable all these behaviors—you won't get to handle things in a "normal" VRML world. In a nutshell, WRIL supports VRML worlds with VREAMScript interactive extensions. It uses Microsoft's Reality Lab for Super-Fast Performance— 100,000 polygons/sec on a 90Mhz Pentium. If you're into computer graphics and programming, you might be impressed to know that WIRL uses real-time Gouraud and Phong Shading, real-time Z-buffering, real-time perspective corrected texture wrapping, and multiple light sources and lighting models. You get full DDE, OLE, and MCI support under

Windows 3.1. The promise support for multiple interface devices (mouse, head-mounted displays, gloves, etc.) for an ultra-realistic VR experience.

WIRL is currently available only for Win95 from **http://www.vream.com/3dl1.html**.

Other VRML browser plug-ins

There are more VRML plug-ins than any other type and, frankly, most of them are pretty much "me too." Still, some offer a few special features, and since VRML browsers (like Web browsers) are pretty much a personal preference thing, here's a list of some others you might want to check out:

SuperScape's Viscape lets you grab objects, do walkthroughs, and hear sounds in VRML worlds. It's available for Windows 95/NT at **http://www.superscape.com**.

Integrated Data Systems' VRealm VRML plug-in also adds some features to VRML worlds, like object behaviors, gravity, collision detection, autopilot, and multimedia support. For Windows 95/NT, it can be downloaded from **http://www.ids-net.com/ids/downldpi.html**.

Topper supports the VRML VRBL extensions, for dynamic 3D interactive worlds with keyframe animations and proximity triggers. Topper also supports 3DS and DXF file formats. Windows 95/NT users can download it from **http://www.ktx.com/products/hyperwire/download.htm**.

Template Graphics Software's WebSpace/VRML plug-in is adapted from Silicon Graphics' VRML browser. WebSpace supports the complete Open Inventor 2.x feature set plus the VRML 1 subset. For Windows machines, you can download WebSpace from **http://www.sd.tgs.com/~template**.

Liquid Reality for Win95, Win 3.1, and Mac is located at **http://www.dimensionx.com/products/lr/index.html**.

Cybergate for Win95 supports multi-user interaction, chat, and "Avatars" in VRML worlds delivered by servers equipped with their Cyberhub server. It can be found at **http://www2.blacksun.com/beta/c-gate/download.html**.

Paragraph 3D for Win95 allows users to view ParaGraph Virtual Home Space Builder Files, which are VRML worlds that can include animations, sounds and behaviors. Find it at **http://russia.paragraph.com/vr/d96html/download.htm**.

Virtus Voyager, at **http://www.virtus.com/voyager.html**, is currently a stand-alone VRML viewer, but a plug-in is promised for Netscape.

Finally, Terraform Free is a VRML browser plug-in for Internet Explorer. (However, we understand that many plug-ins are interchangeable between the two programs.) For more information, check out the Brilliance Labs home page at **http://www.brlabs.com/files/terraform.zip**.

Productivity plug-ins

"Productivity" is a nebulous category which includes real-world tools like word processors and spreadsheets, development systems that let you create your own integrated controls and programs, and miscellaneous tools like clocks and calculators. Most of these are already available as Netscape plug-ins, and I'm sure the rest will come along in time.

Acrobat Amber Reader

If you're like most Web users, you've got a lot of files sitting around that you'd like to put up on the Web. Problem is, they're in a wide variety of formats, and the prospect of translating that much content into HTML files is intimidating, if not impossible.

Never fear. There are a wide variety of document viewer plug-ins becoming available for Netscape. No matter if your information is in the form of Word documents, Excel worksheets, Adobe Acrobat portable documents, or what-have-you, the odds are good that there is—or soon will be—a Netscape plug-in that can display it.

On the CD

Adobe's "Amber" version of the Acrobat Reader lets you view and print Acrobat Portable Document Format (PDF) files. What are "PDF" files? In a nutshell, they are viewable documents that have the visual integrity of a desktop-published document that has been printed on paper. PDF viewers are available for UNIX, Macintosh, and Windows platforms, and each displays PDF documents identically. If the integrity of your documents is important to you (as it is, say, to the IRS, which uses Acrobat to distribute accurate tax forms over the Web), then PDF files are for you.

Amber differs from the stand-alone version of the Acrobat reader in that it will, under the right conditions, display PDF pages in real-time, without waiting for the entire file to download. This requires that the server sending the document be able to "byteserve" the PDF files a page at a time to the Amber reader plug-in. The PDF files themselves must also be "optimized" for progressive display and maximum file compression.

Barring all this, Amber will also happily wait for a non-optimized, non-byteserved standard Acrobat file, and display it as a piece when it's done downloading.

Progressively displayed PDF files let you see the text first, then the images, then embedded fonts—it's similar to the way Web pages appear in "pieces." Fonts are displayed in a substituted format first, then the proper outline font is blitted over the substitute for final display. The final text is antialiased for a crisper on-screen appearance.

The Amber plug-in itself has a plug-in called Weblink, which, when added in, allows PDF files to include hyperlinks to URLs. In other words, it lets you create Acrobat files that act, in many ways, like HTML Web pages.

When the Amber plug-in is activated, it creates a dockable Toolbar in the Netscape window with controls for zooming, printing, and navigating the Acrobat document (see fig. 10.13).

The Amber plug-in is available for Windows 95. Macintosh, and Windows 3.1, with a UNIX version in the wings. It can be downloaded from the Adobe Web site at **http://www.adobe.com/Amber/Download.html**.

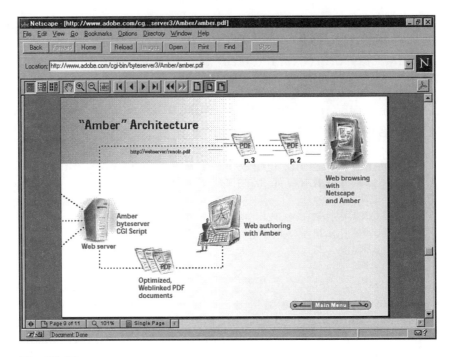

Fig. 10.13
The Adobe Acrobat Amber PDF reader plug-in in action in Netscape Navigator 2. It brings up a full set of Acrobat navigational and viewing controls.

Envoy

With Tumbleweed Software's Envoy plug-in, you can view Envoy portable documents in Navigator inline. Envoy documents, like Acrobat PDF files, maintain their look and feel no matter where or how they are displayed, and an Envoy document is generally much smaller than the original document.

So what can the Envoy plug-in do? Live Hypertext links allow you to jump to other URLs. Zoom features let you fit your document to the width or height of the browser, and move in and out of the document from 3–2000% magnification. You can scroll or pan the display, and jump to different areas of the document using buttons or the scrollbar. Envoy even lets you search for text strings within a document. You can use any application to create your document; you publish it in Envoy format using a custom printer driver that translates the content into an Envoy format file.

You can download the Envoy plug-in from **http://www.twcorp.com/ plugin.htm**.

Formula One/NET

Visual Components' Formula One/NET is an Excel-compatible spreadsheet plug-in for Navigator. It allows you to display fully functional worksheets which can include live charts, links to URLs, formatted text and numbers, calculations, and clickable buttons and controls (see fig. 10.14). It's absolutely amazing—I am blown away that they can place the functionality of a full spreadsheet program inline in Navigator! This thing has all the fancy formulas, all the formatting options, and even all the charts and graphs you need to do everything from simple forms to the quarterly taxes for General Motors.

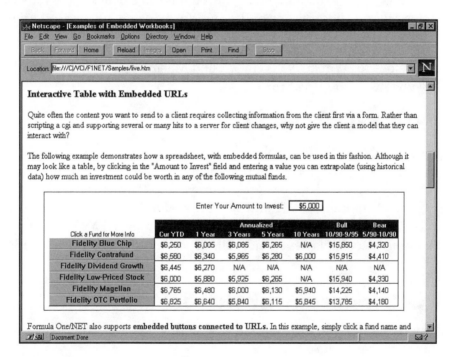

Fig. 10.14
This embedded spreadsheet displayed by the Formula One/NET plug-in looks and acts just like an Excel spreadsheet. Unlike a form, data doesn't have to be transmitted back and forth to a server if you make changes and want to update your calculations.

Formula One/NET is the plug-in for viewing spreadsheets, and Formula One/Net Pro adds a pop-up inline designer for creating them. The pro package also comes with a stand-alone version of the program that adds the ability to read, write, and work with Excel workbook files all for $39. A professional version of the whole works with OLE controls is available for $249.

Formula One/NET is available for Windows 3.1, Windows 95, or Windows NT. It can be downloaded from **http://www.visualcomp.com/f1net/ download.htm**.

Word Viewer

Inso's Word Viewer plug-in displays Microsoft Word 6.0 or 7.0 documents in Netscape Navigator 2 inline. Based on Inso's Quick View Plus viewer, this plug-in lets you copy and print Word documents with all original formatting intact.

Versions for Win95/NT, Win 3.1, and Macintosh can be found at **http:// www.inso.com/plug.htm**.

KEYview (Win95)

The KEYview Netscape plug-in from FTP Software lets you view, print, and convert nearly 200 different file formats. That's right: 200 formats. Name one, and I'll almost guarantee you, as they say on TV, "It's in there." Windows 95/NT and Win 3.1 evaluation versions can be downloaded from **http://www.ftp.com**. The upcoming KEYviews version 5 promises to display even more file types, including popular multimedia formats.

Other document viewers

Here's a roundup of some of the other document viewers available as Netscape plug-ins:

PointPlus displays Microsoft PowerPoint presentations within the Netscape browser window. You can view slide-by-slide manually, or presentations can be displayed hands-free on auto-play. For more information, check out the PointPlus Home Page. **http://www.net-scene.com**.

Not to be outdone by a third party, Microsoft has their own PowerPoint Plug-in for Windows 95 at **http://www.microsoft.com/mspowerpoint/ internet/player/default.htm**. This special viewer is for compressed PowerPoint files which can include audio. They have also made the publisher for these files available, so if you have PowerPoint 95 you can save slides in this new format. Even though this plug-in is from Microsoft and intended for Internet Explorer, it seems to work great with Netscape!

Texture Viewer plays interactive files created with the Texture program. For Win95, this one's at **http://www.futuretense.com/viewdown.htm**.

Techexplorer is an exciting new Netscape plug-in from, of all places, IBM. Techexplorer processes and displays a large subset of TeX/LaTeX, the professional markup language used for typesetting and publishing in education, mathematics, and many of the sciences. Tuned for on-screen readability, Techexplorer provides many options for formatting and customization. Because it formats on the fly, Techexplorer source documents are small, often just one-fourth the size of documents in Acrobat format. Techexplorer can help authors and publishers rapidly and if you publish in TeX, this plug-in will let you put your files right on the Web. It's available at **http://www.ics.raleigh.ibm.com/ics/techexp.htm**.

Navigational aids

The Web is huge, and it's easy to get lost. What was that site you visited early this morning that was so funny? Where did you find that information on the new model Ford cars? You read a great inside scoop on your competitor's new product, but where?

What you need is a plug-in that will help you track, organize, and recall the sites you've visited. And the more automatic it is, the better. Brother, are you gonna *love* the following plug-ins!

ISYS HindSite by ISYS/Odyssey Development remembers everywhere you've been and everything you've seen. You can perform full-text plain English searches on the contents of all the Web pages you've visited. For example, to find previously accessed Web documents relating to bananas, type in "Where did I see bananas?" HindSite indexes and saves the text content of all Web pages visited in a timeframe you set—a week, a month, or six months, for example. Menu-assisted query lets you quickly build accurate queries with push button operators. ISYS HindSite can also display a structured tree outline of every previously accessed URL. It's available for Windows 95/NT and Windows 3.1 from **http://www.isysdev.com**.

Iconovex (**http://www.iconovex.com**) will be releasing an AnchorPage Client plug-in, which will automatically index and abstract all HTML documents read by Navigator. AnchorPage is built from ICONOVEX's Syntactica engine that incorporates the semantic and syntactic rules of the English language to analyze HTML documents. AnchorPage then extracts the significant phrases and concepts and automatically creates the HTML links from those phrases and concepts to their occurrences within the source document. Finally, AnchorPage generates four Content-Driven Navigation views of the documents (Table of Contents, Abstract, Phrase, and Concept views). Check their Web site for availability.

HistoryTree for Windows and Win95 records your web explorations in a tree, not just a list. It can be found at **http://www.smartbrowser.com/**.

DocuMagix's HotPage, captures, organizes, and manages World Wide Web and Intranet information and content. With DocuMagix HotPage, you can view saved Web pages off-line, link back to the original sites without needing to remember the exact URL, organize Web pages, and merge them with other Windows documents. You can search for a particular Web page that contains references to a particular topic, forward a Web page document by fax or e-mail inside your company, mark annotations on a Web document, or even add URL links to any Windows documents. Available for Windows or Windows 95, you can get it at **http://www.documagix.com/**.

Remote PC access

Lots of companies use Carbon Copy, Timbuktu, or other remote access programs to let their field service personnel log into remote computers for troubleshooting or control. These programs require a modem on each end and dialup access. Now, there are Netscape plug-in versions of both programs that work with any computers connected to the Internet. No more long distance dialup charges, no more dedicated modem lines, no more dialing hassles. I know guys would be willing to kill to get these programs because they'll make their lives that much easier. Fortunately, you don't have to kill anyone to get them. You can download them right off the Web.

Carbon Copy/Net is Microcom's plug-in version of its extremely popular Carbon Copy remote access program. In brief, it lets you remotely control another PC over the Internet. You can run applications, access files, and view or edit documents on a remote PC as though they were on the PC in front of you. Your screen looks like their screen; what you type goes to their computer. Carbon Copy/Net is an ideal tool for remote access to Windows applications, collaboration, remote software demonstrations, remote support, and remote file transfer access to CD-ROMs and other data. The only requirement is that both machines must be running a copy of Carbon Copy/Net, and (for security reasons, of course) the machine being accessed must be set up to allow remote access. It is currently available for Windows 95 and Windows 3.1 at **http://www.microcom.com/ cc/ccdnload.htm**.

On the CD

Not to be outdone, Farallon has released a plug-in based on its equally useful Timbuktu Pro remote access package. It's called Look@Me (cute name!). Look@Me gives you the ability to view another Look@Me user's screen anywhere in the world in real time. From within Navigator, you can view a remote computer screen and watch the activity taking place. You can edit documents, go over presentations, review graphics, or provide just-in-time training and support via Netscape Navigator and the World Wide Web. Look@Me is also available as a stand-alone application for use outside a browser in Win95, Win 3.1, or on a Macintosh. The plug-in is available for Windows 95 only at **http://collaborate.farallon.com/ www/look/download.html**.

Miscellaneous tools

There's no end to things that can be implemented as Netscape plug-ins. I'm sure we'll see quite a few that make us wonder just what their creators had in mind. But until then, here are a few of the miscellaneous plug-ins available for Netscape 3.

POWER PACK

Starfish Software's *EarthTime* plug-in is a world clock that displays the local time and date in eight cities of your choice. It features a dynamic world map that shows the day and night regions, and it automatically adjusts for daylight savings time. EarthTime also includes a conversion calculator that translates distances, weights, volumes, power, and other measurements between U.S. and metric measurement systems.

You invoke EarthTime from Navigator by selecting File, Open File (Ctrl+0) from the menu, selecting the new filetype "EARTHTIME, .ETC," and loading file:///C|/Program Files/Netscape/Navigator/Program/ PLUGINS/EarthTime/Earthtim.etc. This brings up the World Map shown in figure 10.15. While I might have preferred something a little more intuitive (like a button on the toolbar), this does keep the world clock just a few keystrokes away. The best thing to do is to set it up once, then bookmark it. Then all you need to do is select EarthTime from the Bookmark menu and it comes up quickly and easily.

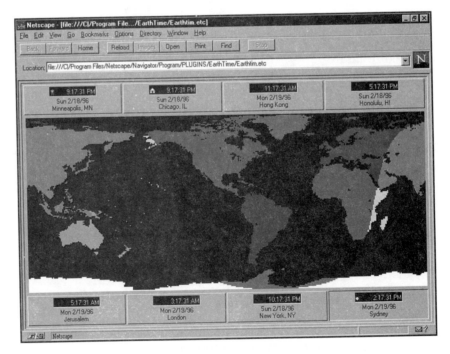

Fig. 10.15
EarthTime is a cool world time clock plug-in for Navigator 2 from Starfish Software.

For the Win95/NT version of Netscape 3 only, EarthTime is a self-installing file. It's handy for determining just what time of day it is in that far-off place you're browsing through. You can get it at **http:// www.starfishsoftware.com/getearth.html**.

The *PointCast Network* is a free online service that broadcasts up-to-the-minute news and other information via the Internet. Their PointCast Network plug-in lets this content be delivered inline in Netscape. This service provides headline news stories, sports, financial news (including stock indices), and lifestyle stories, as well as weather forecasts for 250 cities and business news covering both individual companies and entire industries. The PointCast Network also includes Time-Warner's Pathfinder channel, which presents daily news from Time, People, and Money magazines. If you live in New England you can also see stories from the Boston Globe newspaper, and those in Southern California have access to the Los Angeles Times. The PointCast Network supports live URL links in all news stories, so you can jump right to relevant Web sites. Available for Windows 95 and Windows 3.1, with a Mac version under development, you can download the PointCast Network plug-in from **http://www.pointcast.com**.

The *Argus Map Viewer* displays vector-based maps composed of multiple layers of information. These are dynamic, interactive, vector-based scalable maps which change based on your inquiries. With ARGUS Map Viewer, you can zoom in on items of interest and the map in front of you is automatically redrawn to display new and more detailed information matching the scale of view. Each item on the map is a dynamic object which is selectable. Information on selected objects can be viewed in reports. URL links attached to map objects can be activated taking you directly to other maps, documents, images, and web sites. If you go to **http://www.argusmap.com/mbr_main.htm**, you'll find versions for Win 3.1 and Win95.

Globalink provides translation services and software, and now they've added a set of Netscape plug-ins that are truly impressive. These perform bi-directional translation that convert between English and French, Italian, German, or Spanish. Yes, that means you can jump into a site written in German and see it translated into English on your screen. This is a tremendous step in making the World Wide Web truly world wide. When you encounter a foreign site, just clicking a button will get you a translated page. Translated pages maintain all graphics, hotlinks and formatting. These translations can be created online, while surfing, or alternatively, pages can be downloaded and saved to be translated and viewed off-line. The dictionaries for Web Translator have been specially prepared for use on the Web and include Internet terminology which enhances the accuracy of the translation. Globalink comes on a single CD-ROM which includes both domestic and localized versions. Though not available as a downloadable demo, the price is right at $49.95. You can get further information from Globalink's Web site at **http://www.globalink.com**. (Now, Globalink, how about Japanese?)

The *JetForm Filler* plug-in lets users fill out online forms designed with JetForm Design. Windows, Win95, and Macintosh versions are planned. Check out **http://www.jetform.com/** for more information on this product.

On the CD

It's interesting to note that Netscape Corporation's official IRC (Internet Relay Chat) solution isn't a plug-in, but a helper application. Though their Netscape Chat application auto-configures, it's a separate program. If you want to do your IRC chatting inline in the Netscape window, you need the *ICHAT IRC* Plug-in for Windows from **http://www.ichat.com/**. With ICHAT installed, Web pages can become chat rooms. When you visit a chat-enabled Web page, the plug-in opens a frame in the lower part of the browser window. Within that frame, ICHAT displays a real-time, on-going chat session among all the visitors to that page. Users can enter the conversation and communicate with each other simply by typing. This is a hot product, and I think we can expect to see Netscape trying to play "catch up" soon.

Groupware applications

Groupware is software that allows people in groups (usually on corporate intranets) to exchange information and to collaborate on projects. It's one of the hottest areas of software development right now. There are already a couple of Netscape plug-ins that can be classified as legitimate, powerful groupware applications.

Lotus Notes is the best-established groupware solution for corporations. Brainstorm Technology's *Groupscape* is a visual, object-oriented development tool for building and extending Lotus Notes workgroup applications to the Web. This lets organizations standardize on Netscape clients as the integrated front-end to the World Wide Web and their existing Lotus Notes infrastructure. Groupscape provides corporate users with the ease-of-use of Netscape clients combined with the security and replication strengths of Lotus Notes.

As a demo of what Groupscape can do, Brainstorm has released the free Groupscape Notes Browser, an interactive Netscape/Groupscape application which lets corporate users view, browse, and surf internal Lotus Notes networks. This plug-in provides a sample of the types of applications that can be built using Groupscape. The Groupscape Standard development system is priced at $995.00 per developer with no run-time fees, but the Notes Browser is free for the downloading from **http:// www.braintech.com/gscape.htm**.

Galacticomm Worldgroup, for Windows 3.1 and Windows 95, is a Netscape plug-in that supports dozens of off-the-shelf groupware applications. These can range from real-time video conferencing to on-line fax-back services, questionnaires with graphed results, and more. In fact, its focus is on information, commerce, multimedia databases, and other real-world, corporate-level solutions. Secure buying and selling via the Web is supported, as is forms management, powerful document searching, etc. **http:// www.gcomm.com/wgsupb4.exe** Galacticomm has an impressive list of high-profile clients in business, industry, and the government. If you're looking to bring your big business onto the Web in a big-time way, with more than just a set of Web pages for the public to peruse, it looks like you should look into Worldgroup. You can find out more and download the plug-in from **http://www.gcomm.com/show/plugin.html**.

ActiveX

What if there isn't a plug-in that does what you want it to do? Well, you can always write your own from scratch. There's information about the Netscape plug-ins SDK (Software Developer's Kit) online at the Netscape site at **http://www.netscape.com**. But there are other solutions. If you're mainly concerned about delivering to Windows platforms (all types), there are four plug-ins that let you launch OLE applications inline in Netscape.

ExCITE's NCompass division has created a Navigator plug-in for Windows 95 that lets you embed OLE controls as applets created using standard programming languages and development tools like Visual C++, Visual Basic, and the MS Windows Game SDK.

With the OLE Control plug-in, a software developer can create a version of any Windows standard OLE compliant program that is customized for

use with Netscape and the Web. For example, games, investment programs, multimedia players, and just about anything else can be created for
Windows, then compiled in a version for the Web.

Because OLE plug-ins use compiled native Windows code, Internet
applications can run just as fast as stand-alone Windows 95 applications
while also supporting data exchange and data updating over the Web.

NCompass provides several examples on their Web site, including a
multiplayer DirectX game, a real-time OpenGL rendering of a robot arm,
inline AVI movie player control, and more (see fig. 10.16).

The OLE plug-in requires a 486 DX33 with 8MB RAM, 14.4KB Internet
connection, and Windows 95 or NT. You can download it from **http://
www.excite.sfu.ca/NCompass/nchome.html**.

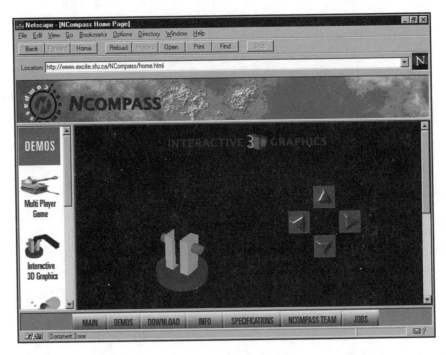

Fig. 10.16
That's a Windows 95 program running in the Netscape window, courtesy of NCompass's OLE Control
plug-in.

OpenScape

Business@Web's OpenScape plug-in is similar to NCompass's OLE Control plug-in in that it lets developers create OLE/OCX compatible applications that run inline in Netscape over the Web. However, OpenScape applications must be created using the OpenScape development system rather than Visual Basic or C++.

There are four versions of the OpenScape product for actually creating the applications that the OpenScape plug-in runs. OpenScape is for individuals who want to build Web pages using Visual Basic-style tools. It lets you create reusable and customizable OCXs with a Visual Basic-compatible scripting language. OpenScape can also be used to create stand-alone desktop applications with embedded OCXs, OLE 2.0 servers, and DLLs. OpenScape Professional adds the ability to actually create OCXs and OLE 2 servers. OpenScape Workgroup is for creating applications that can be distributed securely across a network. Finally, OpenScape Enterprise is for large, corporate development work.

The OpenScape Navigator plug-in is currently downloadable for both Window 95/NT and Windows 3.1. You can get it at **http:// www.busweb.com/download/f_down.html**.

QuickServer

QuickServer, by Wayfarer Communications is for high-performance intranet and Internet client-server applications developed with Visual Basic, PowerBuilder, C++, and Java. Applications developers can build the client component of Internet applications using the leading development tools and run them inside Netscape Navigator using this plug-in. QuickServer reduces development time by leveraging the leading client/ server development tools, such as Visual Basic, PowerBuilder, Visual C++, Delphi and Java, and by eliminating the complexity of communications programming.

You can download the 30-day evaluation version of the QuickServer SDK (Software Developer's Kit), and you can download StockWatcher, a demo application in Visual Basic using Wayfarer's plug-in, to see live, dynamic stock quotes inside Netscape Navigator. For Windows 95/NT, both are available at **http://www.wayfarer.com/**.

WinFrame

Citrix Systems' WinFrame plug-in for Windows 3.1 and Windows 95 actually allows you to execute Windows programs over the Internet. With the WinFrame client, you can publish applications as easily as you publish Web documents. Just download this plug-in, run the setup program, and you can try it for yourself on standard Windows applications like Microsoft Access, Lotus Notes, and Adobe Acrobat. Check it out at **http://www.citrix.com**.

Netscape Helper Applications

● **In this chapter:**

● **Which file types require helper applications, and which don't**

● **What kind of helper applications are right for you**

● **Where to get helper applications**

● **How to configure helper applications to work with Netscape**

We can't always single-handedly manage everything that comes our way—sometimes we need a little help from our friends. Netscape is no different. It can't handle every single file type that it encounters on the World Wide Web. Sometimes it needs a little help from helper applications.

Fortunately, it's pretty easy to configure helper applications for Netscape. The hard part is figuring out which ones you need and where to get them. This chapter should help with that first dilemma, the enclosed CD-ROM should help you with the second.

The following sections will help you choose the best Netscape helper applications for:

- Sound

- Graphics

- Video

- VRML (Virtual Reality Markup Language)

- SGML (Standard Generalized Markup Language)

- Adobe Acrobat and other Portable Document Formats

- File decompression

What are helper applications?

Though Netscape 3 is a pretty versatile Web browser, you'll still run into files on the Web that it can't display. Although this newest release of Netscape incorporates support for more file types and includes plug-ins (see chapter 10) to use even more, there are still some video files, audio files, odd graphics files, strange document formats, and even compressed files that Netscape can't display. To display or play these files, you need to set up helper applications.

A helper application is simply a program that can understand and interpret files that Netscape can't handle itself. Almost any program can be configured to act as a helper application for Netscape. The trick is figuring out which ones will be the most useful to you.

All Web browsers need helper applications. There are simply too many different file types on the Web for a browser to be able to handle them all internally.

Think about this: On a daily basis, you probably use a dozen or more different programs for word processing, spreadsheets, database management, electronic mail, graphics, and many other different applications. Each of these programs produces a different kind of data file, yet only a few of your applications are able to import even a limited number of different file types from other applications. And we're only talking about one person's files on a single computer! It's just not possible for Netscape to handle all the thousands of different file types it might encounter on the Web all by itself.

There is a key difference between helper applications and plug-ins. Plug-ins can display or use the files they work with directly in Netscape. A plug-in becomes almost like a part of Netscape. When using helper applications, the helper application is started and runs as a separate application, in its own window just as if you had started it from the Program Manager or Windows 95 Start Menu.

For that reason, your plug-ins are really the preferred way to work with the extra file types in Netscape. Where you have a choice, you are better to install a plug-in application (as described in the previous chapter) than to use a helper application. As more plug-ins are written, the need for helpers will decrease even further.

Configuring a helper application

No matter what helper applications you choose to add, they all configure the same way. It takes only a few simple steps to set one up.

If you look at table 11.1, you'll notice that Netscape can't display .BMP and .PCX image files. These are pretty ubiquitous file types, and you'll run into them fairly often on the Web. A helper application is definitely in order.

Fortunately, Microsoft includes a program in Windows 95 that does a great job of displaying .PCX and .BMP files: Microsoft Paint—called Paintbrush in Windows 3.1 (see fig. 11.1).

Fig. 11.1
Microsoft's Paint comes with all versions of Windows. It makes a dandy Netscape helper application for viewing .BMP and .PCX image files.

To configure Paint as your .PCX/.BMP helper application for Netscape, follow these steps:

1 Open Netscape's Options menu, and select General Preferences.

2 Click the Helpers tab to bring it to the front (see fig. 11.2).

3 Scroll down the list of MIME types until you see the image/x-MS-bmp entry. Click it to highlight it. The extension "bmp" appears in the file Extensions field (see fig. 11.3).

4 Click the Browse button. A dialog box appears. Find your Windows directory and double-click Pbrush (see fig. 11.4).

5 The full path name for the Paint program appears in the application box beside the Paint icon, and the Launch the Application radio button is auto-selected. If you choose OK now, Paint will be configured as Netscape's helper application for .BMP files. But we want to use it to view .PCX files, too, so we'll go on.

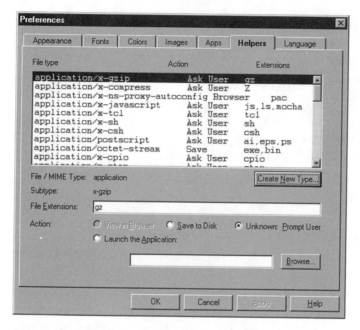

Fig. 11.2
The Helpers tab.

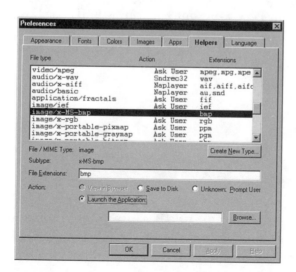

Fig. 11.3
Select the file type from the variety of types available.

Fig. 11.4
Find the Pbrush.exe file and double-click it.

6 Scrolling up and down through the list of MIME file types reveals that there is no entry for a file type with a .PCX extension, so we have to define our own. Click the Create New Type button to bring up the Configure New Mime Type dialog box. We can enter only one of the seven official MIME types in the Mime Type windows, so choose Image. We must make up our own MIME subtype because none is listed. Any "unofficial" MIME subtype must begin with "x-," and we need to follow that prefix with something unique, so let's just use the file name extension. Type **x-pcx** into the Mime SubType box and then click OK (see fig. 11.5).

Fig. 11.5
The Configure New Mime Type dialog box.

7 In the File Extensions box, type **pcx**. Because you already know the full path name for Paint, just type it into the File Path box, or enter it like you did before by Browsing. If the radio button labeled Launch the Application isn't auto-checked, check it manually (see fig. 11.6).

8 Click OK to finish.

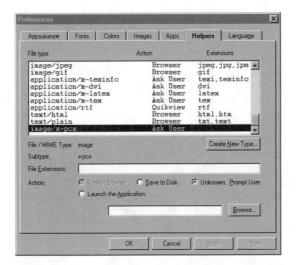

Fig. 11.6
Choose your file extension here.

That's it! Paint is officially a Netscape helper application. The next time Netscape encounters a .PCX or .BMP image, it will automatically launch Paint to view it (see fig. 11.7).

You can also tell Netscape to automatically save a particular file type to disk whenever it is encountered, rather than configuring a helper app to display it. During the configuration process, just click the radio button labeled Save to Disk instead of the one marked Launch Application. You'll probably want to pick Save to Disk for files with an extension of .EXE (MIME: application/octet-stream) because these are usually executable programs.

There is another way to configure helper applications. Rather than going through all of the above steps, you can just wait until you encounter an unknown file with Netscape. When that happens, Netscape will display an Unknown File Type dialog box. Click the Pick App button and you will get a small dialog box to enter the path and filename for the application (or click browse like step 4 of the previous procedure). Once you enter the filename for the program, click OK and you're done. This saves you from having to deal with MIME types, subtypes, and file extensions as Netscape fills these in automatically. This way, you just set up new helper applications as you need them. However, you do have to have the correct helper application installed on your computer.

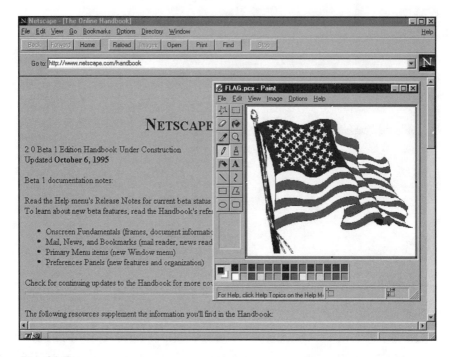

Fig. 11.7
Paint, now fully configured as a Netscape Helper application, displays the flag.

What kinds of files are on the Web?

Just about every type of file you can imagine exists somewhere on the World Wide Web (see Table 11.1 for some examples). But this doesn't mean you'll run into them all.

Web pages themselves are almost always composed of just two elements: HTML-formatted text and inline graphics. All Web browsers can handle these, including Netscape; you don't need to worry about configuring helper applications just to be able to read Web pages. The problem comes when you try to access an external file by clicking a link to something other than a Web page.

Even then, the problem does not loom as large as you might fear, because the Web is mostly a compendium of hypermedia documents. That is, the hyperlinks on most Web pages jump to files with some sort of multimedia content: text, audio, graphics, or video. Even if these are in formats that Netscape doesn't speak natively, once you've configured helper applications for the half dozen or so most common multimedia file types, you may be able to go for months without encountering anything your Netscape configuration can't handle. (For some great online info about multimedia file types, follow the link in figure 11.8.)

However, even if you do your best to avoid exotic file types, the day will come when you'll find a site that provides a link to some killer, must-have file that exists only in some weird format that you've never heard of before. Never fear. By configuring the proper Netscape helper application on the spot, you'll be able to play or display it properly. That's the beauty of helper applications. They make Netscape infinitely open-ended, extensible, and expandable.

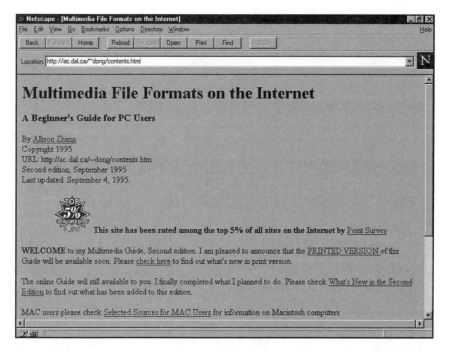

Fig. 11.8
An excellent reference to the kinds of files you'll run into on the World Wide Web is Allison Zhang's online book Multimedia File Formats on the Internet at http://ac.dal.ca/~dong/contents.html.

Netscape's built-in capabilities

Before we get into the topic of the helper apps you need, let's take a moment to find out which ones you don't need. Netscape already includes the built-in ability to display the three most-used graphics file formats on the Web, and bundles plug-in that plays the most popular audio file types, as well.

Built-in GIF, JPEG, and XBM image display

You don't have to configure helper applications for GIF, JPEG, or XBM images. Netscape displays all three of these graphic file formats just fine all by itself.

There are good reasons for having graphics support built right into Netscape, though (see fig. 11.9). Web pages are more aesthetically pleasing if they combine text with inline graphics. But you'd be stuck with separate windows for text and graphics if Netscape had to launch a helper application every time it displayed an image. All Web browsers have to be able to display at least one graphic image format internally if text and graphics are to stay together on the page.

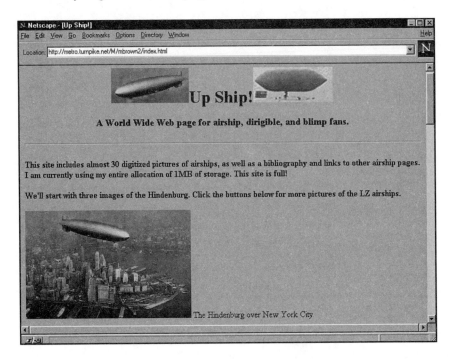

Fig. 11.9
Netscape 3 doesn't need a helper application to display inline GIF, JPEG, and XBM images like these.

TIP **Have you ever wished that Netscape could display an inline graphic in** *its own window instead of inline? It can! Right-click the image and you'll see the menu of options shown in figure 11.10. Select View this Image and it will be displayed in its own window. You can also choose Save this Image As to save the image to disk, or choose Copy this Image Location to copy the URL of the image to the Windows Clipboard.*

Fig. 11.10
Click the right mouse button on an inline image to open this helpful menu of options.

Most of the inline graphics on Web pages are GIF (Graphics Interchange Format) images, because that's what early Web browsers could display. Like all Web browsers, Netscape has built-in support for GIFs. But by today's image compression standards, GIF image files are just plain big. And when you're talking about a time-intensive medium like the Web, smaller is better.

JPEG images are much smaller than GIFs—in fact, a 16-million color JPEG graphic can be as little as 1/4 the size of the same GIF image in only 256 colors! That's why Netscape added built-in JPEG image display capability to its browser a couple of revisions back. Due in no small part to Netscape's support for the JPEG format, many Web sites now include inline JPEGs on their pages, which results in faster page downloads and much better-looking Web sites.

TIP **Look for sites with JPEG images in the new Progressive JPEG format** *supported by Netscape 3. They load up to three times faster than GIFs, and preview faster, too!*

What about XBM images? Well, XBM is a monochrome image format used mostly on X Window systems running under UNIX. Frankly, these days you'll only run into XBMs on older UNIX sites where they haven't bothered to convert their images to GIFs or JPEGs yet. Because most Web servers are UNIX machines (with Windows NT and Windows 95 up-and-coming contenders), XBM isn't dead yet.

GIFs, JPEGs, and XBMs currently account for almost 100 percent of the inline graphic images on Web pages. With built-in support for all three, Netscape faithfully displays most of the images you encounter on the Web without requiring you to configure a single external helper application.

CAUTION **If you are designing your own Web pages, don't entirely abandon GIFs** for JPEGs! There are still some people out there using older browsers that can't read JPEGs. And for small, simple images with few colors, GIFs can often be even smaller than JPEGs. Not only that, but GIFs support background transparency, which can improve the look of your pages—JPEG doesn't (at least not yet).

Netscape's included LiveAudio plug-in

Multimedia just isn't multimedia without sound. Text, graphics, and animation only stimulate the eyes, but sound brings a whole different sense into play. By combining graphics with sound, you activate more of the brain and get your audience more involved. (Not convinced? Try watching TV with the sound muted!)

Starting with version 3, Netscape includes a new audio player in the form of a plug-in. This plug-in, called LiveAudio, is configured by default to play AIFF, MIDI, WAV, and AU sound formats. For more about this plug-in, see Chapter 10.

Other built-in formats

Netscape also supports Microsoft's AVI Video for Windows file format for movies directly. With the Live3D plug-in included with Netscape, many VRML worlds also display without the need for any other helper applications or plug-ins.

How does Netscape know when it needs a helper application?

Before Netscape can tell if it can handle a file internally or whether it has to launch a helper application, it has to determine what kind of data it's dealing with.

If you've been using a PC for very long, you can probably identify many file types by their file name extensions. You know that a file named foo.exe is an executable program because the file name ends in ".EXE," and that one named boo.doc is a Microsoft Word document because it ends in ".DOC."

NOTE By default, Windows 95's file-handling dialog boxes hide file name extensions. For example, a file named "picture.gif" is listed as "picture." File types are identified by icons. To tell Windows 95 to display file name extensions in all its file dialog boxes, follow these steps:

1 Run Windows Explorer.

2 Select the View, Options menu.

3 Choose the View tab.

4 Uncheck the Hide MS-DOS File Extensions box.

CAUTION Not every file type can be correctly identified by its file name extension. Some different file formats share the same extension, and there are also many files on the Web that have arbitrary or misleading file names. Be sure to check for "context clues" that will help you identify a file's real file type. For example, if a file has the file name extension .exe but the text identifies it as an archive file, the odds are good that it's not an executable program, but a self-extracting archive.

Netscape can identify files on the Web by their file names, too. But that is only its backup method of determining what kind of files it's dealing with. Its primary method is by referencing a file's MIME type.

A brief course in MIME types

MIME is an acronym for Multipurpose Internet Mail Extensions, but this is a little misleading. MIME type definitions are not just for Internet mail; they are used to identify any file that can be transmitted over the Internet.

A MIME type definition consists of two parts:

> type/subtype

Here's a real-world example:

> image/jpeg

It's pretty easy to see that this MIME type definition describes an image file in JPEG format.

Before a Web server sends a file to Netscape, it sends the MIME type definition for that file. Netscape reads this definition and looks it up to see if it can handle the file internally, or if there is a helper application defined for it. In the case of the preceding example, Netscape knows that the file it is about to receive is an image in JPEG format, which, of course, it can interpret internally; it won't try to launch a helper application.

If the server doesn't send a MIME type along before transmitting the file, Netscape uses the file name extension to identify the file type.

Q&A *I thought I clicked a link to a graphic, but Netscape displayed a screen of unreadable text instead.*

If Netscape has to identify a file by its file name extension rather than its MIME type, it can make the same kind of misidentification that a human would make with a misnamed or ambiguously named file. If Netscape tries to display a misidentified file typed in its own display or in the wrong helper application, all you see is a garbled mess.

If this happens to you, hover over the file link with the hand pointer and read the file name in the status bar at the bottom of the Netscape window. If the file name extension looks wrong for the type of file you're trying to view, that's probably the problem.

In the rare case where you get a garbled inline image, you can view the file name by right-clicking the image. The file name will be displayed in brackets beside the View this Image choice on the pop-up menu.

You can also see file names by selecting View, By Document Source from the Netscape menu and looking for the file name in the HTML code.

If you can't figure out why a link isn't working right, you can always save the suspect file by holding down the Shift key and clicking the link. Then you can work with it later.

You can see a complete list of the MIME types that Netscape recognizes by choosing Options, General from the Netscape menu, then selecting the Helpers tab (see fig. 11.11), or you can look at table 11.1 for a list of some of the more common types that you may encounter.

Fig. 11.11
Netscape can display this scrolling list of the MIME types it knows about. Just select Options, General Preferences from the menu and click the Helpers tab.

Table 11.1   MIME types that Netscape recognizes

Type/Subtype	Extensions	Description
application/postscript	.AI, .EPS, .PS	PostScript Program
application/octet-stream	.EXE, .BIN	Binary Executable
application/x-zip-compressed	.ZIP	Zip Compressed Data
application/x-stuffit	.SIT	Macintosh Archive
application/mac-binhex40	.HQX	Macintosh BinHex Archive
*video/x-msvideo, video/msvideo	.AVI	Microsoft Video
video/quicktime	.QT, .MOV, .MOOV	QuickTime Video
video/mpeg	.MPEG,.MPG,.MPE, .MPV, .VBS, .MPEGV	MPEG Video
video/x-mpeg-2	.MPV2, .MP2V	MPEG Level 2 Viedo
*audio/x-wav	.WAV	WAV Audio
*audio/x-aiff, audio/aiff	.AIF, .AIFF, .AIFC	AIFF Audio
*audio/basic	.AU, .SND	ULAW Audio Data
audio/x-pn-realaudio	.RA, .RAM	RealAudio
audio/x-mpeg	.MP2, .MPA, .ABS, .MPEGA	MPEG Audio
audio/x-midi, audio/midi	.MID, .MIDI	MIDI Musical Instrument
image/x-png	.PNG	Portable Network Graphic
image/x-MS-bmp	.BMP	Windows Bitmap
*image/x-xbitmap	.XBM	X Bitmap
image/tiff	.TIFF, .TIF	TIFF Image
*image/jpeg	.JPEG, .JPG, .JPE	JPEG Image
*image/gif	.GIF	CompuServe Image Format
application/rtf	.RTF	Rich Text Format
*text/html	.HTML, .HTM	Hypertext Markup Language
*text/plain	.TXT, .TEXT	Plain Text

Type/Subtype	Extensions	Description
*x-conference/x-talk	.ICE	CoolTalk real-time audio conferencing
application/x-director	.DXR	Shockwave for Director
*x-world/x-vrml	WRL	Virtual Reality 3D Worlds/Live 3D files

Files that Netscape handles internally or via included plug-ins in version 3 are marked with an asterisk ("*"). In addition, there are plug-ins to handle QuickTime, MPEG Video, Shockwave (there is no helper application for this type), Real Audio, Portable Network Graphics, TIFF, BMP, EPS, PCX, and MIDI. You probably won't need helper applications for any of these types.

So, what you may find is that there aren't many common file types left. Your only option is a helper application. The most likely thing that you'd want to configure a helper for is for dealing with compressed files (like a software program you download).

Types and subtypes

There are only seven sanctioned MIME types: text, audio, image, video, multipart, message, and application. If somebody comes up with some hot new program or data file type, they have to fit it into one of these seven MIME types if a MIME-enabled application is going to recognize it.

However, there are both "official" and "unofficial" MIME subtypes. Official subtypes appear on the list without an "x-" prefix. That kind of gives away the fact that "x-" is the official way to label an unofficial MIME subtype. That a MIME subtype is "unofficial" in no way makes it a second-class citizen, however. It just means that the Internet Working Group, the organization that oversees the MIME standard, hasn't defined an official subtype for it yet.

Missing MIME types

If Netscape encounters a file with an unknown MIME type and a file extension that is not on its internal list, it may try to display it as text. In most cases, this is definitely not what you want it to do. If you run into this problem, you can configure Netscape so that it automatically saves files of that type to disk by following these steps (see fig. 11.12):

1 Select Options, General Preferences from the Netscape menu.

2 Click on the Helpers tab to bring it to the front.

3 Choose the Create New Type button.

4 Enter a MIME type in the Mime Type field, and a MIME subtype in the Mime SubType field. (This should begin with an "x-.")

Fig. 11.12
You must define both type and subtype for any new MIME type you define for Netscape.

5 Enter the proper file extension(s) in the File Extensions field.

6 Click the Save to Disk radio button.

7 Click OK when you're done.

CAUTION Once you've set up a new MIME type/subtype, you can't get rid of it—there's no Delete button in the Helper Applications configuration window. You can change the name of the application or the file name extension, and you can change the Action to Save to Disk or Ask User, but you can't get rid of it. The only way to do so is to manually edit the NETSCAPE.INI file under Windows 3.1 or the Registry under Windows 95.

Q&A *I configured a helper application for "type/subtype," but Netscape doesn't always seem to use it. And I sometimes get a* Warning: unrecognized encoding *message. What's going on?*

If this problem is only occasional, it's probably not Netscape or your helper application configuration that's at fault. The problem may be with the way the Web site you're connected to is sending MIME type information. Netscape may be receiving a self-contradictory or confusing MIME type identification, and it's trying to interpret the file without really knowing what it is. If you regularly run into this problem on a particular site, e-mail the Webmaster (usually webmaster@site) and inform him of the problem.

What kinds of programs can you use as helper applications?

Almost any program can be configured as a helper application for Netscape. But that doesn't mean you should go ahead and configure every program you own. Keep in mind effectiveness, efficiency, and utility.

Should you use DOS, Windows 3.1, or Win95 helpers?

If you're running under Windows 95, stick with Win95 helper applications as much as you can. If you're running Windows 3.1, use Windows 3.1 helper apps. I can't think of a single reason to ever use a DOS program as a Netscape helper. DOS applications don't integrate well with Windows. They don't make good use of system resources and don't multitask well with Windows applications like Netscape.

If you're running under Windows 95, you'll find that Windows 3.1 applications don't handle long file names, don't multitask efficiently, don't run as fast under Win95 as native 32-bit applications, and don't use the standard Win95 file dialog box.

Both you and Netscape will be happier in the long run if you use the most advanced, up-to-date programs your system can run as helper apps. But don't forget that you want your helper applications to be quick and resource-friendly, too.

Programs you already own

The first place you should look for helper apps is in the treasure trove of programs you already own. Both Windows 3.1 and Windows 95 come with a handful of small, efficient bundled applications that make excellent Netscape helper apps.

Earlier in this chapter, we discussed how to set up Paint, another program that is included with both versions of Windows, as a helper app for viewing .PCX and .BMP image files. With Netscape's native support for .GIFs, .JPEGs, and .XBMs, the addition of Paint instantly sets you up for viewing the Web's five most popular graphics image file types.

Windows 3.1's Notepad and Write can be handy helper apps for text file formats you want to display in a separate window. Windows 95 users can use QuickView or Wordpad, which also display Microsoft Word documents.

Freeware and shareware solutions

You should also be prepared to mine the Web itself for helper applications. There are literally thousands of freeware and shareware programs out there, free for the downloading. The chapters in this section discuss dozens of freeware and shareware programs that you can use as Netscape helper applications.

NOTE **What's the difference between freeware and shareware? Freeware is** just that: free. You can download it and use it forever without ever paying anyone a dime. Shareware, on the other hand, is software you can try for free, but if you continue to use it, you're expected to pay the author for the privilege. If you use it past the trial period stated in the program's license agreement, you are effectively stealing the program, just as if you had shoplifted it from a store shelf. Fortunately, most shareware license fees are so reasonable that they won't put much of a strain on your pocketbook.

So where do you go to get freely distributed helper applications?

First of all, check out the CD included with this book. It includes most of the helper applications discussed in this chapter. The odds are good that you won't have to go any further to get all the helper applications you need.

You might also want to check out the helpful advice that Netscape offers on its own Web site. While you're connected to the Web, choose Help, Release Notes from the Netscape menu and you'll find information on some of the most popular Netscape helper applications, as well as directions on how to download them.

Here are some other software archive sites to try on the World Wide Web:

- **http://vsl.cnet.com**—The Virtual Software Library

- **http://pcwin.com**—Randy Burgess's Windows 95 Resource Center

- **http://www.pcworld.com/win95/shareware**—PC World Online

- **http://www.netex.net/w95/windows95**—Unofficial Windows 95 Software Archive

- **http://www.csusm.edu/cwis/winworld/winworld.html**—CSUSM Software Archive

- **http://www.mcp.com/que/software**—Que Publishing's Software Library

For additional information on how to download files from the Web, see chapter 2, "Moving Around the Web." For more about finding files, see chapter 3, "Finding Information on the Web."

CAUTION **Watch out for files you download that have an .EXE file name** extension. Most are self-extracting archives, not usable executable files!

Commercial programs

Of course, you could actually spend some money and buy programs to use as helper applications. If you're a real control freak, you might be considering using PhotoShop, PhotoStyler, PhotoFinish, or some other "name brand" commercial graphics, sound, or video program as a Netscape helper app.

But you should be aware that most of the programs you can buy for multimedia use are huge and eat up a lot of system resources. For most people, it would certainly be overkill to buy anything like the programs mentioned above just to use as Netscape helper applications.

But if you can find a small, elegant commercial program that you really like, there is certainly no reason why you can't buy it and configure it as a Netscape helper. If you're inclined to go this way, I advise you to read the reviews in popular computer magazines for guidance on which ones might be right for you. But try to steer clear of the huge "professional" packages. Odds are that they would just get in the way of browsing the Web.

Configure now or later, or not at all

If you want, you can try to anticipate your needs and find and configure helper applications for all the file types you think you're likely to encounter in the future. Or you can just wait for Netscape to tell you that you need a helper app.

As you may have noticed when we talked about MIME types, the scrolling list of file types that Netscape maintains under the Action heading also tells you what it will do when it encounters each of them (refer to fig. 11.6). If it handles the file internally, this entry says Browser. If it has been configured to launch a helper application, it lists the name of the application. Most entries are simply labeled Ask User.

If you try to display a file that you haven't configured a helper application for (one that lists Ask User as its Action), Netscape displays the Unknown File Type alert shown in figure 11.13.

Fig. 11.13
The Unknown File Type alert lets you configure a helper application on the fly.

If you want, you can simply back out at this point by choosing Cancel, which returns you to the Netscape main window without viewing the file. You can also choose Save File to load the problem file into your favorite application later. But if you select Pick App, Netscape jumps directly to the Helper Application configuration dialog box shown in figure 11.14, just as though you'd selected it from the menu.

TIP **Advanced users may want to take a look at Netscape's helper** application configuration settings in the Windows 95 Registry. You can do so by running RegEdit (in the Windows directory) and viewing HKEY_CURRENT_USER/ Software/Netscape Navigator/Viewers.

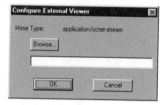

Fig. 11.14
You'll be able to browse for a helper application if you choose the Pick App button.

Checking your work—the WWW Viewer Test Page

How can you make sure your helper applications are configured properly? Test 'em out!

The easiest way to test a Netscape helper application is to select File, Open File from the Netscape menu and try to open a file of the type you want to test from your system. If Netscape launches the right helper app and the file is displayed properly, you're in business.

If you don't have a file of the type you want to check, or if you simply prefer to test your helper app "under fire" on the Web, go to the Lawrence Livermore Labs Web Viewer Test Page at **http://www-dsed.llnl.gov/ documents/WWWtest.html**. This page presents a menu of buttons that send you dozens of different files to exercise just about any helper application you can think of (see fig. 11.15).

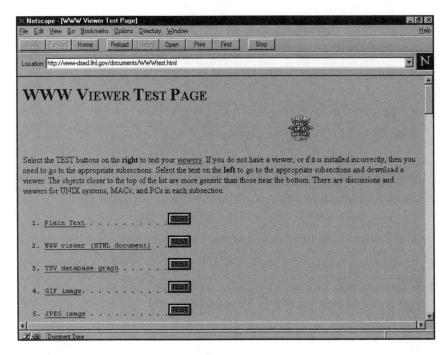

Fig. 11.15
You can test your helper applicatoin configuration by pointing Nestcape to the Lawrence Livermore Labs Web Viewer Test Page.

Popular helper applications

We'll finish off this chapter by listing some of the most popular programs that you may want to use as helper applications. As noted before, there are many plug-ins that will provide most of this same functionality. There are only a couple of reasons that I can think of that would cause you to want to use a helper instead of a plug-in. Those are:

- You don't have a lot of free space on your hard drive and would rather set up one program that handles many file formats (like Paint Shop Pro for many graphics file types) than having several plug-ins. In addition, many plug-ins are just viewers and you might still need an additional application if you want to edit files.

- You have a helper application that has more functions and abilities than the plug-ins.

Of course, you may have other reasons. But what ever your reasons, here is the short list of the best helper applications. You'll find many of these on the CD-ROM included with this book. Others, you can find at any of the sites listed in "Freeware and Shareware Solutions" earlier in this chapter.

Table 11.2   Popular helper applications

File Type	Program Name
MPEG Audio	XingSound
Many Graphics formats	Paint Shop Pro
Many Graphics Formats	LView Pro
MPEG Video	VMPEG
MPEG Video	MPEG Play
SGML	Panorama
PostScript	GhostScript
ZIP, ARJ, LZH, Z, TAR, and other compressed files	WinZip
UUEncoded Files	WinCode

Online Conferencing with CoolTalk

● **In this chapter:**

- Whether or not it's realistic to use the Internet for voice communications

- The hardware requirements for setting up your computer to talk on the Internet

- How to get and configure CoolTalk, which is the official, Netscape-sanctioned program you need to use the Internet for phone conversations

How would you like to have free long-distance telephone service for life? "Wow! Is this a prize in the lottery?" you ask. Not exactly. All you need is Internet access and a sound card to be able to call anyone, anywhere, anytime, for free.

Of course, there are a few catches. The people you call also have to have Internet access and a sound card. They need to be connected to the Internet when you try to call. They have to be running the same Internet telephone software you are. It's not as easy as just picking up a phone and dialing. (Though if you think about it, the requirements are similar; you can't call someone on the phone if he is not connected to the phone system or doesn't own a telephone.) If you have a cousin in France, a fiancé in Alaska, or just like to talk to your Mom back home in Biloxi for a couple of hours every night, these shortcomings may not mean much compared to the savings you'll realize.

Using the Internet for phone calls

The whole purpose of the Internet is to transfer data from one computer to another. The Net is blithely unaware of what that data represents. Text, graphics, audio—all are the same to the Net. So holding a phone conversation over the Internet is mostly just a matter of turning your voice into digital data at one end and turning that data back into audio at the other. In between, it's just data, and the Internet can transfer that just fine no matter what it represents.

System requirements

If your computer is capable of browsing the Web, the odds are excellent that you already have the one additional component that you need to be able to digitize your voice to transmit, and then to convert the data you receive from the Net back into voice—a sound card.

Of course, in addition to a sound card you'll need a dialup or direct connection to the Internet. You'll also have to have the following:

- At least a 50 MHz CPU
- 12-16 MB of RAM
- A set of self-amplified speakers

- A microphone (preferably with an on/off switch)

- A relatively fast connection to the Internet

CAUTION   **Real-time voice communication on the Internet is a real system hog.** It uses lots of CPU time, hardware resources, and RAM. If you're going to be talking on the Internet, it's best if you refrain from running any other tasks. Otherwise, your audio feed is likely to "break up."

NOTE   **Contrary to popular belief, you don't have to have a direct TCP/IP** connection to the Internet to use CoolTalk. You can talk just fine over a SLIP or PPP dial-up connection via a 14.4 or 28.8 Kbps (kilobits per second) modem. Voice communications doesn't use nearly the bandwidth that graphics and video do, so chatting over the Internet on a dial-up connection not only is realistic, but under ideal conditions is indistinguishable from communicating over a direct connection.

Your sound card

All sound cards can convert digital data to audible audio, and most can also digitize audio in real-time from a microphone input. Almost any sound card that can do both can be used with CoolTalk.

A 16-bit stereo sound card is best; although an 8-bit card may work, a 16-bit card is more likely to give you trouble-free compatibility. Creative Labs' SoundBlaster 16 is the industry standard; if you have a SoundBlaster card or compatible hooked up to a microphone and a set of speakers or headphones, you're all set for holding conversations on the Internet with CoolTalk.

CAUTION   **Windows 95 multitasking doesn't mean you can use two programs that** use the sound card at the same time. For example, you can't play MIDI music files while chatting on the Internet.

Most sound cards operate in *half duplex* mode; that is, you can record audio or play audio, but you can't do both simultaneously. This means that your Internet conversations will be limited to a one-way-at-a-time mode. Most people have experienced this type of conversation when using a CB radio or speakerphone; while one person is talking, the other listens. Participants in a conversation must take turns.

There are a few sound cards on the market that support *full duplex* mode; that is, that can record and play sound simultaneously. With such cards, CoolTalk supports full telephone-style two-way conversations. Unfortunately, full duplex sound cards are relatively rare and expensive. Some that are currently on the market are the Gravis UltraSound Max, the ASB 16 Audio System, and the Spectrum Office F/X (which is an all-in-one fax, modem, and sound card). As DSP (Digital Sound Processor) chip technology becomes more prevalent in the PC marketplace, we're bound to see more, less expensive full duplex sound cards.

You can easily test your sound card to see if it supports full duplex operation by using Sound Recorder, an application included with all versions of Windows. Here's how:

1 Open a copy of Sound Recorder, which is located in your Windows directory. Then load a .wav file using File, Open.

2 Open a second copy of Sound Recorder, and press the record button on the toolbar of this second copy.

3 Now press the play button on the toolbar of the first copy of Sound Recorder, the one that you loaded the .wav file into in step one.

4 If you get the warning dialog box shown in figure 12.1, you've got a half duplex sound card, like most of us. Sorry. However, if the .wav file plays okay, you're one of the lucky ones—your card is working in full duplex mode!

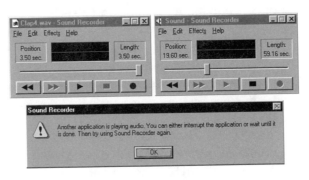

Fig. 12.1
Run two copies of Windows Sound Recorder to test whether you have a full duplex audio card. If you see this warning dialog, your card is only half duplex.

CAUTION A few Internet telephone packages purport to provide full duplex operation with a half duplex sound card. This requires the installation of special software drivers, and can potentially result in compatibility problems with other programs that use your sound card. It's probably best to settle for half duplex operation in most cases rather than trying to "push" your sound card to do something it's not intended to do.

What CoolTalk is

CoolTalk is a stand-alone program that lets you talk and listen to others over the Internet. Note that it is a totally independent program—it doesn't require Netscape to run. You can run it all by itself. However, when you install Netscape 3, CoolTalk is also installed, and is configured as a helper application for Netscape.

When you run CoolTalk—or when Netscape invokes CoolTalk as a helper application—it connects to another user on the Internet and lets you hold a conversation. It uses your computer's sound card and a microphone to digitize your speech, which is then sent via your Internet connection to the party you're talking to. At her computer, the data that represents your spoken words is translated back into sound using her sound card.

CoolTalk also has some impressive additional features. There is an Answering Machine, which can take CoolTalk messages for you when you're connected to the Internet but unable to answer. The Chat Tool option lets you communicate with another CoolTalk user by typing in text. The White Board is probably CoolTalk's coolest option—it lets you load up graphics (even snapshots of your work screens) and share them over the Net. Better yet, you can both mark up the screen and see the comments you both make. This sort of functionality is called "collaborative software" by groupware developers, and it's currently one of the hottest areas of software development.

Installing CoolTalk

CoolTalk comes with Netscape Navigator 3, and is included as part of the Netscape distribution file. When you run the Netscape installation program, CoolTalk is automatically installed as well.

If you didn't get CoolTalk with your copy of Navigator—if, for example, you downloaded a "minimal distribution" version of Navigator without CoolTalk— you can download an installation file containing only CoolTalk from **http://home.netscape.com/comprod/products/navigator/cooltalk/download_cooltalk.html**.

Setting CoolTalk options

During the CoolTalk installation process, you will be asked if you want to install the CoolTalk Watchdog in your system StartUp directory. This Watchdog program runs in the background, waiting for someone to try to call you using CoolTalk. If it detects an incoming call and CoolTalk is not running, it automatically launches CoolTalk so you can receive your call.

Installing the Watchdog only makes sense if you are always (or almost always) connected to the Internet while not running Netscape. If this doesn't describe you, the Watchdog just senselessly uses up system resources. However, if you are connected to the Internet full-time, the Watchdog makes sure that you'll never miss a CoolTalk call. If you expect to be using CoolTalk a good portion of the time, it makes sense to let the setup program put a copy in your StartUp directory.

When the Watchdog is active, its icon will appear in the TaskBar Status Tray. To suspend the Watchdog, double-click on its icon. When it's suspended, a red stop sign will appear over its icon.

If you change your mind later, you can manually delete or move the file Wdog.exe from the Windows\Start Menu\Programs\StartUp directory. (You can likewise add the Watchdog at any time by moving or copying Wdog.exe from Program Files\Netscape\Navigator\Cooltalk to the StartUp directory.)

Once CoolTalk is installed, you'll want to run it and select <u>H</u>elp, Set<u>u</u>p Wizard from the CoolTalk menu. This brings up the CoolTalk Setup Wizard (see fig. 12.2).

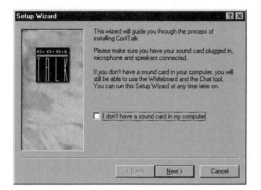

Fig. 12.2
The CoolTalk Setup Wizard helps you configure your CoolTalk options to match your system.

The Setup Wizard first gives you a chance to select a checkbox to tell it that you don't have a sound card, in which case you can't use CoolTalk anyway, so the setup program will abort, leaving the default settings in place.

Assuming you do have a sound card, selecting the Next button takes you to a screen that asks you to indicate whether you have a 9600, 14,400, or 28,800 baud modem. A press of the Next button then auto-detects the type of sound card you have installed, and begins a series of tests of your sound card at different playback and sampling rates. (You'll need to have a microphone connected to your sound card mic input for these tests.)

When done with the audio tests, the Setup Wizard will check your overall system performance.

Provided your system passed all these tests, the Setup Wizard will configure CoolTalk for proper operation depending on how you answered the test questions.

When you're done with the Setup Wizard, you'll want to select Conference, Options from the CoolTalk menu. This lets you set your Conference, Answering Machine, Audio, and Business Card settings.

The Conference options (see fig. 12.3) tab lets you set up phonebook behavior, dialup speed, and call answering options.

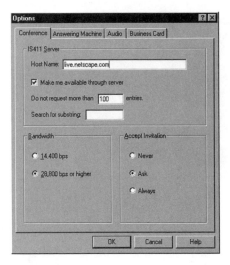

Fig. 12.3
The conference option dialog controls server settings, connection speed, and call answering setup.

The IS411 area under the Conference tab lets you set options for the "411" or "phonebook" server for CoolTalk. The Host name field should contain the URL **live.netscape.com**. This is the default IS411 phonebook server for CoolTalk, and is hosted at Netscape Communications Corporation. Other servers may be made available, and you can select one of them instead if you know the address. If the "Make me available through server" checkbox is selected, when you run CoolTalk you'll be entered automatically into the Host server listing so that others may call you. If you don't want to be bothered, leave this box unchecked and you won't be listed. Every time you run CoolTalk, the status field near the bottom of the CoolTalk window tells you that it's resolving your address. People with dialup connections to the Internet generally get a different IP address assigned to them each time they dial in. CoolTalk resolves this address for the current session and, if the "Make me available" box is checked, registers your currently active IP address with the Host name listed in the dialog. This way, people can call you using CoolTalk whenever you come online, no matter what your IP address is for the current session. This is a very clever setup, and neatly bypasses the problem of floating IP addresses for dialup connections.

The "Do not request more than [n] entries" field lets you control the number of IS4111 listings you view. The "Search for substring" field limits the listings to those that contain only the substring you specify.

The Bandwidth box contains just two radio buttons, which let you select either a 14.4 or 28.8 Kbps (kilobits per second) connection. Make sure this selection matches your modem speed.

The Accept Invitation buttons let you choose to "Never" accept an invitation to chat, or to "Ask" or "Always" accept.

Click on the Answering Machine tab (see fig. 12.4) to set up your answering machine, which can record messages for you whenever you're connected to the Internet, but unable to take calls personally.

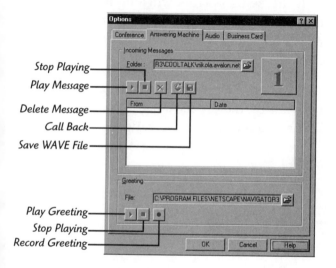

Fig. 12.4
You set up the Answering Machine with this dialog, which lets you record your own outgoing message and define where to save incoming ones.

TIP   **You'll have to have either CoolTalk or the Watchdog program running** in order for your Answering Machine to work properly.

The Incoming Messages field lets you browse to set a Folder that will contain your incoming messages. Below the Folder field is a set of message playback buttons. The large window in the middle of the dialog displays your list of incoming messages. The buttons let you play, stop playing, delete, call back, or save a WAVE file of any messages on your machine. Near the bottom of the dialog are buttons to play, stop, and record your outgoing greeting; there is also a browse button for selecting the filename under which your greeting will be saved to disk.

Selecting the Audio tab brings up a dialog for setting your sound card options. While it's unlikely you'll have more than one Recording Device or Playback Device set up under Windows, this dialog will let you choose which to use if you do. The Sliding control bars let you adjust Recording Sensitivity and Playback Amplification. Both can also be adjusted in the main CoolTalk window by using the up and down arrow buttons on the right end of the bar graph displays. Also in this dialog is the "Recording/ Playback Autoswitch" checkbox. If checked, CoolTalk will automatically switch back and forth from transmitting to receiving audio, determined only by the setting of your Silence Level slider. If this box is checked, you can't manually select to transmit or receive.

The Business Card tab (see fig. 12.5) lets you input personal information, which can be displayed by you or your partner by selecting Conference, Participant Info from the CoolTalk menu during a conversation.

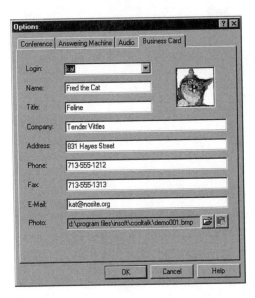

Fig. 12.5
Sharing your personal information by filling out the Business Card fields makes you a real cool cat!

Using CoolTalk

The CoolTalk window (see fig. 12.6) is small and well-organized, with only a few easy-to-use buttons and tools.

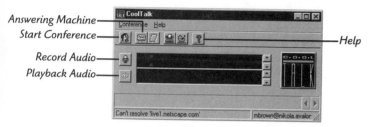

Answering Machine
Start Conference

Record Audio
Playback Audio

Help

Fig. 12.6
The CoolTalk window is unobtrusive and uncluttered, but it packs a lot of power in a small space.

The Start Conference button is equivalent to the menu selection Conference, Start. It is, logically enough, the control you'll use to initiate conversations.

CoolTalk's Answering Machine can be set to answer and log messages when your computer is connected to the Internet but you're not available to answer calls. It's turned on or off using the Answering Machine button. The Read Messages button is used to retrieve messages that have been left on your Answering Machine.

The Chat Tool button brings up the text chat window and the White Board button invokes the collaborative graphical white board tool. These handy tools augment CoolTalk's voice chat with real-time collaborative text and graphic tools.

The Help button—which corresponds to selecting Help, Help Topics from the CoolTalk menu—brings up CoolTalk's extensive help system.

The little microphone is, as you'd expect, a push-to-talk button. You click on it when you want to talk, unless you've configured CoolTalk to work in automatic mode, where it decides when to automatically kick in the microphone. That's what the arrows on the bar graph are for—they set a "silence level" that determines when your mic kicks in if you're in automatic mode.

The speaker button is what you press to listen to the party you're talking with, if you're not in automatic mode.

Up and down audio level control buttons on the right end of the bargraph displays let you set amplification for recording (top) and playback (bottom) sound levels. It's important to adjust these properly for each conversation, as you're likely to run into a wide variety of quality in your CoolTalk connections. I've had good quality hookups with people overseas who are connected with a 486 computer and a 14.4 dialup connection, and bad-to-the-point-of-unintelligible talks with folks hooked up with a T1 line and a Pentium 166. A lot of external factors can affect your connection, including the other person's CoolTalk settings. If you're both willing to play with these a bit, you can usually achieve a very good connection.

Finally, the box at the right center of the CoolTalk screen shows you the image of the person you're speaking to, if he has set it up in his business card settings.

Calling with CoolTalk

You begin a CoolTalk chat session by calling someone up in one of two ways. Clicking on the Start Conference button (or selecting File, Start from the menu) brings up the Open Conference dialog shown in figure 12.7.

From this dialog you can select your internal Address Book, which includes a list of people you've called before, as well as those you've added to the list manually. Picking a name from the list and choosing OK (or simply double-clicking on the name) will dial that person. If the person isn't on your list, you can simply type in her address manually.

From this dialog, you can also select an IS411 Directory. Picking a recipient from this list works in the same manner as the Address Book.

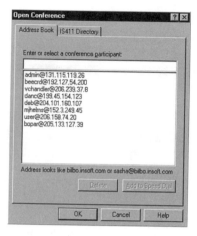

Fig. 12.7
The Open Conference dialog lets you call someone using your internal address book or an IS411 server.

From either list, you can highlight a name and choose <u>A</u>dd to Speed Dial to add the recipient to your speed dial bar near the bottom of the CoolTalk main window (see fig. 12.8).

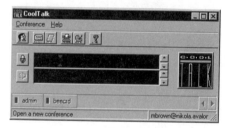

Fig. 12.8
Speed dialer buttons (along the bottom of the CoolTalk window) give you instant access to frequently called addresses.

The second way to call someone makes use of the fact that CoolTalk is configured as a Netscape helper application. You use Netscape to connect to **http://live.netscape.com**, the home page for the IS411 Directory (see fig. 12.9).

Clicking on a link in this alphabetical listing of CoolTalk users will launch CoolTalk and attempt to link you to the listed user.

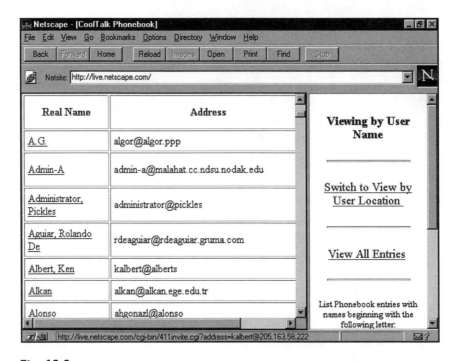

Fig. 12.9
The IS411 Directory page, hosted by Netscape, lists all currently active CoolTalk users who have made their presence known.

"Hey," you may be saying about now, **"this is a bit of a fraud! CoolTalk** doesn't seem to have much to do with Netscape at all!"

You're right. It doesn't. It's really just a stand-alone program, configured to work as a Netscape helper application. Perhaps a future version of CoolTalk will be more integrated into Netscape (as a plug-in, for example), but for the time being, Netscape's Internet telephone application of choice is, indeed, a totally separate program.

The CoolTalk answering machine

We've already covered many of the CoolTalk Answering Machine's features, but it might help to go through the process of using it step-by-step, since its features are really located in different places in CoolTalk.

First, you have to determine if you can realistically use the CoolTalk Answering Machine. It's important to understand that this is not a *telephone* Answering Machine, but a CoolTalk message Answering Machine. That is, it takes CoolTalk calls for you when you're not available to answer them yourself. To be able to do this, you must be connected to the Internet whenever you want it to answer for you. If you're paying for a dialup connection by the minute, obviously the CoolTalk Answering Machine is not for you.

But if you have unlimited access, either through a flat-fee dialup connection or a dedicated line, the CoolTalk Answering Machine can make sure you don't miss important CoolTalk calls.

Once you've decided to set it up, you need to select File, Options from the CoolTalk menu, then click on the Answering Machine tab in the dialog that pops up. Set up a directory to hold your incoming messages and record your outgoing message, as explained in the previous section, "Setting CoolTalk Options."

Back in the main CoolTalk window, click on the Answering Machine button to turn it on.

If you receive any messages while you're away from your computer, the Read Messages button will show you how many you received. Clicking on it will let you play back your messages, and you can choose to delete, save, or respond to them as you wish.

CoolTalk's Chat Tool

Collaboration is a hot word in groupware, intranet, and Internet application circles. All it means, of course, is "working together," and CoolTalk incorporates a couple of great tools for working together over the Internet—the Chat Tool and the White Board.

CoolTalk's Chat Tool is easy to bring up—you just press the Chat Tool button on the CoolTalk Window. Though the Chat Tool button looks like a little telephone, it actually brings up a text-based chat box (see fig. 12.10).

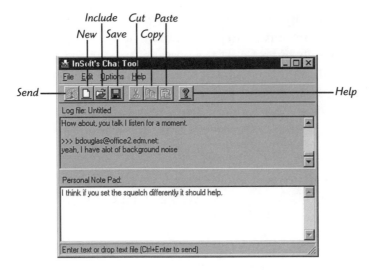

Fig. 12.10
The CoolTalk Chat Tool lets you type messages back and forth or send text files.

You simply type your messages into the lower text box. You can send them by typing Ctrl+E, clicking on the Send button, or selecting File, Post NotePad from the CoolTalk menu. These notes appear on your conversation partner's screen, as well as in the upper Log window of your Chat Tool window. Her messages appear on your screen too, of course. You can save a log file of your Chat session by selecting Save or Save As from the File menu, or clicking on the Save button. Clicking on the New button will clear the text windows and start a new log. Picking File, Include or clicking on the Include button brings up a file browser that lets you send along a text file (though unfortunately not binaries). There are buttons and menu selections for cut, copy, and paste, and the File menu includes Print Setup and Print options.

There is just one selection under the Options menu in the Chat Tool—this is "Pop Up On Receive". If checked, this option will automatically launch the Chat Tool when a text message is transmitted to you.

The Chat Tool is great for exchanging pre-written notes, meeting minutes, and so on, and is a handy backup means of communication if you're having problems with voice transmissions.

CoolTalk's White Board

Clicking on the White Board button brings up CoolTalk's White Board (see fig. 12.11), which at first glance seems to be simply an elementary drawing program. However, a little experimentation reveals it to be an immensely powerful collaboration tool.

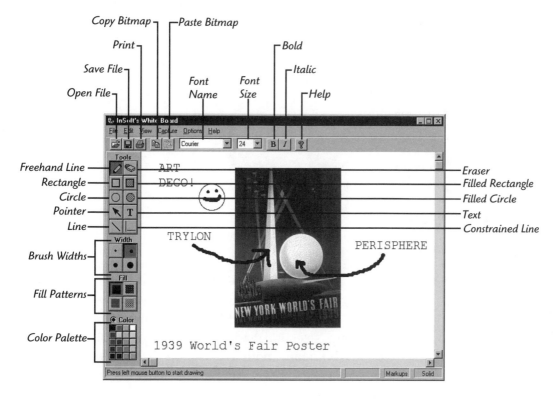

Fig. 12.11
CoolTalk's White Board is a sophisticated collaboration tool with many surprising features.

Of course, you can use the line, rectangle, circle, text, and freehand tools to draw simple illustrations that can be seen by your collaborator. But they can draw on the same workspace. This means you can work on the same image together, trading off one another's ideas. Not only that, but the menus reveal that there are actually two layers to the White Board—one for an image, and one for markups. Either can be changed independently of the other. You can load an image, mark it up, and delete just the markups or the entire white board. You can use the eraser on just markups, too, so you can change your markings any way you wish. At any time, either of you can load in a new image. Zoom controls and even an option to "float" the menu bar give you excellent control over your workspace.

The CoolTalk White Board can load a variety of bitmapped images, including:

- Windows Bitmap
- Compuserve GIF
- ZSoft Paintbrush PCX
- TIFF Revision 5.0
- JPEG
- Sun Raster
- Truevision TARGA

It can also snapshot your desktop, a window, or a dragged-out region of your screen. This means you can load up just about any software program while you're online (CAD, spreadsheet, and so on), capture an image of it with a single CoolTalk menu selection, and share it with your collaborator over the Internet. You can both talk about it, exchange text notes about it, mark it up and change your markups as you work. Then you can quickly move on to the next image under consideration.

I strongly suggest you link up with another CoolTalk user and experiment with the collaboration features embodied in the CoolTalk Chat Tool and White Board. I guarantee you'll fall in love with them. It's a whole new way to communicate.

 NOTE **CoolTalk comes with an extensive set of help files. To find answers to** any CoolTalk questions not answered here, select <u>H</u>elp Topics from the CoolTalk <u>H</u>elp menu. You can also find out more at **http://www.netscape.com**.

The impact of Internet voice communication

Speaking by way of the Internet is still in its infancy, but there is a tremendous amount of potential in such technology. Just as the telephone revolutionized conversation early in this century, Internet talk software could initiate another revolution in the way we converse. Voice communications on the Internet is still in its "hobbyist" stage, much as radio was in the '20s. Though it is currently not practical to make initial contact with people in the business world with Internet phone utilities, that day may come sooner rather than later.

For personal communications, in which price is a major factor in limiting long distance calls, Internet voice chat utilities are already unmatched in economy, if not usefulness. Long distance phone companies have indicated that they are not amused with this emerging technology, and have made their first challenges to it in the courts. Time will tell if they'll be able to shut down Internet telephone before it even gets completely off the ground.

The future

In the near future, we'll see new data compression techniques that will let standard phone twisted pair and CATV coax lines handle phone, live video feeds, cable TV, and Internet WAN (Wide Area Network) connections and still be ready to accommodate lots more data. Fiber optic lines are also being laid in many areas, which will expand these capabilities a thousandfold.

Provided it can survive the legal hurdles, the future of Internet telephony includes these possibilities:

- Conference calling in full duplex
- Call forwarding to other terminals
- Sending files to each other as you talk about something
- Remote talking (so you don't have to be sitting in front of your computer)

Voice communications on the Internet has the potential of becoming as popular as the World Wide Web itself. It is a very possible that on business cards, people will someday have Internet voice contact information right under their e-mail addresses.

NOTE **For more information on the topic of voice communications on the** Internet, check out the Internet Phone FAQ (Frequently Asked Questions) file on Usenet. This file is posted on the 5th and 19th of each month to the Usenet newsgroups **alt.internet.services, alt.bbs.internet, alt.culture.internet, alt.winsock.voice, alt.winsock.ivc, comp.sys.mac.comm, comp.os.ms-windows.apps.comm, alt.answers, comp.answers**, and **news.answers**. The latest version is also available on the World Wide Web at **http://www.northcoast.com/~savetz/voice-faq.html**.

Adding on to Netscape with Power Pack

● **In this chapter:**

● Which plug-ins and helper applications have been included in Power Pack 2

● How to obtain and install Power Pack 2—including information on how to download the free evaluation version

● How to use the four major add-ons included in Power Pack 2

● Where to go in this book for information on using the 15 additional plug-ins included in the Power Pack 2 CD-ROM—and where to download them all for free

Netscape Navigator is a great program, but it doesn't do everything. You can't use it to view inline movies, or listen to live audio streams, or check downloaded files for viruses. You can't chat with other people on the Internet in real-time, and there is no way to monitor Web sites so that you'll be notified when they change.

Of course, that whole introductory paragraph is really just a set-up, because you can, of course, do all of those things with Netscape. But you can't do them with Netscape alone. You need helper applications or plug-ins to add these features to Netscape.

Netscape Corporation, with an eye on enhancing your overall Netscape Web browsing experience, has bundled some of the best helper applications and plug-ins into a commercial product on CD-ROM that they call the Netscape Power Pack.

 TIP **You'll find copies of many of the plug-ins from the Power Pack** on the CD. So, watch for the icon in the margin indicating which programs are on the CD with the book. You may find that you can save yourself the cost of the Power Pack if all of the programs you need are on this book's CD.

What's in Power Pack 2?

Netscape's Power Pack 1 CD-ROM included five add-on applications for Netscape: Netscape SmartMarks 1, Netscape Chat 1.0.1, Adobe Acrobat Reader 2.1, Apple QuickTime 2.0.3, and RealAudio Player 1. Of these, SmartMarks, Chat, and RealAudio have survived into release 2. The Adobe Acrobat Reader and Apple QuickTime aren't on the new CD-ROM, but can be downloaded from the Web for free.

 NOTE **The Adobe Acrobat Amber plug-in for Netscape can be downloaded** from the Adobe Web site at **http://www.adobe.com**.

Apple's QuickTime player is available at **http://www.apple.com**. (Note that this is only a system-level QuickTime player. To actually play QuickTime movies using Netscape, you'll also need to install a QuickTime player plug-in or helper application. See chapter 10 for information on where to download QuickTime player plug-ins.)

 On the CD

Where the Power Pack 1 CD-ROM included only these five Netscape add-ons, Power Pack 2 includes a "main suite" of four add-ons, plus a collection of 15 other Netscape plug-ins. With a total of 19 Netscape enhancements, you could say that there are nearly four times as many useful additions included in package 2.

The main suite of four major applications in Power Pack 2 includes:

- INSO CyberSpell for Netscape Mail
- Norton AntiVirus Internet Scanner
- SmartMarks 2
- Netscape Chat 2

Note that SmartMarks and Chat have both been upgraded to 2 versions in this release. CyberSpell and Norton AntiVirus round out the "top four."

"Where's RealAudio," you ask? Well, you could say that it has been demoted—it's listed as one of the 15 plug-ins also included on the CD-ROM. These are:

On the CD

- ASAP WebShow
- Astound Web Player
- CarbonCopy/Net
- EarthTime/Lite
- Envoy
- FIGleaf Inline Lite
- FormulaOne/NET
- Lightning Strike
- Netscape Live3D
- RealAudio
- Shockwave for Director
- VDOLive
- VRScout

- WIRL 3D Browser
- Word Viewer

Let's take a quick look at the 15 plug-ins first.

The Power Pack 2 plug-ins

The plug-ins included on the Power Pack 2 CD-ROM cover the field as far as adding new capabilities to Netscape is concerned. This set has been carefully balanced to provide at least one plug-in for just about every type of content you can name.

What follows in this section is a summary of the plug-ins included in Power Pack 2, with Web sites where you can download each for free.

The *ASAP WebShow* plug-in from Software Publishing Corporation lets you view business presentations inline in Web pages. You can view, download, and print any document created by SPC's ASAP WordPower report and presentation software package. Available for Windows 95 and Windows 3.1, you can download the latest version from **http://www.spco.com.**

Astound Web Player by Gold Disk plays back multimedia presentations created with Gold Disk's Astound and Studio M products. These documents can include sound, animation, graphics, video, and interactivity. The Astound Web Player features dynamic streaming; the next slide in a presentation is downloaded in the background while you view the current slide. This plug-in is available for Windows 95 and Windows 3.1 from **http://www.golddisk.com.**

Microcom's *CarbonCopy/Net* lets you access and control other PCs over the Internet. You can run applications, access files, and view or edit documents on a remote PC as though they were on the PC in front of you. A plug-in adaptation of Microcom's much-used stand-alone CarbonCopy program, Carbon Copy/Net is useful for collaboration, remote software demonstrations, remote support, and remote access to CD-ROMs and other data. Available for Windows 95 and Windows 3.1, you can download the CarbonCopy/Net plug-in from **http://www.microcom.com/.**

EarthTime/Lite (see fig. 13.1) by Starfish Software is a world time plug-in that displays the local time and date for eight geographic locations from your choice of more than 400 world capitals and commercial centers. Its animated worldwide map also indicates sunrise and sunset boundaries. A Windows 95 and Windows NT version is available at **http://www.starfishsoftware.com**.

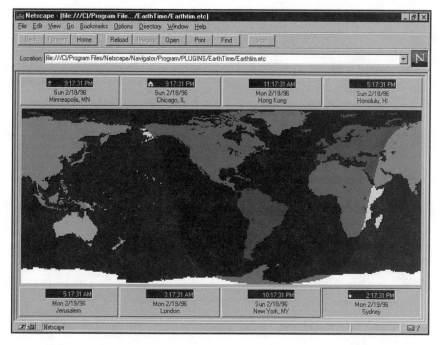

Fig. 13.1
EarthTime *is* a great example of a unique plug-in that *is* both useful and fun.

Tumbleweed Software's *Envoy* is the major competitor to Adobe's Acrobat. That Envoy is in the Power Pack 2 collection, while Acrobat (which was in Power Pack 1) is not, represents a major coup for Tumbleweed. The Envoy plug-in lets you view documents with well-defined and unchangeable fonts, graphics, and layouts. Tumbleweed Publishing Essentials is the commercial program you use for creating Envoy documents, and TW also offers an Envoy Software Developer's Kit for creating customized Envoy document viewers. Access **http://www.twcorp.com** to download versions for Windows 95, Windows NT, Windows 3.1, Macintosh, and PowerMac.

FIGleaf Inline Lite by Carberry Technology lets you view and zoom a wide variety of raster and vector graphics formats. FIGleaf Inline adds rotation of all images in 90, 180, 270, or 360 degrees, and viewing of multipage files. Scrollbars are available when zoomed in on an image, or when the image is too large to be displayed in the default window. Format support includes: CGM (the first vector graphic MIME standard), GIF, JPEG, PNG, TIFF, CCITT GP4, BMP, WMF, EPSF, Sun Raster, RGB, and others. Download a Windows 95 and Windows NT version from **http://www.ct.ebt.com/**.

Visual Components' *FormulaOne/NET* lets you embed and manipulate live spreadsheets and charts on Web pages. This Excel-compatible spreadsheet's worksheets can include live charts, links to URLs, formatted text and numbers, calculations, and clickable buttons and controls. Though probably of limited use on the World Wide Web, this plug-in is sure to get a lot of use on corporate intranets. Download Formula One/NET for Windows 95, Windows NT, and Windows 3.1 from **http://www.visualcomp.com**.

Lightning Strike by InfinitOp lets you view image files compressed with the Lightning Strike optimized wavelet image codec. This alternative to JPEG is said to provide higher compression ratios, smaller image files, faster transmissions, and improved image quality. Available for Windows 95, Windows NT, Windows 3.1, and Macintosh, you can download this plug-in from **http://www.infinop.com**.

It was probably a no-brainer for Netscape to include their own *Live3D* VRML viewer plug-in on the Power Pack 2 CD-ROM. This plug-in lets you fly through VRML worlds on the Web and run interactive, multiuser VRML applications written in Java. Netscape Live3D features 3D text, background images, texture animation, morphing, viewpoints, collision detection, gravity, and RealAudio streaming sound. You can download Live3D for Windows 95, Windows NT, and Windows 3.1 by following the links from Netscape's home page at **http://home.netscape.com**. It's interesting to note, however, that Live3D is not the only VRML plug-in in this collection. The third-party VR Scout and WIRL plug-ins listed below are also included.

Though a major player on the Power Pack 1 CD-ROM and, by comparison, relegated to "me too" status on the 2 collection, *RealAudio* by Progressive Networks—up to version 2 in this release—is an important Netscape plug-in. It lets you listen to both live and rebroadcast audio on the

Internet. It works over 14.4 Kbps or faster connections, and is gaining wide acceptance on the Web. Available for Windows 95, Windows NT, Windows 3.1, and Macintosh, you can download RealAudio from **http://www.realaudio.com/**.

Shockwave for Director by Macromedia lets you play Macromedia Director animations and presentations. You can interact with Director presentations right in a Netscape Navigator window with animation, clickable buttons, links to URLs, digital video movies, sound, and more. Windows 95, Windows 3.1, and Macintosh versions reside at **http://www.macromedia.com**.

VDOLive from VDOnet is for viewing real-time Video for Windows movies over the Internet. VDOLive compresses video images, and the speed of your connection determines the frame delivery rate. With a 28.8 Kbps modem, VDOLive runs in real time at 10 to 15 frames per second. VDOLive is available for Windows 95, Windows NT, and Windows 3.1 at **http://www.vdolive.com/**.

VRScout VR Browser by Chaco Communications is one of three VRML viewers contained in this collection. Download VR Scout for Windows 95 and Windows NT from **http://www.chaco.com**.

The final VRML viewer on the CD-ROM is the *WIRL 3D Browser* by VREAM. This one adds support for object behaviors, logical cause-and-effect relationships, multimedia capabilities, world authoring, and links to Windows applications. Available for Windows 95 and Windows NT, you can download it from **http://www.vream.com**.

Word Viewer by Inso Corporation lets you embed Microsoft Word documents in Web pages. Another plug-in that's more likely to see intranet rather than Internet use, this plug-in can display both Microsoft Word 6 and Microsoft Word 7 documents. It also lets you copy and print Word documents with all original formatting intact. Download the Word Viewer plug-in for Windows 95, Windows NT, and Windows 3.1 from **http://www.inso.com**.

NOTE **For the latest up-to-the-minute information on all Netscape plug-ins,** check out the official Netscape list of available plug-ins at **http://home.netscape.com/comprod/products/navigator/version_2.0/plugins/index.html** or the Plug-Ins Plaza site at **http://www.browserwatch.com/plug-in.html.**

The Power Pack 2 major add-ons

As we said before, the four major add-ons provided in the Power Pack 2 collection are INSO CyberSpell for Netscape Mail, Norton AntiVirus Internet Scanner, SmartMarks 2, and Netscape Chat 2. A free downloadable trial version of Power Pack 2 that includes only these four add-ons is available from **http://home.netscape.com/comprod/mirror/client_download.html.**

INSO's *CyberSpell* provides an integral spell checker for Netscape's Main and News composition windows. This will be a welcome addition for those to whom spelling comes hard. In addition, CyberSpell also provides some basic grammar and capitalization help. CyberSpell features a 146,000 word dictionary with U.S. and British spellings, as well as 13,000 specialized legal, business, and technical terms.

The *Norton AntiVirus Internet Scanner* is an online adaptation of Symantic Corporation's famed Norton AntiVirus stand-alone program. It protects your system from viruses that may come attached to downloaded files or e-mail messages. In addition, it can do a virus scan of your entire system to make sure that you start with a clean slate.

Netscape Smartmarks 2 is an update of the Smartmarks program on the Power Pack 1 collection. It represents Netscape's own attempt to build a better bookmark program. It seamlessly integrates into Navigator's <u>B</u>ookmark menu, providing not only improved bookmark management, but the ability to track Web site changes. You can even automatically download and browse Web sites offline, saving connect time charges. There's also an integrated search tool for searching multiple online search engines with a single query. The whole works is powered by a third party engine from First Floor Software called "Smart Catalog" technology.

Netscape Chat 2 is also an in-house Netscape project, and is, again, an update of a program included on the first Power Pack CD-ROM. This package lets you participate in IRC, or Internet Relay Chat. IRC, a live online chat system, has been around for years, but the Netscape Chat program makes IRC easy to use. If you've made the move from Compuserve or America Online to a standard ISP (Internet Service Provider) and miss the real-time conferences, then IRC is for you. You can initiate one-on-one chats, participate in group conferences, or visit moderated "auditoriums." Netscape Chat includes a special function that lets you share interesting URLs with others in your chat room, launching Navigator automatically so they can browse the Web right along with you. Netscape is even hosting their own IRC server, so you can get online right away.

Installing Power Pack 2

You can purchase the Power Pack 2 CD-ROM online from the Netscape General Store or you can download the trail version which contains just the four main add-on programs. **http://www.netscape.com** is the place to go for either choice.

You'll need at least 8 MB of RAM, a 14.4 Kbps or faster modem, and several megabytes of available hard disk space to install these applications—how much hard drive space depends on how many you choose to install. Let's just say that installing the whole works is another good reason to upgrade to that one gigabyte hard drive you've been wanting.

Power Pack 2 uses the familiar InstallShield Wizard under Windows 95 (see fig. 13.2). Installation on other platforms follows a similar process. You'll need at least version 2 of Netscape before you can use these programs—since this book covers Netscape 3, we'll assume that's the version of Netscape you own, so you probably won't have any problems.

The first thing you'll see is a license window. Read the legalese carefully, then click the "I Agree" button. If you don't agree to the stated terms and conditions, you won't be able to install any of the Power Pack 2 programs.

Once you've been agreeable, you'll see the screen shown in fig. 13.3. Here you can choose which of the four applications to install. All are checked by default; uncheck any you don't want installed, then use the <u>N</u>ext> button to move on to the installation process for each individual program.

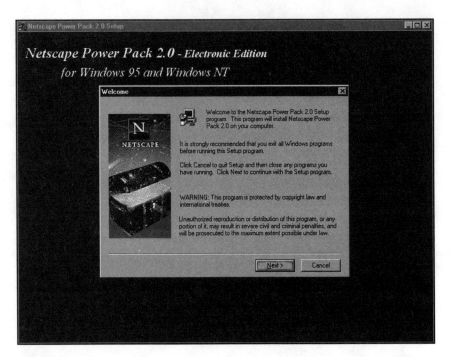

Fig. 13.2
The Power Pack 2 InstallShield Wizard steps you gently through the installation process.

CAUTION **Heed the warning on the program selection window in figure 13.3.**
The InstallShield Wizard is really a shell program that ties together four *separate* and unrelated installation programs, one for each add-on. Some of these will ask you to reboot your computer so that their changes can take effect. *Do not do this!* Instead, always choose the "Do Not Reboot" selection. At the end of the string of installations, you'll be returned to the InstallShield Wizard where you can do a "once for all" reboot to activate the changes.

We'll only step through the installation for SmartMarks here. The installation process for each of these add-ons is similar enough that this should get you by. However, be aware that they do vary some in the details, so be careful to follow the on-screen instructions for each individual program carefully.

The SmartMarks installer first asks you for some personal identification information. Enter your info and select Next> to proceed.

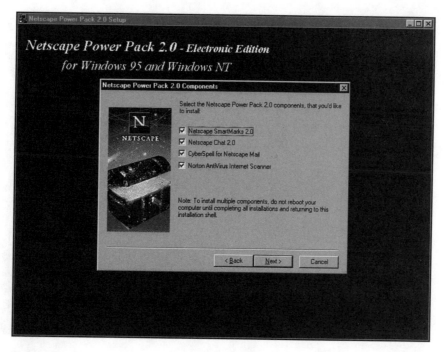

Fig. 13.3
You can install all of the Power Pack 2 applications or none by checking the appropriate boxes in this window.

You're then asked to choose a Typical, Compact, or Custom installation (see fig. 13.4). The default choice is "Typical," and this is the choice you should make unless there is an overpowering reason to do otherwise. For example, if you're a power user you might want to go through the Custom set-up; if you're installing on a laptop with limited resources, you might want to pick Compact.

Finally, you'll be asked to pick a directory in which to install SmartMarks. Again, pick the default unless you have an overpowering reason not to. If that directory doesn't exist, the installer will create it for you. Finally, you review your settings and the SmartMarks files are decompressed and put in their proper place.

CAUTION   **Do not install SmartMarks 2 into your SmartMarks 1 directory, or you** may suffer dire (though unspecified) consequences!

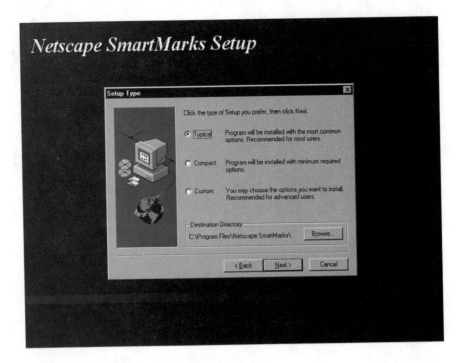

Fig. 13.4
The SmartMarks installer can customize your installation for you.

Once SmartMarks has been installed, the InstallShield Wizard moves on to install the other programs. At the end, you'll be asked to approve the restarting of your computer. Once rebooted, your add-ons are ready to use.

Netscape SmartMarks 2

Like Netscape's built-in bookmarks, Netscape SmartMarks 2 lets you organize bookmarks listing the URLs of interesting sites on the Web. However, SmarkMarks does a lot more for you. It offers more organizational choices, sure. But it also lets you automatically monitor your favorite sites for changes, alerting you when it's time to go back for new information. You can also tell SmartMarks to automatically download a copy of a Web site for you onto your hard drive for offline browsing. If you pay for your Web access, this can save you a lot of connect time charges (albeit at the cost of multi-megabytes of hard disk space). There is an integral search feature that queries many of the most popular online search engines—including Web Crawler, Yahoo, Lycos, InfoSeek, Excite, OpenText, DejaNews, and AltaVista—with a single form. SmartMarks even intelligently imports your own set of personal bookmarks and integrates them seamlessly with its own humongous set of predefined bookmarks.

Much of the magic is accomplished using the licensed Smart Catalog technology from First Floor, Inc.

CAUTION **Note that if you are running Windows 3.x or Windows for Workgroups,** you must use the 16-bit SmartMarks even if you have Win32s installed. If you are running Windows 95 or Windows NT, use the 32-bit SmartMarks. To run the 32-bit SmartMarks, you must have a 32-bit TCP/IP stack.

Getting started with SmartMarks

Figure 13.5 shows the SmartMarks main window.

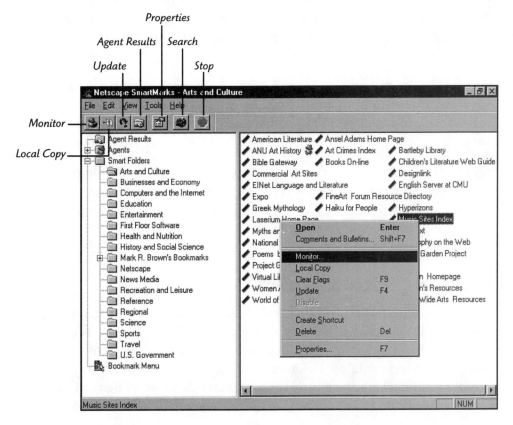

Fig. 13.5
The SmartMarks main window, showing its collection of prebuilt bookmark folders.

For version 2, the main window has been simplified and redesigned to look and work like the Windows Explorer. Your catalog, or collection of bookmarks, is shown as a tree in the left side of the window. Clicking a folder displays its contents in the right-hand window, which the SmartMarks documentation refers to as the "grid." Standard Win95 elements include a menu and toolbar at the top of the screen, and a status bar at the bottom. You can turn off all but the grid window through options under the View menu.

TIP **Windows 95 integration extends to the ability to create a shortcut to** your favorite bookmarks to place on the Win95 desktop. Just right-click a bookmark and select Create Shortcut from the pop-up menu. Now, right from the desktop, you can monitor your favorite Web sites.

The toolbar has buttons for (from left to right): monitoring a site for updates; making a Local Copy of a Web site for offline browsing; updating a site's listing; displaying Agent Results; changing Properties; performing a Search; and Stopping an action.

As you can see from fig. 13.5, right-clicking the mouse over an item brings up a pop-up menu from which you can choose to open, monitor, or create a local copy of a Web site. These choices are also available from the menus.

SmartMarks starts up with a predefined catalog, comprised of folders containing bookmarks for hundreds of interesting Web sites. As you can see from the tree list in fig. 13.5, SmartMarks automatically grabbed my bookmarks and integrated them into its own collection when it was first installed.

Working with the catalog

At its core, SmartMarks is a sophisticated bookmark cataloging system. Because it integrates with Netscape, selecting Add SmartMark from the Netscape Bookmarks menu is all you have to do to add a new Web site to your SmartMarks catalog. Deleting a bookmark can be accomplished by simply right-clicking the mouse on a bookmark and selecting the Delete item, or by clicking and selecting it and pressing the Delete key. Moving bookmarks is as simple as dragging them and dropping them in a new folder.

NOTE　**SmartMarks is only available from the Netscape menu if you have** enabled it. To do so, select Tools, Preferences from the SmartMarks menu, then check the "Load with browser" item under the Options tab.

It's surprising that there's no toolbar button for searching for a bookmark, but it's done easily enough by right-clicking in a blank spot in the grid window and selecting Find, Bookmark from the pop-up menu. You can accomplish the same thing by selecting Tools, Find, Bookmark from the main menu.

To create a new folder, right-click the mouse in a blank spot on the grid window. To delete one, select it and press the Delete key, or right-click it and select Delete from the pop-up menu. Folders can be moved with a simple drag-and-drop.

In general, if you can use Windows Explorer, SmartMarks 2 is a snap. Many of the same commands are available from the menu, toolbar, and right-mouse button pop-up menus.

You gotta have an agent

Agents are a hot topic in programming these days. Basically, an agent is a user-configurable program that will go off and do something you've told it to do in the way you told it to do it, then report back to you with the results. SmartMarks uses agents to tell you when your favorite Web sites have been updated, and to make local copies of them for offline viewing, if you want.

Agents are listed in the left tree window just like folders. Selecting one lists the Web sites it targets in the grid window on the right, just like opening a folder. However, agents are programmable.

SmartMarks comes with three predefined agents: List/Searches, Local Copy, and What's New? Right-clicking any of them in the tree list and selecting Properties (or selecting one and pressing the F7 key) brings up the dialog box shown in figure 13.6.

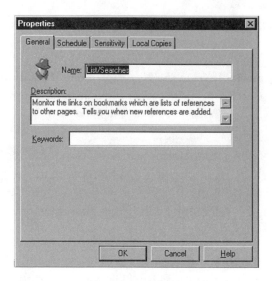

Fig. 13.6
Agents can be programmed using this dialog box to perform a surprising variety of online functions automatically.

Options for an agent include Keywords you can search for, times at which the agent should automatically update its information, how sensitive it should be to changes, and whether or not it should save a copy for local browsing (as well as how much it should save). If you want to keep your current agents' settings, instead of editing an existing agent you can create a new one by selecting File, New, Agent from the main menu.

CAUTION **Don't go crazy setting agents up to make local copies of Web sites.** Depending on your agent settings, each local copy can eat up a horrendous amount of hard disk space. Whole copies can also take a lot of time to download. Keep both factors in mind when using the Local Copy option.

To associate an agent with a bookmark, right-click the bookmark in the grid window and choose Monitor from the pop-up menu. You'll get a dialog with a list of available agents that you can pick from, as well as buttons that let you change an agent's settings or define a new agent on the spot.

NOTE If a Web site uses the HTML feature "bulletins," SmartMarks will tell you more than just the fact that a monitored page has changed—it will tell you *what* has changed! If you're interested in checking out this feature, you will find a SmartMarks-importable list of sites that use bulletins at **http://www.firstfloor.com/catalogs/bulletin.htm**.

Searching the Web with SmartMarks

Another of SmartMarks' nifty features is its ability to perform a search of the most popular Web search engines using a single, simple dialog (see fig. 13.7).

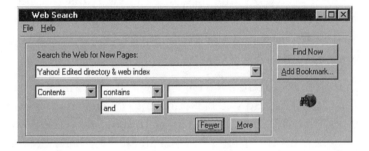

Fig. 13.7
SmartMarks' all-in-one search dialog not only saves you time, it simplifies searches by making the interface the same for all.

You can search the contents, title, URL, or comments of any of the search engines listed for a match of any combination of keywords. Included in the drop-down list of supported search engines are all the most popular Web search sites: Yahoo!, Lycos, InfoSeek, Webcrawler, Excite, DejaNews, OpenText, and Alta Vista.

SmartMarks is a very useful and sophisticated program. Though it can take some time to get comfortable with the controls, if you are a serious Web user, the time you invest in learning to use it right can pay off in time-savings later. SmartMarks' extensive Help system can help you flatten the learning curve considerably.

Netscape Chat 2

Netscape Chat is, like SmartMarks, a product of Netscape Communications Corporation. Also like SmartMarks, Netscape Chat makes a repeat appearance in the Power Pack 2 collection as a v2 revision of a program from the original Power Pack CD-ROM.

Netscape Chat lets you participate in IRC—Internet Relay Chat. This is a live text-based chat system that predates the World Wide Web. By logging onto an IRC server computer system, you can enter discussion "rooms" and hold real-time conversations with other Internet users. These types of services have long been a favorite on Compuserve, America Online, and other for-pay services. But IRC has until recently largely been reserved for those willing to learn how to use the relatively complex UNIX tools you needed to hook up to IRC servers.

Netscape Chat changes all that. It's easy to install, use, and set up. And it integrates with Navigator so you can enter into discussions right from Web page links. Not only that, it adds an option to "share" Web page URLs with others in an IRC room, so you can all effectively browse the Web together! This is not only fun, it can be a great collaboration tool for co-workers, either in the same building or continents apart.

 NOTE One of the best sites on the Net for information about IRC is at http://www.irchelp.org/. Here you'll find a lot of hand-holding help and a complete set of IRC documents, including the IRC FAQ (Frequently Asked Questions list).

Getting set up with Netscape Chat

When you first run Netscape Chat, you'll be asked for a few items of personal information (see fig. 13.8).

IRC works through a series of IRC host computers. You can pick a Host by selecting one from the Address Book, or you can enter one yourself. A good choice is **iapp.netscape.com**, which is Netscape's own IRC server. The Port number for IRC chat is almost always 6667 or, occasionally, 7000—if it's not, you'll be told by your host provider. Table 13.1 lists some of the more popular IRC hosts in the world. Try to pick one close to you.

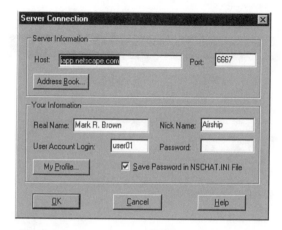

Fig. 13.8
The Server Connection dialog lets you set up your connection information so you can get online.

Table 13.1   IRC hosts

Location	Server name	Port
North America		
Montreal, Quebec	montreal.qu.ca.undernet.org	6667
Netscape Communications	iapp.netscape.com	6667
Austin, TX	austin.tx.us.undernet.org	6667
Bloomington, IN	bloomington.in.us.undernet.org	6667
Charlotte, NC	uncc.dal.net	6667
Chicago, IL	chicago.il.us.undernet.org	6667
Davis, CA	davis.ca.us.undernet.org	6667
Davis, CA	davis.dal.net	7000
Detroit, MI	rochester.mi.us.undernet.org	6667
Hoffman Estates, IL	cin.dal.net	6667
Manhattan, KS	manhattan.ks.us.undernet.org	6667

continues

Table 13.1   Continued

Location	Server name	Port
North America		
Marblehead, MA	**xanth.dal.net**	6667
Minneapolis, MN	**skypoint.dal.net**	6667
University of Oklahoma, OK	**norman.ok.us.undernet.org**	6667
Phoenix, AZ	**phoenix.az.us.undernet.org**	6667
Phoenix, AZ	**phoenix.dal.net**	6667
Pittsburgh, PA	**pittsburgh.pa.us.undernet.org**	6667
Rohnert Park, CA	**groucho.dal.net**	6667
San Jose, CA	**sanjose.ca.us.undernet.org**	6667
San Jose, CA	**mindijari.dal.net**	6668
Tampa, FL	**tampa.fl.us.undernet.org**	6667
Washington, D.C.	**washington.dc.us.undernet.org**	6667
Europe		
Amsterdam, Netherlands	**amsterdam.nl.eu.undernet.org**	6667
Bristol, England	**liberator.dal.net**	7000
Caen, France	**caen.fr.eu.undernet.org**	6667
Delft, Netherlands	**delft.nl.eu.undernet.org**	6667
Espoo, Finland	**xgw.dal.net**	7000
Gothenburg, Sweden	**gothenburg.se.eu.undernet.org**	6667
Ljubljana, Slovenia	**ljubljana.si.eu.undernet.org**	6667
Oslo, Norway	**oslo.no.eu.undernet.org**	6667
Oxford, England	**oxford.uk.eu.undernet.org**	6667
Vienna, Austria	**vienna.at.eu.undernet.org**	6667

Location	Server name	Port
Australia and New Zealand		
Auckland, New Zealand	**auckland.nz.us.undernet.org**	6667
Brisbane, Australia	**brisbane.qld.au.undernet.org**	6667
Wollongong, New South Wales	**wollongong.nsw.au.undernet..org**	6667

The Server Connection dialog is also where you enter personal information. The most important item here is your Nick Name, which is what you'll be known as in your online chats. You can enter additional personal information by clicking the My Profile button. People can view this information by using IRC's Info function, so don't list anything you don't want people to know about you.

 TIP The User Account Login and Password fields may or may not be optional, depending on the requirements of the Chat Server you are connecting to.

The Option menu includes a Preference selection that lets you customize the way NS Chat acts. You can use it with the default settings, but after you've got a bit of experience, you're bound to want to play with the settings. The Help menu includes extensive documentation on how each of the Preferences settings works.

Going online with Netscape Chat

The Netscape Chat main window (see fig. 13.9) includes a menu and toolbar, a chat window, and a console window (shown in fig. 13.10).

Starting a chat session begins with the Connect button on the toolbar. Click it to open the Server Connection dialog we talked about in the previous section. You can change your Host or personal information if you wish, then click OK to connect to the specified IRC server. If everything goes well, the Console window will display a series of messages to let you know you've gotten connected okay, and the Quick Join dialog box will appear (fig. 13.10).

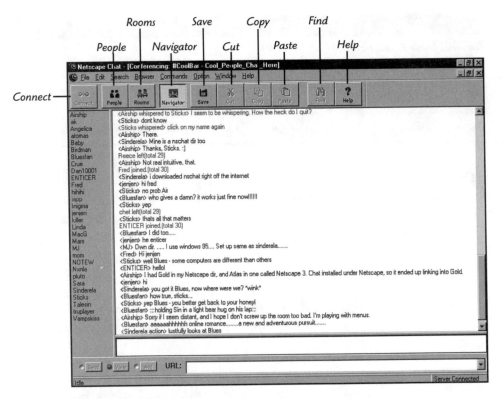

Fig. 13.9
The Netscape Chat main window is clearly laid out and easy to use.

Fig. 13.10
The Console window displays important connection information. The Quick Join dialog gets you chatting right away.

To join the selected chat room, click OK. To pick a different room, click the List button and a list dialog will appear listing all available chat rooms. Pick one and you're online! You can bring up the room list at any time by clicking the Rooms button on the toolbar. Netscape Chat will let you join up to 10 or more rooms at once, depending on the server, but switching among that many conversations can get pretty confusing. To leave a room, select Command, Leave Room from the menu.

You can also create your own chat rooms by simply clicking the Rooms toolbar button and typing a new room name into the Room: name box. You'll be asked to specify if you want this to be a conference room or auditorium. You'll usually specify a conference. An auditorium is a moderated discussion group that you administer—details are available through the NS Chat Help menu.

You type messages into the window above the URL field. Everyone's input is displayed in the large central window. At the left is a list of room participants. You can "whisper" a private message to anyone in a room by clicking their name on the list to highlight it, then typing your message. To turn off whisper mode, click their name again to un-highlight it. Right-clicking a name lets you choose to initiate a private conversation (Talk), turn off their messages (Ignore), or find out more about (Info) that person. All of these options are available for a scrolling list of all persons on the server by selecting the People button from the toolbar.

Because Netscape Chat is linked to Netscape Navigator, you can share an URL with others in the room by typing it into the URL field at the bottom of the window. You can also just click the "Send" button to transmit the URL of the Web page currently displayed in Netscape. Either way, every-one in the room will see the URL and, if they have this feature enabled, their copy of Netscape will jump to the URL you've sent. (Choose Option, Preference, Navigator from the menu and check the Auto View box to activate this feature on your system.) Shared URLs can even be loaded and saved via the Browser, URL List menu selection.

The Navigator button on the toolbar jumps you right to Netscape. The Cut, Copy, Paste, Save, and Find buttons can be used to find and manipu-late text you've highlighted in the chat window. To save an entire session, turn logging on using the Edit, Logging menu selection, then choose Save Transcript from the same menu when done.

When you're done with a session, choose File, Disconnect from the menu.

NS Chat includes a thorough and well-organized Help file that will quickly acclimate you to the program and help you figure out all the niceties and custom settings.

TIP **If you're an IRC old-timer, you'll be happy to know that NS Chat fully** supports access to all standard IRC "slash" commands, as defined in RFC 1459.

CyberSpell

You've probably done it a million times—created a mail message or Usenet news post and only realized after it's gone that you probably misspelled a slew of words. Even so, until now there was no way to spell check your mail and news messages. But CyberSpell changes that. When installed, it integrates seamlessly into your mail and news composition windows, providing you with a new Spelling menu that not only gives you flexible spellchecking, but a degree of grammar, punctuation, and capitalization checking as well.

CyberSpell has been optimized for use on the Web, and knows about URLs, FTP addresses, newsgroup names, e-mail addresses, and specialized Net terminology, so it won't flag them as "errors" like most spell checkers. It even recognizes many "emoticons" (smiley faces).

When you install CyberSpell, it is automatically included in the Windows StartUp group. Under Win95, it appears as an icon in the taskbar. It has no window of its own. If active, CyberSpell appears only as a menu in the mail and news composition windows (see fig. 13.11).

Fig. 13.11
The CyberSpell menu lets you select either of two spell checkers, set options, or get help.

TIP **To display the extensive CyberSpell help file, right-click the CyberSpell** icon in the Win95 taskbar and select Help on CyberSpell.

CyberSpell has two modes of operation. They work alike, and differ only in power. Quick Spell checks spelling only, while Power Spell also checks for punctuation, formatting, spacing, and grammar.

The CyberSpell dictionary has over 159,300 words, including:

- 2,600 technical and computer-related words

- 2,200 names of well-known companies and products

- 8,500 legal, financial, business, and insurance terms

Using CyberSpell should be easy if you've ever used any spell checker. To spell check a composed message, select either Quick Spell or Power Spell from the message composition window's Spelling menu. You'll get the dialog shown in figure 13.12.

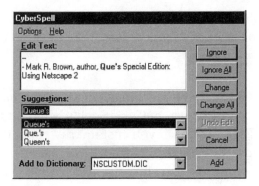

Fig. 13.12
Quick Spell and Power Spell look alike, but Power Spell (shown here) lets you check grammar, punctuation, and capitalization, too.

Quick Spell or Power Spell will scan the document for errors, which you can choose to ignore, correct, or add to a custom dictionary. You can edit or add custom dictionaries by selecting Options from the Spelling menu and selecting the Dictionaries tab (see fig. 13.13).

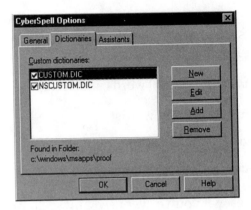

Fig. 13.13
You can Edit, Add, Remove, or create a New custom dictionary from the Options dialog. Other tabs allow you to adjust CyberSpell's overall behavior.

CAUTION **CyberSpell distinguishes between uppercase and lowercase letters in** custom dictionaries. In other words, if you add "Tuna" to a custom dictionary, CyberSpell flags "tuna" as a misspelling.

When you've run CyberSpell for awhile, you may get an offer from its Spelling and Proofing Assistants to custom CyberSpell's behavior to match your historical use. For example, if you customarily allow the word "ain't," after three consecutive approvals CyberSpell will ask if you want it to ignore this word all the time. (I wish all spell checkers had this feature!)

Norton AntiVirus

Viruses are always a concern for computer users, especially when you download a lot of files from the Internet. You always wonder where that file's been, and whether it could have picked up a virus somewhere that will infect your system.

Symantec's Norton AntiVirus Internet Scanner may suffer from an overly long name, but it can help ease your virus worries. It incorporates the same virus hunting and killing technology that has made the stand-alone version of Norton AntiVirus a standard industry tool.

You can run this version of AntiVirus in stand-alone mode. If you do, you'll see the window shown in figure 13.14.

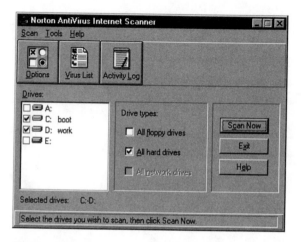

Fig. 13.14
Norton AntiVirus can be used to scan for viruses on your floppies, hard drives, or network drives.

In stand-alone mode, Norton AntiVirus can scan any or all of your disks for viruses. Pick the disks you want to scan and click Scan Now to do so. This takes quite a while, so pick a time when you don't need your system for anything else. If you suspect something in an individual Folder, or even a single File, you can scan these by selecting them from the Scan menu.

The Virus List and Activity Log buttons or menu items (under Tools) fill you in on which viruses AntiVirus knows about and how much scanning you've done, respectively. Though the Tools, Options menu selection (or Options button) gives you a lot of control over the virus checking process, I suggest you leave it alone until you know more about the program. A healthy dose of help from the Info Desk under the Help menu will get you going, as Norton AntiVirus has one of the best and most extensive help systems you'll find anywhere.

Norton AntiVirus is a Netscape helper application, and it automatically sets itself up to check .exe executables, .zip compressed files, and several other file types when it is installed. To see which file types have been configured for automatic checking by Norton AntiVirus, select Options, General Preferences, from the Netscape menu and click the Helpers tab. Then look down the scrolling list of MIME types.

When operating in conjunction with Netscape, Norton AntiVirus is almost invisible. Whenever you download a file or encounter an e-mail attachment, it kicks in invisibly, only popping up briefly to let you know everything's okay, then prompting you where to save the file (see fig. 13.15).

Fig. 13.15
Norton AntiVirus at work, protecting you from nasty viruses in the files you download using Netscape Navigator.

Of course, all this is assuming that it doesn't detect any viruses. But what if it does?

Never fear. Norton AntiVirus can automatically eliminate most viruses. If it can't, it'll tell you so and give you the option of trashing the file instead. Either way, your system is safe from infection.

 NOTE **Symantec engineers track reported outbreaks of computer viruses to** identify new viruses. Once identified, information about the virus (a virus signature) is stored in a virus definitions file. When Norton AntiVirus scans your disk and files it is searching for these telltale signatures. If a file is found that has been infected by one of these viruses, Norton AntiVirus eliminates the virus automatically.

A new virus signature file is available monthly from the Symantec Web site at **ftp://ftp.symantec.com/public/win95_nt/nav/**. You can tell the current virus signature file by the filename, which takes the form mmNAVyy.ZIP, where "mm" is the month and "yy" is the year.

TIP **For more info on Netscape Power Pack 2.0, check out http://home.netscape.com/comprod/power_pack.html**.

Part V: Creating Your Own Web Pages

Creating Web Pages with Netscape Navigator Gold

● **In this chapter:**

- **The basics of Web page creation with Netscape Gold**

- **Creating links and adding graphics in Web pages**

- **Creating tables, lines, and other formatting**

- **Publishing your documents on the Web**

Publishing on the Web is surprisingly easy, and creating your own home page is probably the best first step. It's a great way to get a feel for how HTML works, and you'll produce something you can use, too. How do you go about producing a home page? Well, you can use any of several freeware, shareware, and commercial HTML authoring tools. But in this chapter, you're going to learn about one in particular: Netscape Navigator Gold.

Working with Navigator Gold

Netscape Navigator Gold contains everything that Netscape Navigator contains, plus some great authoring and editing tools that help you create a Web page from scratch or take a Web page that you like and modify it. In this chapter, we've assumed that you are working with Navigator Gold. You can download or order a copy of Netscape Gold from the Netscape Web site.

- Opening the Navigator Gold Editor

- Creating simple Web pages

- Using paragraph and text formats

- Adding links, pictures, lines, and lists

- Entering JavaScript and document properties

How do you open the Editor?

Navigator Gold has a special Editor window. There are two (or more) ways to open this window, as follows:

- To edit a copy of the document you are currently viewing, choose File, Edit Document or click the Edit toolbar button. You'll see a dialog box (which we'll look at in detail in a moment). Click the Save button and the browser window closes and is replaced by the Editor window, displaying the document. (You can reopen the browser window by choosing File, Browse Document, or by clicking the Browser button.)

- To create a new document from scratch from the browser window, choose File, <u>N</u>ew Document, then choose <u>B</u>lank, From <u>T</u>emplate, or From <u>W</u>izard. If you choose <u>B</u>lank, the browser window closes and is replaced by a blank Editor window. The From Template and From Wizard choices only work if you're connected to the Web—they take you to pages at Netscape's Web site that feature pre-built Web page templates and a step-by-step Web page creation Wizard, respectively.

- To edit a copy of a document on your hard disk—a home page that you've created, for instance—choose <u>F</u>ile, Open <u>F</u>ile in Ed<u>i</u>tor, then select a file in the Open dialog box. The Editor window opens, displaying the file you chose (the browser window remains open).

 NOTE If you have both the Editor and Browser windows open, you can close one and the other will stick around. You can always open the other again by using the Browser button from the Editor, and vice versa.

Why would you want to edit an existing document? Eventually you'll want to modify documents you created earlier, of course. But editing an existing document is also a great way to create your first Web document. Find a document that you think looks good—one that you'd like to copy—and edit that document, replacing the original headings with your headings, keeping the images and links you need, and so on. Then save the modified document on your hard disk.

 NOTE If you open a document that contains HTML code that Netscape Gold doesn't understand—for example, Frames—that portion of the page will be displayed as straight HTML code surrounded by "broken tag" icons.

What happens when you open a document in the Editor window? If you opened a file that's stored on your hard disk, the Editor opens and displays the document. If you chose <u>F</u>ile, <u>E</u>dit Document (or just click on the Edit toolbar button), though, you'll see the dialog box shown in figure 14.1.

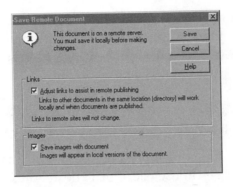

Fig. 14.1
When you open a document from the Web, you have to tell Navigator Gold what to do with the links and graphics.

If you change your mind, simply click the Cancel button. But if you want to continue to modify the document that is currently displayed in the browser, you must decide what to do with the links and graphics in the document. Netscape is going to copy the document to your hard disk, and you need to tell it how. Here are your options:

- **Images: Save images with document**—Make sure this check box is checked if you want to use the images in the document you are copying. Netscape will copy the HTML document from the Web as well as the embedded images. If you know that you don't want the pictures, clear the check box.

- **Links: Adjust links to assist in remote publishing**—If you choose this checkbox Netscape will convert the links in the files to absolute links. For instance, say you are copying a file that contains an HTML link like this:

<a HREF="book.htm">Book Titles</a>

This link points to a file called book.htm—it's what's called a relative link, because it doesn't give the full URL to that document. In fact, the link says "get book.htm, which is in the same directory as the current document." But once the document is on your hard disk, book.htm is no longer in the same directory, so the link won't work. If you chose this option, though, Netscape converts the link, to something like this for instance:

<a HREF="http://www.bigweb.com/books/book.htm">Book Titles</a>

Now the link contains the full URL to book.htm, so it continues to work.

When you click on the Save button, you'll see the dialog box in figure 14.2. This is simply a reminder that you *don't own stuff you find on the Web!* You can click the check box to tell Netscape not to display the message next time, then click OK. Then you'll see a Save As dialog box. Find the directory in which you want to save the copied document, type a filename, then click Save.

CAUTION **You should understand that you don't own something you "borrow"** from the Web. If you borrow something from the Web and simply keep it for your own use, there's no problem. But if you publish Web pages using pictures and text you grabbed from another Web site, you may be guilty of copyright infringement. If you use the borrowed stuff as a template, though, replacing everything in the page with your own stuff, there's no problem in most cases (though it's possible for a particular design to be copyrighted, too).

Fig. 14.2
Netscape warns you that things you find on the Web don't belong to you!

The Editor window

Once you've opened the Editor window, you'll see something like figure 14.3. This shows the current Netscape home page inside the Editor.

The File/
Edit toolbar

The Character
Format toolbar

The Paragraph
Format toolbar

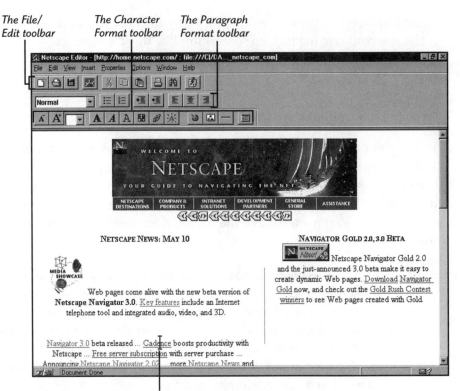

Notice that the mouse pointer hasn't changed to a hand
because in edit mode you can't navigate via the links.

Fig. 14.3
The Editor window provides the tools you need to create or modify a Web page.

Here's a quick summary of what each button does.

- New Document—Click here to open a new blank Editor window so you can begin a new document, or choose to use a Template or the Page Wizard.

- Open File to Edit—Click here to open a file on your hard disk.

- Save—This button saves the document on your hard disk.

- View in Browser—Click here to change back to the browser window.

- Cut—Highlight text in the document and click this button to remove the text, placing it in the Windows Clipboard.

- Copy—This button copies highlighted text to the Clipboard.

- Paste—Click here to paste text from the Clipboard to the document.

- Print—This prints the document.

- Find—Opens the Find dialog box so you can search the document.

- Publish—Transfers your Web page and associated files to the Internet using HTTP or FTP protocol.

- Paragraph Style—The Editor uses a system of styles, much like good word processors. You can click text and modify it by selecting a style.

- Bullet list—This button lets you create a bulleted list.

- Numbered list—Clicking this button creates a numbered list in the document. (Well, it does in theory, but at the time of this writing, it wasn't working correctly.)

- Decrease indent—Use this to move indented text back to the left.

- Increase indent—Click here to indent text to the right.

- Align left—If a paragraph is centered or aligned to the right (right justified), click here to change it to left alignment.

- Center—This button centers the selected paragraph.

- Align right—This button right justifies the selected paragraph.

- Decrease Font Size—Highlight text and click here to decrease the size one level. (There are seven sizes, from –2 to +4, with 0 being the default size. These are relative sizes, not directly related to point size.)

- Increase Font Size—Highlight text and click here to increase the size one level.

- Font Size—Highlight text and then choose a font size setting to make the text larger or smaller than the default for that text style.

- Bold—Highlight text and click here to make it bold (or to remove bold, if the text is already bold).

- Italic—Highlight text and click here to make it italic.

- Fixed Width—Highlight text and click here to change the text to a fixed width (monospace) font, a font in which all characters take up the same space.

- Font Color—Highlight text and click here to change the text color.

- Make Link—Click this button to insert a link in the document.

- Clear All Styles—Highlight text and click here to remove all the text styles, changing the text back to the default font for the paragraph style.

- Insert Target (Named Anchor)—Inserts a target name for frames and links to jump to inside the page.

- Insert Image—This opens the Insert Image dialog box, which helps you insert a picture into your document.

- Insert Horiz. Line—Click here to insert a horizontal line across the document.

- Object Properties—When you click certain objects in your document (images, links, and horizontal lines) and then click this button, the appropriate properties dialog box opens. Highlight text and then click the button to modify general document characteristics (title, colors, and so on).

Entering your text

As an example of how to work with the Editor, let's try creating your own home page—a page that opens when you open the Netscape browser, containing all the links you need. Type the following text into a new, blank Editor window (you can see an example in figure 14.4):

```
My Home Page
This is my very own home page
Really Important Stuff
These are WWW pages I use a lot.

Not So Important Stuff
These are WWW pages I use now and again.

Not Important At All Stuff
These are WWW pages I use to waste time.
```

Right now all you have is basic text; look in the Paragraph Style drop-down list box (the list box on the left side of the Paragraph Format toolbar) and you'll see it shows *Normal*.

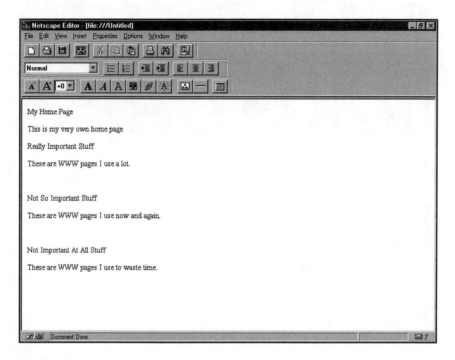

Fig. 14.4
Start typing the headings into the Editor; you'll find it's just like working with a word processor.

You can quickly change the paragraph styles. For instance, try the following:

1 Click the *My Home Page* text, then select Heading 1 from the Paragraph Style drop-down list box.

2 Click the Center toolbar button.

3 Click the *This is my very own home page* text, then click the Center toolbar button.

4 Click the *Really Important Stuff* text, then select Heading 2 from the Paragraph Style drop-down list box.

5 Click the *Not So Important Stuff* text, then select Heading 2 from the Paragraph Style drop-down list box.

6 Click the *Not Important At All Stuff* text, then select Heading 2 from the Paragraph Style drop-down list box.

Now what have you got? Your page should look something like that in figure 14.5.

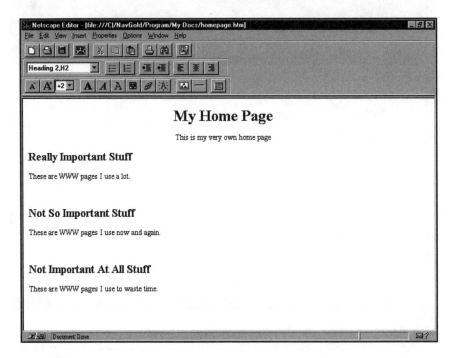

Fig. 14.5
A few mouse clicks, and you've formatted the document.

Before you go on, save what you've done: click the Save button, type a name (homepage, if you wish), then click the Save button. The Editor will save the file with an .HTM extension.

TIP **Want to see what you've just done? Choose Yiew, Document Source,** and you'll see the HTML source document that the Editor has created for you. If you're an HTML purist and want to "tweak" your HTML code by hand, choose View, Edit Document Source instead.

Where did my line breaks go?

Did you create multiple line breaks in your document by pressing Enter? If so, when you finally view your document in the browser window, those line breaks will be gone; the Editor doesn't like multiple line breaks.

For example, try this: Place the cursor at the end of a paragraph (a paragraph that is followed by another paragraph, not the last one in the document) and press Enter several times. Several blank lines appear. Save the document, then press Ctrl+R to reload the document from the hard disk into the Editor. You'll see that the blank lines have gone!

Why? Well, this seems to be a holdover from creating a Web document by entering the HTML codes. Web browsers ignore blank lines in the HTML document. Rather, they only move text down a line when they see a special tag: the <P> or <BR> tag. Of course, there's no reason that the Navigator Gold Editor should do the same; if you entered a blank line, you probably want it there. Nonetheless, that's the way it is.

 NOTE If you've made changes to your document, but want to go back to the way it was the last time you saved it, simply press Ctrl+R or choose View, Reload.

However, there is a way to add a blank line. Place the cursor at the end of line and choose Insert, New Line Break. (Or simply press Shift+Enter.) A blank line appears. This time, if you save the document and then reload it, the blank line remains.

How about links?

Now you're going to get fancy by adding an anchor, a link to another document. For example, you may want to add a link to the Netscape home page. (On the other hand, you may not; you can always choose Directory, Netscape's Home to get there, even if you are using your own home page.) Or perhaps you'd like a link to a favorite site.

 NOTE The HTML tags used to create links are often known as anchors because many people refer to the links themselves in the Web documents as anchors.

Click the blank line below *These are WWW pages I use a lot*, then click the Link button or choose Insert, <u>L</u>ink. You'll see the dialog box in figure 14.6.

Fig. 14.6
Enter the text you want to see and the URL you want to link to. You can choose named targets, too.

In the first text box, type the text that you want to appear in the document: the words that you will be clicking to use that link. In the second box, type the URL of the page you want to link to. The radio buttons let you list named Targets in either the Current <u>d</u>ocument or Selected <u>f</u>ile. To pick one as your link, just click on it and it will appear in the second text box.

You create a Target by highlighting text or placing your cursor where you want a target to appear, then clicking on the Insert Target (Named Anchor) button on the bottom toolbar. You'll get a dialog that asks you for a target name. Links that jump to this target from the same page will have a destination of "#name," while links that jump in from another page will have a destination of "thispage.htm#name."

NOTE **You can find URLs in a number of places. You might press Alt+Tab to** switch back to the browser window, then use the browser to go to the page you want and copy the URL from the Location bar. Remember also that you can right–click on a link in a Web document and choose Copy This Link Location. You can also copy URLs from desktop shortcuts: right–click on the shortcut, choose Properties, click on the Internet Shortcut tab, then press Ctrl+C to copy the URL.

You can also get links from another document or elsewhere in the same document: right-click on a link in the Editor and choose <u>C</u>opy Link to Clipboard.

Notice the <u>B</u>rowse File button; this lets you enter the URL of a file on your hard disk, which is very handy if you are creating a series of linked pages. And there's a <u>R</u>emove Links button, too. This is only active if you click inside a link in your document and then open this dialog box. Clicking the button removes the URL so you can enter a new one, or so that you can retain the document text but remove the link from it.

TIP **Here's another way to create a link: highlight text that you typed into** the document earlier, then click the Link button (or right-click the highlighted text and choose Create <u>L</u>ink Using Selected). The highlighted text will appear in the dialog box. All you need to do is enter the URL and click OK.

More nifty link tricks

You can also create links by copying them from the browser window. Position the windows so that both are visible. Then click a link in the browser window, but hold the mouse button down. You'll notice the link turn red. Now, with the mouse button still held down, drag the link from the browser window over to the Editor window (see fig. 14.7), move the pointer to the position you want to place the link, and release the mouse button.

Finally, why not grab links from your bookmarks? You've probably already created bookmarks to your favorite sites, and you can quickly create links from them. Choose Window, Boo<u>k</u>marks to open the Bookmarks window.

Now you can drag bookmarks from the Bookmarks window onto your document in the Editor. As long as you don't click anywhere in the document—simply drag and release where you want the new link—the Bookmarks window remains above the Editor window.

TIP **To open a browser window containing the document you are editing,** so that you can test the document you've created, choose File, <u>B</u>rowse Document.

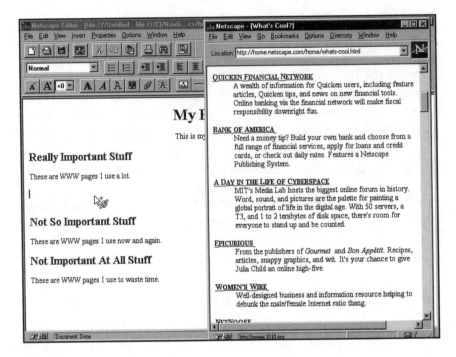

Fig. 14.7
You can drag links from the "What's Cool?" page (or any other Web document) into the Editor.

What about pictures?

No self-respecting Web page would be complete without a picture or two, would it? Luckily the Editor provides a way for you to insert pictures.

Place the cursor where you want the picture, then choose Insert, Image, or click the Insert Image button. You'll see the dialog box in figure 14.8.

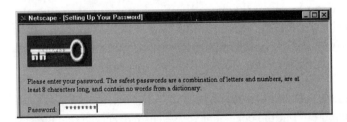

Fig. 14.8
The Insert Image dialog box helps you place the image in just the correct manner.

Start by clicking the Browse button right at the top of the dialog box, and select the image you want to use. (Or you may type a URL into this text box, and the Editor will go out onto the Web to grab the specified file.) If you wish, you can also enter an alternative image in the second text box. This is the image that should be used if the first image isn't available. And you can enter the alternative Text, too, into the third text box. This is the text that is shown if the browser viewing your page is not displaying inline images.

TIP **The alternative image option doesn't work well for all browsers. If the** primary image is not available, some browsers will not be able to display the alternative image, as this is a Netscape feature that has not yet been adopted by all other browser publishers. Also, if you define an alternative image, other browsers viewing your page with inline images turned off may not be able to view the alternative text. The alternative-image information in the HTML file "confuses" them and stops them from reading the text.

The Copy Image to the Document's Location checkbox in the lower left corner of the dialog tells the Editor to copy the picture from its original location to the directory in which the document is stored.

Now take a look at the Alignment box. This is where you define how text on the same line as the image should be wrapped around the image. Each button shows a visual sample of what the image will look like with its designated alignment.

You can now tell the Editor how much space to leave around the image—or whether you want a border around it. The three text boxes under the Space Around Image heading allow you to enter a size, in pixels, between the left and right sides of the image and the text, and between the top and bottom of the image and the text. You can also define the size of a border around the text.

The text boxes under the Dimensions heading let you set the Height and Width of the displayed image. Values of "0" in each mean "original size," which you can also reset by clicking the Original Size button.

The Edit Image button lets you (logically enough) edit the image you've chosen. If you haven't already configured an image editor through the Options, Editor Preferences menu selection, you'll be given a chance to do so automatically.

Finally, how about turning the image into a link to another document? If you want the reader to be able to click the image to view another document, click the Link tab and you can create a link for the image.

When you've finished, simply click OK and the image is inserted into the document. How can you modify the image later? Many ways: double-click the image; click the picture and then click either the Object Properties or Insert Image toolbar button; or right-click and select Image Properties from the pop-up menu.

Do you want to find some icons you can use in your documents? Go to an icon server: a Web site from which you can download icons or even link your documents across the Web to a particular icon. Try the following sites:

http://www.bsdi.com/icons
http://www-ns.rutgers.edu/doc-images
http://www.di.unipi.it/iconbrowser/icons.html
http://www.cit.gu.edu.au/~anthony/icons/

Where are you going to get pictures for your documents? You can create them yourself using a graphics program that can save in a .JPG or .GIF format (many can these days). You can also grab them from the Web, remember! Find a picture you want, right-click it, and choose Save This Image As.

There's a special command that makes sure that text placed after an image appears below the image, not "wrapped" around it. Let's say you've aligned the picture so that the text following it appears on the right side of the picture. You can now place the cursor in the text at the point where you want to move it down below the image, and choose Insert, Break below Image(s). The text that appears after the cursor is now moved down, below the image.

Adding horizontal lines

Horizontal lines are handy. You can use them to underline headers, as dividers between blocks of text, to underline important information, and so on. And the Editor allows you to create a number of different types of lines, as you can see in figure 14.9.

Fig. 14.9
This dialog box helps you create a line; you can see examples in the Editor.

To place a line across the page, place the cursor on a blank line or in a line of text after which you wish to place the line, and click the Insert Horiz. Line button (or choose Insert, Horizontal Line. A line is placed across the page. But what if you don't want a line all the way across the page, or if you want a different style or thickness? You'll have to modify the line.

Select the line; with the cursor at the end of the line, simply press Shift+Left Arrow (or simply click directly on the line). The line will appear to change color or size—it will be highlighted. Now click the Object Properties button to open the Horizontal Line Properties dialog box, which you can see in figure 14.9. Double-clicking on the line, or right-clicking and selecting Horizontal Line properties from the pop-up menu will also bring up this dialog.

There are a variety of controls in this dialog box. First, you can tell the Editor where you want the line: aligned against the Left, in the Center, or aligned against the Right. Notice, however, that by default, the line has a Width of 100 Percent (that is, it's 100 percent of the width of the document's window). The alignment settings have no effect until you modify the width setting. (If a line is 100 percent, how can you center it after all?)

There are actually two ways that you can adjust the line's width: by Percent or by Pixels. Both are selected from the drop-down list to the right of the Width text box. The Percent setting refers to the width of the document (when the window is maximized). So a line that has a width of 50 percent will stretch across half of the document's window.

The Pixel setting is harder to predict, though. A pixel is the smallest unit that your computer monitor can display. For instance, in VGA mode a monitor displays 640 columns and 480 rows of pixels. So if you create a line that's 60 pixels wide, it will be about 10 percent of the width of the document—in VGA mode. But what if the person viewing the document is using a different resolution—1024 by 768, for example? In such a case, the line that was 10 percent of the width in VGA is now about 5 percent of the width. Of course, this doesn't matter if you are creating a home page for your own use, but bear it in mind if you are creating documents that you plan to put out on the Web.

There are two more settings: the Height, which is measured in pixels, and 3-D Shading. The 203-D effect is created by using four different lines to create a "box,"—the left and top lines are dark gray, and the bottom and right lines are white. Clear the 3-D check box, and your horizontal line will be a single dark gray line.

Creating tables

Navigator Gold now lets you easily create tables. Select Insert, Table from the menu and you'll get the dialog box shown in figure 14.10.

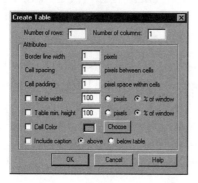

Fig. 14.10
Netscape Gold's table creation dialog makes it easy to define all aspects of a table.

Number of rows and Number of columns each default to 1, but that doesn't make much of a table; set these to the values you want. This is all you really need to define to create a table, but the Create Table dialog also lets you set Border line width, Cell spacing (the number of pixels between cells), Cell padding (pixels of white space inside of cells), Table width, Table minimum height (these two in pixels or as a percentage of window width), and Cell Color. You can also check the Include Caption checkbox to put a caption above or below the table.

Once a blank table is created, you enter information into cells by clicking in them and typing. (Of course, you can also insert images or links into table cells.) You move from cell to cell using the arrow keys.

You can create "nested" tables by moving the cursor into an empty cell and creating a new table there.

Once created, you can modify a table using the menus. From the Insert menu, you can insert a new Table, Row, Column, or Cell at the cursor position. The Properties menu lets you change the properties for a Table, Row, or Cell. The Row and Cell (see fig. 14.11) selections bring up dialogs which let you define text alignment and cell color (both) and column span (cell only). You can also choose Delete Table, Delete Row, Delete Column, or Delete Cell from the Properties menu.

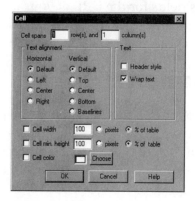

Fig. 14.11
The Cell Properties dialog lets you customize individual table cells.

Publishing your work

Once you've created an HTML page, you'll probably want to publish it on the Web or on an intranet. With Gold, this is now a one-step process. Just click the Publish button on the toolbar, or choose File, Publish from the menu. You'll get the dialog box shown in figure 14.12.

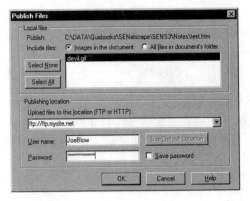

Fig. 14.12
The Publish dialog lets you publish your page on the Web.

From this dialog, radio buttons in the Local files area let you choose to include in your upload only the Images in the Document, or All files in document's folder. A file list lets you choose individual files to include, or you can Select None or Select All using buttons.

The Publishing location box includes fields for the URL of your upload destination, as well as your User Name and Password. When these have been set, a single click on OK uploads your page to its destination.

Creating multiple documents

You may want to create a hierarchy of documents. Create a home page, a page that appears when you open Netscape, with a table of contents linked to several other documents. In each of those documents, you could then have links related to a particular subject: one for business, one for music, one for your kids, and so on.

This is very simple to do. Create and save several documents in the Editor. (I suggest you put them all in the same directory for simplicity's sake.) Each time you finish one, choose File, New Document to clear the screen so you can create the next one. When you have all your documents completed, open your home page document again (click the Open File button or choose File, Open File), and enter links to each page, using the method previously described.

How can I use my home page?

You've created a home page; now how do you use it? Complete the following procedure:

1 Click the Open Browser button, or choose File, Browse Document. The Netscape browser opens and displays your document.

2 Click the Location text box, highlighting the URL.

3 Press Ctrl+C to copy the URL.

4 Choose Options, General Preferences, and click the Appearance tab.

5 Click the Home Page Location option button (in the Startup area).

6 Click inside the text box below this option button.

7 Press Ctrl+V to paste the URL into the text box.

8 Click OK.

Now, the next time you start your browser, you'll see your very own home page. Simple, eh?

Here's a good one—let's change it

Navigator Gold provides a wonderful way to quickly create Web pages—by "borrowing" them from the Web and modifying them to your requirements. If you see a page you like—one that has many links that you'll need in your home page, for instance, or one that uses a particularly attractive format—you can open that page and make changes to it, then save it on your hard disk.

You can work in the document in the same way that you would with documents you created yourself. You can delete text and replace it with your own and change text using the formatting tools.

How do you highlight text? The Editor window works like a word processor. Simply click in the text to place the cursor, then use the arrow keys to move around in the text. You can also hold down the Shift key while you press the arrow keys to highlight text. Ctrl+Shift+Left Arrow and Ctrl+Shift+Right Arrow work (selecting an entire word at a time, though you can't do the same with the Up and Down Arrow keys). Also, you can use the mouse cursor to select text: hold down the mouse button while you drag the pointer across text to highlight it. Or double-click a word to select it.

TIP **As with a word processor, you don't need to highlight text in order to** modify paragraph formats. If you want to change the paragraph style, indentation, or alignment, simply click once in the paragraph and then make your change.

When you've made the changes you need, click the Save button or choose File, <u>S</u>ave and you'll be able to save the document on your hard disk. (No, you can't save it to the original location even if you own that location!)

Lots more formatting

There are a number of formatting tools we haven't looked at yet. You can format a paragraph in many different ways by setting up indents and alignment as well as by choosing a paragraph style. And you can modify particular words or individual characters, too, by changing colors and type styles.

The other paragraph styles

You've only seen a couple of paragraph styles so far, so let's take a look at the others. In figure 14.13, you can see examples of all the different Heading levels as well as Normal text, the Address style, and the Formatted style.

You can apply any of these styles by placing the cursor inside the paragraph you want to modify and then selecting the style from the drop-down list box (or by picking the style from the Properties, <u>P</u>aragraph cascading menu). Note that what you see depends on how you've set up Netscape; other browsers may display these styles in a different way.

NOTE **Browsers normally remove blank lines and multiple spaces when view-**ing a document. The Formatted style tells the browser to keep the text format as it appears in the HTML document. In fact, unless you are using the Formatted style, the Editor won't let you type multiple spaces into a document. Also, long lines of Formatted text will run off the side of the window—the text will not wrap down to the next line.

However, note that Navigator Gold currently doesn't allow you to enter multiple blank lines, even if you've selected the Formatted style.

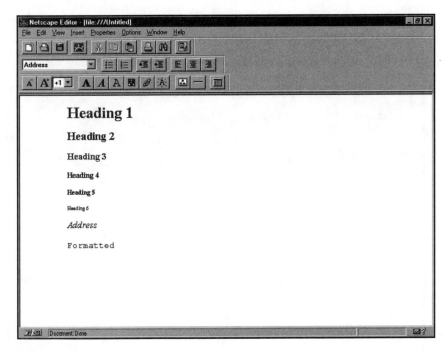

Fig. 14.13
The headers, formatted, and address styles.

How about creating lists?

You can also use the Paragraph Styles drop-down list box and a couple of the toolbar buttons to create lists. You can create bulleted lists, numbered lists, and definition lists.

The quickest way to create a bulleted list is to place the cursor on a blank line and then click the Bulleted List button. You'll see a bullet (a black circle) appear at the beginning of the line. Type the first entry, press Enter, type the next entry, press Enter, and so on. When you get to the last entry press Enter and then select Normal from the Paragraph Style drop-down list box. You can see an example in figure 14.14.

You can create a numbered list in the same way by using the Numbered List button.

Another form of list is the definition list, which you can create by alternating lines between the Description Title, DD and Description Text styles (see fig. 14.14).

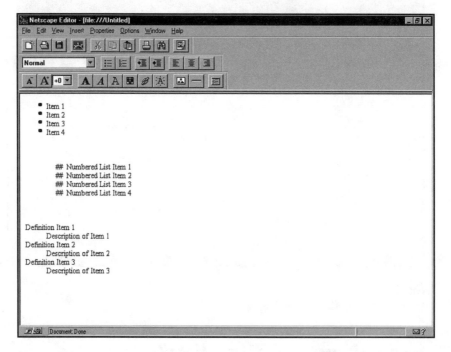

Fig. 14.14
You can create lists using the paragraph styles.

There's another way to work with lists—and other paragraph formats. Here's how to use it. Place the cursor on a blank line and then click the right mouse button. Choose Paragraph/List properties from the pop-up menu. You'll see the dialog box in figure 14.15.

Select the paragraph or list type you want to create in the Paragraph Style drop-down list on the left. If you've selected a List item, pick the Style from the second drop-down list. Finally, select the number or bullet type from the list on the right. Pick Left, Center, or Right alignment, then click OK and the first line is correctly formatted.

This dialog box creates not only numbered and unnumbered lists, but also several other unusual paragraph styles: Block Quotes, Directory Lists, Menu Lists, and Description Lists. Other styles may be added later, too.

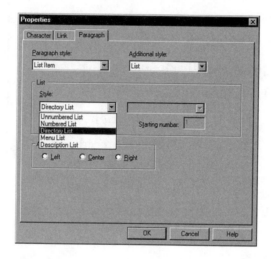

Fig. 14.15
This dialog box allows you to format a variety of paragraph and list types.

Positioning paragraphs

Now let's see how to move paragraphs around the page. You can use the five toolbar buttons on the right side of the Paragraph Format toolbar to indent paragraphs, align them to the left, center them, and align them to the right. You can combine alignment settings and indentations, too. See figure 14.16 for a few examples.

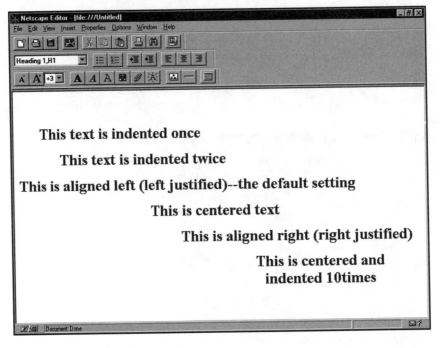

Fig. 14.16
You can position paragraphs in a variety of ways.

How can I modify character formats?

You have quite a bit of control over individual characters. In fact, you are telling your document to override the way in which the browser that opens your document displays the characters. A browser, for example, may have a default text color set, but you can override that color and define your own. Figure 14.17 shows a variety of character formats.

Simply highlight the characters you want to modify, then click the appropriate button (or choose the appropriate entry from the Properties, Character submenu), as follows:

- Font Size—Change a character's size, ranging from –2 to +4. That is, from two "units" below the normal style size, to four "units" above. These are not absolute measurements—it's not –2 points to 4 points, for instance. Rather, they are relative sizes; the browser displaying the document simply decreases or increases the text a certain amount below or above the normal size for that paragraph style.

- Decrease Font Size—Click here to decrease the size one unit.

- Increase Font Size—Click here to increase the size one unit.

- Bold—This changes the character to bold (or removes bold, if the text is already bold). You can combine this with italic to create bold italic.

- Italic—Click here to change the text to italic (or to remove italic).

- Fixed Width—This changes the text to a fixed width (monospace) font, a font in which all characters take up the same amount of space.

- Font Color—You'll see a dialog box from which you can choose a color.

- Clear Styles—Click here to remove all the text styles, changing the text back to the default font for the paragraph style.

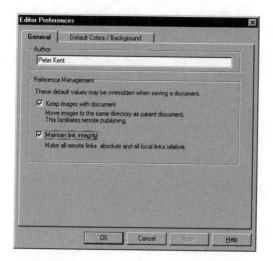

Fig. 14.17
Highlight text and click the appropriate button to modify it.

Here's an example of how to use these tools.

1 In a blank document, type all the text you see in figure 14.17. Don't worry about the different formats, simply type all the text. I've changed the color all the way to fixed width bold italic at the bottom.

2 Now, highlight a few words of the first line, and click the Font Color button. Click the red, then choose OK. The text will change color.

3 Select a letter or several letters on the second line. Then select a size from the Font Size drop-down list box, or click the Increase Font Size or Decrease Font Size buttons. Try several letters, and different sizes.

4 You should have typed all of line three in capitals. Select the first letter of the first word, and increase its size. Modify all the first letters that you want to "capitalize" and increase their size the same amount, to simulate a "small caps" font.

5 Highlight the word bold on the last line and click the Bold button.

6 Highlight the word italic on the last line and click the Italic button.

7 Highlight the words bold italic on the last line and click the Italic button, then the Bold button.

8 Highlight the words fixed width on the last line and click the Fixed Width button.

9 Highlight the words fixed width bold italic on the last line and click the Fixed Width button, then the Bold button, and then the Italic button.

Nonbreaking spaces

Here's one more character format we haven't looked at yet: you can choose Insert, Nonbreaking Space to create a special space between words. This space is treated as part of the two words it divides. When you change the size of the Editor window (or when the person viewing the document changes the size of the Browser window), text has to be wrapped down onto the next line. Now, words are never split in two when Netscape does this wrapping; the text is always broken at a space. But the text won't be broken at one of the nonbreaking spaces—instead Netscape has to break the text at the first normal space that appears before the nonbreaking space.

JavaScript

There are two more character-format types that you may have noticed in the Properties, Character submenu: the JavaScript (Client) and JavaScript (Server) formats.

JavaScript is a special scripting language—a sort of fancy macro language, really. It lets you use some of the power of Java without knowing that programming language. But for now all you need to know is that you can enter JavaScript commands into your documents by choosing Properties, Character, JavaScript (Server) or Properties, Character, JavaScript (Client) formats (depending on which type of command you are entering) and then typing the command. The server commands will appear as blue text, the client commands as red text.

Document Properties—General

Web documents have a variety of properties related not to any particular paragraph or character, but to the document overall. You can modify this by choosing Properties, Document. Click the General tab and you'll see the information in figure 14.18.

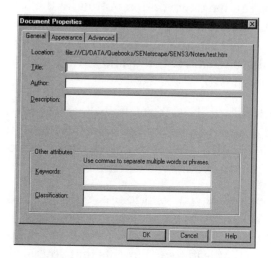

Fig. 14.18
The Document Properties box lets you set colors, the document title, author name, and more.

These are the things you can modify here:

Document property	What it modifies
Title	The title of the document. This is displayed in the browser's title bar, in history lists, bookmark lists, and so on.
Author	This places the <meta name="Author" content="author name"> tag into your document. It's one of the META variables in the Head of the document (see User Variables META, later in this table).
Description	A brief description of the contents of your document. This information can be helpful to readers searching for a specific topic.
Other Attributes	Keywords and Classification that you want searching services such as Yahoo to use to help users locate your document on the Web. Use category names you think best apply to your document.

Appearance

Click the Appearance tab. You have two option buttons at the top. You can choose to either Use Custom Colors (you'll be able to define custom colors and background for this particular document) or Use Browsers Colors (the document will use whatever colors and background are defined by the browser viewing it).

Just below the option buttons you'll see the Color Schemes drop-down list box. From this you can choose from pre-defined color schemes; currently, you can choose about a dozen different color schemes; future versions will also allow you to create and save your own schemes.

Now you can select the text colors you want to use. You can modify the color of Normal Text, Link Text, Active Link Text (this is the color of a link when you point at it and hold down the mouse button), and Followed Link Text (the color of links that lead to documents that you've already been to). Clicking one of these buttons opens the Color dialog box.

Finally, you can modify the background. Either choose a Solid Color (click Choose Color button to select that color), or an Image File—click the Browse button to find a file you want to use as the background image.

Note, however, that there's something a little odd about this color selection system. The way it stands right now you can only set all or nothing. In other words, you can't define a special color for the background, yet keep the browser defaults for everything else. If you change one item, all the other items are also defined as overridden parameters. You can choose colors that are the same as the default colors for Netscape. For instance, these colors will override a reader's settings if they are different from the defaults.

Advanced settings

Power HTML users will appreciate the settings available under the Advanced tab (see fig. 14.19).

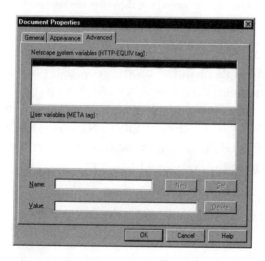

Fig. 14.19
The Advanced tab lets you set system and user variables.

Here's what you can set in this dialog:

Document property	What it modifies
Netscape System Variables	This is information that is sent in a "response (HTTP-EQUIV) header" from a server. A response header is information sent to a browser or other program when it requests information about the document. The information is contained in the HEAD of the document, and may include an expiration date and keywords, for instance. You add this information by clicking in the System Variables box to select it, then typing a value into the Name and Value fields at the bottom of the dialog, and clicking the Add button.
User Variables (META)	The META variables are placed in the HEAD of the document, and are used to identify the document to servers and browsers, allowing them to index and catalog the document.
Name Type	Type a new user variable name here.
Value	Type the user value here, then click the Set button.

You can add more user variables. In fact, you can add variables that a server may want to include in its response header. For instance, you might type Expires into the Name field, then Tue, 24 Dec 1996 into the Value field. When you click Set, the Editor adds this tag to the Head of the document: <META HTTP-EQUIV=Expires CONTENT="Tue, 24 Dec 1996">. (This is the Expiration date shown in the Document Info when you select View, Document Info in the Netscape Browser.

You can also use this feature to add Keywords to your document (so the document can be indexed and cataloged) and a Reply-to address, to create tags such as these:

<META HTTP-EQUIV="Keywords" CONTENT="Art, Sculpture">

<META HTTP-EQUIV="Reply-to"
CONTENT="robinh@sherwood.com (Robin Hood)">

Editor options

You can set default options for the Editor. Choose Options, Editor Preferences to see the Editor Preferences dialog box. Click the Appearance tab to see the same area that we looked at a moment ago (see fig. 14.19); you can use this to define the colors used by new documents you create.

Click the General tab to see the area shown in figure 14.20. This is where you define the default Author name, HTML source and Image editors, and the URL of the HTML document you'll use as a source for your templates (this defaults to a location on Netscape's Web server).

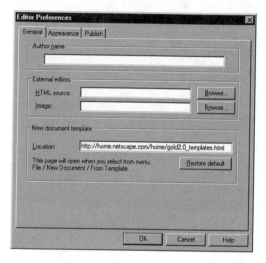

Fig. 14.20
The Editor Preferences dialog box tells the Editor how to set up new documents.

Click the Publish tab to set your Links and Images defaults. You can select the Keep Images With Document check box to tell the Editor that, when you insert an image, you want to move it to the same directory as the document into which it is being inserted. You can also tell the Editor to Maintain Links. Your choice here defines the status of the option buttons in the Save As dialog box that appears when you are opening the editor with a document you have found on the Web.

The Default Publishing Location box is where you enter information about the site where you Publish (upload) your finished pages. Enter the site address, your user name, and password information. (Only check the Save password box if you're sure no one else has access to your system!)

More to come?

You can expect to see many more features added over the next few versions of Navigator Gold. You may find tools that help you create forms, frames, and JavaScripts. You'll also probably be able to create imagemaps—pictures with hotspots on them that lead to other Web documents—special characters, and add sounds and multimedia.

Part VI: Appendixes

Connecting to the Internet

● **In this chapter:**

Getting a connection to the Internet can seem to be an overwhelming problem. There are literally hundreds of Internet service providers (ISPs), many different types of connections, different levels of support, and different pricing plans. How are you supposed to sort through all of it so that it makes sense?

TCP/IP basics

Before we dive into the details of setting up an Internet connection, we need to talk about a few details of the protocols that make the Internet work. In order to understand all the issues involved with an Internet connection, you need to understand the basics of TCP/IP, domain names, and IP addresses.

The suite of widely used protocols known as Transmission Control Protocol/Internet Protocol (TCP/IP) has become increasingly important because international networks such as the Internet depend on it for their communications.

No matter what version of Netscape you are running, they all require a TCP/IP protocol stack to be present in order to communicate with the Internet. TCP/IP is the "language" that computers on the Internet use to speak to each other.

Domain names

With millions of computers on the Internet, how do you specify the one that you want to interact with? You must know the name of the computer, just as you must know the name of someone you want to send a letter to. These names are specified by a convention called the domain name service (DNS), which is described in Chapter 1 in the section "How the domain name service works."

When you hook up to the Internet, you are a part of some domain, whether it is your own domain or that of your company or service provider. You also give your computer a name to identify it as part of your domain. For dial-up accounts with an Internet service provider, you can usually pick the host name for your computer yourself.

Let's look at an example. Assume that you have a personal account through a fictional Internet service provider named SpiffyNet. SpiffyNet's domain name is spiffy.net. SpiffyNet allows you to pick the name for your computer, so in a fit of creativity, you choose to call your computer viper. Thus, the full host and domain name of your computer would be viper.spiffy.net.

IP addresses

Just as you have a name to identify a computer, your computer also has a number that uniquely identifies it to the rest of the world. This number is known as the IP address of your computer. Let's look a little closer at how IP addresses work.

An IP address is a 32-bit value that is divided into four 8-bit fields, each separated by a period. This means that the address would look something like 192.1.5.1. Each computer has exactly one IP address for each physical interface that it has connected to a network.

NOTE   In networking terminology, an 8-bit field is known as an octet.

The IP address of a computer is divided into two parts: a network section, which specifies a particular network, and a host portion, which identifies a particular machine on the network. There now are five categories of IP addresses based on the type of network address. These are referred to as Class A through Class E.

In a Class A address, the first octet has a value between 1 and 126, and the network portion consists of the first octet. This obviously limits the number of Class A networks to 126; however, each network can have more than 16 million computers. Class A networks are limited to major corporations and network providers.

Class B networks use the first two octets to specify the network portion and have the first octet in the range of 128 to 191. This leaves the last two octets free for the host ID. The Class B network space provides for 16,382 network ID numbers, each with 65,534 host IDs. Large companies and organizations such as universities are typically assigned Class B addresses.

Class C addresses use three octets to specify the network portion, with the first octet in the range from 192 to 223. This provides for more than 2 million different Class C networks, but only 254 hosts per network. Class C networks are usually assigned to small businesses or organizations.

In Class D addresses, the first octet is in the range from 224 to 239 and is used for multicast transmissions.

Class E addresses, with the first octet in the range of 240 to 247, are reserved for future use.

When computers communicate using TCP/IP, they use the numeric IP address. DNS names are simply a device that helps us humans remember which host is which and what network it's connected to. When the Internet was first formed, the number of hosts on the Net was very small. As a result, each host had a complete list of all host names and addresses in a local file. For obvious reasons, this system quickly became unwieldy. When a new host was added, it was necessary to update every host file on every computer. With the explosive growth of the Internet, the host files also grew quite large. The mapping of DNS names to IP addresses is now accomplished via a distributed database and specific software that performs the lookup.

Static versus dynamic IP addresses

As you've probably figured out by now, your computer has to have an IP address to communicate on the Internet. How does it get it? Well, in most cases it is assigned by your ISP when you set up your account. Even if you are setting up a whole network of computers, your ISP will probably handle everything for you.

For direct Internet connections, the IP address of your computer is permanently assigned to you. It never changes. These are known as static IP addresses. Most Internet service providers, however, use a scheme known as dynamic IP addressing.

Because most ISPs typically have many more dial-up customers than they do modems, only a fraction of their dial-up customers can be online at any given moment. This usually isn't a problem, unless you want to sit in front of your computer and run Netscape 24 hours a day! In short, this means that an ISP can "recycle" IP addresses by only assigning them when your system dials up to connect to the service. This allows ISPs to get by with far fewer IP addresses than if they were statically assigned.

How does this affect you, the network user? First, you have to configure your networking software differently depending on whether you have a static or dynamic IP address. Second, there are a few things that you just can't do if you have a dynamic IP address. Specifically, because your IP address is dynamic—it changes every time you log in—your host name cannot be registered in a domain name service database along with your IP address. Basically, this prevents anyone out on the Internet from being able to initiate contact with your computer. You won't be able to run an FTP server or a Web server if your computer has a dynamic IP address. Similarly, some commercial database services limit access to specific IP addresses based on subscription. Obviously, if your IP address is changing all the time, this scheme won't work.

Although these limitations don't really affect a lot of people, they can be a real problem if you really want to run an FTP or Web server. Some ISPs charge extra for static IP addresses—sometimes a lot extra. If having a static IP address is a real issue for you, make sure you check with your ISP before signing a service contract.

Types of Internet connections

Depending on how much money you want to spend, you can get many different levels of connection to the Internet. These connection levels primarily differ in the amount of data you can transfer over a given period of time. We refer to the rate at which data can be transferred as the bandwidth of the connection.

There are two categories of Internet connections: dial-up and direct connections. A dial-up connection uses a modem to dial another modem at an Internet service provider, perform some connection sequence, and bring up the TCP/IP network. A direct connection uses a dedicated, data-grade telephone circuit as the connection path to the Internet. Let's look at these in a bit more detail.

Dial-up connections

When you sign up for a dial-up Internet account, you use a modem to dial a telephone number for an Internet service provider. After the modems connect, your computer performs some type of login sequence and the computers start to communicate via TCP/IP.

NOTE **For Netscape to be usable with a dial-up connection, you need, at a** minimum, a 14.4 KBps modem. A faster modem, such as a 28.8 KBps model, is recommended.

The login sequence that your system performs depends on the requirements of your particular ISP. Most of the time, these login sequences are automated by using a script file. (For more information on script files, see "Setting up Windows 95 for PPP" later in this chapter.)

We use a bit of smoke and mirrors when we refer to "starting TCP/IP networking." What this really means is telling the remote system that you want to start communicating via TCP/IP instead of just via ASCII terminal emulation. This is accomplished via a dial-up connection by using a protocol such as PPP.

PPP, the Point to Point Protocol, and SLIP, the Serial Line Internet Protocol, allow you to use TCP/IP communications over a dial-up connection. While either of these protocols works for serial TCP/IP, most ISPs are migrating to PPP, as it is newer and has more robust features. For this discussion, we are assuming you use PPP.

The way you start PPP varies depending on your ISP. In some cases, it starts automatically for you when you log in. In other cases, you may have to execute a command from a login shell on the ISP. Still another way is to make a selection from an interactive menu. It really depends on your ISP.

Direct connections

The other major way of connecting to the Internet is through a direct connection. This method is typically used by large offices and companies to tie their internal networks into the Internet. Quite simply, it requires a lot of money.

A direct connection consists of a dedicated, data-grade telephone line that runs between your location and your service provider. Depending on the bandwidth of this line, the charges from your phone company can be several thousand dollars per month. In addition to this charge, you also have the recurring monthly charge from your ISP, which can also be very expensive. Add to that the cost of the network hardware required, and this option quickly prices itself out of the reach of individuals and small companies.

But let's assume for a second that you have the money to set up a direct Internet connection. How do you do it and what does it buy you? Well, the main things that it gives you are the ability to have a large pipe into the Internet through which to pump data, the ability to assign IP addresses to a whole network of computers, and static IP addressing. As for setting up the connection, most established ISPs have a setup package where they order your phone line, provide the hardware, register your domain name, and get your IP addresses for you—all for a flat fee. It's best to check with the ISP of your choice for more information.

Types of services

Now that we've gotten the basics out of the way, let's look at what services you can get from an ISP. Most ISPs provide dial-up and direct connect services, with a whole menu of services that you can select from.

Dial-up IP

For most ISPs, the basic level of dial-up IP gives you PPP-based, dynamic IP addressing on a public dial-up number. This number is connected to a modem bank, and rotates to the next available modem when you dial in—if there is a modem available. For most ISPs, busy signals are a common problem, especially during the prime evening and weekend hours.

Some ISPs provide a couple levels of service above the basic dial-up PPP account. For example, you may be able to pay an additional fee to dial into a restricted number that has a better user-to-modem ratio. For even more money, the ISP may provide you with a dedicated dial-up line—a phone line that only you can dial in on. It's important to decide what type of dial-up account you are going to need, because this is one of the primary factors that affects the cost of your Internet service.

E-Mail

If you've managed to get this far and set up an Internet connection, you probably want e-mail, right? By using a dial-up PPP account, you can read and send e-mail via the Post Office Protocol (POP). To do this, you get an e-mail client program such as Eudora for your PC and configure it with your e-mail account information and the IP address of your network mail server. If you have a dial-up account, your network mail server is a computer located at your ISP's offices.

 NOTE   **E-mail is transferred between systems on the Internet using a protocol** known as the Simple Mail Transport Protocol, or SMTP. POP is the protocol that a local e-mail client program uses to retrieve mail from a mail server.

Most personal dial-up accounts provide you with at least one e-mail address. Some ISPs even provide as many as five different addresses for personal or family accounts. Other ISPs make you pay an additional monthly charge for extra e-mail IDs. Business accounts usually have a fixed number as well. If you have more than one person who will be using e-mail from your system, you might want to shop around to see what the ISP policies on multiple e-mail addresses are in your area.

News

Just as with e-mail, if your Internet service provider gives you access to UseNet news, you can probably read and post news from your PC by using a newsreader, such as Netscape, that supports the Network News Transport Protocol (NNTP). To do this, simply configure your newsreader with the names or addresses of your mail and news hosts—the computers that you exchange e-mail and news with. Most ISPs provide UseNet news as part of the basic dial-up PPP account service.

Shell access

Another service that is often available with a dial-up account is shell access. This refers to the ability to access a command-line processor on the remote ISP system.

 NOTE   **Because most ISPs use a UNIX system to provide Internet access, and** UNIX command-line processors are known as shells, the term shell access has become rather common.

Your ISP may or may not provide shell access as part of your basic network package. Most people can get by without having shell access. It is useful for accessing your account over the Internet, via Telnet or FTP from another location, as well as doing things like compiling C code. But if you are just running Netscape from home, you can probably survive with out it.

Be aware that some ISPs sell a "shell-access-only" account as a dial-up account. Typically, you cannot run PPP or SLIP from this type of account. Because Netscape needs TCP/IP to run, you need to make sure that you get the right type of service from your ISP.

Web servers

The Web is a hot item—obviously, or you wouldn't be reading a book about Netscape. Another service provided by many ISPs is access to a Web server. Web servers allow you to put home pages on the Web so they can be accessed by people with Web browsers like Netscape. Figure A.1 shows an example of a Web page.

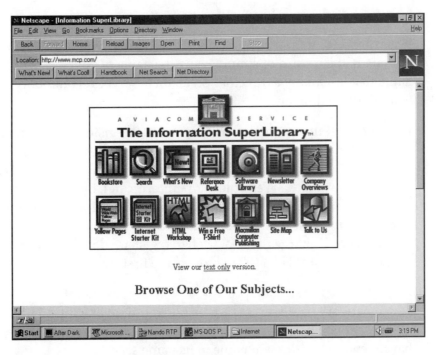

Fig. A.1
The home Web page for Macmillan Computer Publishing.

NOTE **Don't confuse Netscape with a Web server—you can still surf the Net** with Netscape even if you don't have Web server access.

Having access to a Web server means that you can write Web pages in HTML and make them available on the Web. Many ISPs provide their personal account customers the ability to create personal Web pages. Businesses usually have to pay an additional fee for the service.

NOTE **Companies that have a direct connection to the Internet can simply set** up their own Web server on one of their own machines.

If your ISP doesn't provide Web server access, don't give up hope. There are many companies that provide Web services alone, without providing any type of interactive access to the Internet. Basically, you pay a monthly fee to have the Web provider's site place your pages in the World Wide Web. These Web service providers also typically offer consulting and design services to help you create effective Web pages.

Virtual domains

If you are setting up a business account, you may want to use your own domain name instead of simply using the name of your ISP. A domain name that is actually a directory on an ISP's server is commonly referred to as a virtual domain.

In order to set up a virtual domain, you must register your domain name with the Network Information Center (NIC). The NIC acts as the clearing-house for all Internet domain names. You can reach the NIC by Telnet at rs.internic.net, on the Web at **http://rs.internic.net**, by e-mail at **question@internic.net**, or by telephone at 1-703-742-4777. You must fill out a domain name registration template and submit it to the NIC. Currently, the NIC charges a fee of $100 to register a domain, and $50 per year to use the domain. The $100 fee covers the first two years.

As part of the registration process, you must provide information about which network name servers advertise your domain name. In short, this means that you have to find an ISP that provides virtual domains, and have it enter your domain name in its name server.

As with everything else, most ISPs charge an additional fee for supporting virtual domains. If this is a service that you require, make sure you shop around and ask questions.

Finding an Internet service provider

With the explosive growth of the Internet, there are now lots of ISPs to choose from. The services, cost, and customer satisfaction of ISPs vary widely. Some are terrible—a few are wonderful—most fall somewhere in the middle.

National providers

You can divide ISPs into categories based on whether they have a national presence or they are mainly a local company. If you think about it, any ISP has a national presence in the sense that it is connected to the Internet and can be reached from anywhere. What we are referring to is the ability to contact the ISP via a local telephone call. Several of the larger ISPs have local dial access in many different locations, effectively making them national providers.

There are pros and cons to using a national provider. The company is usually larger—not a basement operation—and it usually has competent technical support people working for it. Also, national providers usually have a better uptime percentage than local providers, and also have a better price structure. On the other hand, because national ISPs tend to be larger, it may be harder to reach a technical support person when you have a problem. You may find that their policies are less flexible than local providers, and that they are less willing to make exceptions and work with you. If you are setting up a business connection, your ISP's office may be hundreds or thousands of miles away. If you are the kind of person that values working with a local company, this could present a problem for you.

Regional and local providers

Local and regional providers are ISPs that serve a regional market instead of having a national presence. Like national providers, there are pros and cons here, too. You will probably find that local providers are more flexible on their services and policies. For business, you are usually able to meet face to face with someone in the office to discuss your Internet needs. On the down side, the service quality of local ISPs tends to be less reliable. Sometimes these companies are very small operations, with limited hardware and technical support. You may find that it is difficult to connect due to busy signals during certain times of the day.

Local and regional ISPs are notorious for expanding their customer base faster than their hardware will support. When their servers get overloaded, response creeps to a crawl and uptime suffers. Phone lines are continually busy. If this happens to an ISP, it has to respond immediately or its systems will become unusable.

A word about private information services

Most people are aware of private national information services like CompuServe or America Online. While these services do provide Internet access, including Web access, they did not, when this book was written, provide routed IP access to the Internet. In short, this means that you have to use their tools and interfaces to access the Net. Because you will not have a routed IP connection, you cannot use the network tools of your choice, such as Netscape, via one of these services.

Service levels and cost

As you have seen, there are a lot of things to consider when selecting an ISP. The level of service you need is probably the main thing that affects the cost of your connection. Dial-up modem connections in the general public modem pool are usually cheapest. A restricted modem group is more expensive. A dedicated dial-up line costs even more. Direct connections via leased lines are among the most expensive.

In addition to service level, many ISPs offer different connection pricing plans. Some plans give you a fixed number of connect hours per month and charge you for extra hours. Other plans may give you unlimited hours during a certain time period, and charge you for hours outside of that window. Still other plans give you unlimited connect time for your fee.

Before choosing an ISP, take time to evaluate how you are going to use the service and what level of service you need. Check with computer users in your area to see if they can recommend a local service or a national service that works well.

Netscape and Windows 95

There are several different ways that you can use Netscape to connect to the Internet. You can connect over Microsoft's TCP/IP, a third-party TCP/IP package, or you can purchase one of the bundled starter kits, such as the Earthlink Netscape Total Access package. In this section, we look at how to set up Netscape to run under Windows 95.

Setting up Windows 95 for PPP

If you're using Netscape under Windows 95, you're in luck. Windows 95 includes support for PPP, which enables Netscape to access the Internet. Assuming that you have an account already set up with an Internet service provider, it's not too difficult to configure Windows 95 so that it provides you dial-up PPP support.

There are several bits of information that you need to correctly configure PPP for Windows 95. Your ISP should provide all this information when you set up your account. If you don't know some of these items, contact your ISP for help. You need to know:

- The username that you use to login to your ISP
- The password for your ISP account
- The telephone number for your ISP
- The host name for your computer
- The network domain name for your ISP
- The IP address of your ISP's default gateway or router
- The IP subnet mask of your ISP's network
- The IP address of your ISP's DNS name server
- Whether you have a static or dynamic IP address
- The IP address of your computer, if you have a static address

After you gather all this information, you're ready to start installing PPP for Windows 95. You probably didn't install all the components for PPP when you installed Windows 95, so you need to check to see what's already there and install the ones that are missing.

Dial-up networking, the dial-up adapter, and TCP/IP

The dial-up networking and dial-up adapter items are necessary to set up a dial-up account to the Internet. Make sure you have your installation media handy throughout this process. For simplicity, I'll assume that you are installing from a CD-ROM. To check that dial-up networking is installed:

1 Click the Start button and choose Settings, Control Panel.

2 Double-click the Add/Remove Programs icon.

3 Select the Windows Setup tab. This brings up the section of the Add/Remove Programs dialog box that allows you to install or change various components of Windows 95.

4 Select the Communications option.

5 Click the Details button. This brings up the Communications dialog box showing current configuration of your Windows 95 communications system.

6 Make sure the Dial-Up Networking entry is selected. If it is not selected, select it and click OK.

Now that the dial-up networking package is installed, you need to check for the dial-up adapter. Basically, this program allows Windows 95 to use your telephone to make a network connection. To check that the dial-up adapter is installed:

1 Click the Start button, and choose Settings, Control Panel.

2 Double-click the Network icon. This brings up the Network control panel, which allows you to configure your network setup.

3 Select the Configuration tab. This portion of the Network dialog box allows you to add new network protocols and adapters to your Windows 95 environment. Figure A.2 shows the Network dialog box.

4 Look for TCP/IP and Dial-up Adapter in the list.

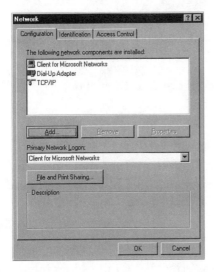

Fig. A.2
The Network dialog box for configuring your network environment.

If you don't see the Dial-Up Adapter in the Network dialog box:

1 Click the Add button. This brings up the Select Network Component Type dialog box, which is where you tell Windows 95 what sort of networking item you want to add to your computer.

2 Double-click Adapter. This brings up the Select Network adapters dialog box. We want to add the Dial-Up Adapter so that we can use dial-up networking.

3 The lefthand scroll box is labeled Select Network Component Type. Scroll this box until you see the Microsoft entry.

4 Select Microsoft from the Select Network Component Type scroll box. Choose Dial-Up Adapter from the righthand scroll box labeled Network Adapters.

5 Click OK.

If you don't see TCP/IP in the Network dialog box:

1 Click the Add button to add the protocol to your computer.

2 Double-click Protocol. TCP/IP is a networking protocol and that is what we need to add. This brings up the Select Network Protocol dialog box.

3 Scroll the left scroll box, labeled Manufacturers, until you see the Microsoft entry.

4 Select Microsoft in the left scroll box and then choose TCP/IP in the right scroll box, labeled Network Protocols.

5 Click OK.

At this point, you should see both TCP/IP and the dial-up adapter in the Network dialog box. Click Properties and then Bindings and verify that the TCP/IP box is selected.

Dial-up scripting

You will probably want to create a script that handles logging in to your ISP's system. This way, you can just double-click an icon and have Windows 95 dial your ISP, log you in automatically, and start PPP. We'll come back to scripting in a bit, but first you need to verify that the Dial-Up Scripting program has been installed.

1 Click Start and choose Programs, Accessories.

2 Look for an entry for the Dial-Up Scripting Tool.

If the Dial-up Scripting Tool isn't installed:

1 Click the Start button, and choose Settings, Control Panel.

2 Double-click the Add/Remove Programs icon.

3 Select the Windows Setup tab. Remember, this is where you add components to your Windows 95 system. We need to install the Dial-Up Scripting Tool from your Windows 95 CD.

4 Click the Have Disk button. This tells Windows 95 that you need to install something from the CD.

5 You will need to enter the path to the dial-up scripting program on your Windows 95 CD. For example, if your CD is drive G:, you would enter **G:\admin\apptools\dscript**.

6 Click the OK button.

Entering the address information

Okay, at this point you should have all the drivers and other programs installed so that you can configure TCP/IP with your network information. A couple of steps in this section depend on whether you have a static or dynamic IP address, so pay attention.

1 Click the Start button, and choose Settings, Control Panel.

2 Double-click the Network icon, and select the TCP/IP Protocol entry.

3 Click the Properties button.

4 If you have a static IP address, select the option labeled Specify an IP Address, type your IP address into the box, and fill in the Subnet Mask box with your subnet mask.

If you have a dynamic IP address, choose the Obtain an IP Address Automatically option.

5 Select Disable WINS Resolution.

6 In the section marked Gateway, type the IP address for your ISP's gateway or router, and then click the Add button.

7 Select the Enable DNS option.

8 Type the host name of your computer in the Host box.

9 Enter the domain name of your ISP in the Domain box.

10 In the DNS Server Search Order section, enter the IP address of your ISP's DNS server.

11 Type the domain name for your ISP in the Domain Suffix Search Order section, and then click the Add button.

12 Double-check all your entries, and then click OK.

13 Windows 95 asks you to reboot your computer. Click Yes.

At this point, your Windows 95 environment should have support for Dial-up Networking, TCP/IP, and the Dial-up Scripting Tool. Hopefully, you were able to successfully add any of those components that were not already installed.

Setting up a connection icon

Now we're almost ready to log on. The connection icon is the icon that you use to initiate your PPP connection. To start configuring it, double-click the My Computer icon on your desktop. Next, double-click the Dial-Up Networking icon, and then double-click the Make New Connection icon. This brings up a wizard box that helps you set up a new connection entry. Simply follow these steps:

1 Enter into the dialog box the connection name that you want to use.

2 Click the Configure button, and then select the General tab.

3 In the Maximum Speed box, set the port speed for your modem. In general, 57600 is a good setting.

4 Make sure that the box marked Only Connect at This Speed is not checked.

5 If you are not going to use a script to automate your login process, select the Options tab. From here, you can have PPP open a login window for you so that you can manually log in to your server.

6 Click OK, and then press Next in the wizard dialog box.

7 Enter the area code and phone number of your ISP in the dialog box and click Next.

8 Click Finish.

At this point, you should see a new connection icon, with the name that you specified, on your system. There are just a couple of more things to do before it's ready to use.

1 Click the right mouse button on your connection icon. This brings up a pop-up menu for the connection icon.

2 Choose Properties from the pop-up menu.

3 Click the Server Type button, and then PPP from the list box.

4 Verify that the TCP/IP box in the Allowed Network Protocols section is checked, and make sure that the Log on to Network box is not selected.

5 Click OK.

6 Click OK again.

We're done configuring TCP/IP. If you want to set your modem to automatically redial, you can do so from the Settings option on the Connections menu in the Dial-Up Networking folder.

Basic scripting

As mentioned earlier, using a script to automate your login process makes things a lot easier. You can start your connection session and run to the fridge while Windows 95 retries your ISP dial-up line and logs you in. Also, scripting is very easy. You can think of a script as telling Windows 95 what to look for from the ISP server. Just as you might look for a login: prompt to type your username, you can have your script do the same thing. Use the Dial-Up Scripting Tool to create scripts to control your dial-up network session. Figure A.3 shows the Dial-Up Scripting Tool.

Fig. A.3
The Windows 95 Dial-Up Scripting Tool.

To make a script, follow these steps:

1 Click the Start button; select Programs, Accessories.

2 Select the Dial-Up Scripting Tool.

3 Click the Edit button to start editing a script.

All scripts start with the line

```
proc main
```

and end with the line

```
endproc
```

Between these two statements, you enter commands that tell Windows 95 what to transmit and what to wait for. There are three basic commands that you need to know in order to write a script: delay, waitfor, and transmit.

The delay statement causes your script to wait for a specified number of seconds. For example:

```
delay 3
```

causes the script to pause for three seconds.

The waitfor statement makes the script wait until the specified string is received. For example:

```
waitfor "ssword"
```

waits for the string "ssword" to be received by your system.

The third statement, transmit, transmits a string to the remote system. It does not automatically send a carriage return at the end of the string. To send a carriage return, you need to transmit the string "^M" to the remote system. Here is an example of a script:

```
proc main
delay 1
transmit "^M"
delay 1
transmit "^M"
delay 1
transmit "^M"
waitfor "name>"
transmit $USERID
transmit "^M"
waitfor "ssword>"
transmit $PASSWORD
transmit "^M"
waitfor "enu:"
```

```
transmit "3"
transmit "^M"
endproc
```

NOTE **It is usually a good idea to only use the last part of a string in a waitfor** statement, in case the first character or two gets garbled by the network. For example, you should use waitfor "ssword>" instead of waitfor "password>".

The previous script waits for one second and then sends a carriage return to the remote system. It then repeats this sequence two more times. The script then waits for the string name> from the remote system. It sends the contents of the special variable $USERID, which contains the user ID that you enter when you start the network connection program. It follows the user ID with a carriage return.

The script then waits for the ssword> prompt from the remote system and sends the contents of the $PASSWORD variable. This variable contains the password that you enter when you start the network connection program. It follows the password with a carriage return. It then waits for the string enu:, and sends the number 5 and a carriage return. That's all there is to it.

Once you have written your script, save it with a .SCP extension. Then, in the Dial-Up Scripting Tool, select the network connection that you want to attach the script to and click Apply. Your script is now associated with that network connection and will be executed automatically any time you run that particular network connection.

You can also select the Step through Script box to be able to step through the script one line at a time to debug it. By selecting the Start Terminal Screen Minimized box, you will see no terminal box displaying the progress of your script. Uncheck this box if you want to watch your script execute as it runs.

Loading and Configuring Netscape

● In this appendix:

● **Installing Netscape from the CD-ROM with this book**

● **Download new versions of Netscape from the Internet when there are upgrades**

● **Get on the Web for the first time**

● **Get help with Netscape products**

Loading Netscape

Of course, you have to install the program before you can catch that first wave. But don't worry; Netscape has included a wizard that guides you through the entire installation process. Netscape has a few system requirements that you must meet to complete the installation and run the program effectively.

Installation requirements

The following list shows all the requirements for installing and running Netscape 3:

- Mouse
- Windows 95, Windows NT (3.5 or higher), or Windows 3.1
- 386sx or compatible machine
- 2 MB of hard drive space
- 4 MB of memory (8 MB recommended)
- LAN or a SLIP/PPP connection to the Internet

CAUTION **These are just the minimum requirements to run Netscape 3 under** Windows 95. Keep in mind that you need more hard drive space if you keep a large list of sites you have visited or if you download lots of images and other files.

The minimum requirements only take into consideration the amount of hard drive space and memory that is required to load and run the program in most situations. When you visit a Web site that has an extraordinary amount of graphics on it, the page takes a long time to load if you only have the "minimum" amount of RAM.

Installing the Netscape browser

The installation process is relatively quick and painless. Because Netscape uses a wizard to walk you through the installation, most of your questions are answered right on-screen. If you experience problems during the installation, call the Macmillan phone number listed in the section titled "Getting Help for Netscape Products" later in this chapter.

1 Close any Windows or DOS programs that are running. Sometimes other programs use files or memory that Netscape needs to use during the install process.

2 Click the Start button or press Ctrl+Esc and select Run.

3 From Windows Explorer, go to the \netscape directory on the CD-ROM. In this directory, there are subdirectories for Windows 95, Windows NT, and Windows 3.1. Change to the directory for your operating system version and double-click the file there. Once the installation files are extracted, the Setup Wizard (which guides you through the installation process) is installed. Once the Wizard's initialization is complete, an introduction and a warning on Netscape appear. Click Next.

4 Netscape requires a specific destination directory, as shown in figure B.1. This is the directory that stores the main portion of Netscape. You can either use the default directory, or you can enter your own directory name.

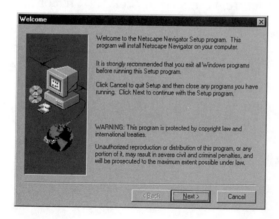

Fig. B.1
The default installation directory for Netscape 2 is C:\Program Files\Netscape\Navigator\.

To specify your own directory, click Browse. You see a list showing your current directory structure, as shown in figure B.2. Select the directory you want to place Netscape into, or type the name of a new directory, and click OK.

Fig. B.2
You can easily select an alternative directory from this Choose Directory dialog window.

 NOTE **The examples in this book use the default path. If you install Netscape** in another directory, please go to that location when you see a reference to c:\Program Files\Netscape.

Whether you choose to create your own directory, or use the pre-defined directory structure, you need to click Next to continue.

5 Netscape now copies the files from the temporary directory to Netscape's permanent location on your hard drive. The scales shown in figure B.3 enable you to keep track of the installation process. When it is done, the Wizard creates a program group folder and shortcut icons that allow you to run Netscape directly from your Start menu.

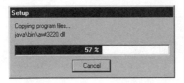

Fig. B.3
Netscape makes it easy to see how your installation is progressing by providing a setup status bar and checks on your available disk space.

6 When you see the short prompt requesting that you finish the Netscape setup by going to their setup site, click Yes. You will be greeted with the How to Setup Netscape page on Netscape's site.

NOTE **The README.TXT file is full of useful information. It guides you through** setting up Netscape to deal with Win32s, and lets you know how to procure and load the appropriate WINSOCK.DLL file. The README.TXT file also gives some basic pointers on where to get more information if you encounter problems using Netscape. Although it does not provide very much helpful information for individuals that are first-time users of Netscape, it may help some old pros fix a new problem.

Now you have Netscape 3 installed. This is the latest shipping version that is currently available.

Downloading Netscape from the Internet

Netscape is frequently updated and there may come a time when you want to get a new version. These new versions are available on the Internet. The best way to download a new version if you ever need one is to use the current version you have installed to go to the Netscape Web site (**http://home.netscape.com**) and download it from there.

1 Go to the Netscape home page at **http://home.netscape.com** and click the Netscape 3 Now button shown in figure B.4. (This number may change when there is a new version.) Or you can go directly to **http://home.netscape.com/comprod/mirror/client_download.html** and skip step number two. This is the address of the Web page for downloading Netscape.

2 Scroll through the document shown in figure B.5 until you find the Netscape Navigator category, which then links you to the Web page for downloading Netscape shown in figure B.6.

3 Netscape asks a series of questions about the product that you want to download.

- Desired product
- Operating system
- Desired language

You need to select Netscape, or Netscape Gold, if you want to look at the latest enhancements in Netscape software.

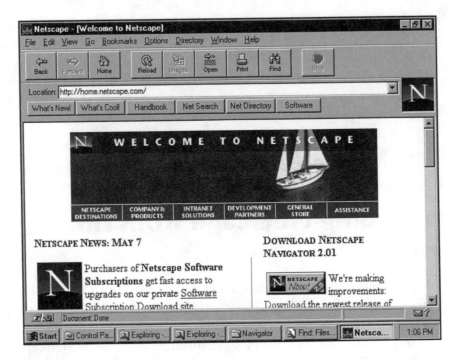

Fig. B.4
The Netscape Communications Corporation's World Wide Web home page.

4 Once you have filled in the above requests for information, you need to click the Click to Display Download Sites button.

5 A list of locations from which you can download Netscape appears. This list includes the majority of the mirror sites listed in the later section titled "The Netscape mirror site list." Select the site closest to your current computer location.

6 Once you have downloaded Netscape, close your Web browser.

Because most of the sites holding Netscape store the program as a self-extracting executable file, you can run the executable by double-clicking it in Windows Explorer. This extracts the compressed files and starts the installation of Netscape. From this point you can follow the instructions in the earlier section entitled "Installing the Netscape browser" to install it. You simply need to refer to the directory to which you copied the Netscape executable file.

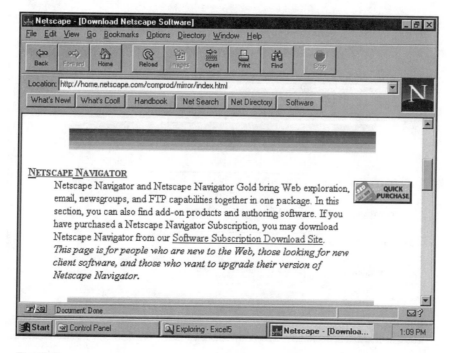

Fig. B.5
The Netscape Communications Corporation's product page.

NOTE **It is always nice to start a new project with some idea about the** amount of time that it is going to involve. The following table shows the average download time I experienced when transferring this file several times while preparing this book. These times should be close to what you will experience, although you should not worry if your times are a bit longer or shorter. These times will vary if the file size of newer versions changes dramatically.

Connection type	Total transfer time
14,400 modem	1 hour
28,800 modem (at least a 24,000 baud carrier)	30 minutes
57,600 network	15 minutes
T1 cable	1 minute

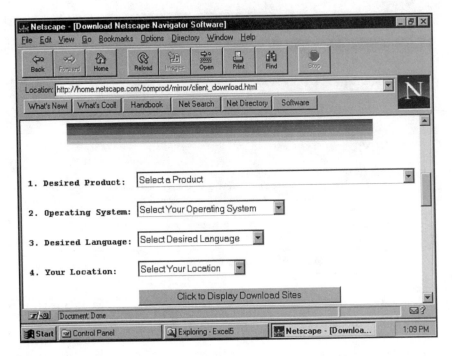

Fig. B.6
Netscape 3 Download page.

The Netscape mirror site list

Netscape allows only a few sites to mirror its information. The following list shows you all the official sites from North America. Of course, you can always download a copy of Netscape from the Netscape Communications Corporation site, listed in the North American section, from anywhere in the world.

Since the most logical place to get a program is from the company that makes it, it would stand to reason that this corporation would have the busiest file servers. This reasoning holds true for the Netscape FTP sites. You will often find that the main Netscape site is busy, even though they have several servers available from which you can download programs. The solution to this information bottleneck lies in the development of mirror sites. Mirror sites provide easy access to information by having copies of files from other computers that could be located across the continent, or on the other side of the globe. Mirror sites draw away from the pool of people that are waiting to get onto the main file server.

- Netscape Communications Corp.—**ftp://ftp.netscape.com/pub/navigator**

- Washington University, St. Louis—**ftp://wuarchive.wustl.edu/packages/www/Netscape/navigator**

- University of Texas at Austin—**ftp://ftp.the.net/mirrors/ftp.netscape.com/pub/navigator**

- University of Texas at Dallas—**ftp://lassen.utdallas.edu/pub/web/netscape/pub/navigator**

- Central Michigan University, Computer Center—**ftp://ftp.cps.cmich.edu/pub/netscape/navigator**

Within the directories listed here, you'll find further subdirectories for various platforms and versions of Netscape. These directory names change from time to time so you'll need to scout your way through them looking for obvious clues like a directory named "windows" for Windows versions and "gold" for the Netscape Gold editor and browser.

Getting on the Web for the first time

The World Wide Web is considered one of the best places to get information on any subject, at any time. To reach this large body of information, you first need to connect to the network of computer systems that makes up the Internet. Use the information in the following sections to connect to your Internet service provider or to your company's network.

Connecting to your service provider

Although the term *service provider* usually refers to a dial-up SLIP or PPP connection, you can also use a standard TCP/IP LAN connection. There are specific details in appendix A, "Connecting to the Internet," that discuss how to set up a working Internet connection for all the operating systems used by Netscape products. The following section covers only the basic steps in the setup process for Windows 95.

Making a LAN connection

When using a Local Area Network (LAN) to connect to the Internet, you must make sure that your computer is correctly configured to use the specific type of network to which it is physically attached. You have to know the specific type of network card that your computer uses and the names of the drivers that are required to run your card. Once this information is obtained you must load those drivers, or tell your computer to do it automatically for you each time it starts, before you can connect to the network. The following steps guide you through the process of getting these drivers loaded and running properly.

1 Open the Control Panel and select the Networks icon.

2 On your Network Properties screen, make sure that you have a TCP/IP protocol loaded for your network card.

NOTE **This protocol needs to be configured with the following information:**

- Your network IP address

- The address of your Internet gateway

- The address of the Domain Name Servers (DNS) used by your facility

Complete the configuration by choosing Properties and filling out the forms on the tab dialog box that appears. See chapter 2, "Moving Around the Web," for detailed information on how to configure these settings.

3 Choose the OK button to exit this screen once you have ensured that the proper drivers are loaded.

4 Double-click the Netscape icon on your desktop. If you do not find this icon, you can open the Start menu, select Programs, and then the Netscape folder, and choose the Netscape icon located on this menu to start the program.

Netscape finds your network and travels through it and out onto the Internet to find Netscape's home page. Once you are there you can travel across the Net to anywhere.

Q&A *Every time I open Netscape I get an error message telling me that I have a Winsock error.*

Generally you get this error when you do not have your TCP/IP protocol properly loaded. Go back to the Control Panel's Network Properties dialog box and ensure that the appropriate TCP/IP and network drivers for your network card are loaded. If you have selected the wrong network card, you will load inappropriate drivers and receive this message. If you just installed your network drivers, you must restart your computer for them to load. Windows 95 does not automatically load the drivers into your computer's memory after you have installed them.

Making a SLIP/PPP connection

Very few home users and relatively few businesses have a direct connection to the Internet, which leaves the majority of the world connecting to the Internet through a SLIP or PPP connection and a modem. Because Netscape does not provide you with a dialing program, you have to use the one that comes with Windows 95, or another third party dial-up connector. Before you attempt to use Netscape the first time, check your dial-up program. It will save you time in the long run.

1 Open the Control Panel and select the Networks icon.

2 Check to ensure that you have the dial-up adapter and a TCP/IP protocol loaded for that adapter. If you do not have these items in your list of network components, refer to Appendix A for assistance in configuring these drivers.

3 Open the Start menu and choose the Programs option, and then choose the Accessories option. This opens the Accessories pop-up menu on which you will find an icon labeled Dial-Up Networking. This is the utility that dials your phone connection for you.

 NOTE The dial-up networking utility actually dials your phone and can log you into your service provider. A detailed discussion of this utility is included in Appendix A.

4 Open the Start menu, select the Programs option, and then choose the Netscape group option.

5 Choose the Netscape option from the resulting menu.

Netscape automatically starts the dial-up networking client, which calls your service provider and establishes a connection. Depending on how you have installed the dial-up client, you might have to manually enter your name and password. When you establish your connection, all the features of Netscape are available.

Getting help for Netscape products

Because Netscape is used by such a large base of Internet users, you can get product support quickly and easily from a variety of sources. If you are using the copy of Netscape provided with this book, your technical support will be provided through QUE and Macmillan Computer Publishing. Netscape Communications Corporation provides technical support to its licensed customers. UseNet newsgroups discuss how to use and configure Netscape to work in various situations. Listserv discussion groups also discuss the use of Netscape and how to make it perform specific required tasks. And once again, there is the World Wide Web. The Web has many sites specifically designed to be viewed with Netscape. Many of these site owners will assist you in configuring Netscape to view their sites in the best possible fashion. You can generally contact the site owners by sending an e-mail message to **webmaster@***the.site.name*.

Receiving technical support from Netscape

Netscape Communications Corporation provides its customers with many ways to get in touch with technical support. These methods include e-mail, World Wide Web pages, its online Help system, a printed handbook (for registered users), and technical voice support over a telephone.

Contacting Que and Macmillan Computer Publishing

If your copy of Netscape is from the CD-ROM included with this book, you must call or e-mail Que for technical support. Please send questions via e-mail to support@mcp.com or call 317-581-3833. Unless you have purchased a copy of Netscape from Netscape, you cannot use the Netscape support numbers listed in this appendix.

Using E-mail

In this world of fast-paced, practically-instantaneous communication, electronic mail is becoming the best way to get information to and from your associates. Technical support services are also starting to jump on this bandwagon. Netscape has quite a few e-mail addresses from which you can get information (see table B.1). Some of them respond with a generic letter full of other important information and answers to the most common questions that people ask. Others respond individually with qualified support or sales personnel.

Table B.1   Netscape corporation electronic mail addresses

For help on...	Department name	E-mail address
Netscape 3 for licensed customers	Technical Support	**client@netscape.com**
Getting information about purchasing products	Sales—automated	**sales@netscape.com**
General product questions and answers	Sales—automated	**info@netscape.com**
Netscape Training programs information		**training@netscape.com**
Bug reports from Windows users	Technical Support	**win31_cbug@netscape.com** **win95_cbug@netscape.com** **winnt_cbug@netscape.com**

When using a manually monitored system, include your name, return e-mail address, and product registration number in your message. Netscape provides support only to individuals who provide this information.

Referring to Netscape's help system

Netscape's help system uses a series of linked HTML pages, some of which are located on your local computer, while others are located at Netscape's Web site. The Help menu in Netscape allows you to jump directly to important product support pages for your version of Netscape (see fig. B.7). These pages include the Release Notes for your version, the related FAQs for Navigator, a Netscape Handbook, and a series of articles on how to get assistance and give feedback on Netscape's products. You can generally answer most, if not all, of your questions by reading these documents.

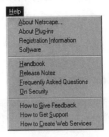

Fig. B.7
The available Netscape Help utilities located in the Help menu.

Using Netscape's World Wide Web pages

Netscape uses its Web site to provide much of its product support, not to mention sales and marketing pushes. You can reach the Technical Support pages by clicking the Assistance portion of the main Netscape image map located at the top of the Netscape home page. The address of Netscape Communications Corporation's Technical Support home page is **http:// help.netscape.com**. Figure B.8 shows you what to expect.

When you get to this page, you are greeted with product FAQs, search engines, a storefront, and a list of all the services Netscape provides for its products. You simply need to find the most appropriate services for the product you have questions on, click its link, and continue down your path to a completely working product.

The Web site contains layers upon layers of information. If you see a topic that just might be helpful, jump to it and read it. If the site does not contain the information you are looking for, choose Back and continue on to your next option. You never know what document is going to provide you with that one clue that solves your problem. Even if it doesn't solve your problem today, it might keep you from having another problem in the future.

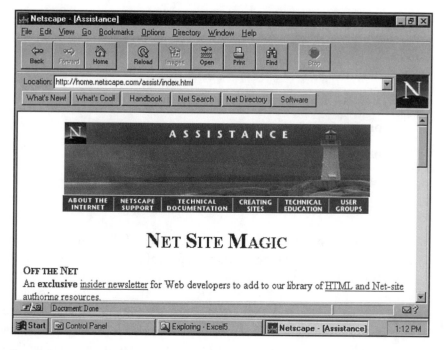

Fig. B.8
The main technical support Web page for Netscape.

Using Netscape phone support

For those of you who want to talk to someone voice to voice, you can get product support over the telephone if you have purchased a copy of Netscape from Netscape via their online store or through a boxed product in a retail store. In that case, you can call with questions about Netscape Navigator at 800-320-2099.

Getting help from UseNet newsgroups

As mentioned earlier, UseNet newsgroups are one of the best ways for people with common interests to get together. There are many different newsgroups that discuss Netscape products. The following list names a few UseNet searching tools with some of the known sites that you can use to get into a UseNet discussion. I have also included specific instructions on how to use Dejanews, a UseNet newsgroup message searching utility that I have found helpful.

- Launch Pad—**http://sunsite.unc.edu/**

  alt.fan.mozzila

  comp.infosystems.www.browsers

- TileNet—**http://www.tile.net/tile/news/index.html**

  comp.infosystems.www.misc

  comp.infosystems.www.users

- Dejanews—**http://www.dejanews.com**

  comp.infosystems.www.browsers.ms-windows

The Dejanews system is very easy to use. The following steps enable you to search its entire message database for information specific to your problem with Netscape.

NOTE **Please remember that vocabulary and spelling are very important. You** may refer to "e-mail" in a search, while someone else calls it "email," and another individual uses the phrase "Internet mail." Your search will not find the messages left by those other individuals. To do a thorough exploration, you need to search on as many different phrases and spellings as you can to get the broadest range of information out of your search.

1 In Netscape, enter the URL above as the address you want to visit.

2 Choose the Power Search! option.

3 Set your search criteria.

- Keywords Match (All/Any)
- Usenet database: (Current/Old)
- Max. number of hits (30/60/120)
- Hitlist detail (Concise/Detailed)
- Hitlist format (Listed/Threaded)
- Sort by (Section/Newsgroup/Date/Author)
- Article date bias (Prefer New/Prefer Old)
- Article date weight (Some/Great/None)

4 Enter your search criteria, such as **Netscape**, and choose the Find button, as shown in figure B.9.

5 Choose Continue from the Security Warning dialog box.

Your screen now changes to a listing of all the messages and UseNet newsgroups that are currently discussing Netscape. This screen should be similar to the one shown in figure B.10. You can read the UseNet discussions by double-clicking the highlighted message subject.

NOTE If you would like more details on using UseNet newsgroups with Netscape, please see chapter 9, "UseNet News with Netscape." To go directly to a UseNet newsgroup, type the address preceded by news: in the URL: field at the top of your Netscape screen.

For example, if you want to look at the **comp.infosystems.www.browsers.ms-windows** newsgroup, place your cursor in the URL: field on your main Netscape screen and type **news:comp.infosystems.www.browsers.ms-windows**. Press Enter to tell Netscape to search for that address.

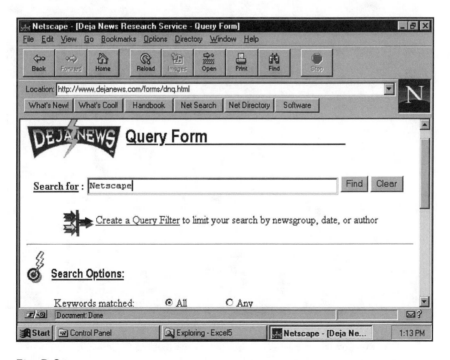

Fig. B.9
The main Dejanews search utility screen configured to perform a search for all discussions of Netscape.

TIP   **Netscape also maintains a set of news groups devoted to help with**
Netscape products. These are called the Netscape User Groups and are easiest
to reach by using Navigator to open this web address: **http://**
home.netscape.com/commun/netscape_user_groups.html. Here you will
find a list of groups and links. Clicking a link will open that group in a Netscape
news window. Be sure to post any questions here only to the appropriate groups.
For example, questions about Netscape Navigator are appropriate in the
NETSCAPE GENERAL TOPIC USER GROUP or NETSCAPE NAVIGATOR USER
GROUP but not in groups related to security, server software, or development
products.

General troubleshooting

There are more "little" problems experienced every day than all the
technical support departments across the country can fix. So when you do
have to call or write for technical support, have the following information
handy to help the process along:

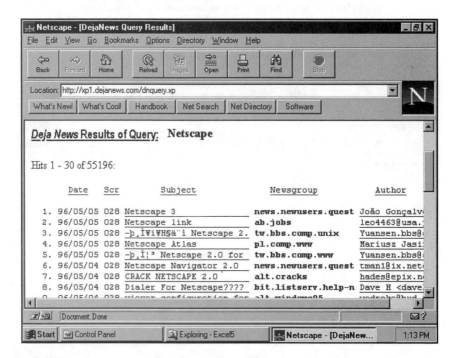

Fig. B.10
The list of the most recent discussions about Netscape that the Dejanews service could find.

- Your name and registration number. Most technical support services will not assist you unless you have a registered product.

- Version of the software you are using. This narrows down the list of known problems so the support specialist can quickly switch gears to help you best with your product version.

- A short description of the problem. For example, "I am able to connect to my service provider, John Doe's Internet Connections, but once I start Netscape I constantly get the following error message: `Netscape is unable to locate server: www.yahoo.com. This server does not have a DNS entry.` Check the server name in the location (URL) and try again." With this information the technician will know if your dial-up PPP connection is working properly, allowing them to narrow down the possible sources of your problem. They will also know the error messages that you are receiving in case this is a known problem they can fix in just a few minutes. When Technical Support personnel have to dig for information on a problem, it needlessly takes more of your time and causes you, and them, more frustration than the problem is worth.

- The name and version of your operating system. If you are running a product designed for Windows 3.1 under Windows 95, you may be having a known conflict with the operating system.

- The type of Internet connection you are using: SLIP/PPP or LAN.

- If you have a SLIP/PPP connection, know the brand and speed of your modem, and the name of the TCP/IP stack you are loading.

  If you have a LAN connection, know the name of the TCP/IP stack you are loading, the type of network card you are using, and the type of connection your network has to the Internet (for example, T1 cable, 57,600 baud line, and so on).

- Try other Internet applications, such as Ping or Telnet, and let the support technician know if they work properly.

- Know when the problem first started, and whether you recently added any new software to your computer around that time. Sometimes installing new software makes your old software not run properly. Many software packages come with their own versions of hardware drivers, and a new software package will often overwrite the version of the driver installed and used by a previously installed package.

Knowing this information in advance helps the technician to diagnose your problem, get you off the telephone, and back onto the Web faster. Without this type of information, you will be extending the time involved in solving your problem. Technical support personnel are highly trained individuals that really know their jobs. Remember that they are people, too, and can't read your mind, nor can they see your computer screen. They are dependent on your descriptions of a situation, or a screen to direct them to a solution. By providing them with as much information as you can, you are helping yourself and all the other people that are waiting on the phone lines.

What's on the CD?

The CD-ROM included with this book is packed with valuable programs and utilities. This appendix gives you a brief overview of the contents of the CD. For a more detailed look at any of these parts, load the CD-ROM and browse the contents.

Netscape Navigator 3

This CD-ROM contains a complete, fully-licensed copy of Netscape Navigator 3.0. This is the full-featured, one-button Web browser/client described throughout this book. Que has licensed this for your use and paid the licensing fee so that you are no longer limited by the Netscape 90-day trial or educational and government usage requirements.

You'll find Netscape for Windows 3.1 in the :\NSCP31 directory on the CD-ROM. You'll find Netscape for Win '95 and Win NT (same version) in the :\NSCP95NT directory on the CD-ROM.

Netscape plug-ins

Plug-ins are great. They were described in some detail in chapter 10 of this book and you've seen what they can do. But finding and downloading these can be a hassle and is definitely time consuming. So, as an added convenience, we've added over 15 plug-ins to this CD-ROM.

Each of the following plug-ins has its own subdirectory in the \plugins directory:

- Acrobat Amber
- ASAP WebShow
- Envoy
- FIGLeaf Inline
- I Chat
- Inso Word View
- Inso CyberSpell
- Lightning Strike
- Look@Me
- Macromedia Shockwave for Authorware
- Macromedia Shockwave for Director
- Macromedia Shockwave for Freehand
- Scream

- Sizzler
- Table of Contents
- TrueSpeech Player
- VDOLive
- VRScout

HTML editors and utilities

There are dozens of good HTML editors and realted utilities available with so many to choose from, you may not know which to use. To help you, we've included a selection of the best of these here. Look for these in the subdirectories in the \html directory:

- Color Manipulation Device
- ColorWiz
- Fountain
- Hot Dog Standard
- HoTMetaL
- Map This!
- Webber
- WebForms
- WebMania

Web utilities, helper applications, and other useful utilities

This next section of software on the CD-ROM includes a carefully selected collection of the best additional utilities that you may find useful when using Netscape. These are in the \util directory:

- Indexer
- NetDate
- PaintShop Pro

- QuickTime Player

- QuickTime VR Player

- Video for Windows Runtime (use for Windows 3.1 only)

- VuePrint

- WebWatch

- WinCode

- WinZip

A Web Directory

If you are looking for a Web site matching a particular category of interests to, look no further than the HTML version of Que's MegaWeb Directory on this CD-ROM. Load this into Netscape like any other Web page and you can search the 18,000 sites listed in this popular book.

Index

Check out Que® Books
on the World Wide Web
http://www.mcp.com/que

As the biggest software release in computer history, Windows 95 continues to redefine the computer industry. Click here for the latest info on our Windows 95 books

Make computing quick and easy with these products designed exclusively for new and casual users

Examine the latest releases in word processing, spreadsheets, operating systems, and suites

The Internet, The World Wide Web, CompuServe®, America Online®, Prodigy®—it's a world of ever-changing information. Don't get left behind!

Find out about new additions to our site, new bestsellers and hot topics

In-depth information on high-end topics: find the best reference books for databases, programming, networking, and client/server technologies

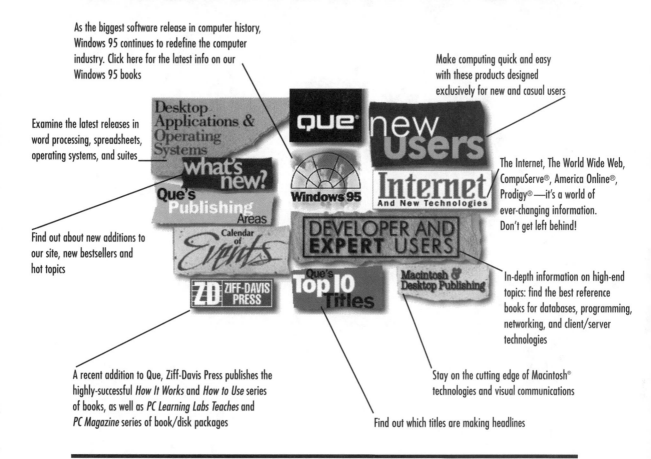

A recent addition to Que, Ziff-Davis Press publishes the highly-successful *How It Works* and *How to Use* series of books, as well as *PC Learning Labs Teaches* and *PC Magazine* series of book/disk packages

Stay on the cutting edge of Macintosh® technologies and visual communications

Find out which titles are making headlines

With 6 separate publishing groups, Que develops products for many specific market segments and areas of computer technology. Explore our Web Site and you'll find information on best-selling titles, newly published titles, upcoming products, authors, and much more.

- Stay informed on the latest industry trends and products available

- Visit our online bookstore for the latest information and editions

- Download software from Que's library of the best shareware and freeware

INTRODUCING A UTILITY THAT WORKS OVERTIME SO YOU MAY NOT HAVE TO.

Quick View Plus. The unbelievably productive utility for Windows 95.

Few things can help you blaze through the day like Quick View Plus. Based on the award-winning Outside In technology, Quick View Plus helps you make the most of the Windows 95 operating system and Netscape Navigator so you can work more productively.

View Everything. Do Anything.

Quick View Plus integrates with Windows Explorer and Microsoft Exchange so you can look at files and attachments without launching, or even having, the original applications.

Quick View Plus lets you view over 200 file formats–from Windows, DOS, and Macintosh programs–including PKZIP, HTML and UUE. It's like having hundreds of applications on your desktop!

And it's WYSIWYG, so what you see is what you get. Quick View Plus gives you instant, fully formatted

display of any file, so you can view text, graphic, database and spreadsheet documents just as they were created in the original applications.

What's more, you can print anything you can see with Quick View Plus. You'll get fully formatted output, with fonts, tables, embedded graphics and OLE objects intact.

Plug in to Netscape.

Quick View Plus plugs in to Netscape Navigator so you have the power to view, copy, print and manipulate virtually any native file from within the Navigator browser window – including word processing, graphic, presentation and compressed formats.

The built-in productivity tool.

Quick View Plus is easy. Quick View Plus is powerful. Most of all, Quick View Plus lets you concentrate on using information instead of acquiring it.

So you can spend your work hours actually working. And your free time doing what you want.

◊Inso®
CORPORATION

330 North Wabash, 15th Floor, Chicago, IL 60611
Toll-free: 800.333.1395, 312.329.0700, fax: 312.670.0820, e-mail: saleschi@inso.com
http://www.inso.com

Starting today, you can feel at home on the Internet

Introducing AT&T WorldNet℠ Service

AT&T

A World of Possibilities...

With AT&T WorldNet℠ Service, a world of possibilities awaits you. Discover new ways to stay in touch with the people, ideas, and information that are important to you at home and at work.

Make travel reservations at any time of the day or night. Access the facts you need to make key decisions. Pursue business opportunities on the AT&T Business Network. Explore new investment options. Play games. Research academic subjects. Stay abreast of current events. Participate in online newsgroups. Purchase merchandise from leading retailers. Send e-Mail.

All you need is a computer with a mouse, a modem, a phone line, and the software enclosed with this mailing. We've taken care of the rest.

If You Can Point and Click, You're There.

Finding the information you want on the Internet with AT&T WorldNet Service is easier than you ever imagined it could be. That's because AT&T WorldNet Service integrates a specially customized version of the popular Netscape Navigator™ software with advanced Internet directories and search engines. The result is an Internet service that sets a new standard for ease of use — virtually everywhere you want to go is a point and click away.

Choose the Plan That's Right for You.

If you're an AT&T Long Distance customer signing up in 1996, you can experience this exciting new service for 5 free hours a month for one full year. Beyond your 5 free hours, you'll be charged only $2.50 for each additional hour. Just use the service for a minimum of one hour per month. If you intend to use AT&T WorldNet Service for more than 5 hours a month, consider choosing the plan with unlimited hours for $19.95 per month.*

If you're not an AT&T Long Distance customer, you can still benefit from AT&T quality and reliability by starting with the plan that offers 3 hours each month and a low monthly fee of $4.95. Under this plan you'll be charged $2.50 for each additional hour, or AT&T WorldNet Service can provide you with unlimited online access for $24.95 per month. It's entirely up to you.

If you're not currently an AT&T Long Distance customer, but would like to become one, please call 1 800 431-0800, ext. 21624.

*The 5 free hours is limited to one AT&T WorldNet Account per residential billed telephone presubscribed to AT&T for "1+ area code + number" long distance dialing. Unlimited usage offers limited to one logon per account at any time. Other terms and conditions apply. Prices quoted are current as of 4/22/96 and are subject to modification by AT&T at any time. Local, long distance, or 800 number access charges and additional access charges and/or taxes that may be imposed on subscribers or on AT&T WorldNet Service will apply to all usage.

Minimum System Requirements

To run AT&T WorldNet Service, you need:

- An IBM-compatible personal computer with a 386 processor or better
- Microsoft Windows 3.1x or Windows 95
- 8MB RAM (16MB or more recommended)
- 11MB of free hard disk space
- 14.4 bps (or faster) modem (28.8 bps is recommended)
- A standard phone line

We're With You Every Step of the Way. 24 Hours a Day, 7 Days a Week.

Nothing is more important to us than making sure that your Internet experience is a truly enriching and satisfying one. That's why our highly trained customer service representatives are available to answer your questions and offer assistance whenever you need it — 24 hours a day, 7 days a week. To reach AT&T WorldNet Customer Care, call **1 800 400-1447**.

Installation Tips and Instructions

- If you have other Web browsers or online software, please consider uninstalling them according to vendor's instructions.

- At the end of installation, you may be asked to restart Windows. Don't attempt the registration process until you have done so.

- If you are experiencing modem problems trying to dial out, try different modem selections, such as Hayes Compatible. If you still have problems, please call Customer Care at **1 800 400-1447**.

- If you are installing AT&T WorldNet Service on a PC with Local Area Networking, please contact your LAN administrator for set-up instructions.

- Follow the initial start-up instructions given to you by the vendor product you purchased. These instructions will tell you how to start the installation of the AT&T WorldNet Service Software.

- Follow the on-screen instructions to install AT&T WorldNet Service Software on your computer.

When you have finished installing the software you may be prompted to restart your computer. Do so when prompted.

Safeguard Your Online Purchases

By registering and continuing to charge your AT&T WorldNet Service to your AT&T Universal Card, you'll enjoy peace of mind whenever you shop the Internet. Should your account number be compromised on the Net, you won't be liable for any online transactions charged to your AT&T Universal Card by a person who is not an authorized user.*

Setting Up Your WorldNet Account

The AT&T WorldNet Service Program group/folder will appear on your Windows desktop.

- Double click on the AT&T WorldNet Service registration icon.

- Follow the on-screen instructions and complete all the stages of registration.

After all the stages have been completed, you'll be prompted to dial into the network to complete the registration process. Make sure your modem and phone line are not in use.

*Today cardmembers may be liable for the first $50 of charges made by a person who is not an authorized user, which will not be imposed under this program as long as the cardmember notifies AT&T Universal Card of the loss within 24 hours and otherwise complies with the Cardmember Agreement. Refer to Cardmember Agreement for definition of authorized user.

Registering With AT&T WorldNet Service

Once you have connected with AT&T WorldNet online registration service, you will be presented with a series of screens that will confirm billing information and prompt you for additional account set-up data.

The following is a list of registration tips and comments that will help you during the registration process.

I. Use the registration code:

- Code for current AT&T Long Distance Customers: L30QIM631

- Code for other long distance customers: L30QIM632

II. We advise that you use all lowercase letters when assigning an e-Mail ID and security code, since they are easier to remember.

III. Choose a special "security code" that you will use to verify who you are when you call Customer Care.

IV. If you make a mistake and exit the registration process prematurely, all you need to do is click on "Create New Account". Do not click on "Edit Existing Account".

V. When choosing your local access telephone number, you will be given several options. Please choose the one nearest to you. Please note that calling a number within your area does not guarantee that the call is free.

Connecting to AT&T WorldNet Service

When you have finished registering with AT&T WorldNet Service you are ready to make online connections.

- Make sure your modem and phone line are available.

- Double click on the AT&T WorldNet Service icon

Follow these steps whenever you wish to connect to AT&T WorldNet Service.

Explore our AT&T WorldNet Service Web site at: http://www.att.com/worldnet

Registration Codes

When installing and registering the AT&T WorldNet℠ Service software, please use the following registration codes:

- Code for current AT&T Long Distance Customers: L30QIM631
- Code for other long distance customers: L30QIM632

Please see the previous pages if you need information about subscribing to AT&T Long Distance service.

Upgrading AT&T WorldNet Service Software to Netscape 3

The version of AT&T WorldNet Service software included on this CD-ROM installs a previous version of Netscape Navigator. In order to use the copy of Netscape Navigator 3 provided by Que on this CD-ROM along with AT&T WorldNet Service, please follow these directions:

I. Follow all of the steps to install the AT&T WorldNet Service software included on the previous pages. You must install the software, set up your account, and register with AT&T WorldNet Service before installing Netscape Navigator 3.

II. Once you have successfully set up your account and registered, install Netscape Navigator 3 by following the directions found in the section "Loading Netscape" in the appendix "Loading and Configuring Netscape" in this book. Windows 3.1 users should select the "Use old Netscape ini file" option when prompted. Choose your WorldNet directory when prompted for the destination path (c:\worldnet). Select the "AT&T WorldNet Services" folder for new items when prompted.

If you choose to use Netscape 3 with AT&T WorldNet Service, you should not call AT&T WorldNet Service customer support for problems relating to Netscape. You will still call them for any support needs related to AT&T WorldNet Service at the number listed earlier under "We're With You Every Step of the Way." For Netscape 3 support, you will call or e-mail Macmillan Technical Support at 317-581-3833 or **support@mcp.com.**

Windows 3.1 users: After following the directions above, use the following steps to configure mail in Netscape 3.

I. Run Eudora light by double-clicking the Eudora light e-mail icon and select the **Special** pull down menu.

II. Select **Settings**.

III. Select the **Getting Started** category.

IV. Write down your POP account information.

V. Cancel the settings and close Eudora Light.

I. Now open Netscape Navigator 3.

II. Select the **Options** pull down menu.

III. Select **Mail and News Preferences...**

IV. Select the **Servers** tab.

V. Select the box to the right of **Incoming Mail (POP3) Server:**

VI. Enter everything after the @ symbol from your Eudora Light POP account information. For instance, if your account information was "Jdoe@postoffice.worldnet.att.net" you would enter "worldnet.att.net" in the box.

VII. Tab to the **POP3 User Name:** box.

VIII. Enter everything before the @ symbol from your Eudora Light POP account information. For instance, if your account information was "Jdoe@postoffice.worldnet.att.net" you would enter "Jdoe" in the box.

IX. Select the **OK** button at the bottom of the Preferences window.

X. You are now ready to use Netscape for e-mail.

After confirming the mail portion of Netscape is configured properly, you may delete the Eudora Light folder from your WorldNet directory, if you choose not to use Eudora Light.

Remember, you can use the copy of Netscape 3 on this CD-ROM with any Internet service provider you choose. AT&T WorldNet Service software is provided as an option for you if you don't currently have an internet provider or would like to switch to AT&T's WorldNet Service.

AT&T WorldNet is a service name of AT&T Corp

Complete and Return this Card
for a *FREE* Computer Book Catalog

Thank you for purchasing this book! You have purchased a superior computer book written expressly for your needs. To continue to provide the kind of up-to-date, pertinent coverage you've come to expect from us, we need to hear from you. Please take a minute to complete and return this self-addressed, postage-paid form. In return, we'll send you a free catalog of all our computer books on topics ranging from word processing to programming and the internet.

Mr. ☐   Mrs. ☐   Ms. ☐   Dr. ☐

Name (first) ☐☐☐☐☐☐☐☐☐☐☐   (M.I.) ☐   (last) ☐☐☐☐☐☐☐☐☐☐☐☐☐☐☐

Address ☐☐☐☐☐☐☐☐☐☐☐☐☐☐☐☐☐☐☐☐☐☐☐☐☐☐☐☐☐☐

☐☐☐☐☐☐☐☐☐☐☐☐☐☐☐☐☐☐☐☐☐☐☐☐☐☐☐☐☐☐

City ☐☐☐☐☐☐☐☐☐☐☐☐☐☐   State ☐☐   Zip ☐☐☐☐☐ ☐☐☐☐

Phone ☐☐☐ ☐☐☐☐☐   Fax ☐☐☐ ☐☐☐☐

Company Name ☐☐☐☐☐☐☐☐☐☐☐☐☐☐☐☐☐☐☐☐☐☐☐☐☐☐☐☐☐☐

E-mail address ☐☐☐☐☐☐☐☐☐☐☐☐☐☐☐☐☐☐☐☐☐☐☐☐☐☐☐☐☐☐

1. Please check at least (3) influencing factors for purchasing this book.

Front or back cover information on book .... ☐
Special approach to the content .... ☐
Completeness of content .... ☐
Author's reputation .... ☐
Publisher's reputation .... ☐
Book cover design or layout .... ☐
Index or table of contents of book .... ☐
Price of book .... ☐
Special effects, graphics, illustrations .... ☐
Other (Please specify): _____ ☐

2. How did you first learn about this book?

Saw in Macmillan Computer Publishing catalog .... ☐
Recommended by store personnel .... ☐
Saw the book on bookshelf at store .... ☐
Recommended by a friend .... ☐
Received advertisement in the mail .... ☐
Saw an advertisement in: _____ ☐
Read book review in: _____ ☐
Other (Please specify): _____ ☐

3. How many computer books have you purchased in the last six months?

This book only .... ☐   3 to 5 books...................... ☐
2 books .... ☐   More than 5 .... ☐

4. Where did you purchase this book?

Bookstore .... ☐
Computer Store .... ☐
Consumer Electronics Store .... ☐
Department Store .... ☐
Office Club .... ☐
Warehouse Club .... ☐
Mail Order .... ☐
Direct from Publisher .... ☐
Internet site .... ☐
Other (Please specify): _____ ☐

5. How long have you been using a computer?

☐ Less than 6 months   ☐ 6 months to a year
☐ 1 to 3 years   ☐ More than 3 years

6. What is your level of experience with personal computers and with the subject of this book?

	With PCs	With subject of book
New	☐	☐
Casual	☐	☐
Accomplished	☐	☐
Expert	☐	☐

Source Code ISBN: 0-7897-0924-4

7. Which of the following best describes your job title?

Administrative Assistant .... ☐
Coordinator .... ☐
Manager/Supervisor .... ☐
Director .... ☐
Vice President .... ☐
President/CEO/COO .... ☐
Lawyer/Doctor/Medical Professional .... ☐
Teacher/Educator/Trainer .... ☐
Engineer/Technician .... ☐
Consultant .... ☐
Not employed/Student/Retired .... ☐
Other (Please specify): _____ ☐

8. Which of the following best describes the area of the company your job title falls under?

Accounting .... ☐
Engineering .... ☐
Manufacturing .... ☐
Operations .... ☐
Marketing .... ☐
Sales .... ☐
Other (Please specify): _____ ☐

9. What is your age?

Under 20 .... ☐
21-29 .... ☐
30-39 .... ☐
40-49 .... ☐
50-59 .... ☐
60-over .... ☐

10. Are you:

Male .... ☐
Female .... ☐

11. Which computer publications do you read regularly? (Please list)

_____
_____
_____
_____
_____
_____
_____
_____
_____
_____

Comments: _____
_____
_____

Fold here and scotch-tape to mai

Fold here and scotch-tape to mail

EXHIBIT B

SOFTWARE LICENSE for QuickTime

PLEASE READ THIS LICENSE CAREFULLY BEFORE USING THE SOFTWARE. BY USING THE SOFTWARE, YOU ARE AGREEING TO BE BOUND BY THE TERMS OF THIS LICENSE. IF YOU DO NOT AGREE TO THE TERMS OF THIS LICENSE, PROMPTLY RETURN THE UNUSED SOFTWARE TO THE PLACE WHERE YOU OBTAINED IT AND YOUR MONEY WILL BE REFUNDED.

1. **License.** The application, demonstration, system and other software accompanying this License, whether on disk, in read-only memory, or on any other media (the "Software"), the related documentation and fonts are licensed to you by Macmillan Computer Publishing. You own the disk on which the Software and fonts are recorded but Macmillan Computer Publishing and/or Macmillan Computer Publishing's Licensors retain title to the Software, related documentation, and fonts. This License allows you to use the Software and fonts on a single Apple computer and make one copy of the Software and fonts in machine-readable form for backup purposes only. You must reproduce on such copy the Macmillan Computer Publishing copyright notice and any other proprietary legends that were on the original copy of the Software and fonts. You may also transfer all your license rights in the Software and fonts, the backup copy of the Software and fonts, the related documentation, and a copy of this License to another party, provided the other party reads and agrees to accept the terms and conditions of this License.

2. **Restrictions.** The Software contains copyrighted material, trade secrets, and other proprietary material. In order to protect them, and except as permitted by applicable legislation, you may not decompile, reverse engineer, disassemble, or otherwise reduce the Software to a human-perceivable form. You may not modify, network, rent, lease, loan, distribute, or create derivative works based upon the Software, in whole or in part. You may not electronically transmit the Software from one computer to another or over a network.

3. **Termination.** This License is effective until terminated. You may terminate this License at any time by destroying the Software, related documentation and fonts, and all copies thereof. This License will terminate immediately without notice from Macmillan Computer Publishing if you fail to comply with any provision of this License. Upon termination you must destroy the Software, related documentation and fonts, and all copies thereof.

4. **Export Law Assurances.** You agree and certify that neither the Software nor any other technical data received from Macmillan Computer Publishing, nor the direct product thereof, will be exported outside the United States except as authorized and as permitted by the laws and regulations of the United States. If the Software has been rightfully obtained by you outside of the United States, you agree that you will not re-export the Software nor any other technical data received from Macmillan Computer Publishing, nor the direct product thereof, except as permitted by the laws and regulations of the United States and the laws and regulations of the jurisdiction in which you obtained the Software.

5. **Government End Users.** If you are acquiring the Software and fonts on behalf of any unit or agency of the United States Government, the following provisions apply. The Government agrees:

(i) if the Software and fonts are supplied to the Department of Defense (DoD), the Software and fonts are classified as "Commercial Computer Software" and the Government is acquiring only "restricted rights" in the Software, its documentation and fonts as that term is defined in Clause 252.227-7013(c)(1) or the DFARS; and

(ii) if the Software and fonts are supplied to any unit or agency of the United States Government other than DoD, the Government's rights in the Software, its documentation and fonts will be as defined in Clause 52.227-19(c)(2) of the FAR or, in the case of NASA, in Clause 18-52.227-86(d) of the NASA supplement to the FAR.

6. **Limited warranty on Media.** Macmillan Computer Publishing warrants the diskettes and/or compact disc on which the Software and fonts are recorded to be free from defects in materials and workmanship under normal use for a period of ninety (90) days from the date of purchase as evidenced by a copy of the receipt. Macmillan Computer Publishing's entire liability and your exclusive remedy will be replacement of the diskettes and/or compact disc not meeting Macmillan Computer Publishing's limited warranty and which

is returned to Macmillan Computer Publishing or a Macmillan Computer Publishing authorized representative with a copy of the receipt. Macmillan Computer Publishing will have no responsibility to replace a disk/disc damaged by accident, abuse, or misapplication. ANY IMPLIED WARRANTIES ON THE DISKETTES AND/OR COMPACT DISC, INCLUDING THE IMPLIED WARRANTIES OF MERCHANTABILITY AND FITNESS FOR A PARTICULAR PURPOSE, ARE LIMITED IN DURATION TO NINETY (90) DAYS FROM THE DATE OF DELIVERY. THIS WARRANTY GIVES YOU SPECIFIC LEGAL RIGHTS, AND YOU MAY ALSO HAVE OTHER RIGHTS WHICH VARY BY JURISDICTION.

7. **Disclaimer of Warranty on Apple Software.** You expressly acknowledge and agree that use of the Software and fonts is at your sole risk. The Software, related documentation and fonts are provided "AS IS" and without warranty of any kind and Macmillan Computer Publishing and Macmillan Computer Publishing's Licensor(s) (for the purposes of provisions 7 and 8, Macmillan Computer Publishing and Macmillan Computer Publishing's Licensor(s) shall be collectively referred to as "Macmillan Computer Publishing") EXPRESSLY DISCLAIM ALL WARRANTIES, EXPRESS OR IMPLIED, INCLUDING, BUT NOT LIMITED TO, THE IMPLIED WARRANTIES OF MERCHANTABILITY AND FITNESS FOR A PARTICULAR PURPOSE. MACMILLAN COMPUTER PUBLISHING DOES NOT WARRANT THAT THE FUNCTIONS CONTAINED IN THE SOFTWARE WILL MEET YOUR REQUIREMENTS, OR THAT THE OPERATION OF THE SOFTWARE WILL BE UNINTERRUPTED OR ERROR-FREE, OR THAT DEFECTS IN THE SOFTWARE AND THE FONTS WILL BE CORRECTED. FURTHERMORE, MACMILLAN COMPUTER PUBLISHING DOES NOT WARRANT OR MAKE ANY REPRESENTATIONS REGARDING THE USE OR THE RESULTS OF THE USE OF THE SOFTWARE AND FONTS OR RELATED DOCUMENTATION IN TERMS OF THEIR CORRECTNESS, ACCURACY, RELIABILITY, OR OTHERWISE. NO ORAL OR WRITTEN INFORMATION OR ADVICE GIVEN BY MACMILLAN COMPUTER PUBLISHING OR A MACMILLAN COMPUTER PUBLISHING AUTHORIZED REPRESENTATIVE SHALL CREATE A WARRANTY OR IN ANY WAY INCREASE THE SCOPE OF THIS WARRANTY. SHOULD THE SOFTWARE PROVE DEFECTIVE, YOU (AND NOT MACMILLAN COMPUTER PUBLISHING OR A MACMILLAN COMPUTER PUBLISHING AUTHORIZED REPRESENTATIVE) ASSUME THE ENTIRE COST OF ALL NECESSARY SERVICING, REPAIR OR CORRECTION. SOME JURISDICTIONS DO NOT ALLOW THE EXCLUSION OF IMPLIED WARRANTIES, SO THE ABOVE EXCLUSION MAY NOT APPLY TO YOU.

8. **Limitation of Liability.** UNDER NO CIRCUMSTANCES INCLUDING NEGLIGENCE, SHALL MACMILLAN COMPUTER PUBLISHING BE LIABLE FOR ANY INCIDENTAL, SPECIAL, OR CONSE-QUENTIAL DAMAGES THAT RESULT FROM THE USE OR INABILITY TO USE THE SOFTWARE OR RELATED DOCUMENTATION, EVEN IF MACMILLAN COMPUTER PUBLISHING OR A MACMILLAN COMPUTER PUBLISHING AUTHORIZED REPRESENTATIVE HAS BEEN ADVISED OF THE POSSIBIL-ITY OF SUCH DAMAGES. SOME JURISDICTIONS DO NOT ALLOW THE LIMITATION OR EXCLUSION OF LIABILITY FOR INCIDENTAL OR CONSEQUENTIAL DAMAGES SO THE ABOVE LIMITATION OR EXCLUSION MAY NOT APPLY TO YOU.

   In no event shall Macmillan Computer Publishing's total liability to you for all damages, losses, and causes of action (whether in contract, tort [including negligence] or otherwise) exceed the amount paid by you for the Software and fonts.

9. **Law and Severability.** This License shall be governed by and construed in accordance with the laws of the United States and the State of California, as applied to agreements entered into and to be performed entirely within California between California residents. If for any reason a court of competent jurisdiction finds any provision of this License, or portion thereof, to be unenforceable, that provision of the License shall be enforced to the maximum extent permissible so as to effect the intent of the parties, and the remainder of this License shall continue in full force and effect.

10. **Complete Agreement.** This License constitutes the entire agreement between the parties with respect to the use of the Software, the related documentation and fonts, and supersedes all prior or contemporaneous understandings or agreements, written or oral, regarding such subject matter. No amendment to or modifica-tion of this License will be binding unless in writing and signed by a duly authorized representative of Macmillan Computer Publishing.

Netscape Navigator End User License Agreement

BY CLICKING ON THE "ACCEPT" BUTTON OR OPENING THE PACKAGE, YOU ARE CONSENTING TO BE BOUND BY THIS AGREEMENT. IF YOU DO NOT AGREE TO ALL OF THE TERMS OF THIS AGREEMENT, CLICK THE "DO NOT ACCEPT" BUTTON AND THE INSTALLATION PROCESS WILL NOT CONTINUE, AND, IF APPLICABLE, RETURN THE PRODUCT TO THE PLACE OF PURCHASE FOR A FULL REFUND.

NETSCAPE END USER LICENSE AGREEMENT

REDISTRIBUTION NOT PERMITTED

This Agreement has 3 parts. Part I applies if you have not purchased a license to the accompanying software (the "Software"). Part II applies if you have purchased a license to the Software. Part III applies to all license grants. If you initially acquired a copy of the Software without purchasing a license and you wish to purchase a license, contact Netscape Communications Corporation ("Netscape") on the Internet at **http://www.netscape.com**.

PART I—TERMS APPLICABLE WHEN LICENSE FEES NOT (YET) PAID

(LIMITED TO EVALUATION, EDUCATIONAL, AND NON-PROFIT USE)

GRANT. Netscape grants you a non-exclusive license to use the Software free of charge if (a) you are a student, faculty member, or staff member of an educational institution (K-12, junior college, college, or library) or an employee of an organization that meets Netscape's criteria for a charitable non-profit organization; or (b) your use of the Software is for the purpose of evaluating whether to purchase an ongoing license to the Software. The evaluation period for use by or on behalf of a commercial entity is limited to ninety (90) days; evaluation use by others is not subject to this ninety (90) day limit. Government agencies (other than public libraries) are not considered educational or charitable non-profit organizations for purposes of this Agreement. If you are using the software free of charge, you are not entitled to hard-copy documentation, support, or telephone assistance. If you fit within the description above, you may use the Software in the manner described in Part III under "Scope of Grant."

DISCLAIMER OF WARRANTY. Free of charge Software is provided on an "AS IS" basis, without warranty of any kind, including without limitation the warranties of merchantability, fitness for a particular purpose, and non-infringement. The entire risk as to the quality and performance of the Software is borne by you. Should the Software prove defective, you and not Netscape or its suppliers assume the entire cost of any service and repair. In addition, the security mechanisms implemented by Netscape software have inherent limitations, and you must determine that the Software sufficiently meets your requirements. This disclaimer of warranty constitutes an essential part of this Agreement. SOME JURISDICTIONS DO NOT ALLOW EXCLUSIONS OF AN IMPLIED WARRANTY, SO THIS DISCLAIMER MAY NOT APPLY TO YOU AND YOU MAY HAVE OTHER LEGAL RIGHTS THAT VARY BY JURISDICTION.

PART II—TERMS APPLICABLE WHEN LICENSE FEES PAID

GRANT. Subject to payment of applicable license fees, Netscape grants to you a non-exclusive license to use the Software and accompanying documentation ("Documentation") in the manner described in Part III under "Scope of Grant."

LIMITED WARRANTY. Netscape warrants that for a period of ninety (90) days from the date of acquisition, the Software, if operated as directed, will substantially achieve the functionality described in the Documentation. Netscape does not warrant, however, that your use of the Software will be uninterrupted or that the operation of the Software will be error-free or secure. In addition, the security mechanisms implemented by Netscape software have inherent limitations, and you must determine that the Software sufficiently meets your requirements. Netscape also warrants that the media containing the Software, if provided by Netscape, is free from defects in material and workmanship and will so remain for ninety (90) days from the date you acquired the Software. Netscape's sole liability for any breach of this warranty shall be, in Netscape's sole discretion: (i) to replace your defective media or Software; or (ii) to advise you how to achieve substantially the same functionality with the Software as described in the Documentation through a procedure different from that set forth in the Documentation; or (iii) if the above remedies are impracticable, to refund the license fee you paid for the Software. Repaired, corrected, or replaced Software and Documentation shall be covered by this limited warranty for the period remaining under the warranty that covered the original Software, or if longer, for thirty (30) days after the date (a) of shipment to you of the repaired or replaced Software, or (b) Netscape advised you how to operate the Software so as to achieve the functionality described in the Documentation. Only if you inform Netscape of your problem with the Software during the applicable warranty period and provide evidence of the date you purchased a license to the Software will Netscape be obligated to honor this warranty. Netscape will use reasonable commercial efforts to repair, replace, advise or, for individual consumers, refund pursuant to the foregoing warranty within thirty (30) days of being so notified.

THIS IS A LIMITED WARRANTY AND IT IS THE ONLY WARRANTY MADE BY NETSCAPE OR ITS SUPPLIERS. NETSCAPE MAKES NO OTHER EXPRESS WARRANTY AND NO WARRANTY OF NONINFRINGEMENT OF THIRD PARTIES' RIGHTS. THE DURATION OF IMPLIED WARRANTIES INCLUDING, WITHOUT LIMITATION, WARRANTIES OF MERCHANTABILITY AND OF FITNESS FOR A PARTICULAR PURPOSE, IS LIMITED TO THE ABOVE LIMITED WARRANTY PERIOD; SOME JURISDICTIONS DO NOT ALLOW LIMITATIONS ON HOW LONG AN IMPLIED WARRANTY LASTS, SO LIMITATIONS MAY NOT APPLY TO YOU. NO NETSCAPE DEALER, AGENT, OR EMPLOYEE IS AUTHORIZED TO MAKE ANY MODIFICATIONS, EXTENSIONS, OR ADDITIONS TO THIS WARRANTY. If any modifications are made to the Software by you during the warranty period; if the media is subjected to accident, abuse, or improper use; or if you violate the terms of this Agreement, then this warranty shall immediately terminate. This warranty shall not apply if the Software is used on or in conjunction with hardware or software other than the unmodified version of hardware or software with which the Software was designed to be used as described in the Documentation. THIS WARRANTY GIVES YOU SPECIFIC LEGAL RIGHTS, AND YOU MAY HAVE OTHER LEGAL RIGHTS THAT VARY BY JURISDICTION.

PART III—TERMS APPLICABLE TO ALL LICENSE GRANTS

SCOPE OF GRANT.

You may:

- ■ use the Software on any single computer;
- ■ use the Software on a network, provided that each person accessing the Software through the network must have a copy licensed to that person;

- use the Software on a second computer so long as only one copy is used at a time;
- copy the Software for archival purposes, provided any copy must contain all of the original Software's proprietary notices; or
- if you have purchased licenses for a 10 Pack or a 50 Pack, make up to 10 or 50 copies, respectively, of the Software (but not the Documentation), or, if you have purchased licenses for multiple copies of the Software, make the number of copies of Software (but not the Documentation) that the packing slip or invoice states you have paid for, provided any copy must contain all of the original Software's proprietary notices. The number of copies on the invoice is the total number of copies that may be made for *all* platforms. Additional copies of Documentation may be purchased from Netscape.

You may not:

- permit other individuals to use the Software except under the terms listed above;
- permit concurrent use of the Software;
- modify, translate, reverse engineer, decompile, disassemble (except to the extent applicable laws specifically prohibit such restriction), or create derivative works based on the Software;
- copy the Software other than as specified above;
- rent, lease, grant a security interest in, or otherwise transfer rights to the Software; or
- remove any proprietary notices or labels from the Software.

TITLE. Title, ownership rights, and intellectual property rights in the Software shall remain in Netscape and/or its suppliers. The Software is protected by copyright and other intellectual property laws and by international treaties. Title and related rights in the content accessed through the Software is the property of the applicable content owner and may be protected by applicable law. The license granted under this Agreement gives you no rights to such content.

TERMINATION. This Agreement and the license granted hereunder will terminate automatically if you fail to comply with the limitations described herein. Upon termination, you must destroy all copies of the Software and Documentation.

EXPORT CONTROLS. None of the Software or underlying information or technology may be downloaded or otherwise exported or reexported (i) into (or to a national or resident of) Cuba, Iraq, Libya, Yugoslavia, North Korea, Iran, Syria, or any other country to which the U.S. has embargoed goods; or (ii) to anyone on the U.S. Treasury Department's list of Specially Designated Nationals or the U.S. Commerce Department's Table of Denial Orders. By downloading or using the Software, you are agreeing to the foregoing and you are representing and warranting that you are not located in, under the control of, or a national or resident of any such country or on any such list.

In addition, if the licensed Software is identified as a not-for-export product (for example, on the box or media or in the installation process), then the following applies: EXCEPT FOR EXPORT TO CANADA FOR USE IN CANADA BY CANADIAN CITIZENS, THE SOFTWARE AND ANY UNDERLYING TECHNOLOGY MAY NOT BE EXPORTED OUTSIDE THE UNITED STATES OR TO ANY FOREIGN ENTITY OR "FOREIGN PERSON" AS DEFINED

BY U.S. GOVERNMENT REGULATIONS INCLUDING, WITHOUT LIMITATION, ANYONE WHO IS NOT A CITIZEN, NATIONAL, OR LAWFUL PERMANENT RESIDENT OF THE UNITED STATES. BY DOWNLOADING OR USING THE SOFTWARE, YOU ARE AGREEING TO THE FOREGOING AND YOU ARE WARRANTING THAT YOU ARE NOT A "FOREIGN PERSON" OR UNDER THE CONTROL OF A FOREIGN PERSON.

LIMITATION OF LIABILITY. UNDER NO CIRCUMSTANCES AND UNDER NO LEGAL THEORY, TORT, CONTRACT, OR OTHERWISE, SHALL NETSCAPE OR ITS SUPPLIERS OR RESELLERS BE LIABLE TO YOU OR ANY OTHER PERSON FOR ANY INDIRECT, SPE-CIAL, INCIDENTAL, OR CONSEQUENTIAL DAMAGES OF ANY CHARACTER, INCLUD-ING, WITHOUT LIMITATION, DAMAGES FOR LOSS OF GOODWILL, WORK STOPPAGE, COMPUTER FAILURE OR MALFUNCTION, OR ANY AND ALL OTHER COMMERCIAL DAMAGES OR LOSSES. IN NO EVENT WILL NETSCAPE BE LIABLE FOR ANY DAMAGES IN EXCESS OF THE AMOUNT NETSCAPE RECEIVED FROM YOU FOR A LICENSE TO THE SOFTWARE, EVEN IF NETSCAPE SHALL HAVE BEEN INFORMED OF THE POSSI-BILITY OF SUCH DAMAGES, OR FOR ANY CLAIM BY ANY OTHER PARTY. THIS LIMITA-TION OF LIABILITY SHALL NOT APPLY TO LIABILITY FOR DEATH OR PERSONAL IN-JURY TO THE EXTENT APPLICABLE LAW PROHIBITS SUCH LIMITATION. FURTHER-MORE, SOME JURISDICTIONS DO NOT ALLOW THE EXCLUSION OR LIMITATION OF INCIDENTAL OR CONSEQUENTIAL DAMAGES, SO THIS LIMITATION AND EXCLUSION MAY NOT APPLY TO YOU.

HIGH RISK ACTIVITIES. The Software is not fault-tolerant and is not designed, manufactured, or intended for use or resale as on-line control equipment in hazardous environments requiring fail-safe performance, such as in the operation of nuclear facilities, aircraft navigation or com-munication systems, air traffic control, direct life support machines, or weapons systems, in which the failure of the Software could lead directly to death, personal injury, or severe physi-cal or environmental damage ("High Risk Activities"). Netscape and its suppliers specifically disclaim any express or implied warranty of fitness for High Risk Activities.

MISCELLANEOUS. If the copy of the Software you received was accompanied by a printed or other form of "hard-copy" End User License Agreement whose terms vary from this Agree-ment, then the hard-copy End User License Agreement governs your use of the Software. This Agreement represents the complete agreement concerning the license granted hereunder and may be amended only by a writing executed by both parties. THE ACCEPTANCE OF ANY PURCHASE ORDER PLACED BY YOU IS EXPRESSLY MADE CONDITIONAL ON YOUR ASSENT TO THE TERMS SET FORTH HEREIN, AND NOT THOSE IN YOUR PURCHASE ORDER. If any provision of this Agreement is held to be unenforceable, such provision shall be reformed only to the extent necessary to make it enforceable. This Agreement shall be gov-erned by California law (except for conflict of law provisions). The application of the United Nations Convention of Contracts for the International Sale of Goods is expressly excluded.

U.S. GOVERNMENT END USERS. The Software is a "commercial item," as that term is de-fined in 48 C.F.R. 2.101 (Oct. 1995), consisting of "commercial computer software" and "com-mercial computer software documentation," as such terms are used in 48 C.F.R. 12.212 (Sept. 1995). Consistent with 48 C.F.R. 12.212 and 48 C.F.R. 227.7202-1 through 227.7202-4 (June 1995), all U.S. Government End Users acquire the Software with only those rights set forth herein.

Before using any of the software on this disc, you need to install the software you plan to use. See Appendix C "What's on the CD" for directions. If you have problems with *Special Edition Using Netscape 3 CD*, please contact Macmillan Technical Support at (317) 581-3833. We can be reached by e-mail at **support@mcp.com** or by CompuServe at GO QUEBOOKS.

Please note that technical support for the copy of Netscape Navigator included on the CD is provided through Macamillan Technical Support at the number or e-mail address listed above. Do not contact Netscape Corporation for Technical Support with this product.

Grab Hold of the Future

...by reading today's #1 magazine dedicated to online solutions!

Written by trail-blazing experts, *INTERNET & JAVA ADVISOR* is your complete technical guide to designing, deploying, and managing applications that use Internet, Intranet, Java, and Web technology to extend your business.

Subscribe Today!

SAVE 41%

NOW MONTHLY
Your Guide to Developing Internet Applications
Firewalls • Security • HTML • Java • Netscape • Intranets
April 1996

INTERNET & JAVA ADVISOR

- ■ Learn to Program Java Applets
- ■ Start Building Your Corporate Intranet
- ■ Understand Firewalls

BUILD HOT WEB PAGES!
Master Netscape's New HTML Extensions

5 New Web Sites You Just Gotta See!

NetWatch:
Exciting New Products Coming Your Way

NEW PRODUCT REVIEWS & TEST DRIVES tell you in detail what's worth buying and why.

FEATURE ARTICLES
reveal expert solutions you can use right now.

NET WATCH
provides advance word on new products coming your way.

DEVELOPER NEWS
keeps you updated on what's new and important.

NET SIGHTINGS
describes useful Web sites you'll want to visit.

COMPANION RESOURCE DISKS
bring you examples, applications, utilities, and other goodies from each issue in ready-to-use electronic form.